The Making of Modern Cynicism

University of Virginia Press *Charlottesville & London*

DAVID MAZELLA

THE MAKING OF MODERN

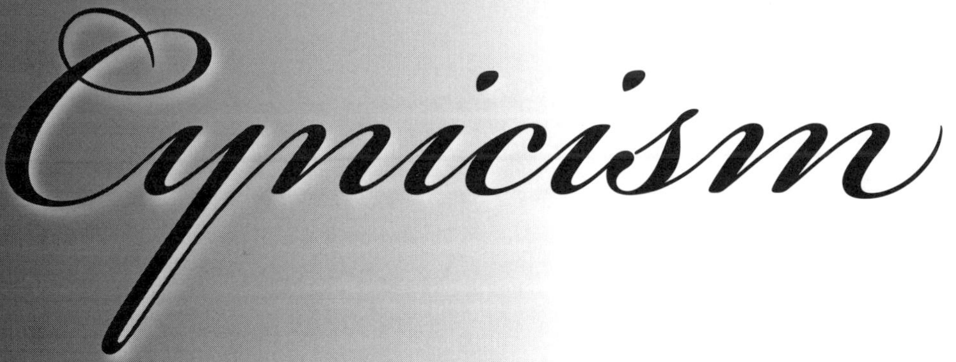

University of Virginia Press

Printed in the United States of America on acid-free paper

First published 2007

9 8 7 6 5 4 3 2 1

Library of Congress Cataloging-in-Publication Data

Mazella, David, 1962–
The making of modern cynicism / David Mazella.
p. cm.
Includes bibliographical references and index.
ISBN 978-0-8139-2615-5 (cloth : alk. paper)
1. Cynicism. 2. Diogenes, d. ca. 323 B.C. I. Title.
B809.5.M39 2007
149—dc22

2006033639

He who loves me, loves my dog.
—St. Bernard

CONTENTS

ACKNOWLEDGMENTS

IN THE TIME THAT IT HAS TAKEN for me to complete this project, I have learned just how many people can be involved in the writing of a single book. I should begin these acknowledgments by thanking all my friends and colleagues at the University of Houston, who have been reading this book, and hearing about its revisions, longer than I care to recall.

First of all, I would like to acknowledge the contributions of the members of my writing group, Hosam Aboul-Ela, Margot Backus, Karen Fang, and especially Maria Gonzalez, for all their encouragement and suggestions during the drafting and redrafting process. Their unstinting generosity to my project has been extremely helpful, and an invaluable instance of scholarly community. Other members of my department, including John Bernard, David Mikics, Jay Kastely, Pat Yongue, and Wyman Herendeen, have read and commented on various portions and at various stages of its drafting, for which I am grateful. Shortly after her arrival here at UH, Natalie Houston suggested that I go look at cynical dandies, and readers will see how indebted I am to her initial suggestion. As departmental chairs, Harmon Boertien, Wyman Herendeen, and John McNamara all strongly supported this project from the start and helped me bring it to fruition. Finally, I am grateful to the English Department's Committee and the Houstoun Fund for summer grants that allowed me to conduct research at the Folger and the Huntington libraries.

This project received a number of college and university grants from its inception through its completion. The writing of this book was supported by University of Houston RIG, LGIA, and Small Grants, some of which allowed me to hire an invaluable assistant, Ms. Eva Ginsburg, during the early stages of the writing and research. The UH Small Grants Program has also contributed a subvention to help defray costs of publication. I must also acknowledge the role of Dean John Antel at CLASS, who was a crucial supporter of my scholarship during a critical time. For their generous help during this period, I gratefully acknowledge the efforts of the late Yale Rosenberg, Irene Rosenberg, Laura Oren, and the late Ross Lence at UH, as well as Mary Burgan of the AAUP.

A portion of chapter 3 first appeared in "Diogenes the Cynic in the Dialogues of the Dead of Thomas Brown, Lord Lyttelton, and William Blake," by David Mazella, in *Texas Studies in Literature and Language* 48: 2, pp. 102–22. Copyright ©2006 by the University of Texas Press. All rights reserved.

My editor at the University of Virginia Press, Ms. Cathie Brettschneider, has also been a warm supporter of the project through its various stages and deserves thanks for her suggestions and advice along the way. My anonymous readers at the Press, one of whom, Adam Potkay, has subsequently identified himself to me, were the book's first audience, and their remarks and suggestions were invaluable for my conception of the book. Their readings have significantly improved the book, though any mistakes remaining are of course my own.

Over the years, I have received warm and generous readings, advice, encouragement, and suggestions from Robert Folkenflik and Bliss Carnochan, who both helped me to recognize the true scope of the project. Michael Seidel also deserves thanks for his support of what he always called my "big think project." Carl Fisher and the rest of the ASECS crew will recognize the scraps and scruds of our conversations in the body of the text and in my footnotes. Similarly, I have benefited from conversations with the Houston-area Rice Early Modern Reading Group, which includes Meredith Skura, Betty Joseph, and Rajani Sudan. It was through Betty and the group that I met Louisa Shea, who is writing her own book on Cynicism in the French Enlightenment. At every turn, I have learned a tremendous amount from the people who were willing to discuss this book's topics with me, including those who listened and responded to its previews in scholarly conferences at ASECS and regional meetings. In particular, I should thank the list members of C18-L, where I discussed some of the topics broached here, and who generously responded with their own comments and suggestions.

Since I began this book, I have been extremely fortunate in my research assistants and my students. Ms. Eva Ginsburg was a huge help while I was mining examples of Cynics and Cynicism in every era of English literary history, and often seemed bemused that so much could be made of a single word. She should see my files now. At the very end of the project, I also received assistance from Scott Wagner, Erin Makulski Sandler, David Raffetto, and Laura Berwick, who did yeoman's work with all the documentation that accumulated (who knows how?) over the years. I am thankful for all the help they provided. Finally I should acknowledge the role of my students in my UH graduate seminar in Cynicism and its literary forms, who helped me learn how to frame this very large topic.

A number of libraries made it possible for me to conceive and execute this project. The UH Special Collections staff (Pat Bozeman, Julie Grob, and Bobby Marlin) have all exerted themselves on my behalf, and the staff at Interlibrary Loan has allowed me to view, if not to possess, a large amount of material to which I otherwise had no access. The staffs and facilities at the Huntington Library, the Folger, and the Library of Congress also provided access and assistance at various times during the writing of this project.

My parents, Dr. Samuel Mazella and Judy Mazella, have always seemed a bit puzzled, but pleased, at the idea of my writing a book. I hope this is what they had in mind. For many, many years, they have given me consistently warm and loving support for my efforts. My children, Helen and Joseph, have enlivened my scholarly days and filled my evenings with joy for some time now. I will never forget how Helen arrived with her mom during a mid-August Houston heat wave, or how Joseph was born just a month after tropical storm Allison. They, too, made their contribution to my life, and my thought, during this period.

Finally, my wife, Beryl Forrest Mazella, learned some time ago that she was living with a book as well as a husband and two kids. She accepted this fate with good humor and grace and has improved me and my book in a thousand different ways. I cannot thank her enough for all that she has provided over the years. This book is dedicated to her.

The Making of Modern Cynicism

INTRODUCTION From the Man of Reason to the Cynical Insider

I reject the cynical view that politics is inevitably or even usually a dirty business.
—Richard M. Nixon, second Watergate speech, August 15, 1973

Learning to Love Your Inner Cynic

When we think about cynicism, we usually think of it as a reaction to the latest political scandal. Viewing it as a mere distraction from more serious business, however, leads us to regard it as an unavoidable part of our present, perhaps an inevitable part of our future, but not necessarily as part of our past. We assume that we are always getting more cynical, or finding that it takes more and more effort to believe what we are told. Each year, we seem to progress toward ever-greater degrees of cynicism, disbelief, or disenchantment. Indeed, this may be the only progress we can discern in our lives.

The place where this disenchantment seems most obvious is, of course, in politics, where cynicism has become a routine part of our everyday political vocabulary, a regular feature of what pundits and newscasters call "the cycle." Yet for all its persistence, cynicism still provokes suspicion, anger, disillusion, and distrust among those who care about politics. Indeed, it is possible to find a news item every day that features one public figure accusing another of cynicism. To give an example from the last primary election season: "To me, there is no room for the cynical politics of manufactured anger and false conviction. I believe in standing for something," the Missouri lawmaker Dick Gephardt said in a speech that heightened his criticism of the Democratic presidential front-runner (at that time, Howard Dean).[1] Yet Gephardt's failed presidential bid demonstrated that his accusations provoked as much cynicism about his own candidacy as they did about his opponent's.

When I considered Gephardt's statement more closely, however, I wondered, just how recent is the manufacture of cynicism? I open a book, for example, called *The Politics of Meaning* (1997), and find Michael Lerner assuring us there that most Clinton-era Americans "are [were?] caught within a web of cynicism that makes us question whether there could be a higher purpose besides material self-interest and looking out for number one."[2] If I am not sure about Lerner's confident diagnosis of America's "hunger for meaning" during the second Clinton administration, I can always turn to Kathleen Jamieson and Joseph Cappella's *Spiral of Cynicism* (1995), which echoes David Broder's 1994 complaint that "cynicism is epidemic right now. It saps people's confidence in politics and public officials, and it erodes both the standing and the standards of journalism."[3] This epidemic, however, dates back at least as far as Jeffery Goldfarb's *The Cynical Society* (1991), which assures us on the first page that the "single most pressing challenge facing American democracy today is widespread public cynicism."[4] Though I do not doubt that repeated viewings of Michael Dukakis riding a tank, paired with round-the-clock Willie Horton ads, would give anyone a "hunger for meaning," I am still not sure that this "pressing challenge" is such a recent phenomenon.

Let us retreat another decade to the mid-1970s, for example, and we will find American political scientists debating the significance of events like the Watergate scandals, Vietnam War protests, and the George Wallace presidential candidacy and wondering whether these events reflected unprecedented levels of "political cynicism" and "alienation."[5] Yet one decade earlier, in the early 1960s, we will find political studies like Edgar Litt's "Political Cynicism and Political Futility." Though the early 1960s have often been treated as a halcyon moment of prepolarized political consensus, Litt was able to write in 1963 that "the politics of Boston glows with a radiance like that of the tubercular patients who lived in the sanatorium of Thomas Mann's *The Magic Mountain*. The corruption, shenanigans, and ineptness of the city's political life have meshed into a continuous political process that has sickened and fascinated observers of its abortive efforts at self-government."[6] Although Litt makes clear how rational his Boston citizens are in their cynicism about local government, we can still step back a few more years and find former Senator William Benton of Connecticut complaining in 1960 that "one of the gravest problems the American people face is the public cynicism about politics and government. We are paying a frightful cost for this unjustified cynicism. Many decent—including many prominent—citizens shy away from assuming civic responsibilities because they mistakenly believe politics and government are generally corrupt and evil."[7] Presumably, the former senator from Connecticut never made the trip to Boston.

If we are still not convinced about how long-standing this kind of complaint is, we can always consult the dictionaries and phrasebooks. The *OED* reminds us of the fundamental alliance of politicians and journalists in the manufacture of cynicism, when we retreat almost eighty years to its examples from 1875 and 1882, and find "a cynical journalist which sneered at every belief," and "the bitter cynicism of the newspaper satirist" (s.vv. "cynical" and "cynicism"). So cynicism has been found lurking in the entanglements of power and publicity for over one hundred years.

Yet we may retreat a decade further to the embittered "Pennsylvania Teuton" who wrote *The Snarl of A Cynic. A Rhyme* (1868), which laments the recent loss of civic virtue among the politicians of his generation:

Our legislation is controlled
  By rogues with fraud and shrewd devices;
Law-maker's votes are bought and sold
        At various prices.

The public good, my mind recalls,
  Once moved the patriot's zeal and passion,
But now in legislative halls
        Quite out of fashion.[8]

These milquetoast cynics, however, will not be outdone by those painted by Henry Ward Beecher in his sermons. In 1853, Beecher (later removed from his fashionable New York church for an affair with a member of his congregation) presented a series of sermons depicting the vices of his age, including, of course, the cynic. In Beecher's portrait, the cynic was a "human owl, vigilant in darkness and blind to light, mousing for vermin, and never seeing noble game."[9] Beecher, never one for understatement, also described the cynic as a "swoln [*sic*] wretch, blotched all over with leprosy, [who] may grin hideously at every wart or excrescence upon beauty" (118–19).

Which leads me to the question that initially provoked this book: Why are we so afraid of cynics? Why should we talk about cynicism in such alarmist tones, when it seems to have been such a stable, persistent, indeed, routine aspect of modern politics for the better part of 150 years? Why should every year bring a round of fresh denunciations, when all previous denunciations have demonstrably failed—or indeed, when their only measurable effect has been to deepen our cynicism? What, precisely, does widespread cynicism threaten? And what problems does the cynic create for other, presumably noncynical people? These were the questions I thought needed answering when I realized that virtually every extant discussion of cynicism took its harmfulness for granted.[10] Yet the precise forms taken by cynicism in these denunciations, and the types of harm for which it seemed responsible, varied drastically from one account to the next, and from one historical moment to the next. I thought, therefore, that a closer, more historical look at these questions might help move the discussion into more fruitful areas.

Now that I have written the book and reflected upon this initial set of questions, I can offer this provisional answer, which the rest of my analysis will have to make good. Cynics are feared because they threaten the public with a genuinely worrying prospect, a future without hope of meaningful change. At the very least, cynics foresee a future in which individuals have little chance of fixing their problems or improving their conditions in life or at work.

Although some have regarded cynicism simply as mere passivity or fatalism, I find such descriptions partial and misleading. The cynic's special psychic burden resides in his[11] conviction that the problems he faces are indeed amenable to intellectual solutions, while also remaining convinced that those concerned will never work together to solve their problems. Without the cynic's tacit recognition of the possibilities for improvement, we would not have the well-known frustration and anger of the cynic—transmuted into the cynic's characteristic irony and aggressive detachment—at the social deadlock that has so thoroughly thwarted him and his desires for change.[12] This is part of the meaning behind the familiar saying that "underneath every cynic lies a disappointed idealist."

The major reason why cynics doubt the possibility of collective action or social change lies in their suspicion of language, particularly language used for political purposes or in public settings generally. The cynic's most characteristic gesture is to doubt the sincerity of others' speech, while refusing to take at face value other people's accounts of their motives or actions.[13] This renders the cynic immune to persuasion by others, and indeed leaves him with doubts about the possibility of persuasion ever taking place. Consequently, the cynic finds little use for the give and take of everyday political discussion.

Interestingly enough, however, the cynic will sometimes garner sympathetic reactions when he announces that the endless talk demanded by the democratic process has become not just unpleasant and time-consuming but futile.[14] (Note that this judgment takes the form of a prediction that is impossible to refute.)

For the cynic angrily watching the TV news or reading the newspaper or getting his news online, all the everyday language of politics—including stump speeches, position papers, primaries, caucuses, sit-downs, block parties, rallies, meetings, coffee-klatsches, news reports, candidate interviews, telephone banks, and so on—all these can be safely dismissed as so much nonsense and persiflage. After all, the cynic knows that the two things politicians really care about, no matter what they tell you, are their own self-interest and their desire for power. Though the cynic may not be alone in this suspicion, he does often seem the only one willing to voice such doubts, because he was never committed to the democratic process in the first place.

The series of denunciations and diagnoses of cynicism I have just surveyed register the persistence of complaints against the cynic, but they also register a recurrent anxiety about this figure. In regularly banishing the cynic from democratic society for his distrust of the system, the denunciations also betray an anxiety, never fully resolved, about the legitimacy and historically and politically progressive nature of democracy, assumptions that lean heavily upon the presumed rationality of public opinion, the quality of democratic procedures of decision making, and the usefulness of political discussion.[15] Cynicism, of course, throws doubt upon all these assumptions. That is why it causes so much anxiety among those committed to the political process in one way or another. Nonetheless, our anxiety about democratic legitimacy and historical progress is only partially satisfied by such rituals of denunciation, denunciations of the cynics and doubters and disbelievers who dare manifest the discontent that many others share about their political institutions, whatever their ideological convictions. In other words, cynics inspire such fear and anxiety not only because of their refusal to believe, but because their distrust and disbelief seem plausible enough to spread like an epidemic throughout the entire system. This is why cynicism is always labeled a "problem" or "challenge" for the democratic political process. The legitimacy of the system hinges on its capacities for change, and cynics question precisely this aspect of the system.

Though I would not have written this book if I shared the belief that political discussion was a futile undertaking, I do not think that we should discount such reactions.[16] Indeed, I wrote this book from the conviction that the only way to make our system more truly democratic would be to address popular cynicism in more effective, less moralistic ways.[17] The persistence of cynicism in contemporary political life points to the often unspoken limits of political discussion: where it can go, what it can say, what it can do. Analyzing cynicism is one of the ways that those desirous of change can make the limits of discussion a matter of explicit reflection, debate, and contestation. Such a process might take us beyond the current deadlocks in discussion, past the legitimation of the status quo, and toward more meaningful, substantive forms of change. An analysis of cynicism will not save us from the demands of politics, but it might be able to give us the historical and conceptual resources to get the hard work of political persuasion restarted.

A Cynic's Lexicon, Part 1: Politics without a Future Tense

A cynic is not merely one who reads bitter lessons from the past, he is one who is prematurely disappointed in the future.

—Sidney J. Harris

So how does the concept of cynicism undermine our hopes for the future? By denying, first of all, that popular discontent with the political system will help drive forward progressive social change. Cynicism, like the poststructuralist antifoundationalism it sometimes resembles, removes the causal and metaphysical links that once undergirded ideologies of historical "progress" in the nineteenth and twentieth centuries.[18] At the most fundamental level of individual political agency and rationality, cynicism questions our ability to foresee the perverse outcomes of our actions, or to plan rationally around those perverse effects.[19] When the cynic considers collective political actions, the threat of hidden agendas or unintended consequences seems enough to overwhelm any possible benefit. In other words, cynicism opens serious doubts about the viability of rational political agency and makes every desire for political change seem equally naïve or uninformed. These kinds of doubts make it difficult to plan for any large-scale social transformation that could improve people's lives on a broad scale.

Cynicism also subverts our desires for collective action and a better future by attacking human institutions and the entire process of institutionalization. Cynicism targets institutionalization for the temporal gap it creates between the institution and the beliefs that helped shaped it. The cynic then *moralizes* this gap by treating institutional settings as hypocritical, soulless, or otherwise devoid of the beliefs that once animated them.[20] To use Certeau's famous distinction, institutions are by definition the place where "beliefs" no longer organize "practices."[21] Yet human institutions can only accumulate the strength and solidity they have by reproducing themselves over time, and, as such, they remain one of the few ways we have for projecting collective decisions into the future.[22] Nonetheless, cynicism recasts one of the key desiderata of politics—institutional stability—into unthinking resistance to time, opportunity, or circumstance. The institutional stability envisioned by cynicism is nothing more than a stalemate or deadlock, an unhappy, unsatisfying state of affairs desired by none of those who helped to create or sustain it. This nightmarish version of stability becomes nothing more than an unending series of arguments or stalled actions.

Cynicism's dramatic recasting of political language, of the future, of the possibilities of collective action, and of institutions generally, suggests its most disorienting quality, its ability to render even the most affirmative terms in our moral and political vocabulary empty and unsatisfying. The political theorist William Chaloupka, for example, has observed that "cynicism clashes with familiar and powerful ways of characterizing social life. It resists and subverts the important social themes, such as faith, rationality, utopia, or reform. It undermines how we think about important concepts: freedom, authority, society, self, change, and stability. As cynicism spreads, discontent takes different qualities" (12). Cynicism defamiliarizes terms like faith, rationality, or reform by detaching them from the emotional satisfactions and robust agency they were once thought to uphold. Cynicism degrades critique, autonomy, and intellectual freedom, for example, into sneering and doubting. It recasts society and traditional social authorities into degraded, time-serving institutions hardly worthy of commitment or respect. Yet cynicism can hardly be considered a celebration of individualism, either, since the cynical self remains too passive and self-divided to sustain any critique of, or distance from, whatever surrounds it. Cynics feel no less cynical about themselves than they do about others.[23]

In other words, cynicism offers a drastic *redescription* of our experience that reverses existing political and moral valuations. What makes such moral redescriptions seem so dangerous, however, resides in the cynic's ability to persuade others of such reductive views and spread the contagion of disbelief widely enough to threaten the entire political system.

For all the troubling political implications of cynicism, I believe nonetheless that its persistence in our political discourse makes it an invaluable critical concept, largely because it complicates some of modernity's most cherished self-images, its myths of rationality, dynamism, and progress. For this reason, cynicism, for all its affinities with conservative thought, has genuine critical potential, revealing the extent to which our key concepts of collective action and planning rely on unexamined assumptions about progress, modernity, and modernization.

A Cynic's Lexicon, Part 2: The Ensemble Effect

Cynics are made, not born.

—Anonymous

So what qualities of cynicism help to produce its supposed nightmarish stability, its stubborn persistence, its kudzulike ability to reproduce and spread in all directions?

The first step to understanding cynicism is realizing that it does not simply refer to an individual's psychological state. In this respect, the *OED* definition seems inadequate when it describes the "cynic" as one who is predisposed "to disbelieve in the sincerity or goodness of human motives or actions, and [who is] wont to express this by sneers and sarcasms" (*OED,* s.vv. "cynic," cynical," "cynicism"). If this were its only meaning, then the cynic would represent nothing more than a specific character type, a kind of updated malcontent or misanthrope for our own era. "Cynicism" does not assume real importance until it is seen as a mass concept, and as an attitude potentially shared by large numbers of people. The term points as much to the kind of social situation productive of cynicism as it does to the cynical reactions and personalities of those marked by that social situation.

Cynicism, in other words, is a social concept, a term that describes interactions, not individuals or their states of consciousness. Chaloupka confirms this when he notes that the unitary term "cynicism" encompasses a variety of attitudes, and attributes its strength and persistence to the fact that it operates as a heterogeneous ensemble. "Cynicism," Chaloupka writes, "is not uniformly an affliction or an injury. Indeed, it is more than one thing, and as an ensemble, cynicism does its work at the core of Americans' relationship to political life. But the ensemble effect is important. The cynicism of leaders does not simply produce or reflect the cynicism of citizens" (xiv–xv).

Chaloupka's point about cynicism's "ensemble effect" suggests why cynicism has been so difficult to analyze or reduce. The notorious difficulty of defining cynicism, or of coordinating its various conflicting meanings, stems from the fact that it refers to an ensemble of mutually reinforcing attitudes rather than a single attitude uniformly held within the ensemble. Its power and persistence reside in its ability to sustain itself as an ensemble even while absorbing various attempts to change the dynamic. This ensemble manages to generate perverse effects for all parties engaged in—and even those abstaining from—processes of political discussion or negotiation.

At the same time, cynicism is not simply reproduced in a mimetic fashion from one power position to the next. It is wrong to think that the cynicism of rulers is a mirror image of the cynicism of the ruled. This is one reason why the usual denunciations actually help cynicism, in Chaloupka's fine phrase, to feed on its remedies. Attacking, for example, the reflexive distrust and apathy of the powerless will only leave the self-seeking of the powerful untouched.[24] To address the workings of the ensemble requires something more: a more comprehensive view of its workings in relation to power and publicity, and more self-reflective strategies about how to alter the internal dynamics of the ensemble.

In the discussion that follows, I will be drawing upon the political theorist Alan Keenan's "taxonomy of political cynicisms," but I would like to extend Keenan's work by showing how the various types he delineates actually function as part of the "ensemble effect" just described in Chaloupka. Following Keenan, we may define the three ideal types as (1) the "master-cynic," who wields power within the political system; (2) the cynical (though disempowered) insiders, whose publicity helps sustain the political system; and (3) the powerless "outsider-cynics," who operate as the passive, excluded "public" of the political system.[25] Each of these cynics maintains a specific relation to the structures of power and publicity, which, in turn, determine the behavior of each cynical type within the political process.

Assuming with Keenan that the content of cynicism can be minimally defined as "the belief that the ultimate motives of human action are self-interest and the quest for power," we can begin by defining each of these three types by their relation to power. Keenan's "master-cynic" (cf. also Sloterdijk) eagerly pursues power and self-interest, but this type is also careful to "take hypocritical advantage of the scruples and ideals of others."[26] "Master-cynicism" is a form of political rationality that predicts behavior by assuming the worst about people, but it is also careful not to operate too much in the open. Although the master-cynic regards the public as completely enslaved by its own blindness, he does not wish to alert them to his operations.

Master-cynicism, for all its reliance upon publicity, is nonetheless shy of publicizing itself and is wary of disclosing its secrets. It is manipulative in that it coolly and rationally exploits the irrationality of the public.[27] It is hypocritical to the extent that it never seriously pursues the beliefs (ideals, norms, codes, or creeds) that it urges others to practice. Master-cynicism pays lip service to the conventional values and moralities of the ruled, but this strategy leaves gaps between its elevated pronouncements and its self-seeking behavior. In other words, master-cynicism leaves enough of its workings in view to foster the cynicism of the powerless.

The next position down would be the cynical mediators, the "insiders" who help confer legitimacy upon the powerful. Members of this group mimic the cynicism of the powerful, but more from fear of losing their position or security than from any power seeking of their own. These are the alienated middlemen, the professional shapers of public opinion and redescribers of reality who are given the job of creating and sustaining the illusions that allow the powerful to rule. Insider cynicism differs from master-cynicism, however, because of its habits of indiscretion. Insiders often take enough pride in their verbal redescriptions to brag of their success, something the truly powerful cynic would never do. The insider-cynic, near but never quite possessing the power he serves, allows the public a precious glimpse into the appalling processes of real power. Emblematic here would be David Stockman's scandalous public admissions about his fictitious budget numbers during the first Reagan administration. This is the abject cynicism of shamelessness, the cynicism that confesses to more than it ever intended.

The least powerful, though by no means the least important, position would be the cynicism of the powerless, or what might be called the cynical public. According to Keenan, these cynics are the "disempowered outsiders," "whose distrust of the motivations of others, especially those with power, would be born of the disappointment with the failure to realize the promises and ideals of democratic politics and a lack of faith in the possibility of positive change. . . . This last variety of cynicism can, in turn, take many forms, including both active hostility towards government and politicians, and alienation, apathy, and abstention from participation."[28] This is the disenchanted, disillusioned cynicism of the alienated and distrustful, those whose opinions are treated instrumentally by the political system, whose expectations are perpetually disappointed and desires thwarted, and those who are more than willing to abstain entirely from a system designed to minimize the impact of their participation.

Breaking up the Ensemble

If my reading of Chaloupka and Keenan is correct, cynicism's ensemble effect is as impervious as it is because we both moralize and psychologize it, focusing our attention upon one symptomatic manifestation after another, without ever recognizing their systemic relation to one another. Paradoxically, by moralizing its most symptomatic expressions in everyday political language, we also depoliticize it, failing to recognize how each part of the ensemble (master-cynic, insider-cynic, cynical public) operates within a political and institutional nexus of power and publicity that helps produce more and more cynicism. And indeed, moralizing denunciations of cynicism, like moralizing accusations of cynicism—or indeed like most proposed moral remedies of cynicism—accomplish nothing more than further, unintended reinforcement of existing cynicism.

So how might we try to break apart the ensemble effect in ways that do not simply deepen existing cynicism? We might begin by recognizing that cynicism is most common in an environment where discussion is routinely conducted through moralizing polemics and the delegitimation of one's opponents.[29] In other words, cynicism is *not* produced by a so-called "belief deficit" in which some or all of the parties to a discussion fail to share some common belief but is instead the result of a breakdown in the social and political institutions that sustain discussion, and ultimately, persuasion. Without such institutions, we often lack the political and discursive forums that make negotiated compromise (*pace* Rawls, *not* consensus) possible.[30] And without the institutional stability that encourages quarreling parties to compromise, we find it far more difficult to produce the creative verbal redescriptions that help move those parties away from their initial negotiating stances toward mutual persuasion. Both polemics and the moralistic obsession with the legitimacy of one's opponents are symptoms of this institutional breakdown. Nevertheless, the only way to break free of the enforced repetition of the cynical deadlock is to conduct a different kind of argument. This kind of argument would discover, first of all, how we have fallen into the traps that have captured discussion thus far, and would use that historical knowledge to get the political process of persuasion restarted.

To accomplish this, I have used the history of this term's varied meanings to write in the mixed historical-literary-philosophical genre of the "genealogy." Foucault took this term over from Nietzsche to describe a form of antiprogressive, antiteleological historical investigation conducted for the sake of understanding one's own historical moment.[31] In the succinct definition of Wendy Brown, genealogy for Foucault is "not merely a method of historical inquiry and political analysis, but . . . an intellectual orientation potentially generative of new political directions."[32]

Like Brown, I see Foucault's commitment to Nietzsche and genealogy as one that runs throughout his career, uniting the quite disparate methods and interests of works like "Nietzsche, Genealogy, and History," *Discipline and Punish,*

The History of Sexuality, and even the reading of Kant in "What Is Enlightenment?" This last example reveals the extent to which Foucault conceived his practice as in some way a "reactivation" (42) of Kant's pioneering attempt to reflect on "'Today' as difference in history and as motive for a particular philosophical task."[33] And indeed, reactivating this philosophical ethos, which Foucault identifies with the Enlightenment, remains one of the goals of this book, even as it investigates the complex historical continuities and discontinuities between cynicism and the Enlightenment in England and Great Britain.

A genealogical response to cynicism's ensemble effect, which could also be called a "conceptual history" of cynicism, would emphasize, first of all, the historicity and therefore the specificity of the situation we now inhabit.[34] Though cynicism describes an interminable, deadlocked state of stalemate and collusion among the powerful, their publicists, and the public, the genealogist would note that the modern concept of cynicism appeared in English at a very specific historical moment, the close of the eighteenth century and the beginning of the nineteenth.[35] In other words, the modern concept of cynicism emerges around the same time that the hopes for an Enlightenment in Great Britain were destroyed first by the French Revolution, then by Britain's Counter-Revolutionary reaction, and finally by the Napoleonic wars.

The historical circumstances surrounding cynicism's emergence might therefore help to reveal dimensions of the concept that are hard to recognize in the present, but which remain relevant to understanding how the concept operates in contemporary culture. Recovering the long-term historical semantic formation of cynicism might also help us to grasp its extraordinary slipperiness in terms of both its meaning and its range of reference and application.[36] It is, to use William Empson's suggestive term, a "complex word" whose range of moral and social implications is broad indeed, and which contains an extensive history that somehow lurks in the background in even the most casual uses.

The Uses of History

This book's largest claim is that the complexities, involutions, and internal structures of a term like "cynicism" are best unpacked through a genealogical analysis of its lengthy semantic history, to see precisely how it assumed its current importance, and hopefully to generate new and more effective political directions. The first step in such an investigation is to recognize the various, and discontinuous, layers of historical meaning encompassed by the seemingly simple, unitary term "cynic."

To begin with the earliest and therefore most unfamiliar portion of that history as it appears in the *OED*, "Cynic" (generally uppercase) has for most of its history simply denoted a follower of the ancient Greek philosopher Diogenes the Cynic (ca. 412–403–ca. 324–321 BC), while "Cynicism" was merely "the philosophy of the Cynics," or, more broadly, a "Cynical disposition, character, or quality" (cf. *OED*, s.vv. "Cynic," "Cynicism").[37] These philosophers "were marked by an ostentatious contempt for ease, wealth, and the enjoyments of life; the most famous was Diogenes . . . who carried the principles of the sect to an extreme of asceticism" (s.v. "cynic"). In one of the earliest *OED* entries, for example, taken from William Baldwin's *A Treatise of Morall Philosophie* (1547–64), we find: "He fel straight to the sect of the cinikes, and became Diogenes scholer" (1.19).[38] A Cynic is a philosophical follower or "scholer" of Diogenes, and consequently denies himself pleasure to instruct others how to live in accordance with virtue.

In the course of this book, I will have much more to say about Diogenes the Cynic and how his singular personality and history helped to instantiate Cynic philosophy for nearly two thousand years. For now, however, I would only like to stress how different this philosopher's character was from the modern cynic, who is a morally compromised, overly accommodating "moral chameleon."[39] This disparity between ancient and modern cynicism is all the more striking because Diogenes was in many respects the most uncompromising of the followers of Socratic philosophy. He was the ancient philosopher who demanded the most from himself and his followers in terms of asceticism, cheerful acceptance of hardship, verbal freedom, and absolute physical and intellectual self-sufficiency. In contrast with Plato's "strategic," institutionalizing reason, which characterized the Cynic philosopher as a "Socrates out of his Senses," Diogenes embodied a "tactical" reason that was itinerant, timely, and opportunistic, uninterested in accumulating either power or possessions in one place.[40]

For this reason, Diogenes was often considered the Greek philosopher who most successfully infused his philosophy with the quality of masculine independence, fighting off the temptations of a corrupt and feminizing society, even when it addressed him in the person of Alexander the Great. In one of the most famous exchanges of antiquity, when Alexander asked the sunbathing philosopher what he could do for him, Diogenes' only response was, "Stand out of my light!" Diogenes therefore set a standard of uncompromising philosophical independence and integrity in his relations with the powerful that no other ancient philosopher could equal.

Diogenes' unwillingness to compromise, however, was not limited to the dictates of power or the temptations of the flesh but extended to the most deeply held beliefs of the community. More than any other ancient philosopher, Diogenes believed that philosophy was obliged to challenge the conventional values, beliefs, and customs of the community—to "deface the currency" of commonly held opinions.[41] Diogenes himself operated fully in accordance with this ethos; living as an itinerant beggar, he took care to flout or scandalize the feelings of the communities wherever he lived. In the anecdotes recording Diogenes' outrageous behavior and jokes at the expense of the citizens of Sinope, Corinth, and Athens, we find the first traces of Cynic philosophy as it was transmitted to subsequent generations. This ancient Cynic philosophy, in its wit, self-denial, and shameless independence, maintained a significant but complex relation to the modern attitude that shares its name.

It is worth reflecting for a moment on the manifest differences between the ancient Cynic Diogenes and his modern, cynical counterpart. The largest difference lies in the modern cynic's evasion of the demands of either philosophical reflection or moral self-regulation, demands that were paramount for the uncompromising ancient Cynics. Diogenes faces down the conqueror of the world; the modern cynic accommodates himself to whoever is in power. The ancient Cynic flouts conventional values because he is a philosophical hero, devoted to the cosmopolitan reason that permits him to recognize the customs, forms, institutions, and authorities around him as local, contingent, even unnatural. The modern cynic, however, has lost all interest in philosophy and lacks the Cynics' asceticism or freedom of speech. The modern cynic has abandoned his counterpart's ideals of reason and philosophy, to take up instead a life of rationalization and intellectual accommodation. By the close of the nineteenth century, Oscar Wilde could label the cynic, "a man who knows the price of everything and the value of nothing" (*Lady Windermere's Fan*).[42] Modern cynicism had come to describe something antithetical to its previous meanings, a psychological state hardened against both moral reflection and intellectual persuasion. This is what Peter Sloterdijk had in mind when he labeled modern cynicism "enlightened false consciousness." This joyless, anti-intellectual, and self-enclosed version of cynicism only travesties the fearless, physically active philosophy of Diogenes the Cynic and his followers.

The enormous ethical, political, and historical disparities between ancient and modern cynicisms, however, only beg the question of how and when these changes occurred. It is the burden of this book's narrative to show how the transition took place, and what surrounding circumstances invested modern cynicism with the discursive power it currently holds.

Our first clue resides in the subsequent, early modern layer of the *OED*'s entries, which defines a "cynic" as a "person disposed to rail or find fault." Such a definition represents an ethical and intellectual narrowing and comic reduction of the Cynic philosopher. These cynics are closely related to the early modern character type of the "misanthrope," "malcontent," or "railer" found in so many of the formal verse satires, character writings, or stage comedies between the sixteenth and eighteenth centuries. These Cynics are not usually presented as conscious or philosophic followers of Diogenes, but instead as men who merely "resemble the Cynic philosophers in contempt of pleasure, churlishness, or disposition to find fault[; men who are] surly, currish, misanthropic, captious" (s.v. "cynical"). Whereas the ancient Cynic is seen to have an ascetic, reasoned basis for his refusals, the early modern type is seen as passionately addicted to complaint. This period's Cynic is synonymous with "misanthrope" or "man-hater," and sixteenth- and seventeenth-century satires are filled with self-consciously learned allusions to the Cynic's doglike nature (for example, Heywood's "Peace Cinicke, barke not dogge" [1632]). These meanings were still current through much of the eighteenth century, as we can see in Samuel Johnson's 1755 *Dictionary* definition of the "Cynick" or "Cynick philosopher": "philosopher of the snarling or currish sort; a follower of Diogenes; a rude man; a snarler; a misanthrope."[43] Though these definitions all retained some connection with Diogenes and Cynic philosophy, they also show how Cynic philosophy had been reduced to a burlesque of itself by the mid-eighteenth century.

The final stage of semantic development in the *OED* citations occurs around 1814, the date of the first recognized usage of "cynic" in its familiar, modern sense of one who demonstrates "a disposition to disbelieve in the sincerity or goodness of human motives and actions, and is wont to express this by sneers and sarcasms; a sneering fault-finder" (s.v. "cynic"). The *OED*'s 1814 entry records the literary historian Isaac D'Israeli's observation that "our cynical Hobbes had no respect for his species." D'Israeli's portrait of the philosopher—whom he calls a "polished cynic"—describes not an ancient but a modern cynic, the unreflective product of mass society. According to D'Israeli, Hobbes's cynical "dogmas," which he links to other modern immoralists like Machiavelli or Mandeville, "only degrade us" in their insistence on selfishness and self-preservation as the universal motives for behavior. According to D'Israeli, these cynical assumptions about human nature constitute a "philosophy true only for the wretched and the criminal." This is cynicism as disbelief, distrust, disillusionment, or disenchantment on the broadest possible social scale. Under that moment's ideological pressure, D'Israeli has displaced over two thousand years of philosophical history and helped detach cynicism permanently from the founder of ancient Cynicism.

Thus, even by the end of the eighteenth century, "Cynic" generally referred to a specific philosophical sect, however construed. At the beginning of the nineteenth century, however, this stable referent for "Cynicism" in philosophical history became less important, and the word "cynic" took on radically new meanings. This phase, we might say, completed the *vernacularization* of cynicism, the process whereby the concept freed itself from its ancient Greek origins and evolved into an important term in the Anglo-British vocabularies regarding the formation of trust and belief.[44] Thus, the most significant rupture in the meanings of cynicism occurred around 1814, when the modern notion of cynicism took on its own autonomy and importance in our moral and political lexicon.

My brief outline of the various semantic layers contained within the *OED* definitions should indicate the histories embedded within the term, but it still leaves open many questions regarding the timing and causes of these various changes, which I hope the following chapters will answer. Why, for example, did cynicism change at this particular moment at the end of the eighteenth century, and why did the change occur so many centuries after the Cynic movement's own historical moment had come and gone? What historical circumstances led to the change? Which features of the premodern Cynic helped invite these transformations in the late eighteenth century and early nineteenth century? And which features of the modern cynic were retained from earlier Cynics, which features were transformed, and which features were entirely new and unprecedented? At a more general level, how does the prehistory of cynicism as an important moral concept—Cynicism prior to 1800—illuminate its subsequent evolution into an important, though underanalyzed, term in the moral and political lexicon of modernity?

Making Cynicism

To counter the philosophic amnesia initiated by D'Israeli, *The Making of Modern Cynicism* confronts the ahistorical modern cynic with the reception-history of his ancient counterpart, Diogenes. In the passage from the uppercase Cynic philosopher to the lowercase cynic, we can observe that the attitude now known as modern cynicism was *made*—in Certeau's sense of *poiesis,* making, but also using—by innumerable writers and speakers out of a variety of ancient and contemporary materials across the centuries. From his lifetime onward, Diogenes the Cynic appeared successively as philosopher, moralist, and intellectual, but for each epoch this figure also represented some version of the "Man of Reason," the heroically or comically "Unmoved Man" who demonstrates his independent Reason by rejecting the opinions of others.[45]

To explain how the modern notion of cynicism was produced by a series of events between the seventeenth and the late eighteenth century, *The Making of Modern Cynicism* reads the conceptual history of these terms within a constellation of related cultural, historical, and literary contexts. These contexts include the cultural history of individuals such as Diogenes or Jean-Jacques Rousseau, whose reputations as famous "Cynics" made them into emblematic figures for English culture (for example, Diogenes or Rousseau as familiar symbols either of "virtuous poverty" or "shamelessness"). Equally relevant is the literary history of the diverse set of genres whose discussions of Cynics influenced the semantic development of the concepts, including pre-eighteenth-century genres (anecdote collections, apophthegms, Dialogues of the Dead); eighteenth-century genres (satiric poems, sentimental novels, essays, political pamphlets); and works by or about certain key authors or fictionalized figures (for example, Lucian, Rousseau, William Godwin).

What all these discursive contexts and genres share is a common interest in the personal ethics of the public Man of Reason, the extent to which the philosopher or author either lives up to or discredits his announced intellectual ideals. To use a favorite metaphor of Michel Foucault, it is a question of how well the philosopher "harmonizes" his doctrine with his life, a quality that can only emerge from a lifelong process of self-"testing." Even modern cynicism honors this notion when it obsessively notes the failures of writers to match the ideals they have so assiduously publicized. Thus, genres like the anecdote, confession, memoir, biography, or semifictionalized secret history play crucial roles in the development of the concept of cynicism, as does the notion of scandalous truth telling (*parrhesia*) first explored by Diogenes as a form of ascetic discipline.[46] Each chapter, however, will focus upon the genres and contexts that reflect most directly the semantic developments in the concept.

The six chapters of *The Making of Modern Cynicism* correspond to the major phases in the concept's passage from premodern meanings to modern ones and show how radically our notions of the intellectual and moralist have changed since the classical era and how problematic this figure's relation to his audience or public has become. What did it mean, for example, to be a Socratic philosopher and moralist in ancient Greece, and how did Diogenes and the Cynics travesty that role in their parodies and serio-comic "philosophizing"? Moreover, how were Diogenes' practices as semiserious philosopher and morally equivocal moralist further ironized and elaborated during the early modern and Enlightenment periods? The first two chapters feature the ancient Greek and early modern English versions of the Cynics; the next three chapters, which constitute the core of the argument, trace the appearances of Diogenes and Cynicism in eighteenth-century British writing through the French Revolution and the Counter-Revolutionary reaction; the final chapter follows the modern, disillusioned cynic from Regency England to contemporary political arguments about democracy and the relation of intellectuals to an increasingly abstract and notional public.

To describe this oddly nonlinear trajectory of "the Cynic" from antiquity to the present, I will draw upon the historiographer Mark Salber Phillips's very useful notion of "reframing," a master metaphor for historical change that works well with Certeau's notions of cultural transmission as collective processes of "making" and "use." Phillips is dissatisfied with our limited range of concepts regarding historical change, discovery, and discontinuity in intellectual history, and wishes to write a less abstract, idealized, and linear version of what he calls "the movement of ideas." To address this need, Phillips offers a less individualistic model of collective intellectual activity and stresses its reliance instead upon the eminently institutional processes of collective discoveries, debates, and accommodations. Phillips therefore describes this process of collective intellectual discussion and discovery as *"reframing"*—meaning the re-use, reconfiguration, and redirection of existing materials—rather than the single-handed invention of novel concepts and arguments. Indeed, once we begin to focus on the irreducibly linguistic (and therefore collective and rhetorical) dimension of knowledge production in fields like politics, history, or literature, innovations gain support largely through such "tactical" devices as *re*framing (in effect, *re*capturing, and *re*directing) existing language and concepts for one's own purposes. As it turns out, many of our notions of modern, degraded cynicism involve this kind of linguistic reframing, in what I have already termed "moral redescription": changing the moral valence of a situation simply by redescribing it in ways more or less acceptable to one's audience.

As an intellectual historian, Phillips grounds his discussion on the observation that "statements identical in form may bear very different meanings depending on the context of questioning." (We may think of the sheer variety of meanings discovered in Diogenes' retort to Alexander, "Get out of my light!") As Phillips states, intellectual change, or the "movement of ideas," occurs chiefly through a "repositioning [of existing elements] that responds to changing contexts and needs."[47] Reframing can cause "familiar but subordinated notions [to] acquire a new centrality, thereby taking on a new meaning and seriousness in relation to other concerns; conversely, "older ideas may slip to the side, though without in any real sense disappearing." Phillips's notion of reframing is the best account I have seen that explains, for example, the extremely divergent ranges of images of Diogenes that have been drawn from a limited repertoire of anecdotes since antiquity.[48] It also suggests how relatively undeveloped hints in the anecdotal tradition concerning, say, Diogenes' misogyny could be expanded into dominant aspects of his reception in subsequent periods. And it seems peculiarly appropriate to use such a methodology to describe the Cynics, who were emblems of intellectual thrift, to explain how they became antiquity's biggest advocates of the principle "use what is present." Hence, each successive chapter of this book will treat a new "reframing" of the Cynic and Cynicism that reorients these literary, philosophical, and historical materials in a decisive new way.

Chapter 1 begins with ancient Cynicism's founder, Diogenes of Sinope, a philosopher whose greatest legacy was the corpus of anecdotes that others told and recorded about him, not in his lost writings. The Diogenes anecdotes embody in the briefest, most vivid way possible the scandalous qualities celebrated by Cynic philosophy's distinctive "way of life": shamelessness, mendicancy, parodic philosophizing, and fearless speech. The Diogenes of this anecdotal tradition constitutes a "philosophical hero" whose entire life demonstrates the superiority of Cynic philosophy's "shortcut to virtue." Diogenes therefore "defaced the currency" of conventional values wherever he found them, whether in the crowds flocking to hear the Cynics preach, in the luxurious courts of tyrants, or in the doctrines of his philosophical rivals. As much as is humanly possible, Diogenes exemplified a philosopher whose "practices" harmonized with his "doctrines," a convergence that allowed him to speak the truth as a parrhesiast, or one who "says all" despite the risk to himself.

As early as Lucian's satires on the Cynics, however, Lucian's succession of cheerful philosophical frauds competed with the truth-telling "philosophical hero" as the dominant image of the Cynic philosopher. In Lucian's influential counterimages of Cynic philosophy, particularly in his satirical portrait of the effeminate semi-Christian crowd-pleaser Peregrinus Proteus, we find for the first time some of the attributes of the modern cynic: fraudulence, intellectual opportunism, and an eagerness to use elevated philosophical language to rationalize his bad behavior. The imposter Peregrinus's public suicide shows what happens to Cynic shamelessness when it is no longer underwritten by the Man of Reason's integrity, self-sufficiency, or harmonization of words and deeds: it has ceased to exist as true "lived philosophy" and devolves into a hypocritical "verbal philosophy" fit for haranguing crowds and leaping onto pyres.

The second chapter describes the initial phase of vernacularization of Cynicism in the early modern period, when Diogenes anecdotes and Lucianic dialogues played an important role in the rhetorical curriculum used in the English grammar schools. The early modern Diogenes cannot be understood outside the rhetorical forms and frames that used the Cynics to represent a plainspoken yet "tactical" wit that always remained foreign to the imperatives of courtly life, civility, and power. We find the Cynics repeatedly used and reused in tropes like the Diogenes-Alexander encounter to represent the rhetorically trained "counsellor" addressing (and potentially improving) his audience of one, the sovereign. In such humanist fantasies, the Cynic philosopher is, for the first time, located *inside* a system of persuasion and power, which is associated with the flattering potential of *paradiastole,* or positive moral redescription.

Yet this period also witnesses a host of displaced vernacular cynics and misanthropes who deny rhetoric's association of persuasion with power. Some have simply been driven away from the courtly centers of power, while others represent the breakdown of the entire model of rhetorical power and agency assumed by the earlier writers. This is clearest in Shakespeare's *Timon of Athens,* which portrays the "churlish philosopher" Apemantus as a false and uninspiring Cynic who has concealed the conventionality of his views from everyone but his enemy Timon. Because it demonstrates the irrelevance of both intellectual reflection (Apemantus) and heroic action (Alcibiades) in the general breakdown of persuasion that has taken place in Athens, *Timon* anticipates the modern, disillusioned cynicism that has lost all hope of ameliorating social problems with reasoned political solutions. *Timon* therefore represents one of the first attempts to outline the workings of the "ensemble effect" in the early modern period.

In the third chapter, the collapse of rhetoric and the breakdown of persuasion hinted at in *Timon* had become literally true during the general collapse of inherited authorities during the Civil Wars. One of the products of this collapse was the burlesque Cynic, who found himself outside such conventional values of the post-Restoration era as modernity, progress, politeness, commerce, and "improvement." Yet these burlesque Cynics, once they were freed from that dependence upon the sovereign, remained enemies of the indeterminate modern public or "multitude," as Davenant's pleasure-hating Puritan Diogenes proves in his *First Day's Entertainment.* By the time we reach Lyttelton's demagogic Diogenes in his Dialogue of Diogenes and Plato, we see a Diogenes capable of governing a mob himself. Lyttelton's Diogenes, inspired perhaps by the popular agitations of Wilkes in the 1760s, debates Plato to a standstill on the question of whether philosophers owe more obligations to "the people" or their rulers. Thus, the single largest factor in the transformation of the Cynic between the early modern through the Enlightenment period was the collapse of rhetorical humanism's stratified model of face-to-face interaction, and its replacement by the new, postrhetorical configuration of power and publicity demanded by a vernacular print culture.

In the fourth chapter, Jean-Jacques Rousseau plays a unique role in the formation of the concept of cynicism in English, since he is one of the few figures accused of being a Cynic in both the premodern and modern senses of the term. In the first, Diogenical phase of his career, his radical critique of the luxury and effeminacy of modern civilization made his contemporaries compare him to the rudeness, shamelessness, or misanthropy of the ancient Cynics. In the second phase, Rousseau's popularity as a writer of sentimental fiction, combined with his public break with the philosophes, led to a new and more polarized set of public images of Rousseau: Rousseau the sentimental truth-teller versus Rousseau the liar or hypocrite. In the final decade of his life, however, the English publication of his autobiographical writings, which were parrhesiastic and temporizing by turns, left even his sympathetic readers shocked and silenced. Rousseau permanently alienated his supporters by offering a self-image that challenged their heavily sentimental idealizations of their hero. Accordingly, his French and British detractors used his writings to assemble a public image remarkably close to the features of what would be known as the modern cynic: atheistic disbelief, habitual distrust of others, shameless indifference to conventional morality, and a hypocritical gap between word and deed.

The polarizing career and reception of Rousseau inflected D'Israeli's innovative use of the term "cynicism" in the previously mentioned *Quarrels of Authors.* D'Israeli offers a psychological portrait of Hobbes modeled upon Rousseau's criticisms of his fellow philosophes. D'Israeli labels Hobbes a cynic not because he is rudely independent, but because he is a misanthropic enemy of the human race who has crawled into a position of great power. More damning still, Hobbes is too comfortable with the powerful and too politically flexible to attain true philosophic greatness. D'Israeli's Hobbesian modern cynic is not impolite, but selfishly conformist, and unwilling to sacrifice anything for the sake of his ideals. Hobbes has become, in D'Israeli's words, a "polished cynic" in the manner of La Rochefoucauld, Machiavelli, or Chesterfield. Though D'Israeli describes this entire group of immoralists as "cynics," ten or twenty years earlier they would not have been brought together in this manner; they are all writers who excelled at redescribing their societies in unflattering ways. In D'Israeli, cynicism has become synonymous not with philosophy or virtue, but with petty, conformist, self-seeking behavior rationalized in plausibly elevated "philosophical" terms. In other words, D'Israeli's description of cynicism no longer suggested independent philosophic reflection, critique, or even satirical abuse, but Hobbes's supposed qualities of accommodation, self-seeking, and servile publicity for those in power.

The sixth and final chapter takes up the polished cynics and cynical dandies of Regency Britain and beyond, to trace the concept to its final moment of semantic development around the beginning of the twentieth century. At this point, every term in the ensemble identified by Chaloupka and Keenan has fallen into place: master-cynics, cynical insiders, and cynical public. The dandies who modeled themselves upon Beau Brummell introduced a new dimension to cynicism: a cool indifference to conventional codes of masculinity that was almost indistinguishable from polite accommodation. It is this parodic, even scandalous dimension of dandyism that Oscar Wilde exploited in his fiction and his life and that caused him to be labeled a bad cynic, a disbeliever, and a supremely dangerous example to the nation's youth.

After Wilde's prosecution and exile, one of the last reflective cynics and aphorists disappeared in Anglophone writing. Instead, cynicism became a regular feature of mass culture, entering the marketplace of opinions as yet another disillusioned and disillusioning voice in the era of Bierce and Mencken.[49] After 1913, when Webster's *Dictionary* formally related cynicism to a belief in the universality of self-seeking or self-interest, the semantic development of the concept reached the point where it remains today. Cynicism was no longer the exclusive possession of the philosopher but that of the unreflective media expert. The cynical media insider or "talking head" becomes the perverse legacy of Diogenes' heroic philosophy and Rousseau's tortured quest for autonomy.

ONE

Diogenes of Sinope and Philosophy as a Way of Life

To pervert Plato is to side with the Sophists' spitefulness, the rudeness of the Cynics, the arguments of the Stoics, and the fluttering visions of Epicurus. It is time to read Diogenes Laertius.
—Michel Foucault, "Theatrum Philosophicum"

To describe the process that transformed ancient Cynicism into modern cynicism, we should start with the "life and opinions" of Diogenes of Sinope (ca. 412–403 to ca. 324–321 BC), who was one of the first philosophers to be labeled a Cynic, or "dog" (*kuon*).[1] It was the memorable personality and behavior of Diogenes that established the distinctive practices and purposes of Cynic philosophy for the next two-and-a-half millennia. The characteristically "cynical" attitudes and practices attributed to this movement helped define "cynic" and "cynicism" long after Diogenes and the canine metaphor had disappeared from everyday usage.

Along with a brief biography of Diogenes, this chapter will also offer some contexts for understanding Cynic philosophy as it was practiced in antiquity, focusing on the characteristics that most powerfully affected its reception in later periods: its character as a philosophical "way of life" emblematized by the ascetic "philosophical hero" Diogenes; its missionary character; its reliance upon satiric or farcical language and gestures to communicate its serious philosophic message; its programmatic hostility to political power, conventional values, and rival philosophies. Then I will conclude with an account of how the satires of Lucian systematically invert many of these characteristics, most crucially the "philosophical hero," to create a gallery of hypocritical or sneering would-be Cynics. Once Cynic philosophy had become firmly associated with *both* the philosophical hero Diogenes and the unphilosophical antiheroes of Lucian in the second century AD, we have the cluster of contradictory meanings that accompanied discussions of ancient Cynicism through the end of the eighteenth century.

We must preface any so-called "biography" of Diogenes with an acknowledgment of the limits to our historical knowledge of this semilegendary figure. Since all of Diogenes' own writings were lost in antiquity, the single most extensive historical source is the "Life" contained in Diogenes Laertius's *Lives and Opinions of Ancient Philosophers* (ca. 230? AD), a "compilation of compilations" written at nearly five centuries' remove from the philosopher's lifetime.[2] Though Laertius's collection of Diogenes lore offers us a fascinating hodgepodge of historical fact, legend, and outright fabrications, there is enough corroborating evidence from other sources and traditions to give us some degree of confidence in the narrative that follows. Nonetheless, we should always keep in mind how drastically the historical image of Diogenes has been shaped by the demands of oral, anecdotal transmission over many centuries.

A "Simple Life"

According to Laertius and other sources, Diogenes was born around 400 BC in Sinope, a bleak little commercial outpost on the edge of the Black Sea, far from the metropolitan centers of the Greek world and tied through trade to a variety of non-Greek peoples in what is now Turkey and India.[3] Diogenes was exiled for counterfeiting the public coinage, an act that was committed either by himself or his father, Hicesias (DL 6.20).[4] This well-known incident, which is supported by numismatic evidence, probably inspired his most famous philosophic motto, "deface the currency!" (meaning literally to "scratch the face off" the coinage).[5] In his wanderings, Diogenes was later taken and sold as a slave to Xeniades, and when asked what he could do, replied, "Govern men" (DL 6.29). Diogenes then tutored Xeniades' children, devoting as much time to their physical training as to lectures and recitations (DL 6.30–31).

At some point, Diogenes decided to become a philosopher. As he often does, Laertius records two different versions of how Diogenes was initiated into philosophy. First he describes Diogenes demanding instruction from Antisthenes, a one-time disciple of Socrates.[6] When Antisthenes tried to refuse, Diogenes "offered his head with the words, 'Strike, for you will find no wood hard enough to keep me away from you, so long as I think you've something to say" (DL 6.21). Afterwards, Diogenes, though an exile, became Antisthenes' student and took up the "simple life," meaning a philosophical "way of life" on the model of Socrates.[7]

Laertius immediately follows this anecdote with another, perhaps more fanciful story of how Diogenes saw a "mouse running about . . . , not looking for a place to lie down in, not afraid of the dark, not seeking any of the things which are considered to be dainties." According to Laertius, this mouse taught Diogenes "the means of adapting himself to circumstances," one of the hallmarks of Cynic philosophy (DL 6.21). After this incident, Diogenes stressed the importance of adapting easily and cheerfully to one's circumstances, and praised such adaptability as the best way to a life lived according to nature (*phusis*) rather than human conventions (*nomos*). "He would often insist loudly that the gods had given to men the means of living easily, but this had been put out of sight, because we require honeyed cakes, unguents, and the like" (DL 6.44).

For Diogenes, the example of the mouse becomes a signal lesson in the distinction between nature's needs, which can be met without fuss, and the artificial fears, desires, and dependencies imposed by human society, with all its essentially arbitrary conventions and customs. The Cynic philosopher therefore continually trains himself in a starkly minimal lifestyle, the so-called "shortcut to virtue," so as to maximize his freedom and self-sufficiency (*autarkeia*). The Cynic abjures not only material possessions, however, but every conventional human attachment, in order to reduce his dependency on others to the absolute minimum. In accordance with the Cynic principle of adaptation ("use the things that are present"), begging for one's subsistence remains the best way for the philosopher to remain free of false values, though as we shall see, there are other reasons why the Cynics begged for their living.[8]

After taking up philosophy, Diogenes was content to live openly in the marketplace in a "tub" (literally a *pithos* or wine-jar) instead of a house, dressing himself in a simple cloak, and carrying his only possessions, a walking staff and a beggar's pouch, with him wherever he went (DL 6.22–23). This mendicant lifestyle, unkempt appearance, and minimal outfit (cloak, staff, and pouch) became the uniform of Cynic philosophers in antiquity, as we will see in Lucian's satires on the Cynic philosophers of his own era some five hundred years later.

Diogenes was called "the Dog" for the meanness of his physical existence and for his barking ridicule of vice and absurdity, but just as important was his conscious refusal of conventional Greek attitudes of shame (*anaideia*) for their arbitrary and unnatural basis in human convention. Consequently, he performed natural acts like eating, urination, defecation, or masturbation in public, with the shamelessness of a dog (DL 6.69). Diogenes spent the rest of his long life as a philosophical celebrity, challenging crowds, fellow philosophers, and even rulers like Alexander the Great to lead better, more self-sufficient lives. He both preached and exemplified a philosophical life of severe self-restraint and freedom from luxury, living in the open and alternating between Corinth and Athens until his death in his eighties or nineties around 325 BC.

A number of resonant themes appear in Laertius's account of Diogenes' life that will recur in many other accounts throughout antiquity: exile, asceticism, self-sufficiency, and shamelessness, all practiced for the sake of a philosophic mission wholly devoted to following nature and rejecting human convention. When Diogenes "defaced the currency," moreover, he flouted conventional values as much in his speech as in his actions. His extraordinary capacity to embody his philosophical principles, fully and without remainder, made him both a legendary figure and a philosopher whose manner of living constituted the greatest expression of, and justification for, his philosophy. As Laertius comments: "he acted [in accordance with his speeches], adulterating currency (*nomisma*)[9] in very truth, allowing convention no such authority as he allowed to natural right" (DL 6.71).

In Laertius's conflicting anecdotes of Diogenes' first introduction to philosophy, we might reflect for a moment upon the specific forms of resistance and adaptation demanded by the Cynic philosophy. In the first story, Diogenes will not politely acquiesce to Antisthenes' command to leave him alone because he knows he needs to learn philosophy from his chosen teacher, Antisthenes. In the second, Diogenes immediately adapts himself to the deprivations experienced by the mouse because he realizes that to live a free and virtuous life he must learn indifference to the "dainties" that other men take for granted. Diogenes therefore inverts the conventional man's habits of accommodation by adapting willingly to the demands of nature, while resisting just as fiercely the dictates of human morality or custom. This is yet another way that he "defaces the currency" as much in word as in deed.

Having set forth this philosophy of self-denial, we might expect Diogenes' philosophic practice to have been cold, aloof, humorless, pleasureless, or self-isolating, but exactly the opposite seems to have been the case. Diogenes publicly, even joyfully performed his independence and self-sufficiency in front of the large urban crowds he wished to educate, just as he had once governed Xeniades and his children. In fact, Diogenes' way of life demanded something that went beyond the severest self-discipline and physical "training" (*askesis*) from its followers. It also required those professing Cynic philosophy to have the courage to communicate it to the widest possible audience, in order to shock them out of their false conventional values. In other words, the ostentatiously shameless style of Cynic philosophy was motivated by its *mission-*

ary character, which transformed the private drama of the philosophical hero's self-mastery into a public spectacle and made the crowd itself an important part of the performance.[10]

The public, missionary character of Cynic shamelessness, the Cynic philosophers' decided preference for preaching to large crowds and public gatherings, and the Cynics' concern with challenging the false values of their massed audiences all help to explain the distinctively Cynic emphasis upon the crowd in their philosophy. The anecdotal traditions concerning Diogenes are filled with descriptions of the gawkers, gapers, and onlookers who react to his provocations, and who collectively embody the false conventional values that he opposed at every turn. This is clearest in Laertius's story of what happened when Diogenes entered a theater at the wrong time: "Meeting face to face those who were coming out, and being asked why, 'This,' he said, 'is what I practice doing all my life'" (DL 6.64). Thus, the presence of an audience, whether sympathetic or not, became an indispensable part of the drama of Cynic philosophic practice, and Diogenes, who needed very few things, nevertheless needed a crowd, an audience whom he could harangue and entertain, and whose most cherished opinions he could ridicule.

In one important respect, the presence of a crowd helped transform Diogenes from a single eccentric vagrant into a philosophical hero, a man capable of "governing men." It did this by showing the philosopher heroically risking their rejection and disapproval, all in the hope of transforming his audience in some fundamental way. In fact, Diogenes treated the desire for approval like any other desire, and systematically trained himself to regard it with indifference: "He once begged alms of a statue, and, when asked why he did so, replied, 'To get practice in being refused'" (DL 6.49). Indeed, the numerous stories of Diogenes' famously gruff and unpleasant manner of begging enact this dynamic on the smallest possible scale, in the transaction between the paradoxically independent beggar-philosopher and his client-donor: "Being short of money, he told his friends that he applied to them not for alms, but for repayment of his due" (DL 6.46).

Hence, the paradoxically governing yet mendicant relation of Cynic philosophy to its nonphilosophical audience dictated its shameless yet missionary approach to preaching, which in turn demanded that Cynic philosophers directly challenge their listeners' opinions in order to make the listeners' assent ethically meaningful. It was this consciously paradoxical and scandalous style of preaching that became known, in Michel Foucault's coinage, as "parrhesiast" (*parrésia,* or *le franc parler*), and can be translated as "saying all," "free-speaking," or "truth telling." *Parrhesia,* which Diogenes once called "the most beautiful thing in the world" (DL 6.69), became another distinctive attribute of Cynic philosophy in antiquity, and an important part of its verbal and philosophical legacy to subsequent generations.

Michel Foucault on *Parrhesia*

Many of these themes regarding Diogenes, *parrhesia,* and the Cynic way of life were brilliantly synthesized in Michel Foucault's 1983 lectures on *parrhesia,* which culminated in the lectures regarding *parrhesia* and Cynic philosophy that were sadly interrupted by Foucault's death in 1984.[11] Though various transcriptions and redactions of these materials are now beginning to appear in print and on the Web, the most convenient source available in English right now is a valuable account published by the philosopher Thomas Flynn, who attended the 1984 lectures and provides readers with a detailed synopsis of, and commentary upon, the course's content (*FP* 102–3).

In Flynn's summary of Foucault, Cynicism as a philosophy cannot be communicated in the form of verbal doctrine but only as the visible *effect* that the Cynic "way of life" has had upon the lives of those who embrace it. Foucault, who had earlier acknowledged his general indebtedness to the Hellenist Pierre Hadot's scholarship on philosophy as a "way of life" or "spiritual exercise" in antiquity, seems to have been drawing extensively upon these notions in his treatment of the Cynics.[12]

According to Foucault/Flynn, the Cynic emphasis upon the philosopher's manner of existence rather than his verbal products (for example, in the form of axioms, systems, or theories) has important consequences for its transmission, which comes primarily in the form of stories, or better yet, *anecdotes* about famous Cynic philosophers rather than their own writings.[13] Foucault/Flynn describes the transmission process in the following way: "The Cynics' scheme of life is difficult to summarize theoretically. It is expressed and transmitted by stories, paradigmatic figures like Hercules, and case histories. Because what is to be communicated is a way of life more than a doctrine, the philosophical hero becomes of prime importance and philosophic legend is common coin" (*FP* 110). By viewing Cynic philosophy as a "way of life" rather than a theoretical construction, Foucault helps explain the peculiar status and function of Diogenes as the "philosophical hero" or "paradigmatic figure" around whom innumerable "stories" and "case histories" are told, even when none of his own writings survive.

Flynn summarizes Foucault's view of Cynic truth telling and the true life in the following, extremely compressed description:

> Foucault sees the Cynics' extreme, indeed scandalous, pursuit of the true life as an *inversion* of, a kind of carnivalesque grimace directed toward, the Platonic tradition. This, he believes, is the meaning of the Delphic Oracle's gnomic advice to Diogenes: "Change the value of the money" [or, as Branham has translated it, "Deface the currency."]. For the forms and habits of common life one must substitute the philosophers' principles, but *lived to the point of scandal.* Far from random grossness, the Cynics' practices challenged philosophers to live radically different lives from those conforming to the received wisdom of their contemporaries. For the Socratic "other world" they substituted an "other life," the truly philosophical life, the "true life." (*FP* 110; Flynn's emphases)

As we can see, Cynic *parrhesia* constitutes a philosophy devoted not merely to truth-telling but to active pursuit of the "true life." As Foucault noted, Diogenes' pursuit of the "true life" can be traced back to Socratic *parrhesia,* with its interest in the philosopher's harmonization of one's "doctrine" with one's "life." Harmonizing one's doctrine and life, however, is accomplished not by any single moment of contemplating the truth but by an ongoing process of *testing.* In the words of Foucault/Flynn: "this alternative care of oneself denotes a manner of living as well as a self-knowledge of a quite different sort than the contemplative: it involves a practical proof, a testing of the manner of living and of truth-telling that yields a certain *form* to this rendering an account of oneself, a life-long examination that issues in a certain *style of existence*" (*FP* 108–9; Flynn's emphases).[14]

The "truth" around which Cynic life is organized systematically inverts the Platonic or contemplative understandings of such terms or activities. The Platonic life of philosophic transparency, purity, conformity to the rule, and fixity is upended in Cynic practices, which insist that the pursuit of truth is best served in actively "defacing the currency" of others' false values and in living a life demonstrably different than that prescribed by "received wisdom." In other words, to merit the title "parrhesiast," a philosopher must continually and publicly demonstrate his willingness to test himself and all around him, risking scandal or even death by his very public words and deeds.[15] Or, to align Foucault's terms here with those of Certeau quoted in the introduction, we might say that the parrhesiast Cynic, because he harmonizes his doctrine and life through an ongoing process of testing, represents the philosophic school in antiquity whose "beliefs" most thoroughly organize their "practices" (*PEL* 178).

In one of Foucault/Flynn's most important formulations, the Cynics substitute for the Socratic "other world" an "other life," a life whose difference from other lives resides in how it was lived, not in how it was conceived and justified and elaborated. To this formulation I would add that Diogenes and the Cynics' decided preference for an "other life" accords well with both Cynic minimalism and naturalism, which derive ultimately from the Cynic principles of "adaptation" and "use what is present" described earlier. For their concentration upon an ongoing "style of existence" rather than metaphysical speculation, the Cynics were often labeled as gross, libertine, or unphilosophical by their philosophical rivals, but Foucault rightly restored the submerged historical and philosophic context that motivated their scandalous behavior and unified their various activities: truth telling or *parrhesia* as a philosophic "style of existence."

One of the most interesting effects of the parrhesiast hostility to conventional values appeared in the characteristic language and style Cynics used to "deface the currency," a philosophical style that distinguished itself from other schools' styles with its uninhibitedly ironic, shameless, and satirical tone, though these violations of linguistic and social decorum were intended to serve higher ethical purposes. Such stylistic paradoxes and contradictions seem implicit in the traditional description of the ancient Cynics' style as "seriocomic."[16] Yet we should never forget how, to use Nietzsche's terminology, parrhesiastic speech enacts the "transvaluation" of existing values in the most ostentatious and public fashion possible. Parrhesiastic speech accomplishes this by extending the risky project of Cynic "testing" to the everyday language of his audiences (*FP* 108).

For example, in many anecdotes, Diogenes takes some commonplace name for something and *redescribes* it in ways that render it shocking or absurd, often by reversing its conventional moral valuations, so that what seems virtuous to the unreflective observer is renamed as something vicious, and vice versa. As Laertius recounts: "He would ridicule good birth and fame and all such distinctions, calling them showy ornaments of vice. The only true commonwealth was, he said, that which is as wide as the universe. He advocated community of wives, recognizing no other marriage than a union of the man who persuades with the woman who consents. And for this reason, he thought sons should be held in common" (DL 6.72). Good birth and fame are renamed "ornaments of vice," and what might have been called "whoring" is simply renamed a "community of wives." Diogenes therefore uses a risky strategy that I call "moral redescription" to transvalue core concepts of Greek culture like birth, fame, marriage, and family, in order to test them, and thereby reveal their flimsy basis in local custom and circumstance rather than nature.[17]

It might be easier to understand this ongoing process of testing through transvaluation by analyzing one of the most famous anecdotes concerning Diogenes. When Diogenes "lit a lamp in broad daylight," he said, "I am looking for a man" (DL 6.41). In the words of the Hellenist A. A. Long, Diogenes' linguistic strategy is to turn "names that are primarily descriptive into words that only pertain to those who *merit* the description."[18] Diogenes searches the city's crowds to find those few who truly deserve to be called "men," meaning those capable of following his philosophy. This gesture is designed not only to gain every man's attention (the missionary dimension) but also to test them to see who is willing to relearn the meaning of "man," "manhood," or "humanity" on Diogenes' strict terms.[19]

As Long concludes, "in rejecting the standard denotations of certain terms and in renaming certain things, he indicated the gulf between current ethical discourse and what he took to be the natural meaning of terms." This notion of the gulf between the conventional and the natural meanings of terms becomes an important trope for the Cynic philosopher, who is always testing those around him to measure the *disparity* between the names applied to things and what he understands as the natural meanings of those terms. "Being asked where in Greece he saw good men, he replied, 'Good men nowhere, but good boys at Lacedaemon [Sparta]'" (DL 6.27). And, of course, the Cynic philosopher was sometimes obliged to call things by their right names, even if it meant redescribing them to restore the distinction of virtue and vice that had been lost in ordinary or polite language: "Some one took him into a magnificent house and warned him not to expectorate, whereupon having cleared his throat he discharged the phlegm into the man's face, being unable, he said, to find a meaner receptacle" (DL 6.32).

The linguistic dimension of Cynic *parrhesia* and its elaborate strategies of renaming should bring to mind the other great rivals to Cynic philosophy in ancient Greece, the Sophists and rhetoricians. At one level, this perceived affinity is historically warranted, especially when we consider Diogenes' discipleship with Antisthenes: before his relationship with Socrates, Antisthenes had been a student of the rhetorician Gorgias; Antisthenes was also deeply interested in the neo-Eleatic logic and wrote on rhetorical topics; moreover, it was the fifth-century Sophists who first elaborated the distinction between nature and convention (*phusis/nomos*) that later became so important for Diogenes and the Cynics.[20]

For all those affinities, however, Dudley and subsequent historians of Cynicism are surely correct to point out the dramatic differences between Diogenes and the rhetoricians, differences amplified by their rivalry for the attention of the Athenian public: Diogenes would characteristically wonder, for example, "that the orators should make a fuss about justice in their speeches, but never practice it" (DL 6.28).[21] As Foucault points out, this divergence stems from the parrhesiastic demand that the Cynic philosopher harmonize his doctrine and life, even while scandalizing his audience with both. The ancient and early modern rhetorician was not expected to speak from a position of personal belief, nor did he seek to "share in the thoughts and feelings that he [sought] to produce in his audience"; indeed, the rhetorician's "creative role" lay precisely in "the bridging of this difference."[22] In contrast, just because of his lived relation to the truth, the parrhesiast was able to act on others "so that they [could] come to build up a relationship of sovereignty to themselves, with regard to themselves."[23] In other words, both the Cynics and the rhetoricians manipulated language, including the moral valences of language, to influence crowds and individuals, but the rhetoricians never shared the Cynics' project of testing themselves and their audiences in the hopes of their ethical transformation.

In Foucault/Flynn's terminology, the rhetorician is the "open contrary" of the parrhesiast because he is a professional who is well-paid for his services, with nothing at stake if his message is rejected; the rhetorician, moreover, has no need to harmonize his doctrine with his life and never invites his audience to embark upon the difficult task of ethical self-scrutiny and -transformation (*FP* 103). To use one of Foucault's examples, the parrhesiast philosopher chiding a tyrant, unlike the grammarian safely teaching a lesson to a student, exposes himself to genuine danger by speaking the truth.[24] In fact, the well-paid professional rhetorician often succeeded by manipulating precisely those unreflective opinions that the Cynic was obliged to challenge. In this respect, Diogenes directed the same "ridicule" toward the Sophists and rhetoricians as he did toward every other ethically useless form of knowledge: "The school of Euclides he called bilious, and Plato's lectures a waste of time, the performances at the Dionysia great peep-shows for fools, and the demagogues the mob's lacqueys" (DL 6.24). None of these arts and sciences tested or transformed their audiences the way that Cynic philosophy did.

Cynic *Parrhesia* versus Tyrants, the Polis, and Rival Philosophers

In the course of their "critical preaching," Diogenes and his Cynic followers discovered three major obstacles to their project of "defacing the currency": tyrants, the crowds in the polis, and rival philosophers. In each instance, the anecdotal literature shows Diogenes in his typically caustic mode of *parrhesia,* testing these representative defenders of conventional values to see whether they can withstand his truth telling. At the same time, we should view the Cynic's verbal aggression as essentially missionary, even therapeutic: this is why he could be called a "doctor of souls."[25] To invoke Foucault's terms once again, the Cynic's "critical preaching" remains a call for an ethical transformation, not destruction, of those to whom he addresses his criticisms.

This reading of the Cynics' criticisms as therapeutic rather than destructive is bolstered by the fact that the Cynic parrhesiast, in his exiled, propertyless, powerless, vagrant state, administers his criticisms from a consciously assumed position of social inferiority, even abjection. It is in this juncture that we can understand Cynic shamelessness not simply as an outward assault against its audience's values but as part of the larger process of total dispossession, and as necessary preparations for the "shortcut to virtue." This seems to be one of its most important divergences from the Platonic tradition, with its fear of democratic rule and its gravitation toward imagined philosopher-kings and real-life tyrants like Dionysius of Syracuse. As Foucault observed in his 1983 Berkeley lectures: "The *parrhesia* comes from 'below,' as it were, and is directed towards 'above.' . . . [W]hen a philosopher criticizes a tyrant, when a citizen criticizes the majority, when a pupil criticizes his or her teacher, then such speakers may be using *parrhesia.*"[26] In other words, a Cynic does not merit the term "parrhesiast" without running the risk of rejection and real physical harm.

Tyrants

Because tyrants, who emblematize state power, present the most obvious instance of a threatening audience for the Cynic philosopher, we should begin with Diogenes' confrontations with them and their values, as these values are localized in a courtly setting. Here the conventional values of an entire city or state have been gathered together and armed, so to speak, in the person of a single, very powerful yet fallible man surrounded by flatterers and parasites eager to put his wishes into effect. From the point of view of the vagrant

Cynic philosopher, it is the Cynic and not the tyrant who possesses the most freedom, since the tyrant is necessarily imprisoned within the conventional values of a retinue afraid to challenge him. The danger for everyone is that the ruler's whims and desires essentially dictate local opinion, so that he lacks any possible corrective of his errors or wayward desires. The ruler needs precisely what he is least likely to receive: honest and, more important, un-self-interested criticism, and this is what the Cynic, the "doctor of souls" administers, whether he is asked to or not.

These encounters also clarify the distinction between a democratic, political *parrhesia*, which is inseparable from the free speech practiced among the qualified citizens in the polis, and Diogenes' own philosophical *parrhesia*, which is associated with the subsequent decline of the polis and the emergence of tyrants and their courts as hierarchical centers of power in the ancient world.[27] In a courtly milieu of luxury, implicit violence, and omnipresent flattery, the Cynic philosopher is valued because he abjures self-serving rhetoric and flattery in his "free speech."[28]

The inevitable point of reference regarding *parrhesia* and political power remains Diogenes' encounter with Alexander the Great, one of the best-known stories in the anecdotal tradition. Diogenes had been outside sunning himself when Alexander approached and asked what he could do for him; Diogenes' only response was, "Stand out of my light" (DL 6.38). Alexander, unlike other recipients of Diogenes' reproofs, was not at all displeased with this treatment and told his men that if he were not Alexander, he would be Diogenes (DL 6.32). As Foucault noted in his 1983 lectures, this is a paradigmatic moment of parrhesiastic confrontation, in which the philosopher bluntly informs the ruler how little he needs him. Note, however, that Diogenes does not try to displace the ruler from his position of power, nor does he wish to disturb existing hierarchies of political power, but only forces Alexander to acknowledge his independent existence and thereby "internalize [the] parrhesiastic struggle—to fight within himself against his own faults, and to be with himself in the same way that Diogenes was with him."[29] In Laertius's version of the anecdote, Alexander affirms their shared desire for independence, along with their equivalent status as governors of men. Alexander conquered the world, and Diogenes his own desires. This parallel, however, only emerges in the risky moment when Diogenes challenges the emperor, while making no attempt to abolish the essential asymmetry of their respective speaking positions. In this respect, *parrhesia* is a "philosopher's virtue," adapting to what is present, taking for granted the huge disparity in power between philosopher and tyrant, and reminding even the ruler of the possibility of an "other life."[30]

The Polis

The second category of encounters, Diogenes' risky addresses to the crowds in the polis, shows the philosopher militating against every conventional form of attachment, from marriage and family all the way up to the polis and empire, while striving to remain a friend to the whole of humankind. In these, the philosopher's ambiguously mendicant yet governing relation to the crowd is extended to the polis and ultimately to the whole of humanity. For example, Diogenes arrives at *philanthropia* (or love of humankind) through exile, an exclusion that he characteristically reversed and adopted in the form of an itinerant, cosmopolitan lifestyle. As Laertius recounts, "when some one reminded him that the people of Sinope had sentenced him to exile, 'And I them,' said he, 'to home-staying'" (DL 6.49).

Diogenes' exile and his rejection of the disgrace offered by the city of Sinope helped transform him into a philosopher, a man capable of a philosophical "way of life" inextricably caught up with the care of others. Though exile was usually considered in antiquity to be one of the greatest evils to befall someone, for the Cynic philosopher it becomes the best possible training for philosophy: "When some one reproached him with his exile, his reply was, 'Nay, it was through that, you miserable fellow, that I came to be a philosopher'" (DL 6.49).

Exile, or at the very least a cosmopolitan existence, introduces a real disparity between the philosopher and the rest of humanity, but this disparity paradoxically transforms the philosopher into a "guard dog," devoted to the welfare of others, a friend of humanity in its widest possible sense, and therefore, in Diogenes' famous words, a "citizen of the world" (DL 6.63) (*FP* 111). Again, as Diogenes put it:

> All the curses of tragedy, he used to say, had lighted upon him. At all events he was
>
> > A homeless exile, to his country dead.
> > A wanderer who begs his daily bread.
>
> But he claimed that to fortune he could oppose courage, to convention nature, to passion reason. (DL 6.38)

Unlike other philosophers, Diogenes refused to participate in the politics of the city or polis, refused to own property, and refused to perpetuate the social institutions of marriage or child-rearing except in their properly Cynic, communal form. Diogenes discovered freedom in his rejection of every kind of attachment, even if that meant considerable sacrifices of comfort and economic security. Nonetheless, I concur with the judgment of the classicist John Moles that the missionary nature of Cynic philosophy appears most clearly in its cosmopolitan "indifference to place" and its embrace of kinship with humanity in the broadest possible sense, over and against the numerous divisions introduced by human conventions and institutions.[31]

Rival Philosophers

The last series of confrontations with conventional values involve Diogenes' philosophical rivals, whose doctrines he considered intellectually distracting and ethically useless—in other words, purely verbal philosophies. In the absence of the parrhesiast drive to harmonize one's life with one's doctrine, the conventional philosopher could easily become what Diogenes once accused Plato of being, "one who talked without end" (DL 6.26). And yet what distinguished these confrontations from Diogenes' challenges to the polis or tyrants was the fact that he was addressing those with a similar status and function as his own, without the possibility (or the risk) of criticizing them parrhesiastically, "from below." To supply the necessary risks of rejection, then, Diogenes introduced a number of doubts about whether he himself merited the title "philosopher": by treating his own claims to the title "philosopher" with an aggressive irony, by practicing philosophy in parodic, serio-comic forms, and by ironically inviting others to treat him as a fraud or a counterfeit philosopher. Consequently, when Diogenes made his parrhesiastic challenges to his philosophic rivals, it was not from the safety of an elaborated theoretical system of his own but as a would-be "philosophizer" and parodist, making incursions on their home turf.

A "Socrates out of His Senses"?

To understand Diogenes' fraught relations with his philosophic rivals, we might begin with Plato's well-known description of Diogenes: a "Socrates out of his senses" (DL 6.54). This label, though dismissive, has the virtue of recognizing the indubitably Socratic origins of Diogenes' parrhesiastic role as satiric gadfly, while calling attention to the manifest differences between the two. In the words of Dudley, "Diogenes represents the Socratic *sophos* [sage or wise man] with its chief features pushed to extremes."[32] In Plato's description, Diogenes operates as *both* a legitimate disciple of Socrates' model of the philosophic life, *and* as a potent symbol of philosophical reason fallen into self-reflection, excess, or even madness.[33] The anecdotal clashes of Diogenes with Plato can therefore be read as genealogical documents of the struggles to decide who constituted the genuine heir to Socratic philosophy.

The deliberate extremity of Cynic philosophy begins to look less idiosyncratic, moreover, once we consider the social context in which the Cynics competed for the public's attention. Our first clue comes from Hadot's assertion, seconded by other scholars of Hellenistic philosophy, that "philosophy as a way of life" was an assumption more or less shared by virtually every major school of philosophy in antiquity.[34] In the midst of a noisy and contentious philosophical scene, one that had witnessed the state execution of Socrates during Antisthenes' lifetime, and to which Antisthenes was a companion and an eyewitness, the Cynics took the shared assumption of the philosophical "way of life" but pushed it to a degree that the other philosophical schools were unwilling to emulate.[35] Accordingly, Hadot has remarked that in Cynicism we have a "highly revelatory example" of a "limit case," a philosophy that was "exclusively a choice of life," and in which "philosophical discourse was reduced to a minimum"—an unsurprising development, once we remember the normative status of the minimum in both Cynic doctrine and practice.[36]

Diogenes therefore assumed the simple but strenuous life of a philosophical hero to demonstrate to his rivals and the public just how little theory or philosophical discourse one really needed to live virtuously. This is the philosophic equivalent of the philosopher throwing away his cup after he saw a little boy drinking from cupped hands, exclaiming, "a child has beaten me in plainness of living" (DL 6.37). Yet we should also note the very Greek overtones of athleticism and competitive striving in these stories of Diogenes, overtones equally present in the pivotal Cynic concept of *askesis* (training).[37]

Philosopher or Philosophizer?

We can see, moreover, that Diogenes, when challenged to defend his claim to the term "philosopher," played a variation on his usual games with the conventional and natural meanings of words: "To the man who said to him, 'You don't know anything, although you are a philosopher,' he replied, 'Even if I am but a pretender to wisdom, that in itself is philosophy'" (DL 6.64). In a gesture resembling his denial of the term "men" to the crowds of Athens, Diogenes denies that he himself merits the title of "philosopher" and settles instead upon the more equivocal title "pretender to wisdom." The force of this slightly puzzling remark is perhaps clearer in William Baxter's 1688 English rendering than in the standard Loeb translation: "If I do but pretend to Wisdom, even that is to Philosophize (or affect Wisdom)."[38] Regarding Diogenes, the intransitive verbal form "philosophize" seems a more fitting description of his activities than the flat static noun "philosophy." This subtle distinction between philosophy as an activity rather than an abstraction coincides with Hadot's observation that philosophy as a way of life names the philosopher's continual preparation for a form of wisdom that nevertheless remains distinct from philosophical discourse.[39] Hence, "philosophizing" may very well be the best term we have in English to describe the characteristically ironic Cynic interpretation of philosophy as a lifestyle, introducing a hint that the "philosophizer" could be a fraud or a counterfeit who merely affects, or pretends to, a philosophy.

By describing himself as nothing more than a pretender to Wisdom (but not necessarily its possessor), Diogenes locates his philosophic practice somewhere between Wisdom and outright parody. This suggestion of a disparity between the term "philosopher" and his own practice indicates first of all that Diogenes conceives his self-training and -testing to be lifelong processes—what we have already seen described as a "style of existence." More important, this refusal to fix his identity securely either as philosopher or fraud forced his philosophic rivals to draw the distinctions for themselves. By alternating in this way between jests and earnest behavior, Diogenes maintained in his life as well as his speech a "serio-comic" style that consistently blurred the boundary between serious philosophy and witty philosophizing.[40] Mingling sense and nonsense together in this fashion is an aggressive act along the lines of Freud's "tendentious jokes," one designed to expose one's audience as they attempt to distinguish between outward nonsense and underlying insult.

Strategies or Tactics?

To develop further this distinction between Platonic philosophy and Diogenical philosophizing, we might recall Certeau's valuable distinction between the rationality of "strategies" and that of "tactics" (*PEL* 29–42). According to Certeau, a strategy is the "calculus of force-relationships which becomes possible when a subject of will and power (a proprietor, an enterprise, a city, a scientific institution) can be isolated from an 'environment.' A strategy assumes a place that can be circumscribed as proper and thus serve as the basis for generating relations with an exterior distinct from it" (*PEL* xix). In both military and philosophical practice, to draw boundaries, police borders, and establish a place as one's own is to lay the foundations for a nexus of knowledge and power capable of growth and endurance. In Certeau's terms, establishing "the proper" (in French, *propre,* proper, correct, related of course to *propriété,* estate, ownership, property) is the first step toward winning a "triumph of place over time" (*PEL* 36).

Hence, Plato's philosophy can be seen as a strategic rationality because it creates and regulates its own theoretical realm, that of "Ideas," that it designates as its own "proper," at the same time that it becomes localized in an institution, the Platonic school or Academy that reproduces itself in writing, teaching, and the training of students. The Platonic Academy therefore becomes a site of institutionalized transmission and a model for subsequent philosophy up to the present. Most important, Plato's philosophy establishes itself in such a way that it becomes invested with what Certeau calls the "power of knowledge" (*PEL* 36), a hankering after power and influence that expresses itself most vividly in Plato's abortive attempts to counsel the tyrant Dionysius.

In contrast, Diogenes' philosophizing "tactics" rely on a calculus that does not belong to the localized place or institutional setting of "the proper" because his tactical rationality lacks borders, property, or possessions of its own. Certeau describes the rationality of tactics in the following manner:

> The place of a tactic belongs to the other. A tactic insinuates itself into the other's place, fragmentarily, without taking it over in its entirety, without being able to keep it at a distance. It has at its disposal no base where it can capitalize on its advantages, prepare its expansions, and secure independence with respect to circumstances. . . . On the contrary, because it does not have a place, a tactic depends on time—it is always on the watch for opportunities that must be seized "on the wing." Whatever it wins, it does not keep. It must constantly manipulate events in order to turn them into opportunities. (*PEL* xix)

Certeau's remarks on the rationality of tactics forge a significant connection between Diogenes' cosmopolitan "indifference to place," his shameless refusal of distinctions or boundaries between private and public behavior, his lack of interest in theoretical system-building, and his transient, emphatically temporal mode of philosophizing, which wins its battles opportunistically, "on the wing," and always on another's turf.

Certeau, moreover, citing Clausewitz and Freud, makes three further points about tactics as an "art of the weak" that could be taken over and applied to Cynic *parrhesia:* tactical thinking demands a capacity for surprise, guile, makeshifts, ruses, and cunning to win skirmishes against the more powerful and persistent forces of strategic rationality; tactical thinking is therefore analogous to "wit" in the verbal realm, when a sudden "legerdemain" or sleight of hand takes an order by surprise, and finally, tactics represent yet another link to the verbal juggling of ancient rhetoric, the Sophistic art of making "the weaker argument seem the stronger" (*PEL* 37–38).

Even if we accept Foucault's strictures against conflating the parrhesiast with the orator, the deliberately weakened position of the parrhesiast seems to demand a certain kind of verbal wit, intellectual creativity, even adaptability, from the Cynic speaker. It is this quality of quick-witted persuasiveness—which I earlier identified as moral redescription or renaming—that the parrhesiast necessarily shares with the orator, a coincidence that will have important consequences for the subsequent reception of Cynicism in classical rhetoric. Nonetheless, the contrast of Diogenes the tactician with Plato's institutionalized, strategic philosophy seems clear.

Consequently, parody and performance, not written philosophic systems of his own invention, remain Diogenes' preferred method for testing the views of his opponents: "Plato had defined Man as an animal, biped and featherless, and was applauded. Diogenes plucked a fowl and brought it into the lecture-room with the words, 'Here is Plato's man.' In consequence of which there was added to the definition, 'having broad nails'" (DL 6.40).

As is usual with the "serio-comic" anecdote, there is more to this episode than what appears on the surface, something beyond a mere clash of personalities.[41] When Diogenes ambushes Plato, he rudely invades Plato's lecture room, his rival's "proper" space of philosophical transmission, to refute his rival's definition with a single unforgettable gesture. We could not ask for a better image of the moral and philosophical disparity between conventional and natural meanings of words—the noble term "man" matched with the sorry sight of a plucked chicken. Diogenes' quarrel with Plato involves not simply the terms of the definition but the failure of Plato's philosophy to capture the most salient aspects of the human creature he would define. Diogenes' opportunistic parody of Plato's definition takes the featherless biped outside the realm of words and confronts the students dutifully applauding in the lecture room with the paltriness (poultriness?) of the definition.

We should take note of an especially fateful aspect of Diogenes' showdown with Plato: Diogenes' insistence on *moralizing* the gap between his own ethically driven *parrhesia* and Plato's institutionalized version of philosophy, a philosophy of the lecture room but not a way of life. In essence, Diogenes asserts that Plato's lectures do not produce a "man" but only a travesty of a man, "Plato's man." Thus for Diogenes the entire process of institutional transmission and reproduction constitutes an evasion of the ethical demands of philosophy and produces neither philosophers nor philosophizers but a sorry-looking succession of "Plato's men." From Diogenes' point of view, the institutionalization of philosophy represents not the triumph of philosophy over time but a thoroughgoing perversion of its characteristic "style of existence," its program of self-testing. Diogenes confronts Plato to show how the institutional transmission of philosophy actually reproduces the moral infirmities of convention (*nomos*) rather than the philosophic *activity* of "defacing." By the time we reach modern cynicism, we can see this concern translated into a series of assumptions about institutions and their "triumphs over time" that echo and generalize Diogenes' critique of Platonic philosophy: that institutions routinely generate disparities between the conventional and natural meanings of words, that the demands of institutional self-reproduction, not beliefs, organize the practices taking place there, and, consequently, that such institutions do not merely neglect, but actively betray their founding ideals or values.[42] Nonetheless, each of these assumptions about institutions will need to be revisited in order to analyze the dynamics of modern cynicism.

I should make one final point before we leave Laertius's account of Diogenes as philosophical hero, and consider how the parrhesiastic impulse and the anecdotal form combined to affect the historical reception of Cynicism. The parrhesiastic exploration of the arbitrary and essentially local nature of shame helped to foster both negative and positive images of the Cynic philosopher that persisted long after the movement itself had died off as a viable "way of life." Though one portion of their audience willingly overlooked the outrageous, trivial, or unimpressive aspect of Cynicism, another portion consistently refused this interpretation, and interpreted the scandalous behavior or language of the mendicant philosopher as "uncharitably" as possible.

The parrhesiast dimension to Cynicism therefore demands that we treat it not as a self-contained verbal artifact, tradition, or philosophical "school" but rather as a series of "philosophizing" gestures. These acts of "philosophizing" were performed upon, and in conjunction with, an audience free to express its moral disapproval, rejection, or abuse of the philosopher. This "philosophizing," moreover, also included a series of hostile and parodic incursions onto the territory of other philosophers, who were not shy about answering Cynic wit in kind. The result of all these factors is that the hostile, unsympathetic, or dismissive historical responses to Cynic philosophy constituted a peculiarly large portion of its historical legacy, since such responses represent important evidence for the success of its parrhesiastic mission to "deface the currency."

The polarized images and counterimages of Diogenes, moreover, were reinforced and amplified by their anecdotal form, which encouraged a largely anonymous, long-term process of telling and retelling, collecting and re-collecting before and after Laertius. In this respect, Laertius is only one of the few surviving examples of what once must have been a long succession of compilers, and his "Life" of Diogenes shows all the signs of such shuttling back and forth between oral and written transmission: the biographical anecdotes and traditions, which rarely agree with one another, were preserved piecemeal over time because each helped illustrate some particular quality of Diogenes' distinctive philosophical ethos, however understood, and came to be clumped together without any authorial attempt to resolve their conflicts.[43] Because Diogenes and the Cynics never bothered to produce a canonical literary document or authorized foundational statement of beliefs along the lines of Plato or Aristotle's texts and never possessed a "property" that would help to classify subsequent texts as either faithful or unfaithful to the tradition, the legacy of Cynicism was transmitted as a vast, contradictory corpus of anecdotes—stories without authors or authority—whose meanings could never be organized into a coherent or univocal "tradition."

Thus, the Cynic's ironic silence regarding the value of his philosophy also helped structure the terms in which the stupid or the insensible could dismiss him. That is how images of the Cynic as a philosophical hero proliferated alongside images of the Cynic philosopher as a sham, phony, madman, or libertine. In these curiously matched images of the Cynic philosopher coexisting in the anecdotal tradition, we find the common origin of what one Renaissance scholar has called the "High View" and "Low View" of Diogenes the Cynic during the Renaissance.[44] In effect, both images were authorized and reinforced by Cynic *parrhesia,* both images were transmitted piecemeal through the vast corpus of anecdotes and collections of which Laertius is only a part, and both images pervade the work of one of the most important responses to Cynicism in antiquity, the satires of Lucian of Samosata.

Lucian's Passing of Peregrinus Proteus

As I have just argued, the anecdotal images of Diogenes as a philosophical hero were always shadowed by potentially negative responses to his shamelessness and truth telling. Yet the late-Roman satires of the Syrian-born, Greek-speaking rhetorician Lucian of Samosata (ca. 120–180 AD) formalized, and in some sense, thematized the tensions between the competing views of Diogenes as philosophical hero and as fraud. Lucian presents a series of "genuine" (meaning, unambiguous) philosophical frauds who, lacking the true Diogenical paradox of inverted greatness, are nothing more than hypocrites or shams, pathetic wannabe philosophers. Lucian, however, is too practiced in the technique of satiric inversion, which he directed toward the latter-day Cynics of his own era, and too conversant with Cynic literary forms like the Menippean journey or dialogue, to be regarded in a simplistic way as an anti-Cynical writer.[45]

The single most important difference between Laertius's and Lucian's accounts, produced in roughly the same period of Imperial Rome, is that where Laertius attempted to reconstruct and restore the true philosophical "way of life" emblematized by Diogenes in the fourth century BC, Lucian decided to stress the unbridgeable historical distance between his own era and that of Diogenes. Lucian therefore registered the now historical as well as ethical disparity between the genuine Cynicism of Diogenes and the fraudulent pseudo-Cynicism of "modern Cynics" of his own era like Peregrinus Proteus. In this respect, Lucian "tests" Peregrinus to see whether he merits the term "Cynic" and finds him absurdly outmatched by his historical predecessors.

One of the implications of Lucian's satires upon the modern Cynic is the impossibility, or even absurdity, of practical imitation of the Cynic lifestyle, and a turn instead toward a *literary* re-creation of the Cynic through what the philosophical historian Niehues-Pröbsting has called "conscious imitation of particular Cynic gestures, in the avowal of Cynic maxims and attitudes, in the literary relation to Cynic motifs and the figure of the Cynic, [and] in the use of this figure as one of projection and identification."[46] This represents yet another fragmentation and dispersion of Cynicism through the isolation and elaboration of particular gestures, maxims, and motifs in literary forms rather than in the holism of the philosophical life. Though Cynicism remained in fact a popular philosophical movement throughout this period, the subsequent historical trajectory of Cynicism lay in the historicization and ironization of the Cynic philosopher-turned-fraud that led eventually to the self-seeking, unbelieving modern cynic.

Lucian's attitude toward the Cynics alternated between admiration (*Dialogues of the Dead*) or dismissal (*Sale of Philosophers*). Moreover, we recognize in Lucian's split attitude toward the Cynics the distinctively rhetorical approach of the professional advocate looking either to prosecute or defend a particular client.[47] It is this rhetorical approach that sustains and reinforces the coexistence of the positive and negative images of the Cynic found in the anecdotal tradition, and that feeds into the Renaissance High and Low Views of the Cynic.

Nevertheless, in this satire Lucian is clearly out to prosecute the false Cynic Peregrinus for his crimes against philosophy. *The Passing of Peregrinus* offers a trenchant critique of the Cynics' ethos of philosophical heroism and lived philosophy that goes beyond the earlier polarities of parrhesiastic reception.

The premise of Lucian's *Peregrinus* is simple: Lucian writes to his friend about a recent newsworthy event. In this case, the event is the very real and very public suicide that the notorious Cynic Peregrinus Proteus had staged for himself at the Olympic Games. This piece includes another skeptical observer's history of Peregrinus's actions prior to the suicide, an unsympathetic description of one of his followers, Theagenes, praising his master, then a jeering and explicit description of the unpleasant physical details of Peregrinus's self-immolation. Though the description of Peregrinus and the circumstances of the suicide seem more or less factually accurate, Lucian nonetheless chose to present Peregrinus's character and background as unsympathetically as possible, producing in effect an example of "ancient invective" designed, in the manner of ancient rhetorical practice, to discredit its target utterly and without reserve.[48]

Lucian's psychological study of Peregrinus, a former Christian and would-be Cynic, anticipates many of the paradoxes surrounding modern, disillusioned cynicism. For one thing, Proteus's story is not so much about a philosophic way of life as about the temptations of falling into a degraded, unreflective, hypocritical, pseudo-philosophical pose: Peregrinus is an antiparrhesiast who has absolutely refused to harmonize his life and doctrine, deceives others with his sham philosophy, lacks all integrity, and conceals his deeply conventional values underneath a superficially outrageous exterior. Peregrinus may have considered himself a follower of Diogenes, but he was widely known to be, in one spectator's words, "a man who only used philosophy as a cloak," running through a succession of identities grounded in pathetic outcast groups such as Christians or the urban poor.[49] Hence, Peregrinus represents a perversion of earlier Cynic attitudes toward adaptability, or "use what is present," by flouting conventional values without any sense of purpose or risk about his feckless philosophizing.

When Lucian writes his account of the man, Peregrinus had been reduced to a final trick to gain the mob's attention, a publicly announced suicide (in imitation of the end of the Cynic icon Heracles), where he would immolate himself on a pyre before the crowd already gathered to watch the Olympic Games. Lucian used the risible tale of this "new Diogenes" to demonstrate the Cynic's continual need to parade his independence before the crowd. Hence,

Peregrinus, as a would-be leader of what increasingly appeared to be a religious cult, violated the aspects of Cynicism that always provided its distance from political power or religious authority.[50] To use Foucault's description of the struggle between Diogenes and Alexander, Peregrinus is a false parrhesiast to the extent that he has betrayed the distinction (hence, the struggle) between "political power" and "the power of truth" and assumed both forms of power for his own selfish purposes.[51] In the words of two recent commentators on the Cynics, "Peregrinus's theatrical imitation of Heracles" threatened to turn Cynicism "into just another cult; and indeed that is always what it is in danger of becoming merely in virtue of reproducing itself over time, a process that entails imitation and easily lapses into mere conformity to a type."[52] Lucian, in other words, has taken on the same role of "watchdog" that Diogenes once assumed in the plucked chicken episode, ensuring that any modern pretenders to the name "Cynic" merited the title and warning against a process of reproduction that travestied philosophy.

Yet Lucian's satiric character study also reveals how Peregrinus became entangled in his own deceptions while facing death: when finally confronted by his own funeral pyre, Proteus is visibly shocked when the crowd fails to call him back from his public suicide. Much to his disappointment, this professional manipulator finds that the crowd is contentedly waiting for the spectacle of his death. Instead, Peregrinus must proceed with the public suicide he had never really planned on committing. When the impatient crowd finally begins to shout for him to "Carry out your purpose!" Proteus is forced to perform his Cynicism in the most practical way, even if his final suicidal act has been provoked by the very shame that he had once disavowed.[53] Peregrinus's last act is an unwilling parody of the parrhesiastic harmonization of doctrine and life and ultimately forces him to match his actions with his words in a pointless suicide. Though Diogenes had once derived his very livelihood from the crowd, false Cynics like Peregrinus Proteus are punished for their need to shock and scandalize their audiences.

Lucian's early portrait of Peregrinus helped to harden the distinction between true and false cynics, a reworking and stabilization of the distinction implicit in Laertius's discussions of Diogenes as a self-conscious philosophizer, a purveyor of both sense and nonsense. Lucian's influential distinction between true (ancient) and false (modern) Cynics would accompany discussions of Cynicism for the next two thousand years. Lucian has shown what Cynic shamelessness would look like in the absence of masculine reason and self-possession, and lacking the parrhesiastic drive to harmonize one's doctrines with one's life. Peregrinus Proteus has in some way ceased to be a governor of men, in the manner of Diogenes, and has become instead a captive and slave to the crowd that screams for his death. Peregrinus Proteus does not die because the crowd is vengeful, or because he has risked anything in his flattering addresses to them, but because they are bored. These are the consequences, Lucian seems to suggest, of living and dying for the sake of publicity.

TWO Diogenes the Cynic as "Counsellor" and Malcontent in Early Modern England

Hence then with those Athenian Timons, those Diogenical cynics, that make their private mansions the public monuments of their living carcasses and so retire themselves from all occasions of intercourse that the very doors of their habitation do seem to challenge by way of anticipation the inscription from their tombs.

—Daniel Tuvill, "Of Civil Carriage and Conversation" (1608)

WITH THIS CHAPTER we begin the story of the extraordinarily long afterlife of Cynicism, when Cynicism ceased as a philosophic movement but persisted in the form of stories, sayings, and images of Cynic philosophers. For a philosophy more interested in actions than theories, the fading public presence of the movement was especially troubling because it eliminated one of the most important elements in the transmission of Cynic values: the public example of the Cynics' self-testing "style of existence" (*FP* 109). In the absence of written systems or theories, the disappearance of new philosophers attempting to emulate the Cynic way of life reduced Cynicism to the recorded acts and sayings of a handful of names. Consequently, transmitting narratives about the movement without any corroboration from ongoing Cynic practice eliminated a crucial dimension of *parrhesia*, its lived tension between the verbal and ethical interests of Cynic philosophy. The loss of this tension, as it was embodied in the exemplary lives of Cynic philosophers, irrevocably altered the balance between Cynic philosophy and the language in which it was transmitted. At the same time, this reduction of Cynic philosophy to stories about the Cynics helped to disperse and even perpetuate their legacy, in the form of innumerable lives and writings tinged with some recollection of Cynicism.

Cynic language did not lose its association with the obscene wit or fearless comments of the Cynic philosophers, but it did add to these styles the oral, textual, and literary tropes first found in Lucian and other writers from the Imperial Roman era. These tropes focused mainly on the difficulties and paradoxes of transmitting ethical models across great stretches of time, and included literary and philosophical imitations of Cynic gestures, avowals of Cynic maxims, allusions to Cynic motifs, and, most important, treatments of the Cynic philosopher that turned him into an object of authorial projection and identification.[1]

Cynicism therefore lost the holistic force of a philosophic way of life, and was fragmented and spun centrifugally into innumerable Cynic stories, tropes, and gestures. These were told and retold within a vast oral and anecdotal tradition, which in turn fed the more individualized and literary responses found in writers like Lucian and Dio Chysostom. But we should recognize from the outset the centrality of the anecdote, oral communication, and rhetorical training in the preservation and transmission of knowledge about the Cynics between antiquity and the early modern period.[2]

The Cynics attained this ubiquity in the early modern period because of the enduring cultural prestige of rhetoric, which exposed students to Cynic anecdotes at a number of points in their careers. At the earliest and most rudimentary level, ancient gnomologies and literary collections of the sayings of Diogenes and the Cynics (known as *chreiai* or apothegms) were incorporated wholesale into the rhetorical handbooks that trained young students in their beginning compositions and declamations from the Hellenistic period onward.[3] These collections of carefully graded exercises, known as the *progymnasmata,* were still being compiled, revised, expanded, and reprinted in the seventeenth century in England and on the Continent.[4] Beginning students of rhetoric in the early modern period could also find Cynic anecdotes in numerous printed commonplace collections, most notably Erasmus's influential Latin *Apophthegmata,* or, as it was translated into English, his *Apophthegmes* (1531; translation 1542).[5] At more advanced levels of rhetorical instruction, authorities like Cicero had long recommended that aspiring orators themselves collect philosophic opinions and maxims on a variety of issues, so that they could quickly work up a philosophic foundation for their arguments on either side of a topic (arguments *in utramque partem*), a practice of capital importance for both Ciceronian eloquence and Renaissance humanism.[6] Despite Cicero's marked distaste for the Cynics, such philosophic compilations may have also served as additional repositories of Cynic lore. All these rhetorical uses of the Cynics had important effects on early modern interpretations of the Cynic movement.[7]

The disappearance of Cynicism as a viable way of life in late antiquity and its persistence in early modern rhetorical and literary forms *recentered* this period's treatment of Cynic philosophy in four respects.[8] With respect to language, it minimized the former opposition between ancient Cynic truth telling and classical eloquence and introduced the Cynic concept of *parrhesia* into the rhetorical training of ancient and early modern orators.[9] With respect to institutional and disciplinary location, it assimilated Cynic philosophy into the *ars rhetorica* and transformed the rude and shameless Cynic philosopher into a "counsellor" holding forth at court.[10] With respect to the public addressed by Cynicism, it refocused Cynic philosophy's potential audience from the anonymous urban crowd to what was essentially an audience of one—the sovereign. Most important, with respect to the moral qualities attributed to the Cynic philosopher, Cynic philosophy itself took on an increasingly equivocal appearance, alternating between images of high virtue and deep shamelessness that led eventually to the familiar split between the Renaissance High and Low Views of Diogenes.[11]

One cause for this split may have been the Cynics' usefulness in training orators to argue both sides of a case, so that one morally polarized view of Diogenes was always deployed to counter the other, preserving both traditions in tandem.[12] Nonetheless, it was also during this period that the rhetorically inflected Low View of Diogenes developed into the vernacular, postclassical image of the Cynic who is not a true philosopher, but merely, in the words of the *OED,* "A person disposed to rail or find fault" (s.v. "cynic").[13] Thus, the two most important contributions of the early modern period to the meanings of "Cynic" were the *rhetoricization* that reworked this figure to reflect the demands of classical eloquence, and the *vernacularization* that remade him into an early modern English railer, misanthrope, melancholic, or malcontent.[14]

This chapter describes how the rhetorical uses of the Cynics and Cynicism in the early modern period preserved its tropes but distanced it from its ancient contexts, helping to split the Cynic into two distinct figures: a classical Diogenes whose philosophic powers of reflection, self-control, and freedom from flattery made his speech more effective than that of conventional courtiers, and a vernacular Cynic whose unreflective violations of civility and decorum left him a misanthrope railing impotently against his fellow men. After a quick review of contemporary definitions of "Cynic," I describe first Cicero's influential rejection of the Cynics, then this period's tactical alliance of Cynicism with eloquence in the Diogenical "counsellor." Emerging doubts about the limitations of eloquence, however, produced new images of the Cynic as mere hectoring malcontent or misanthrope. I will then conclude with a discussion of Shakespeare's *Timon of Athens,* which effectively distinguishes between its lead character's eloquent misanthropy and the ineffective speech of its false would-be Cynic, Apemantus.

Some Definitions

Evidence for the conceptual splitting of the Cynic during this period can be found in its vernacular dictionaries, which had only recently come into use.[15] "Cynic," like "opportune" or "artefact," was a word that still retained a foreign flavor in 1604, and it appeared alongside similar imports from Latin or Greek in the "hard word" dictionaries designed for those lacking classical languages.[16] As unimpressive as such books may seem today, humble compendia like Cockeram's *English Dictionarie* (1623), along with a wide variety of literary and rhetorical sources, helped to introduce and sustain a vernacular discourse concerning Cynics and Cynicism throughout the sixteenth and seventeenth centuries, a discourse dominated by the rhetorical compilations and commonplace collections in Latin and English used by schoolboys to expand their compositions and declamations.

Diogenes' sayings were prominently featured in many of these early modern compilations, which were descended from the proverb collections and "sayings of the philosophers" used in England since at least the twelfth century, and in Greek and Roman antiquity long before that.[17] As Adam Fox has argued, these kinds of source-texts of "proverbial wisdom" had been dramatically reinvented, systematized, and expanded by humanist educators like Erasmus in a whole series of rhetorical collections like the *Apophthegmata* or *Adagia.* These immensely popular works demonstrate Erasmus's pivotal role as an intellectual mediator between the humanistic New Learning and the orally and scribally transmitted proverbial wisdom contained in older works like the *Dicts and Sayings of the Philosophers.*[18]

This meant in practice that early modern depictions of the Cynics gained enormously from humanist projects of editing, translating, and imitating classical texts, particularly from this era's editions of Laertius, Lucian, and Plutarch.[19] Where Cynicism's fate diverged from the rest of the classical heritage, however, was in its lack of authoritative foundational texts or doctrines, which left it unusually open to topical, popular, or vernacular interpretive pressures.

Because of the cumulative work of scholars on the chronological and philological problems of textual transmission, humanist editors and commentators on Plato or Aristotle were only beginning to distinguish between genuine, garbled, and wholly invented works attributed to these philosophers, but this kind of philological analysis could never reach the orally transmitted core of Cynic philosophic practice.[20] It is this crucially oral and popular dimension of the Cynics, I argue, that made it possible for the concept of Cynicism to expand well past its classical parameters and take on new, vernacular meanings during this period.

For example, because of its pedagogical usefulness in teaching students good manners via comically exaggerated bad examples, this vernacular discourse often reinforced and exaggerated the Low, shameless View of Diogenes and the Cynics at the expense of the High and virtuous View, so that the ancient philosophic contexts were subsumed under more contemporary discourses of misanthropic railing or melancholic "humours." Comparing these vernacular dictionaries with the *OED*'s historical examples also confirms that the firmly postclassical, vernacular sense of the Cynic as railer or melancholic seems to have emerged alongside a vernacular tradition of comic or satiric Cynics sometime in the 1580s or 1590s.[21] In other words, the emerging meanings of "Cynic" as a humours-character, or at best a would-be satirist, philosopher, or moralist, seems to have been a by-product of the early rhetorical training of such vernacular writers as Samuel Rowlands, John Lyly, John Marston, or even William Shakespeare.[22]

Bullokar's 1616 dictionary shows, for example, how "Cynike" was taken to mean "Doggish or currish," a sense given a straightforward etymological and historical gloss: "There was in Greece an old sect of Philosophers so called, because they did oversharply barke at mens vices, and were not so respective in their behavior as civilitie required. The chiefe of this sect were Antisthenes and Diogenes."[23] In this way, the "Cynike" was associated as much with uncivil railing (or barking) as with philosophy and philosophers, often because the obscene or aggressive nature of his speech led him toward a rough, currish misogyny.[24] Likewise, Erasmus in his *Apophthegmes* explained that "[the Cynics] did with their foule mouthes represent the currisheness of Doggues," "Because thei were ever moste importunelie barking and railling againste the vices of menne or els because in woords of rebaudrie and shamelesse speaking [they acted currishly]."[25] Erasmus, who, as we will see, admired Diogenes, nonetheless admitted the Cynics' shamelessness, while allowing for two possibilities regarding its causes: either the Cynics' "barking and railling" were loudly (and justifiably) directed against men's vices, or their "woords of rebaudrie and shamelesse speaking" were "foule," currish, and truly doglike, in the sense of reflexively barking, snarling, snapping, and so on.

Needless to say, Diogenes' "currish" rejection of local customs or ordinary civility seemed very different when ascribed to a hatred of vice rather than indifference to social and moral codes. But this kind of unresolved moral ambiguity ran through most of the early modern accounts, which, as Lievsay observed, maintained the Low View of Diogenes as a "brute" and a "dirty, ill-tempered, snarling cur" at the same time as it propagated a High View that considered him a "corrector of manners and morals, [and] a kind of Greek Cato."[26] Indeed, the coexistence of such morally polarized interpretations of Diogenes makes more sense when we recall that these moral readings were sustained chiefly in the telling, retelling, and expansion of individual anecdotes rather than in holistic presentations of his life or personality. In the words of one scholar of Renaissance drama, the rhetorically expanded anecdote functioned as "an independent unit of narrative or dramaturgical energy" that could be used in multiple ways to produce multiple meanings, so that even within a single work authors might include positive and negative readings of Diogenes without any concern for building up a larger or more consistent picture of the philosopher.[27]

Nevertheless, this was also the period when the term "Cynical" (perhaps because of its increasing detachment from the historical referent Diogenes) came to be treated as a rough synonym for a whole set of English terms associated with doglike incivility. Synonyms for "cynical" included "Doggish,"[28] "currish,"[29] and even "canine,"[30] and there were further extensions like "froward"[31] (meaning opinionated or obstinate) and "clownish" (meaning unmannerly or rude).[32] It is also true that many if not most of these extensions of "Cynic" were metaphorical rather than historical, and seemed to draw more from the complex contemporary associations of the dog in this period (as self-sufficient rogue, for example) than the historical associations of ancient Cynic philosophy.[33]

Whether classical or vernacular, however, all these definitions and examples demonstrate how these Cynics' rude shamelessness made them formidable symbols of resistance to this era's normative codes of civility.[34] In a word, this was because Diogenes' philosophy or the vernacular Cynic's personality made them "singular," meaning unamiable, unpleasing, uncourtly, and insistent upon voicing their opinions to superiors and inferiors alike.[35] The early modern emphasis upon the Cynic philosopher's extraordinary verbal freedom suggests how much deference was ordinarily demanded in verbal interactions between different social ranks.[36] And yet under certain circumstances such boldness in speech, or singularity of manner, was not merely forgiven, or licensed, but admired. This is how Diogenes continued to serve as an emblem of parrhesiastic "freedom of speech" in this period's rhetorical and literary works, even while vernacular Cynics were denounced for their violations of the norms of civility.[37]

Ciceronian Eloquence, the Retired Cynic-Misanthrope, and Verbal Action

Now that we have seen how the High/Low or Classical/Vernacular splits in the "Cynic" are reflected in this period's vernacular dictionaries, we might wish to reflect upon the causes of these splits and how they were sustained across the entire period. To do this, we need to abandon the notion that the divergent interpretations of the Cynics objectively coexisted "inside" a unitary concept, and instead consider the divergences as products of the various and distinct lessons that the Cynics taught early modern readers.[38] Nonetheless, whether positive or negative, both sets of images were derived from the Cynics' relation to rhetorical training, Ciceronian eloquence, and verbal effectiveness.

In the case of the uncivil Diogenes, such figures appear in satires, character writings, or courtesy books as negative examples demonstrating the importance of propriety to effective speech, a propriety as much physical as it is verbal.[39] In the absence of such self-control, these writings argue, the Cynic loses his verbal powers along with his social status, becoming nothing better than a sour misanthrope.

This kind of negative treatment can be traced back at least as far as Cicero, who ruled out the Cynics as potential models for Roman education because of their deliberate violations of *decorum* (seemliness) and *verecundia* (sense of shame). As a result of this hostility, Cicero's influential synthesis of philosophy and rhetoric in both the *De officiis* and *De oratore* left Cynic philosophy largely outside his canon of philosophers useful to the orator. After all, the Cynics did little to promote the kinds of wisdom or eloquence sought by Cicero's orators-in-training. Nonetheless, this exclusion was consequential because it was Cicero's expansive view of the orator's education that helped determine the enormous scope of the humanists' later pursuit of eloquence, which in its turn influenced many details of the verbal and social interactions dictated by early modern civility.[40]

Cicero's importance as an architect of, and model for, subsequent rhetorical practices meant that his works did not merely convey opinions about Hellenistic philosophy but helped to institutionalize a set of oral and textual practices that constituted what has been described as rhetoric's "extraordinarily long-lived theory of verbal action."[41] These verbal strategies maximized the "profitable" use of the classical past by treating it as a verbal territory requiring rigorous demarcation, categorization, cultivation, regulation, and so forth.[42] Its policing of these boundaries, however, did not so much serve the classical past as use it instrumentally, in order to master fully the "changeable conditions of persuasion that lead to ethical or social action."[43]

Following Cicero's notion of the profitable uses of the past, the humanistic orator could ill afford to pursue a solitary or retired wisdom that led to inaction. Instead, he pursued wisdom insofar as it led to eloquent and effective public speech, which led in turn to the more effective exercise of power in an active public life. In such an account, eloquence gave the orator ascendancy over other men in public assemblies, made him a better leader in military and civic crises, and invested him with an irresistible power over others.[44] In a paradigm of philosophy that insisted that wisdom was useful to the extent that it acted as the willing rhetorical instrument of power and property for the sake of collective action, the half-naked Cynic sitting in his tub or the querulous cur barking in his kennel would seem to have little place.

For the sixteenth- and seventeenth-century English commentators who accepted Cicero's dismissals, the Cynics, like other malcontents, simply lacked the propriety and decorum that provided the prudence and worldly wisdom that they so admired in Cicero and his followers.[45] In a word, the Cynics lacked Ciceronian *honestas*, or "honorableness," a crucial component of early modern notions of civility, and which comprehended such values as "a show of 'reverence' to others, 'considerateness,' self-control of the passions *and* attention to one's dress and deportment."[46] This lack of civility left the Cynics and their imitators unsuited for the friendly exchanges of "civil conversation" that Cicero had endorsed throughout the *De officiis*.[47]

When we view the early modern Cynic as a negation of that neo-Ciceronian blend of eloquence and civility, we find that the culturally dominant form—the active, eloquent orator—could only acknowledge Cynicism as one of its despised antitypes, the solitary, melancholic, malcontent in retirement.[48] Nonetheless, the outlines of the original ideal of eloquence remain recognizable, even in its negation. Barnabe Rich, for example, calls his melancholic "malecontent" "a right *cornish Diamond*" (that is, a counterfeit) who ostentatiously walks "with sad and sober aspects," so that others will cry, "Loe, yonder goes the melancholy gentleman: see there vertue and wisedome both despised and neglected."[49] Hence, in the background of these satires on the malcontent lay the venerable classical-humanist debates about the virtues of the active versus the contemplative life, with the malcontent living in a state of displaced, unhappy, self-deluded "retirement" parodying the contemplative lifestyle of the classical-Humanist retired poet or moral philosopher.[50]

It is worth reiterating that melancholy was a vice imputed to the leisured gentlemen who consoled themselves with ancient philosophy, not the ancient philosophers themselves. Rich's "malecontent" is therefore described as "singular in his owne conceit[; he] will sometimes withdraw himselfe into retired places, forbearing speech and conversation, reprooving the vanities of the world but with a word, and the manners of the people with a shrug." Nevertheless, the uncivil Cynic, and especially the scholarly Cynic in retirement, represent a warning to those who would use their classical knowledge not for worldly "speech and conversation" and the orator's proper sphere of public activity, but for the unprofitable pastime of "reprooving the vanities of the world." From this perspective, the disillusioned Cynic converges with the misanthrope, eagerly though impotently "barking and railling againste the vices of menne," to quote Erasmus once again.

For this reason, many early modern accounts of the uncivil Diogenes compared or equated him with Timon, an equation that made most sense when both were viewed as melancholics.[51] Though I will have much more to say about these two types when we reach Shakespeare's *Timon of Athens,* here I will merely note that condensing these two figures together into the single compound Cynic-misanthrope introduces two new qualities to the Cynic's personality that we have not seen before, and that run counter to what little we know about the personality and life story of Diogenes: first, *an attitude of melancholy or disillusionment with human viciousness,* appropriate for Timon but not for the man who said that it was exile that taught him how to be a philosopher, and whose philosophic mission demanded he preach to large crowds; second, *ineffective speech,* once again, appropriate for Timon's rants against the human race, but strangely inapt for a man whose fame rested as much on his witty repartees as on his ascetic lifestyle.

But what if a humanist writer of neo-Ciceronian dialogues, eager to argue "the other side of the case," decided to present an "honest" Cynic in the full, early modern sense that included friendliness or heartiness as well as candor?[52] Or treated Diogenes not as a negation of civil conversation and decorum but as the fullest embodiment of the ideal? This is what happened in Stefano Guazzo's extremely popular courtesy book *The Civile Conversations* (1581/1586). Guazzo's comparison of the retired and active life contained discussions of Diogenes and Timon that were echoed by many other sixteenth- and seventeenth-century English writers.[53] Unlike other treatments of the two figures, however, Guazzo insisted on strongly distinguishing Diogenes' conversational philosophy from the misanthropy of Timon.

At the beginning of their dialogue in book 1, Guazzo's brother William admits that he suffers from a melancholy caused by an inordinate love of solitude. His physician and friend Anniball, however, warns that the antisocial pleasures of melancholy, unlike those of company and conversation, are not real. An inordinate love of solitude could even drive him to the folly of committing suicide like the "melancholike Athenian" Timon, who refused human conversation even in death, leaving behind a tombstone that rudely told passersby to drop dead.[54]

In the course of his therapeutic conversations with Anniball, William proudly offers as one of his authorities the "[Philosophers who] flie . . . the Conversation of Men," noting in particular the case of Diogenes, "who going to the church doore, as the people went out, thrust into the midst of them, . . . saying, it was the part of such as he was, to be always contrarie to the multitude: which was to shewe, that we ought according to the saying of the Poet, To follow the fewer sort, and not the common crue" (26–27).

To this, Anniball responds that "the doing of Diogenes, which you have rehearsed, served wel to shewe, that a Philosopher is contrary to the multitude, but not to disallowe conversation, which hee more accounted of then other Philosophers did" (31). Though Guazzo presents symmetrically opposed arguments regarding this philosopher's misanthropy, he concludes that Diogenes, unlike the fearful Timon, did not "flie" conversation with the "learned," but actually valued it more highly than other philosophers, since so much of his philosophy took the form of witty give-and-take with his listeners.

I believe that it is through Guazzo's recasting of Diogenes as Ciceronian conversationalist that we may trace one of the proverbial phrases concerning Diogenes: that he wandered the streets at noonday "searching for an honest man." As far as I can tell, this familiar yet unattributed phrase stems from Guazzo's devoted plagiarist and fellow-devotee of Diogenes, Samuel Rowlands, whose most famous couplet appears on the title page of his *Diogenes Lanthorne* (1608): "Athens I seeke for honest men; But I shall finde them God knowes when. / Ile search the Citie, where if I can see / One honest man; he shall goe home with me."[55] With this inaccurate though durable version of the *quaero hominem*—a true vernacularization of Diogenes' most famous saying—Rowlands has remade Diogenes into a Ciceronian seeker of company, even if the philosopher has to walk up and down the filthy streets of "Athens" to find what he has been searching for, a man worthy of his respect and friendship. Naturally, he can find this only when he encounters Alexander the Great.

Profitable Wisdom: Diogenes' Witty Counsel in Erasmus's *Apophthegmes*

When Diogenes refused Alexander's gift and told the emperor of the world to "Stand out of my light" (DL 6.38), this episode was endlessly told and retold by rhetoricians to teach the value of fearlessly speaking truth to the powerful. And yet the meaning of this incident in the early modern period, along with the *parrhesia* it exemplified, had radically changed from the democratic practice or "philosopher's virtue" it had represented in fifth-century Athens or Imperial Rome.[56] From Cicero and Quintilian onward, *parrhesia* had been transformed from the hard-won virtue of the ancient philosopher to a rhetorical figure or stratagem in its own right, a formal request to a powerful listener for the right to speak freely in his presence.[57] Seen in this light, the Diogenes-Alexander encounter served as an emblem of the highly stratified speech situation faced by any speaker who wished to address the riskiest and most beneficent of all possible audiences, the monarch. By highlighting the inherent stratification of speech in all rhetorical address, as well as the risks created by such stratification, this episode taught young students both the dangers and opportunities that accompanied the practice of eloquence in the real world of position and power.[58]

This episode, however, held another, more unsettling implication for those able to hear it: that what Erasmus had termed Diogenes' "pleasaunte mirthe" (xxvi) is not merely a pleasing ornament or turn of phrase but is another version of tactical wit, or what Certeau called *legerdemain,* the rhetorical "sleight of hand" that allows the "the weaker argument seem the stronger," or the weaker position displace the more powerful one (*PEL* 37–38). It is this tactical wit, this capacity for verbal cut-and-thrust that allows the rhetorically trained speaker to exploit his opponent's momentary weaknesses, even when their social positions are unequal. These are the destabilizing implications for rhetoric that Diogenes and Alexander endlessly reenact, though the positive treatments of Diogenes tried to address them by subordinating his wit to the demands of "counsel." Nonetheless, Diogenes was an irreplaceable symbol of verbal resourcefulness and self-sufficiency for a rhetorical pedagogy devoted, in Ong's terms, to inculcating the values of both masculine "toughness" and an agonistic, committed eloquence eager to take sides and debate competing positions.[59] The male independence of the Cynic, moreover, helped to banish some of the effeminizing implications of courtly service.

Consequently, images of this encounter were repeated in poems, paintings, emblem books, essays, orations, and other forms throughout this period.[60] As Francis Bacon observed, the incident raised "one of the greatest questions of moral philosophy: whether the enjoying of outward things, or the contemning of them, be the greatest happiness."[61] (Note Bacon's rhetorical framing of the question as a general thesis for debate.) Bacon, however, felt no need to point out what may have seemed to him the most obvious implication of the anecdote: that the "outward things" condemned by the ascetic Diogenes include all the blandishments of power and position that a training in rhetoric was supposed to provide. In other words, Diogenes' ascetic refusals had become entangled with the temptations not just of worldly pleasures but of worldly power and service to the state.[62]

Interestingly, this positive image of Diogenes and his parrhesiastic yet dutiful "speech," like the negative image of the uncivil Cynic's "barking and railling," stressed his indecorous talk but excused it to the extent that Diogenes' reproofs served the dual moral and political purpose of counseling the sovereign toward more virtuous behavior. Moreover, having such a blunt counsellor actually benefited the sovereign, by helping him sort through the ubiquitous flattery directed at him by his courtiers and subjects. Such a reading of Diogenes accorded well with the English humanists' project of defining "the role of the active, rhetorically trained citizen as a 'counsellor' of the ruler."[63]

The figure of Diogenes, however, further sharpened the discourse of counsel by making its users more self-reflexive, more aware of its inherent tendencies toward flattery, courtly dissimulation, and self-serving speech and conduct.[64] In such instances, Diogenes symbolized an *anti*-rhetorical and *un*civil impulse that actively pursued truth and virtue while remaining critical of the values of accommodation and "seemliness" enforced by Ciceronian eloquence and civility.[65] Thus, Diogenes appeared in a satiric work like the *Ars Adulandi, or Arte of Flattery,* specifically to distinguish between his own "truthful praise" and the "lying flatterer['s]" "cloak of feigned eloquence."[66]

The unresolved tension between the rhetorical and antirhetorical aspects of *parrhesia* ran through the most distinguished humanist treatments of Diogenes and the Cynics, which included More and Erasmus's translations of Lucian, Erasmus's apothegmatic collections of Diogenes lore, and culminated in the playwright John Lyly's *A Most Excellent Comedie of Alexander, Campaspe, and Diogenes.*[67] Accordingly, these rhetorical and literary treatments of Diogenes did not emphasize his smooth and accommodating conversation in the manner of Guazzo, but a bold yet reflective wit, capable of telling the truth so pleasantly that it became hard to refuse. Erasmus therefore praised the philosophy of Diogenes for his "pleasaunte mirthe" (xxvi), while More extolled wit as a peculiarly powerful form of eloquence when handled by a wise and virtuous counsellor.[68]

We can see this convergence between the various modes of wit and the tricky political maneuverings of the counsellor in the prefaces to More's and Erasmus's rhetorical works. In More's preface to their joint translations (1506), he argues the moral usefulness of translating and teaching both the Cynics and Lucian (whose dialogue *Cynicus* appears here). While the Cynics receive straightforward praise for their near-saintly self-denial, Lucian is presented as a useful stylistic and conversational model for those who wish to respond honestly to vice without offending decorum or surrendering one's integrity.[69] More writes that Lucian "everywhere reprimands and censures, with very honest and at the same time very entertaining wit, our human frailties," yet the satirist manages this so deftly that his jabs never incur resentment.[70] With this observation, More has revealed a tactic for overcoming one of the gravest difficulties facing the aspiring counsellor: how does one point out faults of conduct to one's social superiors without risking offense? More's suggestion is that an aptly turned piece of wit allows the satiric moralist to speak honestly, so long as he is sufficiently entertaining. Hence, a ready wit allows the counsellor to overcome one of the chief dangers of stratified speech without surrendering his role as moral "watchdog." And yet More's later career as lord chancellor and martyr should remind us how difficult it was to survive as a truth-teller or wit at court.[71]

Erasmus's preface to the *Apophthegmes* (1531; translation 1542) similarly treats the training and exercise of wit as part of a practical grounding in oratory and eloquence, equally necessary to the worldly ambitions of both the nobility and those who served them.[72] Erasmus, however, seems to have designed his collection for a younger, less sophisticated audience than the potential readers of Lucian's dialogues (the volume's initial dedicatee, William of Cleves, was then fifteen).[73] The *Apophthegmes* were, in fact, the classical past reduced to collections of "sentences" organized by speaker and alphabetically indexed for easy searching. Erasmus therefore designed the *Apophthegmes* to serve the practical needs of students at the lower levels of the rhetorical curriculum, who needed a ready stock of "commonplaces" derived (in his words) from such sources as "celebrated apophthegms of the ancients, or from proverbs, or from fables, or from similes and metaphors" to use as patterns and examples for the construction and expansion of assigned themes.[74] Erasmus's preface to the *Apophthegmes* makes it clear that the point of such rhetorical training in what still amounted to "proverbial wisdom" was not scholarly achievement but social advancement, in order to teach young men how to act in a very specific political environment—the courtly world of real power and position.

In Erasmus's description in the preface, the student must take the conventional or "commonplace" meaning of a standard saying and use his wit to dig down and find a deeper one underneath: "The principall beste sorte of *Apophthegmes* is that saiyng, whiche in fewe woordes, doeth rather by a colour signifie, then plainly expresse a sense, not comen for every witte to picke out, and soche a saiyng, as no manne could lightely feigne by studie, and whiche the longer ye doe consider it in your mynde, the more and more it dooeth still delite you" (xxii). Because the apothegmatic form often contains as much action or gesture as it does verbal content, it demands that the student expand, elaborate, or amplify the anecdote to clarify its point to an audience already familiar with the story.[75]

Consequently, the apothegm's demand for the speaker's and audience's shared engagement in the reconstruction of its meaning makes it excellent training for those "princes and noble menne" (xi) who must incorporate the common understanding of things into their eloquence, even while using their "witte" to discover new meanings within that common understanding. The apothegm is thus the ideal genre for training the man of state whose time for reading is limited and who must learn not to take men at their flattering word.

To demonstrate just how much can be drawn from even the least impressive apothegm, Erasmus uses the emblematic example of Diogenes: "More over, those saiynges that seme most fonde thinges of all to laugh at, by well handelyng, become matters of sadnesse. For what could bee a more fonde thyng to laugh at, then *Diogenes* goyng from place to place, with a candle in his hande at high noonetide, saiyng still, that he did seke a man?" (xxiii). As we saw earlier with Diogenes' serio-comic presentation of the Cynic philosophers in chapter 1, the appearance of nonsense on the surface conceals a more serious sense beneath: from the idiot's statement "I seek a man" in broad daylight, to the more reflective "how can I find a man worthy of the name?" "But in the meane tyme by laughyng, we learne that he is not by and by, in all the haste a manne, that hath the figure and shape of a manne (which Images also of wood and stone have) but to find out a manne, the botome of the harte and mynde must bee founde out" (xxiii).

The answer is that to "find out" a man, one must be able, like Diogenes, to look past appearances and sound out the very "botome of the harte and mynde." So, too, we must look past the appearances of Diogenes to find out what lies underneath the surface of any apothegm. Erasmus's recurring metaphor of the philosopher's wisdom as buried treasure is anticipated in his earlier comparison of Plutarch's apothegm collection to "golde in the veines under the yearth," patiently gathered by the counsellor and presented to the young prince for his pleasure and edification (xi).

In this instance, we find that it is Diogenes himself who serves as the truest model for the man he nonetheless seeks: "If the harte and minde bee guided by reason and discrecion, rather then lead by willful appetite: then and els not, haste thou founde out a manne" (xxiii). In other words, we find in this passage a more expansive ethical justification of wit, one that focuses on the heroic self-sufficiency of Diogenes, and rests ultimately on a view of the witty Diogenes as a paragon of intellectual autonomy, reason, and freedom from "appetite," one that even "Princes and noble menne"—perhaps even Alexander himself—would do well to reflect upon and imitate.

John Lyly's *A Most Excellent Comedie of Alexander, Campaspe, and Diogenes*

With John Lyly's *Campaspe* (1584), we reach the end of one trajectory involving Diogenes and the beginning of another. As mentioned earlier, the play depicts Diogenes as a good counsellor and follows in many respects the rhetorical and pedagogical models of eloquence I have identified with More and Erasmus. At the same time, Lyly's presentation of these themes explores some of the limits that these paradigms had encountered in his own era and identifies a newly relevant audience for the Cynic's wit, the "populus," or people. This, I should point out, was the same "multitude" that Guazzo's Diogenes (translated just three years earlier) "[was] always contrarie to."[76] Thus, in a surprising tub-sermon delivered to a jeering urban crowd, Lyly's Diogenes suddenly reclaims his missionary zeal, turning himself into an orator and quasi-Puritan preacher, while attacking the civility, accommodation, and verbal redescriptions that have corrupted Athenian language and manners since Alexander's arrival.

Whether we read Lyly as emulating or satirizing the courtly lifestyle and careers of his contemporaries, there is no doubt about the centrality of wit, learning, and rhetoric in his best-known prose fiction and plays.[77] These works are gorgeously contrived vehicles of wit and classical allusion and represent one of the high points of the "oratorical" high style that dominated much of this era's best writing.[78] In keeping with the heavily ornamented, logically elaborated, antithetic style of Euphuism, Lyly's fiction and early drama also display what his best critic, G. K. Hunter, has called an "aesthetic of the apopthegm."[79] This anecdotal, indeed, antinarrative mode of presentation displaces its action almost entirely into various forms of debate, proceeding by way of "dialogues, soliloquies, and alternating orations" rather than progressive plot- or character development.[80]

At this point, it should be clear that what Hunter terms this era's "aesthetic of the apophthegm" was created and sustained at least in part by the productive alliance of humanistic training in eloquence and the long-standing appeal of "proverbial wisdom," an alliance that helped to elevate Diogenes as a symbol of independent and therefore morally effective speech. And yet when we compare Lyly's play to Erasmus's treatment of the philosopher, something has vanished from Lyly's presentation of Diogenes and Alexander: the classical humanist ideals of eloquence, persuasion, or rhetoric as a form of verbal action. Quite simply, under a monarch like Alexander, there is little to discuss, and even less to debate, in what Lyly's Alexander defiantly terms "king's causes" (1.3.89). Hence, in the latter part of Elizabeth's reign, the classical-humanist "counsellor" of Elyot, Erasmus, or More seemed not just implausible but slightly ludicrous and obsolete, and Lyly's depictions of the court-philosopher Diogenes, the courtly artist Apelles and his lover Campaspe, and the vacillating monarch Alexander all reflect this state of affairs.[81]

As both Hunter and Pincombe acknowledge, between the era of Lyly's famous grammarian-grandfather and his own historical moment, there had been an unmistakable devaluation of the classical, largely literary training in eloquence that had provided earlier generations of scholars access to preferment.[82] As Hunter sums it up, "The literature of the 'eighties and 'nineties is, in fact, largely a product of frustration. As we see with the students of the Parnassus Plays, literature is only a stopgap, one stage better than divinity perhaps, but not the real end of learning."[83] Similarly, Pincombe views *Euphues* as essentially describing the obstacles facing the young wit aspiring to advancement through learning, governmental service, or literary reputation. The concerns of rhetoric had been displaced into literature and literary form, thereby emptying out the once-viable ideal of the "humanist courtier" to which earlier scholars could at least aspire. All that remained of eloquence was the brusque wit of Diogenes and his menials. Because critics like Hunter, Saccio, Pincombe, and Scragg have so effectively canvassed the play's tripartite plotting of honor, love, and philosophy, my focus in the rest of this section will be the two competing images of the wit's audience: Alexander and the crowd, along with the characteristic style with which each audience is addressed.[84]

In Lyly's treatment of the wit's reception at court, Diogenes is described as "dogged but discreet, I cannot tell how, sharp with a kind of sweetness, full of wit, yet too, too wayward" (2.2.168–70). Diogenes uses his wit to distinguish himself from Alexander's courtiers and parasites, not least Hephestion, Alexander's loyal soldier and friend, and the source of this ambivalent description.[85] Diogenes' "sharp" yet "wayward" wit shows how the Cynic philosopher beats the courtiers and other philosophers at their own game: his "sweetness" is not an overrefined amiability, but something closer to the term's older senses of "pleasant feeling, delight, pleasure."[86] He therefore offers the sovereign a pleasingly paradoxical blend of doggedness and discretion, Cynicism and "seemliness."

The occasion of this description is Alexander's famous first meeting with the philosopher, which concludes with the emperor's famous "wish to be Diogenes" (2.2.167–68).

> *Alexander.* If Alexander have anything that may pleasure Diogenes, let me know, and take it.
>
> *Diogenes.* Then take not from me that you cannot give me, the light of the world.
>
> *Alexander.* What dost thou want?
>
> *Diogenes.* Nothing that you have.
>
> *Alexander.* I have the world at command.
>
> *Diogenes.* And I in contempt.
>
> *Alexander.* Thou shalt live no longer than I will.
>
> *Diogenes.* But I shall die whether you will or no.
>
> (2.2.155–64)

Lyly's version of this incident is so compressed that his theater audiences could easily miss his carefully arranged thematic juxtapositions: Alexander offers the world's sensual pleasures, while Diogenes prefers its philosophic light; Alexander has the world in command, while Diogenes holds it in contempt. The effect of this rapid series of juxtapositions is to minimize the differences between the two men, stressing their parallels and temporarily suspending the enormous social disparity between philosopher and king. This may seem, therefore, like Erasmus's treatment when he described how Alexander "talked familiarlye with [Diogenes] manie thynges" (93).

As many readers of Lyly have noticed, however, the treatment of the sovereign's relationship to the philosopher is more psychologically complex than in Erasmus. For one thing, the discourse of counsel generally predicates such parrhesiastic freedoms on a preexisting relationship of "amicitia" or "friendship," the "strictly moral" and voluntary obligation of the ruler to listen to the openly expressed opinions of his friendly counsellors, men like Hephestion or his onetime teacher Aristotle.[87] And yet Lyly shows Alexander resisting Hephestion's good advice throughout the play and treating the greatest philosophers in antiquity, including Aristotle, like a burlesque vaudeville revue. Most significant of all these gestures is Lyly's discreet inclusion of the historical figures Clitus and Parmenio, two loyal officers of Alexander whom the emperor later slew after the events of the play. These are the not-so-random members of the rank and file who serve as an unhappy chorus to Alexander's developing love affair with Campaspe.[88] Though there are no overt references to their eventual fates within the play's frame, their comments build up dramatic irony around the play's ongoing discussion of Alexander's character, even while allowing Lyly to maintain courtly decorum. Lyly can therefore exhibit a sovereign onstage who learns to renounce love and embrace duty, while also exploring the implications of Alexander's continual refusal to listen to any counsel but Diogenes' misogynist jokes.

At the same time, the clipped tone of these exchanges shows that Diogenes, unlike every other character except Campaspe and Apelles, understands the dangers that follow from too-close proximity to the sovereign and his desires. This makes Diogenes' task a delicate one. Unlike the hapless vaudeville troupe of famous philosophers that Alexander questioned and threatened by turns, Diogenes expertly engages in his own defensive tactics, fending off questions, yet keeping his retorts brief enough to satisfy the emperor's vanity. Diogenes does not wish to humiliate the emperor, nor does he wish to befriend him. Instead, this scene plays out like a martial-arts film, with a master batting away every blow his young disciple can offer and finishing as serenely as he began. Consequently, the philosopher's rhetorical victory serves a pedagogical purpose for the headstrong Alexander, though Diogenes remains too tactful and entertaining to present it as anything other than a victory over himself. This is how he disarms his audience of one, the sovereign, and avoids Callisthenes' fate.

The second major image of an audience's reception occurs when Diogenes addresses the "populus"—the Athenians as an undifferentiated crowd—and denounces them for their meek acceptance of an aristocratic decorum that conceals foul behavior under seemly language. Here the rhetorical values of tact, decorum, and verbal inventiveness come in for heavy antirhetorical criticism for their emptiness, hypocrisy, dissimulation, accommodation of vice, etc. Diogenes delivers his "diatribe" in its proper Cynic form as an "argumentative monologue with imagined interlocutors."[89] He therefore baits the crowd with ambiguous language, promising them an attempt "to fly," then abusing them for assembling for such a stupid purpose. Though there are plenty of classical analogues for this scene in Laertius, the flying objects ("dog, dog, take a bone!"), hissing, and allusions to other forms of "rough music" offered by the early modern crowd argue for more popular vernacular sources like contemporary jest books or the Guazzo passages discussed in the previous section (Guazzo 26–27).[90]

In a vein of Cynic preaching little acknowledged in either the early modern vernacular or humanist treatments, Diogenes denounces those assembled for their vicious though perfectly conventional behavior and challenges them to act as if they were men:

> *Diogenes.* Ye wicked and bewitched Athenians, whose bodies make the earth to groan and whose breaths infect the air with stench, come ye to see Diogenes fly? Diogenes cometh to see you sink. Ye call me dog; so I am, for I long to gnaw the bones in your skins. Ye term me an hater of men; no, I am a hater of your manners. Your lives dissolute, not fearing death, will prove your deaths desperate, not hoping for life. (4.1.25–32)

This passage answers a number of popular accusations made against the philosopher throughout this period: about his doggish incivility, his misanthropy, and his status as a mere jester devoid of moral instruction. Moreover, by attacking the conventional decorum followed by everyone in Athens, Diogenes suddenly assumes an almost Calvinist language of moral and even religious absolutes, and attacks the crowd for its worldly "manners."[91] Intriguingly, the corrupt worldliness he attacks here resembles the civility practiced with little comment in the rest of the play. In the wake of Diogenes' parrhesiastic preaching, the rhetorical arts of verbal accommodation and self-idealization are revealed to be the characteristic vices of Alexander's court. Diogenes tells the crowd:

> You flatter kings and call them gods; speak truth of yourselves and confess you are devils. From the bee you have taken not the honey but the wax to make your religion, framing it to the time, not to the truth. Your filthy lust you colour under a courtly colour of love, injuries abroad under the title of policies at home, and secret malice creepeth under the name of public justice. (35–42)

Diogenes' denunciation of the "colours" used to paint over vice recalls the rhetorical manuals' ambivalent definitions of *paradiastole,* the reversal of moral distinctions for the purposes of swaying the crowd.[92] This technique consists of the artful substitution of names, so that certain moral distinctions may be quietly forgotten. Lust is therefore transmuted to a "courtly colour of love," for example, and Lyly creates a master trope for rhetoric in the overaccommodating wax that "frames [itself] to the time, not to the truth," forming a would-be religion of flattery that leads inevitably to the worship of Alexander himself.[93]

This amounts to a moral redescription of the earlier events of the play, one that argues the other side of the case about Alexander and his increasing entanglement with the lovers Apelles and Campaspe. Alexander appears in a new guise, as the emperor who once demanded to be worshipped as a god, a switch in sources from Erasmus's *Apophthegmes* to Lucian's *Dialogues of the Dead.* Along with Alexander the counterfeit god, whose "injuries abroad" are colored "under the title of policies at home," we may also in this speech recognize the whole series of rhetorical substitution made possible by *paradiastole:* "All things are lawful in Athens" (47–48), announces Diogenes, since "swearing cometh of a 'hot mettle,' lying of a 'quick wit,' flattery of a 'flowing tongue,' undecent talk of a 'merry disposition'" and so on (45–47).[94] Though any rhetorical argument has the potential to undo fixed moral distinctions, Diogenes refers to a much more sweeping and dangerous force that has corrupted the morals of his city and destroyed its language: the unrestricted power of Alexander. And yet Diogenes uses his own rhetorical powers of moral redescription, his own misleading figures of speech, his own *parrhesia* and *paradiastole,* to counter Athens' moral and linguistic confusion. Nonetheless, none of the major characters witness or react to this scene, and the play's celebration of aristocratic decorum goes on to its preordained conclusion (Alexander will *always* give up Campaspe), unaffected by this brief appearance of an antirhetorical, moral perspective in its midst.

Lyly's Diogenes, for all his divergences from the ancient Diogenes, still represents an undiminished normative perspective able to measure others by his own values. Diogenes' philosophic independence is never an empty, abstract, or metaphysical quality, because it is always an independence that has to be recaptured, one joke at a time, from those who already hold power. Nonetheless, even the most idealizing early modern accounts of Cynicism recognized that Cynic "freenesse of speache" must always be practiced in a world ruled by the enemies of independence; therein lies its genuine philosophical heroism.[95]

This self-imposed demand meant that Diogenes or his imitators must practice their philosophy in the world *as it stands*, without the option of simply *imagining* their philosophy as it would be practiced in some metaphysical Cloud-Cuckoo-land where philosophers can fly whenever and wherever they desire. This is what Foucault meant when he talked about the ancient Cynics aspiring to an "other life" (*FP* 110). Yet it is always possible to see this antimetaphysical strain of Cynicism as an accommodation with power rather than its critique, especially when ambitious intellectuals like Bacon praised Diogenes for an independence that in no way threatened the sovereign's inherent power.

Useless Knowledge: Vernacular Cynics and Malcontents in John Marston's "Cynick worke"

In the early career and writings of John Marston, we can see how a writer identifying himself with the Cynics abandoned eloquence and civility and embraced wholeheartedly their most stigmatized traits, including misanthropy, personal satire, and railing. Most important for our history of the concept of Cynicism, Marston's choice suggests that the role of a would-be Diogenes and moralist had degenerated into the cheapest forms of pamphlet moralism, in the manner of Rowlands's warmed-over rehashing of Guazzo and Aesop. Instead, Marston proudly presented himself as a fully vernacular Cynic, a "humorous" and up-to-date malcontent and satirist who signed his *Scourge of Villainy* (1598) as W. Kinsayder, or in effect, as a modernized, transliterated "Cynick."[96] This self-identification with the currish, uncivil side of the Cynics, which may be taken equally as a gesture of self-authorization and preemptive self-abasement, was soon confirmed by his fellow satirists, who ridiculed Marston as a shameless, impotent, barking Cynic until the Bishops' Ban in 1599 interrupted the exchanges.[97]

The reasons for this epidemic of accusations of currish Cynicism were multiple, though we can point to contributing factors like the economic unrest and credit panics of the 1590s, as well as the extraordinary surge in satire and libels that provoked the Bishops' Ban.[98] New anxieties surrounding the luxury and effeminacy of the upper classes had made Diogenes topical again, and the currish philosopher was enlisted to critique the bad habits of the aristocratic class from an outsider's uninhibited, shamelessly unaristocratic perspective.[99] Much of the self-censoring wit that had once softened such critiques was now gone. Diogenes was no longer the philosopher defining his role in a courtly milieu, but a compromised figure wandering far from the centers of power. Once displaced, writers using this kind of Cynic persona had no need to demonstrate their wit, prove their autonomy, censor themselves, or impress their social superiors. To that extent, the vernacular Cynic once again reveals the close, mutually reinforcing relationship of classical humanist eloquence, civility, and Ciceronian decorum or "seemliness."[100] Once he loses access to power through eloquence, the Diogenes of the rhetorical traditions abandons the self-control or wit he once demonstrated, leaving a shameless, uncivil vernacular "Cynick" in his place.

The *Scourge of Villainy* portrays both the Cynic moralist and Cynic satirist as malcontents and firmly links the Cynic style with both sexual obscenity and uncontrolled railing. Nevertheless, Marston, whose satiric stance always contained a touch of the self-defeating and paradoxical, maintained that he had written his *Scourge of Villainy* as a moral corrective to the corruptions he (all too joyously) described.[101] After Marston's promise in the *Certain Satires* (1598) to "turne [his] tub against the sunne" ("Parua magna, magna nulla"), Diogenes and the Cynics appear in his satires as historical precedents for Marston's blunt and aggressive style, armed against detraction with even heavier weapons of detraction.[102] The humanist-inspired culture of eloquence and civility, which earlier friends of the Cynics like Erasmus and Guazzo had done so much to construct, had now become the chief target of the Diogenical satirist.

For Marston, his identification with Diogenes authorizes him to attack head-on the conventional values of decorum and civility that had once underwritten persuasion, particularly verbal accommodation. Instead, the writer assumes a plainspoken persona interested in scourging immorality, not his own social advancement, or even appearance of virtue. Marston writes:

> Where I but strive in honest seriousnes,
> To scourge some soule-poluting beastlines.
> So you will raile, and finde huge errors lurke
> In every corner of my Cynick worke.
> ("In Lectores prorsus indignos," *Scourge,* lines 67–70)

Appropriately, Marston's "Cynick worke" offers an encyclopedic range of dog imagery, depicting the snarling dogs of satire, as well as the barking or hand-licking dogs that the satirist must chastise:

> Envies abhorred childe, *Detraction,*
> I heare expose, to thy all-taynting breath
> The issue of my braine, snarle, raile, barke, bite,
> Know that my spirit scornes *Detractions* spight.
> ("To Detraction," *Scourge,* lines 3–6)

All these flattering or detracting dogs descend from the remark of Diogenes dividing men up into wild and tame dogs, or rather, detractors and flatterers (DL 6.51). Consequently, the melancholic Cynic is a detractor who wishes to attack other detractors for their detraction, rather like Roger Sharpe's "Second Diogenes," who "cals each man knave he meets, but be it knowne, / That title he doth give them, is his owne."[103] This suggestion of the Cynic's self-hatred and psychological projection is significant because it suggests that we are dealing with a specific "sociological" category rather than an individual "psychological" type. Marston's "Kinsayder" persona reflects the anxieties of an educated professional class whose marks of classically informed "distinction," and therefore their professional prospects, were rapidly dwindling.[104] In Marston's querulous tone, we can hear the displaced intellectuals of the Elizabethan and Jacobean era discovering their own uselessness to the social and political order, so that resentment spurs them onto even freer and less decorous speech. As Marston's displaced, disguised, disgraced, and exiled malcontent Altofronto/Malevole announces:

> Well, this disguise doth yet afford me that
> Which kings do seldom hear or great men use—
> Free speech; and though my state's usurped,
> Yet this affected strain gives me a tongue
> As fetterless as is an emperor's.[105]

In his "Kinsayder" persona, Marston never bothers to articulate why his detraction differs from that of his targets. Unconcerned by this confusion, however, Marston portrays himself as a "barking Satyrist," snarling at the "changing Proteans" who populate the fashionable world, and who govern and are governed by Opinion, the opposite of the neo-Stoic Reason that supposedly governs his writing ("The Author in Praise of the Preceding Poem," lines 45–46).[106] Though Marston himself never quite spells it out this way, Caputi's account of Marston's neo-Stoic distinction between reason and opinion at least makes Marston's criticisms of others more intelligible. In Marston's terms, the "all-taynting breath" of his *enemies'* detraction is ruled by "the worlds mightie Monarch, Good Opinion," to whom he had sarcastically dedicated the *Certain Satires.* But the very offensiveness of Marston's writing guarantees that it will never be mistaken for courtly flattery or the bland opinions circulating easily through the thoughts of fashionable or effeminate "Proteans."[107] In this respect, Marston has identified himself with the Diogenes who as a matter of principle goes "contrarie to the multitude," now firmly identified with a fluctuating realm of Opinion. And yet the personal self-control of the Cynic philosopher, and his uses as an ethical model, are gone, replaced with the misanthropic desire to annihilate the semi-demi-men he abuses. And, of course, their continued shameless existence in the face of such angry satire testifies to both the ineffectiveness of his railing and the depth of the corruption surrounding him.

The *Scourge*'s Satyre VII, "A Cynicke Satyre," combines Laertius's anecdote of Diogenes and the lamp at midday with Shakespeare's *Richard III.* This poem returns to the question that Erasmus had earlier broached in the *Apophthegmes:* where to find a real man? Marston answers in the negative: not in ancient Athens, nor in contemporary London:

A *Man, a man, a kingdom for a man.*
Why how now currish, mad *Athenian*?
Thou Cynick dogge, see'st not streets do swarme
With troupes of men? No, no: for *Circes* charme
Hath turn'd them all to swine. . . .
("Cynicke Satyre," lines 1–5)

Marston's writing is designed to reflect at least two kinds of flux and disorder: the monstrous condition of contemporary London's fashionable society and the disordered state of the "currish, mad Athenian" Diogenes. This Diogenes, of course, functions as a persona for the currish, mad, "barking Satyrist" Marston. Though Marston's writing has been criticized because his claims as a moral censor seem bizarrely mismatched with his obscene style, his lapses in decorum are better understood as symptoms of the corruptions he depicts *involuntarily,* through his breakdowns in style. The violence of his outbursts, then, registers how deeply he has been affected by the effort of representing such sins. In other words, the violated decorum, contorted style, and obscene content of Marston's "Cynick worke" reflect how much the satirist himself has been made into an impotent, railing misanthrope by his own subject matter.

Profitless Wisdom: Cynic vs. Misanthrope in Shakespeare's *Timon of Athens*

Betweene treasure buried under the ground, and wisedom kept hidden in the heart, there is no difference at all.

—Stefano Guazzo, *The Civile Conversation of M. Steeven Guazzo*

Shakespeare's *Timon of Athens* (1607–8?) represents the culmination of many of the themes pursued in this chapter.[108] It demonstrates, first of all, how classical humanist rhetoric helped to create a vernacular, postclassical discourse of the Cynic through a series of linguistic and historical displacements, moving the Cynics from Greek to Latin to English. Consequently, the play builds its plot around the false Cynic Apemantus without ever mentioning Diogenes or even the word "Cynic," though audiences and critics have long recognized the "churlish philosopher's" affiliation with some form of Cynicism. These affiliations were recognized through the play's recurrent references to dogs, its debates over who deserves the name "man" and whether such men are superior to beasts, and its concern with honesty and "plain dealing."[109] The play also takes as its starting point the early modern conflation of Timon and Diogenes, while deriving its Timon lore from many of the same vernacular and commonplace sources that had also conveyed Cynic lore into the rhetorical curricula and textbooks (for example, North's Plutarch, Erasmus's *Apophthegmes*, Erasmus and More's Lucian).[110] *Timon's* rather stylized version of the classical past therefore shows traces of what one historian of rhetoric has termed "vernacularity," the tendency of vernacular translation and exegesis to "displace the source which it proposes to serve."[111] In this play, the misanthrope Timon does not agree with the Cynic Apemantus, but quarrels violently with him, ultimately displacing the Cynic from his classically authorized function of calling virtue and vice by their real names. Timon does this by revealing Apemantus's tacit complicity with the rhetorical doublespeak and moral accommodation that have by now thoroughly corrupted Athens and its institutions.

Since *Timon* is one of the least discussed plays in the Shakespearean canon, I should briefly review its rather hectic plot: Timon is a rich man who is so generous that he resists the good counsel of everyone around him and bankrupts himself in gifts to supposed friends. Once his money runs out, he cannot persuade his former "friends" to reciprocate. In the meantime, the general Alcibiades pleads unsuccessfully with the Athenian Senate on behalf of one of his soldiers and ends up getting banished himself. Then Timon names himself "Misanthropos" (4.3.54) and runs into the woods to shun mankind. While digging for roots, Timon discovers enough gold to resume his former life but decides he will use it to buy the destruction of Athens instead. Timon's former dependents suddenly reappear, but Timon beats them and sends them away. Apemantus arrives, too, hoping to taunt him, but the two just bicker until Timon drives him away. Finally, Timon rejects the Athenians' pleas to stave off Alcibiades, who is preparing to invade Athens. Instead, Timon withdraws to the seashore to die alone, whereupon Alcibiades conquers Athens, only to find the grave of Timon.

As this summary indicates, the plot turns on a series of moments of failed persuasion that might have halted Timon's and Athens' march toward a common destruction: Timon's resistance to his steward's counsel; the stubborness of the Athenian Senate; Alcibiades' decision to invade rather than accept banishment; Timon's refusal to take up the Athenian senators' request to oppose Alcibiades; Timon's decision to die rather than rejoin his city or the human race. This series of test cases in failed eloquence suggests an equivalent series of failures of intellectual reflection to influence individual or collective actions, in a play evidently devoted to the unshakeable folly of the wise and the great. Into this context of failed reflection and stalled action enters the false Cynic Apemantus, who is as unpersuasive as he is unreflective.

The ineffectiveness of Apemantus, however, only reflects the more general paralysis affecting the social institutions and leadership of Timon's Athens, which are uniformly incapable of acting on behalf of their city. The Athenians' general state of institutional collapse and incapacity, moreover, should be seen as Shakespeare's rebuttal of the more grandiose claims on behalf of the orator, namely, that the trained man of eloquence is an agent of civilization who helps raise mankind out of its former beastliness.[112]

On the contrary, in *Timon* we witness the unraveling of a recognizable civilization, a collapse caused by a breakdown in Athens' once-celebrated practices of rhetorical persuasion, and which results in Timon's hope that "beasts / May have the world in empire!" (4.3.393–94). *Timon* demonstrates that in a so-called "community" where every conversation is either empty or futile, disagreements cannot be managed, and so even the most trivial disputes lead to unregenerative violence like Alcibiades' invasion of his own city. *Timon*'s depiction of the failure of persuasion in Athens anticipates Chaloupka's discussions of how cynicism's "ensemble effect" simultaneously degrades a society's language, institutions, and capacity for collective action.[113] Hence, Shakespeare's *Timon* becomes an important, though untimely, document of the transition from the classical-humanist Cynicism of Lyly to the modern, vernacular cynicism that was emerging out of the rhetorical tradition's dissolution.

Hence, *Timon*'s strategies of displacement begin with his classical sources, but they also overtake the historical mediations of rhetorical culture, critiquing the values endorsed by Erasmean humanism to show their obsolescence in a postclassical version of "Athens." The displacements of rhetoric occur in three important scenes: in the marketplace of flattery that the pseudo-diatribes of Apemantus only reinforce; in Timon's denunciation of gold, which identifies the morally destabilizing effects of rhetoric with those of gold; and finally in the confrontation between Timon and Apemantus, which takes the form not of rhetorical debate but verbal dueling.

In the play's opening scenes, Shakespeare seems to offer the conventional or literally "commonplace" view of the Cynic's role when he opposes Apemantus to the flatterers surrounding Timon.[114] As with Lyly's more tactful depiction of Alexander's military court at Athens, the civility, deference, and decorum enforced by stratification encourage a dishonest flattery when the Monarch or Great Man is not careful about his friends and dependents.[115] Timon, of course, is prodigally careless about his dependents and remains greedy for their praise, no matter how hypocritically offered.[116] Timon therefore surrounds himself with a carnival atmosphere of flattering deceit where crowds of people stand in line to praise him and receive outsized rewards. It is in this complacent environment of ubiquitous flattery that Apemantus's blunt and uncourtly diatribes have their greatest effect, though they are far from the "plain dealing" (1.1.210–11) he claims for himself. Where Shakespeare diverges most radically from Lyly's version of a courtly Athens is in his Lucianic treatment of Poet, Artist, and Cynic philosopher, which reduces them all to frauds and to flatterers, though Apemantus tenders his "services" in the form of pleasing self-abasement: "Apemantus, that few things loves better / Than to abhor himself—even he drops down / The knee before him [Timon]."[117] As David Colclough has argued, classical and early modern rhetoricians were well aware of the possibility that parrhesiastic free speech could serve rhetorical purposes of dissimulation, and Apemantus's split between his publicly Cynic exterior and private self-seeking seems to reflect such a reading of *parrhesia*.[118]

After the Poet and Painter reveal their mutual emptiness and admiration in conventional allegories of a "sea of wax" (1.1.42–50) and Fortune on a Hill (65–96), Apemantus's churlishness does provide a genuine relief from this market in praise:

Timon. How lik'st this picture, Apemantus?

Apem. The best, for the innocence.

Tim. Wrought he not well that painted it?

Apem. He wrought better that made the painter, and yet he's but a filthy piece of work.

Painter. Y'are a dog.

Apem. Thy mother's of my generation. What's she, if I be a dog?
(1.1.195–202)

The pervasive dog imagery in this play follows Marston's standard opposition of detraction and flattery, in which the barking, currish, displaced Cynic becomes the implacable enemy of his fawning, flattering, lapdog counterpart ("Thy mother's of my generation").[119] And just as we saw in Marston, the generally degraded condition of poetry, painting—and, we will soon learn, philosophy—have collapsed the usual distinctions between courtiers and philosophers, so that we view the plight of an entire class of dependent intellectuals in Timon's would-be "court."

Yet Apemantus at the close of act 1 reveals himself to be a counterfeit Cynic, a conscious negation of Cynicism's values. Once Timon vows to ignore his ineffective warnings and his railing against mankind, Apemantus makes a final vow in what seems like a Iago-like aside:

So. Thou wilt not hear me now; thou shalt not
then. I'll lock thy heaven from thee.
O that men's ears should be
To counsel deaf, but not to flattery.
(1.2.248–51)

For all their roughness, these lines suggest that Apemantus has explicitly abandoned the "counsel" that would save Timon from flattery.[120] The philosopher refuses to warn the Great Man about his future dangers ("thou shalt not then") and will therefore deny him "heaven" (that is, future happiness).[121] This refusal of the Cynic's early modern role of "counsellor," however, introduces a note of positive and personal malice into Apemantus's character, while the withholding of "counsel" makes him vengefully complicit in Timon's looming catastrophe. Apemantus is no longer the detached observer he pretends to be (1.2.33–35), but a participant in Timon's downfall, since his silence allows Timon to advance unimpeded toward doom. With this deliberate choice of silence, complicity, and inaction—the choice, we might say, of the modern, degraded, small "c" cynic—Apemantus has sided himself with everything corrupt in Athens, including the parasites and usurious senators he otherwise abhors. It is a betrayal not just of Timon but of the Cynic philosophy he professes and the "counsellor's" role he travesties in his lame banquet speeches.

The next great displacement of rhetoric occurs when Timon, having lost money and friends, flees the city, digs for roots, and finds enough gold to restore his "fortune" (4.3). Timon has naively uncovered the cause underlying all the terrible changes overtaking both him and his city: gold.[122] Gold, in its powerfully nonmaterial incarnation as currency or debt, governs Athens more powerfully than any feeling of trust, duty, or moral obligation.[123] Timon has symbolically discovered the power of gold, not just as a force that drives and transforms human behavior but as a powerfully reductive way to explain it. Timon's digging, in other words, has discovered something like Marxian materialism, a universal explanatory scheme that partakes of the same tension between materialism and abstraction as what it would diagnose.[124]

At the same time, Timon's gold travesties another kind of buried treasure, Erasmus's "golde in the veines under the yearth," so that we can recognize Timon's gold as a universal persuader of the most degraded sort, the only kind of eloquence understood in Athens. This reading of Timon's gold as a debased form of eloquence is reinforced when we see how Timon's diatribe against gold resembles Diogenes' rant against Alexander in *Campaspe,* similarly focusing on the power of gold to inspire moral redescriptions (*paradiastole*) designed to flatter or mislead one's audiences. Timon exposes the amorality buried underneath *paradiastole*'s "mannerly interpretation" when he exclaims:

> Thus much of this [gold] will make
> Black, white; foul, fair; wrong, right;
> Base, noble; old, young; coward, valiant.
> . . . .
> This yellow slave
> Will knit and break religions, bless th'accurs'd,
> Make the hoar leprosy ador'd, place thieves,
> And give them title, knee and approbation
> With senators on the bench. This is it
> That makes the wappen'd widow wed again:
> She whom the spital-house and ulcerous sores
> Would cast the gorge at, this embalms and spices
> To th'April day again. Come, damn'd earth,

Thou common whore of mankind, that puts odds
Among the rout of nations, I will thee
Do thy right nature. (4.3.28–30, 34–45)

Beginning with its brisk reversals of names, gold is figured as incorrigibly rhetorical, seductive, political, and monstrous.[125] Unlike the masculine powers of eloquence, action, and virtue, however, the mutability of gold carries all the socially disintegrating powers of female sexuality, which translate, as in Marston, into a monstrously androgynous form of political action coupled with corruption.

Yet Timon's misogynist speech only exaggerates the defensive suspicion of the courtly female that we saw before in Lyly's Diogenes, a suspicion shared by many other early modern Cynics who jealously guarded their independence against potential effeminacy. Timon's misogyny, however, extends as wide as the "damn'd earth . . . common whore of mankind." The all-too-mutable values represented by rhetoric, gold, and prostitutes have inspired him to seek something outside this economy, something whose value cannot fluctuate. Unlike the classical Diogenes, the melancholy Timon covets a condition that puts him well outside the reach of fortune: namely, the grave.

The third displacement of rhetoric occurs in act 4, during the series of visits Timon receives from those whom he knew during his previous fluctuations of fortune. Though many critics have noted the static, antiprogressive nature of these scenes, they may represent a kind of travesty of the rhetorically driven drama that we have already seen in Lyly. The difference is that the "dialogue" figured here is postrhetorical, unregulated by traditional rules of decorum, and concerned largely with the Cynic and Misanthrope's competing claims to intellectual freedom and independence.

In other words, Timon and Apemantus's quarrels depict what Peter Sloterdijk has called the "struggle with opponents disinclined to dialogue."[126] This kind of struggle recurs at moments of political and institutional deadlock, when ideological critique steps in to diagnose the precise reasons that dialogue has come to a halt. In Sloterdijk's suggestive formulation, the failure of dialogue caused by deadlock encourages the formation of competing ideological critiques. When these critiques duel, they seek, in Sloterdijk's words, "not merely to 'hit,' but to operate with precision, in the surgical and military sense, to outflank and expose opponents, to reveal the opponents' intentions. Exposing implies laying out the mechanism of false and unfree consciousness."[127] Needless to say, in such a verbal duel, what we are witnessing is not dialogue, nor is it speech conducted for the sake of persuasion, but mutual attempts at unmasking. Shakespeare therefore offers an untimely depiction of cynical ideological critique, one that concludes with Timon's exposure of Apemantus's "false and unfree consciousness."

Though critics have long prized act 4's confrontation between Apemantus and Timon, they have sometimes failed to note that the scene's dramatic power comes from its fusion of intellectual debate with character revelation: we feel that we are witnessing a completely credible and evolving argument between two characters while we follow the dialogue's exploration of the strengths and weaknesses of two distinct intellectual positions, Alienation versus Accommodation.[128] In critical terms, this means that Shakespeare's dramatic goal seems not to have been to seek a resolution or clear "winner" of the debate but to lead the audience to discriminate more thoughtfully between the two characters and their competing positions.

When seen in this light, it's easier to see why Apemantus's opening charge against Timon is that he has imitated Apemantus's form but not his philosophic substance: "Thou dost affect my manners, and dost use them" (4.3.201). In Apemantus's view, Timon's misanthropy offers nothing but an unreflective imitation of Cynic philosophy, a form of counterfeit Cynicism brought on by a few disappointments and a case of the vapors. Timon's "Cynicism" can be changed as easily as a suit of clothes, though Apemantus maliciously suggests that Timon, as someone born to privilege, is more suited to flattery than philosophy:

> This is in thee a nature but infected,
> A poor unmanly melancholy sprung
> From change of future. Why this spade? This place?
> This slave-like habit, and these looks of care?
> . . . .
> . . . Shame not these woods
> By putting on the cunning of a carper.
> Be thou a flatterer now, and seek to thrive
> By that which has undone thee. . . .
> . . . .
> . . . 'Tis most just
> That thou turn rascal; hadst thou wealth again,
> Rascals should have't. Do not assume my likeness.
> (4.3.204–7, 210–13, 218–20)

What Apemantus does not recognize is that Timon never imitated anyone's pose and was never interested in anyone's philosophy. Instead Timon is expressing a rage rooted in an experience of deep betrayal. Apemantus's accusations, moreover, only conjure up the possibility that *he* is the one who has put on the "cunning of a carper," and that Timon's presence has only made his behavior look imitative, parodic, unfree by comparison. Who better deserves the name of false Cynic, after all? We suspect Apemantus even more strongly when he orders Timon to give up the woods and return to his former, unreflective life. Once again, Apemantus sides himself with the most conventional, unreflective, and corrupted values of Athens even while he assumes (incorrectly) that Timon has not been transformed by his experience. The audience, however, could not have a more direct demonstration of how Apemantus's false Cynicism has caused him to discount the possibility of any genuine change, either in Timon or in Athens.

Timon's damaging response is classically Cynic in that it interrupts a fine stream of eloquence with a rude gesture:

> *Apem.* What, think'st
> That the bleak air, thy boisterous chamberlain,
> Will put thy shirt on warm? Will these moist trees,
> That have outliv'd the eagle, page thy heels
> And skip when thou point'st out? . . .
> . . . .
> O thou shalt find—
>
> *Tim* A fool of thee. Depart.
>
> (4.3.223–27; 234)

As a would-be moralist, Apemantus assumes that all other men aspire to his behavior and deviate from it only because of their weakness. Yet Timon shocks Apemantus when he interrupts the philosopher's lectures and asks him to leave. It is a theatrically arresting moment, because with one word, "Depart," Timon has demonstrated that Apemantus's greatest desire is not to withdraw from society but to stay and lecture him. Timon has uncovered Apemantus's unacknowledged desire for, and dependence upon, an audience. Unlike a genuine Cynic, however, Apemantus has no interest in the ethical fate of his listeners. Timon, of course, has been permanently cured of this kind of need for others, which is why he wishes to plunge himself, his city, and the whole human race into a grand fiesta of self-annihilation. And yet for all Timon's craziness, who is the more effective speaker? Apemantus, whose low jests have never managed to depress a banquetgoer's appetite, or Timon, whose speech to the Bandits inspires the Third Bandit to say: "[He's] almost charm'd me from my profession, by persuading me to it" (4.3.454)?[129]

All that is left for Timon to do is to make the final break from human society, the melancholic withdrawal that Apemantus ceaselessly talks of but can never accomplish. When Timon flings stones at Apemantus and calls upon his gold—that "visible god" (4.3.389)—to set men at odds and finally grant dominion of the world to beasts, Apemantus murmurs: "Would 'twere so! / But not till I am dead" (4.3.395–96). Then Apemantus promises to tell everyone in town about the "treasure" so that Timon will be miserably "throng'd to" (4.3.397). It is Apemantus's final gesture of solidarity with Athens over and against the misanthrope who has rejected them both.

When Samuel Johnson analyzed this scene, he observed, "I have heard Mr. Burke commend the subtility of discrimination with which Shakespere distinguishes the present character of Timon from that of Apemantus, whom to vulgar eyes he would now resemble."[130] What Johnson and Burke seem to have recognized is that both these characters make competing claims to represent the values of freedom, independence, and autonomy from conventional values, but this outward resemblance does not survive their quarrel. Apemantus boasts of his superior philosophical independence in comparison with Timon's merely reactive, disordered state of mind, but Shakespeare, unlike earlier writers on the "philosophical hero," does not leave the discussion there. Like Diogenes and the Cynics, Timon has seen through the conventionality of local values, but these values now include the Cynic/Stoic ideal of the Unmoved Man.[131] If we take Apemantus as representative of this ideal, an unmoved man is one who has used his philosophy to defend himself all too well against the disappointments of experience. The sheer violence of Timon's rage makes Apemantus's philosophizing seem defensive, distrustful, and mean, a reflex masquerading as a philosophy.

When the critic G. W. Knight singled out Apemantus's odd decision to seek out Timon so that he could "join in a dilettante festival of cynicism," he pinpointed the play's reversal of the usual treatments of Cynic and Misanthrope. The most interesting twist in this regard is the play's suggestion that Apemantus secretly nurses some sort of envious admiration for Timon's more authentically alienated condition. This suggestion of envy might explain Apemantus's puppy-doggish insistence on following Timon in spite of his insults and stone throwing. We know what Apemantus is—and what he lacks—by what he envies about Timon.

In the corruption and flux of Athens, the would-be Cynic philosopher has become an advocate for the community's compromised values, while the Misanthrope's more absolute rejection of Athens has actually made him appear more heroic and less dissimulating than his railing counterpart. In the final contrast between Cynic and Misanthrope, the supposedly superior "philosophy" of Apemantus is revealed to be no philosophy at all, but a mere rationalization of private self-seeking and public malice toward others. Apemantus's "philosophy," one hardly worthy of the name, is a false philosophy content with discounting the painful experiences of others and every possibility of future change. Apemantus, in other words, has become an early, untimely example of a modern, small "c" cynic, in the sense of philosophic reason degraded into rationalized self-seeking, effective speech and action degraded into impotent railing, and the public harmonization of word and deed degraded into dissimulation and self-concealment. With this depiction of Apemantus's effect on those around him, *Timon* nicely captures the consequences of cynicism's "ensemble effect" and how it leads to institutional deadlock, stalled dialogue, and a passive complicity with moral and political corruption.

THREE From Rude Cynics to "Cynical Revilers"

Diogenes once passing neare to Hell
Beheld Mydas, that sometime liv'd a King,
Now in Infernall Beggery to dwell,
Base, ragged, dispossesst of ev'ry thing;
And laughing said, ah ah my golden Asse,
Ist possible the world comes thus to passe?
—Arthur Warren, "Poverties Patience" (1605)

This chapter takes up the story of Cynicism about fifty years later, in the middle of the seventeenth century, the moment when the breakup of rhetoric reduced Diogenes and Cynic philosophy to burlesque figures, doubly displaced parodies of a once-robust philosophy. Under the dual pressures of disciplinary division and political turmoil, classical rhetoric had transferred most of its historical commonplaces to the realm of literature, where they survived for another 150 years. Yet this switch from rhetorical to literary uses of the Cynics entailed a dramatically different ethical attitude of the writer toward the material. From the point of view of imitation, for example, a merely literary imitation of a commonplace ignored the possibility of identifying strongly with the Diogenes of the anecdotes, or of debating the meaning of his sayings, the two rhetorical practices that had provoked the most compelling reflections upon the Cynics during the previous era.

As the single most important tradition that had preserved and transmitted information about the Cynics, classical rhetoric had lost its cultural preeminence, with a number of reasons lurking behind its visible decline.[1] Rhetoric had suffered serious epistemological challenges from science and philosophy, when these had claimed their independence as fields of knowledge,[2] at the same time it had been forced to compete with print media for an expanding and increasingly heterogeneous literate public. Most damagingly, like every other inherited language of tradition and authority during the Civil Wars, classical rhetoric had shared in the general humiliation of elite culture that occurred during that time, when those inherited languages proved incapable of keeping Charles I's head attached to his body.[3] The result was a crisis in legitimation that provoked elites to reassess the effectiveness of a classical eloquence that had once served as the primary verbal armory for projecting, defending, and sustaining power in early modern England.[4] Thus, the self-conscious modernity of many of the antirhetorical thinkers of this period, particularly Royalist writers like Hobbes, Butler, and Davenant, had an edge of political resentment to it, while these thinkers sought to find new verbal strategies to protect a newly restored political power and authority from incursions from "the people."

With these changes to the status of rhetoric, the most familiar aspects of the rhetorical treatment of the Diogenes anecdotes and commonplaces were lost. The former tension between the rhetorical and antirhetorical aspects of Diogenes disappeared, as did the distinction between the Renaissance High and Low Views. For the most part, only the Low View of the rude or fraudulent Cynic remained relevant to this period's writers.[5] These shifts reduced the Cynics to literary characters of a rigidly satiric and predetermined type, still informed by early modern notions of the "humours" or melancholy, but with little connection to contemporary concerns in literature or philosophy. The Cynic was out of date, out of sorts, a relic of obsolete manners and false philosophy. In the words of the Royalist Samuel Butler, the "Cynique coynd False Money, and for feare / Of being Hangd for't, turnd Philosopher."[6] Yet the "Mad Phantastique Gambols" of Diogenes and "th' antique Greek Forefathers of the Trade . . . were not much Inferior to the Freaks / Of all our Lunatique, Fanatique Sects."[7] Diogenes appears in this "satyr" on the abuses of learning as one of the dealers in "False Money," that is, prejudice and error, who simply deserve to be expunged from an up-to-date curriculum.

Consequently, the writers depicting the Cynics in this period organized their depictions around the clustered notions of commerce, modernity, politeness, progress, and "improvement."[8] Once released from the synchronic rhetorical practices of reading and imitation, the Cynics were now seen diachronically, as historical figures at some remove from the present. Yet this insight did little to spur further curiosity in their philosophy: in the Royalist Thomas Stanley's massive doxographical *History of Philosophy* (1655–60), the prefatory "Life of Stanley" reassures the reader that the author has faithfully described Diogenes' "odd manner of living in a Tub," the various "pleasant Incidents of his Life," and the "Singularity of his Maxims."[9]

As a portion of philosophic history too oral, proverbial, collective, and popular—in other words, too "common-place"—to fit comfortably into either side of the emerging Enlightenment distinction between "Ancients" or "Moderns," the Cynics landed instead in this era's catch-all category of the "burlesque"—formerly authoritative historical figures persisting in a degraded and "residual" fashion into the present.[10] Consequently, the burlesque Cynic became identified with all that a normative, "improving" modernity tried to exclude: the malcontented, the rude, the misanthropic, the "common-place," and the antisocial.[11]

Moreover, since politeness was aligned throughout this period with an assumption of modernity's superiority over the past, the Cynic's rudeness was critiqued not merely in the unmannerly senses of "currish or churlish"[12] or "crabbed and severe,"[13] but also as unrefined, uncivilized, or primitive, symptomatic of a cruder era's *mores*. When viewed this way, the Cynics' out-of-date manners and outmoded notions of ascetic virtue could only confirm this era's historicist assumptions about the progressive refinement of society since antiquity.[14] Yet these same assumptions made this sect unsuitable for imitation in the present. What had once been viewed as the Cynic philosopher's limited and licensed transgression of courtly codes of "civility," or the vernacular Cynic's impotent railing against a rigid courtly *decorum* and "seemliness," was now viewed as a misanthrope's unreflective hostility toward this era's more expansive and generalized notions of "civility," "sensibility," "sociability," or "politeness."[15]

While the historical Cynics were being fragmented or flattened in this way, however, the concept of Cynicism began a new line of development that involved Enlightenment notions of the social. These uses of the Cynic seem to have coincided with moments of political crisis, when political disagreements inspired various opposition groups to claim authority from "the people," though the identity, allegiance, precise definition, and boundaries of "the people" remained contentious questions.[16] Consequently, we find Diogenes addressing himself to a series of crowds, or describing his relations with the multitude to interlocutors like Aristophanes, Alexander, or Plato. Some of these episodes recall Lyly's and Guazzo's antirhetorical retelling of Diogenes and the theater crowd, but they all stage fascinating confrontations between the Cynic and "the multitude." The Cynic's recurrent opposition to the multitude, however, paradoxically led to Cynicism's closer association with the multitude, in much the same way that the Cynic's former negations of rhetoric led to his assimilation into rhetorical culture, as discussed in the previous chapter. Thus, the meanings of Cynicism decisively changed once it was used to critique some of this era's morally inflected notions of the social, which took such forms as "the polite," "the public," "the people," "the multitude" or "the mob." The result was that the Cynic was transformed from an opponent of the mob to one of its most dangerous leaders.

To describe the Cynics' engagement with these morally inflected images of "the people," I will begin by showing how in Davenant's and Shaftesbury's works a rude Cynic is ridiculed for his resistance to a morally improving commercial modernity, even while he points to the menaces of "the multitude" who threaten polite society with revolutionary violence. In the Lucianic Dialogue of Diogenes and Alexander, Fielding reconceives their confrontation so that it is no longer the humanist debate between Temporal Power and Moral Reflection, but a more equal match between two verbally agile men who are *both* searching for an audience and the power that comes with it. Finally, Lyttelton's dialogue of Diogenes and Plato opens up an entirely new set of associations for the concept when it presents Diogenes as a leveling demagogue ready to use the mob instrumentally for his own purposes. Thirty years before Burke's debate with the philosophes over the political stakes of Enlightenment reason, Lyttelton's Cynic has become an exponent of a suspect philosophical reason fascinated with the power to shape others' beliefs. Because of his continual contacts with the "the people," the burlesque Cynic was transformed into a disbelieving Cynic, able to move the multitude to imitate his "cynical reviling." The Cynic has moved from being a figure of ridicule to an object of fear.

Sir William Davenant, *First Day's Entertainment at Rutland House*

Sir William Davenant was one of the earliest English writers to represent Diogenes as a rude moralist who worried over the political consequences of addressing "the multitude"—or, in what amounted to the same thing—of conjuring up a virtual "multitude" in the theater or in print so soon after the Regicide had shown what real, active multitudes could do. Davenant's staged debate took place near the end of Cromwell's rule, while plays were still banned by the Protectorate.

Accordingly, Davenant staged at his own residence a "public entertainment" entitled *The First Day's Entertainment at Rutland House* (performed 1656; published 1657).[17] Davenant's entertainment, really a set of staged declamations interspersed with concert music and songs, featured Diogenes debating with Aristophanes the value of the theater, which Davenant had carefully termed "public entertainment, by moral representations."[18] In this rhetorically framed pair of declamations, Diogenes plays his usual metacritical role, allowing Davenant simultaneously to impersonate and respond to the enemies of the theater. Davenant's rhetorical strategy of critique via impersonation was particularly prescient, since the regime had sent spies to monitor the performance.[19] Assigning the speeches against the theater to a figure like Diogenes was another smart tactical move, since it made it even harder for Davenant's audience to locate him as either supporting or opposing the Puritan ban on theater.[20]

Davenant may have chosen Diogenes because this philosopher represented a safely secularized image of a moralist whose antiquated notions of virtue and vice left him indifferent to the civilizing pleasures of commercial modernity.[21] In this respect, the *Entertainment,* like other texts in this period, uses the ambiguous trope of the Cynic to participate in the long-running Enlightenment debates about luxury, which focused on the fate of virtue or morality in a society devoted largely to the pleasures of consumption.[22] Diogenes' obvious excesses as a moralist make him an ideal opponent of Aristophanes' (and Davenant's) justifications for theatrical representations.

I should begin this discussion of the *Entertainment* by noting the most significant absence: Alexander the Great, or in effect, any mention of the sovereign or Protector. Davenant had prudently moved Alexander out of view during a ban on theatrical entertainments by a Puritan regime that had executed a monarch not so long ago. Instead, Diogenes directly addressed the crowd facing him, at the historical moment when Cromwell's Protectorate was looking less and less like "the people" and more like the previous regime.[23]

Diogenes, however, is not impressed by what he sees. His first question is whether "the multitude" should even form themselves into a public.[24] Can Englishmen gather into assemblies without harming themselves or their betters? Diogenes rudely reminds the crowd before him of "their" recent disorders:

> Can any entertainment divert you [he asks the crowd] from the mischief to which you are excellently inclined when you meet in public? Are not the winds your orators, and you their many headed waves that meet not but in foam and rage? Have you not yet distinguished the modesty and wariness of solitude from the impudence and rashness of assemblies? . . . As if the mingled breath of multitude were so contagious, that it infected reason as well as blood. (199–200)

As critics have long noted, these arguments reach well beyond the theater to the very nature of the social and political institutions of the Protectorate. Is there such a thing, Diogenes demands, as a public assembly free of "impudence and rashness"?[25] Does every member of an assembly risk losing his "reason" to the wind, foam, and rage of some "orator"? This is where Davenant's dissatisfaction with rhetoric, like Hobbes's, focuses upon the irresponsibility of the "orators" (both in- and outside of Parliament) who manipulate the people into disorders.[26] Is there simply too much risk in bringing crowds together into a "public," when they might decide to coalesce together and collectively *act* as a "multitude"?

When Diogenes describes the multitude, all he finds are winds, waves, foam—even diseased breaths—all metaphors of mob violence, contagion, and irrationality run amok. Davenant echoes the language of Barnabe Rich's Jacobean tract *Opinion Diefied* (1613), which describes how Diogenes chastised the "vulgare people" for their capacity for "violent tempestes" and opposed himself to the loosely held opinions of the "multitude."[27] And yet Davenant's greatest fear is not the multitude's "tempestes" but their potential for violence or their capacity for concerted, independent action like the previous decade's regicide.

This reading of Davenant is reinforced when we consider another potential source for Diogenes' accusation against the "multitude." Davenant might also be thinking of the moment in Hobbes's *Leviathan* (1651), published just five years earlier, when Hobbes defines "Rage" as "Vehement opinion of the truth of any thing" and gives the following example:

> When many of [those convinced of their own inspiration] conspire together, the Rage of the whole multitude is visible enough [in clamoring, fighting, and destroying those who protect them.] . . . And if this be Madnesse in the multitude, it is the same in every particular man. For as in the middest of the sea, though a man perceive no sound of that part of the water next him; yet he is well assured, that part contributes as much, to the Roaring of the Sea, as any other part, of the same quantity.[28]

It may be mere coincidence that Rich, Davenant, and Hobbes all compared the multitude's overwhelming noise and violence to the rage of the sea, which was no doubt a commonplace metaphor found in other writers as well. Yet Hobbes's treatment of the sea metaphor shows that the most fearsome capacity of the multitude lies in its ability to act collectively, in ways for which "no particular man" can be punished. And this may be the greatest potential danger of allowing orators to address the multitude. "O number, number," exclaims Diogenes, "when it consists of men, how accurst are those who trust to it? If for wisdom, who will rely upon determination, where the difference of opinions doth often equal the variety of faces?" (200). Consequently, "the multitude" represents an unpredictable force, difficult to influence, and harboring an irremediable, and therefore dangerous, "diversity of opinions."[29]

In the midst of this declamation to the modest paying crowd at Rutland House, Davenant's Diogenes has singled out one of the chief differences between the addressees of rhetorical speech and those of print: the open-endedness, anonymity, and, consequently, the *impunity* of the print audience. In John Bender and David Wellbery's suggestive account of this issue, rhetorical address is always marked by specific stratifications of power and property and remains irrevocably bonded to speech as it was conducted in the formalized and hierarchical spaces of a premodern society, notably in Parliament and other "assemblies." This inherent stratification (which, as Bryson reminds us, entails deference, accommodation, and decorum)[30] contrasts dramatically with emerging Enlightenment models of transparent, apparently positionless language addressed to an "audience" conceived in some fundamental sense as anonymous, heterogeneous, unpredictable, and therefore unknowable.[31] As Michael Warner has described the conceptual structures of "the public" in modernity, a "public" is "always in excess of its known social basis. It must be more than a list of one's friends. It must include strangers."[32] Rich, Hobbes, and Davenant all fear this contingency and open-endedness of "the multitude," a dynamic force unleashed by print, and best represented by the violent rolling of waves.

Moreover, Davenant's treatment of these competing conceptions of the public (present coterie vs. absent multitude) permits him an interesting double game. Diogenes can insult the absent mob's irrationality while flattering his paying theatrical audience's wisdom, though it might be hard strictly to distinguish the two. Nonetheless, Diogenes reminds the audience of their "annual feast where you devour your governors, or shift them nimbly as your trenchers before they are foul" (200). It is possible to see this passage, however, as not merely fear of the multitude but also a description of how the indeterminacy of the print public—its contingency and open-endedness—leads to a continual "commotion, change, and dissolution" in the modern body politic. When Aristophanes answers these charges, however, his rejoinder takes up the nature of the public and claims that people naturally behave better in public than they might in private. The same qualities of modernity feared by Diogenes—publicity and stranger-sociability—become the foundation for Aristophanes' (and Davenant's) trust in the public's openness to improvement.[33]

Soon enough, however, this Diogenes shows how the censorious moralist can become the greatest enemy of the virtue and moral improvement he endorses, when the philosopher derides Davenant's project of moral reformation via the theater: "But you [the theater audience] would meet to receive entertainment from such as represent the virtuous actions of the heroes. Is not virtue esteem'd in Athens but as the particular humour of philosophers? And, though it may please some few who study it, yet, because 'tis singular, it doth offend the generality; and 'tis safe in popular governments to content the people" (201). By arbitrarily restricting virtue to philosophers like himself, Diogenes has sarcastically opposed it to "popular government" and "the people," while travestying it as a mere "humour" or "singularity" of philosophers.

When Diogenes calls for Lady Virtue to "shrink up her white shoulders, put on her black hood, and retire to her closet," he argues against precisely the "amiable" and sociable notions of virtue amenable to an "improving" commercial modernity (202). The traditional early modern image of the withdrawn, misanthropic Cynic has been given a new veneer of antisocial religious impulses, remaking the solitary philosopher into one of the eighteenth-century's favorite ideological enemies, the Protestant "enthusiast."[34] Thus the moral rigor of Diogenes, which demands a "sullen" or melancholy withdrawal from enriching human interactions, places the philosopher squarely in opposition to this period's emerging values of sociability and commerce.[35]

Diogenes' final target is the stratified notion of "civility" that Davenant would expand into the more public, anonymous, and contingent notion of politeness (202). The Cynic philosopher now takes a rather anti-aristocratic tone, warning his listeners against all the courtly "excesses of civility" that will result from the opera's introduction. "Let the people be rude still," he exclaims, "for if by suffering it to be taught in public we refine their craftiness with civility, you must ere long fling away your night-caps and sleep in your helmets" (203). By arguing against the historical and ethical improvements offered by politeness, Diogenes ironically acknowledges one of the greatest anxieties an unstratified politeness could provoke among a defensive elite culture: its strategic usefulness for dissimulation, self-seeking, social emulation, and class mobility. By placing such complaints in the mouth of the reclusive antisocial philosopher, however, Davenant has helped legitimize precisely this era's transformation of virtue from a self-denying, solitary virtue to an eminently polite and sociable virtue better suited for modern, commercial societies.

We can recognize some of the historical and discursive forces at work behind this travestying of Diogenes when his opponent Aristophanes chooses not to label his opponent's "deform'd disposition" as a moral failing and redescribes it instead "under the pleasant shape of humour" (208). As a humourist and melancholic rather than a moralist, Diogenes is, in spite of his grave pronouncements, perfectly isolated, unauthoritative, and harmless. Aristophanes' and Davenant's easy dismissal of the philosopher shows how confident they are in their grasp of the future. Aristophanes confirms this when he jokes about "giv[ing Diogenes] authority, and let[ting] him have time and countenance to breed and enlarge a melancholy sect . . . till it multiply to extremes" (208). After such an increase in the "melancholy sect," "we should all grow most courageiously sad, and very bountifully hang and drown ourselves at our own charge" (208). The burlesque cynic has as much chance of multiplying himself as he does of persuading his audience to go hang themselves.

Davenant therefore uses Diogenes as a register of historical change, articulating the strongest objections to the postrhetorical, open-ended, contingent public, the sociable virtue practiced in a commercial society, and the politeness that tacitly undergirds both virtue and self-seeking in such a society. The result is that Davenant has redefined the active part of "the people" from the dangerous multitudes outside Rutland House to all those who are, in Aristophanes' words, "not misgovern'd by passion," and who "have an instinct to communication, that by virtuous emulations each may endeavour to become the best example to the rest" (206). In other words, Davenant addresses not "*the* people," but its most moral and active subset, "a polite and commercial people" (to use Blackstone's famous phrase) who are genteel enough to contribute to the improvements wrought by modernity.

The result of this kind of revaluation of Diogenes' rude virtue will be attitudes like the following remarks of Bernard Mandeville, who argued that such an out-of-date conception of virtue had no place in commercial modernity:

> When a Man from the greatness of his Soul (or an obstinate Vanity, which will do as well) resolving to subdue his Appetites in good earnest, refuses all the Offers of Ease and Luxury that can be made to him, and embracing a voluntary Poverty with Chearfulness, rejects whatever may gratify the Senses, and actually sacrifices all his Passions to his Pride in acting this Part, the Vulgar, far from contemning, will be ready to deify and adore him. How famous have the *Cynick* Philosophers made themselves, only by refusing to dissimulate and make use of Superfluities?[36]

In a passage like this, Diogenes represents nothing more than the conventional claims of an "antique or Christian ethic of self-restraint," the same self-deceiving ethical tradition that Mandeville had enjoyed demystifying in the *Fable of the Bees.*[37] Though Mandeville would be one of the first writers to be retrospectively labeled a modern cynic in the nineteenth century (cf. chapter 5), in his own writing he is dismissive of Diogenes' so-called virtue, which he terms the "subdu[ing of] Appetites." Mandeville is happy, moreover, to describe such feats of "voluntary Poverty" as mere stunts done to satisfy "the Vulgar." In this way, he tacitly brings the "polite" portion of the audience over to himself, by tagging Diogenes' natural audience as credulous, worshipful, and, of course, "vulgar." By their public ye shall know them.

Shaftesbury's Notebooks and the *Soliloquy*

When Anthony Ashley Cooper, 3rd Earl of Shaftesbury, formulated his influential vision of a "polite philosophy," he, like Davenant and Butler, took up Diogenes and the Cynics along with much else from philosophical antiquity, to mark the proper boundaries of modern politeness and learning. The result of this reading, however, was the disappearance of the "serio-comic" style that had characterized so much of their philosophy and reception since antiquity.[38] Shaftesbury insisted that the true, decorous core of Cynic philosophy had been concealed by its reputation for low, plebeian jests, rendering most of the anecdotal and commonplace traditions inauthentic. This is another sign that Shaftesbury has moved away from the rhetorical paradigms that sustained the morally polarized view of the Cynics, even as he offers his own polarization. Shaftesbury's sundering of the traditions was an influential one, so that for the rest of the century writers reduced the Cynics either to jesting burlesques or idealized, un-Diogenical Citizens of the World.[39] Nonetheless, because the concept's line of semantic development followed the burlesque Cynic rather than the Citizen of the World, we will pursue the Lucianic, travestying line of descent that leads to modern cynicism.

Though Shaftesbury spent much of his career writing against Hobbes, he shared with his antagonist the ambition of developing a distinctive new philosophical style that would supersede earlier, now ineffective modes of ethical and rhetorical persuasion. Unlike Hobbes's apparent exclusion of earlier philosophical authorities, Shaftesbury selectively appropriated the Cynics and incorporated them into his larger project of using philosophical history to reimagine the domain of the social in the present. In a further contrast with the Royalist writers and wits of Hobbes's generation, Shaftesbury's post-1688 classicism had a Whiggish cast to it that avoided the nostalgia, gloom, or disillusionment—-in a word, the antimodernism—of the Restoration-era writers. Instead, Shaftesbury continued to elaborate the possibilities of the same polite and sociable "virtue" that Davenant's Diogenes had mocked some sixty years before.

Nonetheless, despite the relative sunniness of Shaftesbury's views of human nature, the inescapable frame of reference for Shaftesbury's social thought remained the disaster of 1649 and the possibility of its recurrence through a breakdown in the compromises negotiated in 1660 or 1688. Shaftesbury's notions of politeness therefore regulated the social behavior of persecutory churchmen or enthusiastic sectarians to prevent the destabilizing effects of unconstrained, subjective religious belief. Thus, when we see this writer's interestingly comic and idealizing treatment of Diogenes in the "Maxims" contained in the Notebooks that make up the so-called *Philosophical Regimen,* we must read this in the context of other passages regarding the ferocity and violence of plebeian crowds, a violence always implicit within their capacity for collective laughter, seen by Shaftesbury as a prelude to violent collective action.[40]

Under the heading of "Laughter," Shaftesbury argues against a coarse and violent laughter, productive of "Savageness, barbarity, [in?]humanity, brutality, tyranny," and argues instead for a kind of joyful laughter more oriented toward the social, which he typically equates with the polite part of the people.[41] "How happy would it be, therefore, to exchange this vulgar, sordid, profuse, horrid laughter for that more reserved, gentle kind, which hardly is to be called laughter, or which at least is of another species?" (226).

Shaftesbury's selective picture of Diogenes must be read in the context of his ethical and social redefinition of laughter, which accompanied his project of broadening aristocratic decorum to encompass the polite, or genteel, classes. The violence and sadism of plebeian laughter, which he identifies with the crowds thronging around the gallows at public executions, must be regulated by some more general principle of humanity: "baulks, snubs, ill come-offs, strippings, whippings, executions, and all this with humour, raillery, wit, a comedy" (225). For Shaftesbury, this kind of coarsening, low comedy, "rustic, barbarous, immane," should be exchanged for something more "civil, polite, humane" (226).

Then Shaftesbury recalls Diogenes as a potential ethical model, but one that corresponds to that other "species" of decorous laughter, which is "benign, courteous, and kind" (226): "Remember [Shaftesbury urges himself] Socrates and laugh with Apollodorus in the prison. —Remember that [laughter] of [the Cynic] Demonax, which even Lucian sees, and Diogenes, which no one now sees, or understands, with the rest of that sweet kind. And remember what a happiness, improvement, enjoyment, to reserve all that is humorous and pleasant in the temper for such geniuses as those" (227).

To attain this level of authority, Diogenes is firmly located within a Socratic succession that offers the "sweet kind" of laughter and is followed by the late, idealized Cynic Demonax, who was memorialized in Lucian's work of that title.[42] As in Davenant, Shaftesbury opposes Diogenes to the violence and inhumanity of the crowd. What is more, Shaftesbury intriguingly claims that "no one now sees, or understands" the Cynic philosopher's "sweet" yet decorous wit.

When Shaftesbury turned to the more public genre of the *Soliloquy* in 1711, he continued his selective appropriation of the philosophical past. Shaftesbury drew up a historical succession of philosophers, beginning with the "philosophical patriarch" Socrates and culminating in his own version of "polite philosophy," a philosophy whose "familiar airy muse was privileged as a sort of counter-pedagogue against the pomp and formality of the more solemn writers."[43] Shaftesbury identified polite philosophy with a specific, gentlemanly role that remains independent of the earlier associations and affiliations that had sparked the Civil War. Shaftesbury's Polite Philosopher refuses to join either with the warring Protestant sects or persecuting Anglican clergy, rejecting both sectarian controversy and ungentlemanly isolation.

In the *Soliloquy*'s comparison of Diogenes and Antisthenes, Shaftesbury depicts a rude, meanly born, and satiric Cynic [Antisthenes] being superseded by a "better-humoured and more agreeable successor" [Diogenes].[44] The oddity is that Shaftesbury chose to depict Diogenes, rather than a later successor, as an "agreeable" and "comic" character who softens the reproving role defined by his rude predecessor. This is yet another instance of this era's tendency to view politeness in historical terms, as the result of further development. Once Shaftesbury's politeness became a dominant term in eighteenth-century England, however, this revisionist view of a "sweet" Diogenes disappeared. Most writers tended to dismiss Diogenes and the Cynics altogether as buffoons, while popularizing instead a number of decorous, un-Diogenical variants like the Citizen of the World or the sentimental Cynic.[45]

Diogenes and the Public in Two Lucianic Dialogues

Surely these proud people never think what a short stage life is; and that, with all their vanity, a time is coming, when they shall be on a level with us. The philosopher, who looked upon the skull of a king, and that of a poor man, saw no difference between them.

—Samuel Richardson, *Pamela* (1740)

When Davenant died in 1668, the London wits amused themselves by imagining his lukewarm reception in the underworld. Richard Flecknoe describes Davenant's uncomfortable meeting to gain admission to the Poet's section of Elizium: "When [Davenant] added, He was a Poet Laureate, they laugh'd, and said, Bayes [laurels] was never more cheap than now; and that since Petrarch's time, none had ever been legitimately crown'd."[46] Davenant, as unperturbed in death as he was in life by insults, makes his way instead to Pluto's court, where he was made "Superintendent of all their Sports and Recreations: So as, onely changing Place and Persons, he is now in as good Condition as he was before; and lives the same Life there, as he did here."[47]

Flecknoe uses the Lucianic device of the Voyage to the Next World to adjust the oversized reputation of his deceased rival and to exhibit the unctuous and fawning character of Davenant. Not even death could disrupt this essential aspect of Davenant's character, which the Lucianic genre is designed to expose. Thus, in Lucianic satires, death is the moment when publicity ends and reputation begins. The Lucianic Dialogue of the Dead or Voyage to the Next World turns the genre of burlesque into a device of historicization, by pairing Ancients with Moderns and encouraging their debate. In this respect, they are but one of many instances of "desacralization" occurring in the literary, political, and cultural spheres during the Restoration era and beyond. Desacralization describes how once-respected figures and institutions lose their sacred aura, whether through the passage of time, conscious critique, or the historical outcomes of their actions or words. In mid-seventeenth-century England, desacralization began with the person of the executed king and moved outward from there.

After the regicide, which signaled a momentous and permanent "desacralization of the monarchy,"[48] this blow to political authority resonated through English culture for another 150 years. The desacralization of the monarchy did not end with the struggles of the Interregnum, however, but was paradoxically confirmed and extended by the compromises imposed upon Charles II upon his Restoration in 1660 and subsequent reign. It is for this reason that desacralization (*pace* McKeon, not to be confused with secularization) marks so many of the characteristic literary genres and strategies of the Interregnum and Restoration eras, including travesty, burlesque, mock epic, or political satire.[49]

It is through this notion of desacralization that we can begin to link up the political and intellectual repercussions of the English Civil Wars with the satiric dimensions of the European Enlightenment. These linkages are particularly manifest in skeptical English and continental treatments of history writing between the seventeenth and eighteenth centuries. In both instances, the advances of modernity strip away the fame of the great exemplary figures of history, inverting their reputations and degrading them into parodies. Though this desacralization—or what we might call "historical ironization"—is recognizable in many of the Enlightenment's skeptical treatments of sacred or official histories, it finds its paradigmatic form in the Enlightenment vernacular versions of the Dialogue of the Dead, one of Lucian's most important legacies to seventeenth- and eighteenth-century writings in English, French, and German.[50]

In spite of these satiric origins, the Dialogues of the Dead became a favorite "polite" genre across Europe after Fénelon and Fontenelle offered their very popular imitations in 1683 and 1700. These French authors' versions of the genre became at least as familiar to eighteenth-century readers and writers as those of Lucian and his humanist imitators Erasmus, More, and Rabelais. The considerable cultural authority of Fénelon and Fontenelle therefore remade the genre into a favorite of polite, vernacular audiences, even while these works retained certain metacritical links to the genre's ancient, humanist, and rhetorical roots by citation, allusion, and so on. Whether as translations, imitations, or extensions of Lucian, however, these new-style Dialogues of the Dead would sometimes introduce Diogenes in order to mark their generic affiliation with earlier Dialogues of the Dead. It is in such moments of self-conscious filiation that we find the most extensive *literary* discussions of the Cynic philosopher during this period.[51]

It is important to remember, however, that the Enlightenment genre of the vernacular Dialogue of the Dead is a *post*rhetorical genre that uses the historical commonplaces of humanism to critique rhetoric's lack of historical or ethical understanding. In other words, the Enlightenment Dialogue of the Dead is only part of a much larger set of changes, whereby the rhetorical tradition was critiqued by the emerging vernacular genres of literature, philosophy, and history for its various inadequacies.[52] The Dialogue of the Dead is one of the best examples of how the stock of rhetorical commonplaces had been given a new, and postrhetorical, function, by literature.

In contrast with the humanist strategy of eliding the difference between the exemplary past and the contingent present, the Enlightenment Dialogues of the Dead highlighted the dramatic historical differences separating the ancient from the modern eras. As a contributor to the *Westminster Journal* wrote in 1741–42, "The Dialogues of *Lucian* have been universally esteem'd excellent Pieces of Humour; but few have consider'd them as historical Satires on the Men and Times he wrote in. Tho' he lays his visionary Scenes among the *Ely-*

sian Shades . . . and the Characters who speak are the Ghosts of dead Men; yet I believe his Cotemporaries [*sic*] were very well acquainted with every Character they drew."[53] It was the presence and pressure of the topical and the historical that transformed the vernacular Enlightenment Dialogue of the Dead into a distinctly modernizing genre.

Hence, the eighteenth-century Dialogue of the Dead should be viewed as a transitional genre that sprang up during the passage from rhetorical to historicist understandings of the past. As a vehicle of satire and historical desacralization, it inevitably exposed superstition and belief as symptoms of human delusion, credulity, and shortsightedness, and delighted in the small humiliations of the great and the powerful in the pagan underworld's "democracy of death."[54] Yet in at least two important instances, the story of this genre intersects with another story involving belief in the seventeenth and eighteenth centuries.

This story concerns the emergence of a highly literate class of lay intellectuals whose function was to direct the beliefs of "the public" and who were charged with shaping the realm of "public opinion."[55] In these instances, both these dialogue writers chose Diogenes to represent this intellectual class, which specialized in publicity and which understood the ways in which publicity could either serve power or undermine its foundations. The growth and professionalization of this class of pamphleteers and hack writers in the early eighteenth century suggests the desire on all political sides to strengthen the belief of "the public," to increase the numbers of the believing, and to regulate those beliefs so that they fell in line with the agendas of those groups. This is how the concept of public opinion came into being, as much through the desire to manage it as to observe its fluctuations.

To understand this stage in the history of opinion formation, we need to draw yet again from the work of Michel de Certeau. Certeau has outlined a two-part historical pattern regarding belief, whereby the collective energies of beliefs are regarded in one phase as both "inexhaustible" and "transportable toward other objects and ends, just as waterfalls are harnessed by hydroelectric plants" (*PEL* 178). We might consider the writings of Davenant, Hobbes, and Shaftesbury as part of an early Enlightenment impulse that attempts to "capture" the energies of religious belief and "transport" them toward commerce, the state, sociability, or some other institution or activity that might replace religion's recognized role as "social cement." This goal of capturing and transporting belief seemed especially urgent in the Restoration era, once religion was definitively acknowledged to have failed that role during the Civil Wars.

This is why Hobbes, for one, began to develop a political rationality on new grounds, by reducing every divergent interpretation of religious conscience to matters of private opinion, which are linked thereby to human mediations of faith and authority rather than an immediate experience of religious truth: "To *have faith in,* or *trust to,* or *beleeve a man,* [argues Hobbes] signifie the same thing; namely, an opinion of the veracity of the man: But to *beleeve what is said,* signifieth only an opinion of the truth of the saying."[56] Hobbes's prime example for this problem is the historian Livy's insistence that the Gods once made a cow speak. If "we believe it not; wee distrust not God therein, but Livy."[57] Thus, when Hobbes concludes that our beliefs "drawn from authority of men onely," constitute a "Faith in men onely," he suggests the political stakes of the historian's skepticism toward the excesses of popular belief, in the context of religious Civil War.[58]

Certeau, however, has observed a distinctly different phase of this problem, which occurs when elites discover that belief is not as common as it once was, and not plentiful enough to be exploited or redirected at will by churches and politicians (not to mention corporations and advertisers). Instead, belief in this other phase represents a precious store of mass credulity whose energies may not always be convertible to new ends or assignable to new ideals. This is the moment when "there are now too many things to believe and not enough credibility to go around" (*PEL* 179). What Certeau may not have realized, however, is that this perception of "too many things to believe" may not represent a deficit of credulity among a wary public but simply an unmanageable increase in the tempo or volume of printed communications, such as occurred in the pamphleteering wars of the Interregnum or the Opposition to Walpole in the 1720s and 1730s.[59] This overload of potential beliefs creates the need for a new, mediating class of functionaries and publicists who can reduce the complexity to a more manageable size and tempo and thereby make it possible for large and indeterminate publics to respond and act collectively. Writers help to create this illusion of a responsive virtual public by directing and accelerating the circulation of opinions into a temporal flow that can itself become the subject of further discussion and feedback.[60] In the 1730s, it was Bolingbroke's unique position as an ideologist and publicist for his own unstable coalition, buttressed with a brilliant marshaling of literary and journalistic forces writing alongside him, which lent his writing its immediacy and force.

"Too many things to believe" seems a good way to describe the Lucianic version of history offered in the Dialogues of the Dead, where Christian and pagan figures appear side by side in a vague netherworld devoted to intellectual conversation, not eternal punishment. Of course, in the ethically and temporally suspended universe of this genre, that is not a bad thing. For once, belief and its eternal consequences are not the issue here, nor do we worry much about the before-and-after of strictly linear historical time. Thus, it seems appropriate that it is in this "scoffing" genre, the Lucianic dialogue, and in its postrhetorical forms of historical skepticism, that we begin to see the modern, disbelieving cynic being developed in the mid-eighteenth century. In the dialogues of Lyttelton and Fielding, both produced out of their hard experiences of eighteenth-century party politics in Bolingbroke's Opposition, we find both men creating versions of Diogenes with an unmistakable political valence.[61] For these writers, Diogenes has become a complex symbol of a political rationality that paradoxically unites elite disbelief with mass credulity, so that he resembles nothing less than Keenan's "insider-cynic."[62]

Henry Fielding, *A Dialogue between Alexander the Great and Diogenes the Cynic*

Henry Fielding's *A Dialogue between Alexander the Great and Diogenes the Cynic*, printed in his *Miscellanies* (1743), though not strictly speaking a Dialogue of the Dead, remains one of Fielding's closest Lucianic imitations. At the same time, it is also a renewed meditation upon the difficult relations between power and intellectual reflection—polarities conventionally represented by Alexander the Great and "Diogenes the Cynick" in the rhetorical commonplace tradition.[63] Yet the circumstances determining both governance and reflection had changed dramatically since the humanist confrontations of Erasmus and Lyly, a massive set of changes that can be summed up in the related developments of "desacralization" and "print culture" in the mid-seventeenth century. As a result, the task of this dialogue is not to push the monarch into self-reflection, but to reveal both philosopher and monarch as fallible men (what Hobbes would call "men onely") whose power derives equally from opinion, Davenant's "mingled breath of multitude." In other words, both men are equally dependent upon their respective "followers," whose support lends them whatever power they may wield in political argument.

Of course, Fielding's historical reference points for the monarchy were not Davenant's would-be absolutists Charles I or Charles II, but the phlegmatic Hanoverians George I and George II. Yet the losses were not just on the side of the monarch. During the period between the reign of Charles II and the Hanoverians, the print culture of Georgian England had helped create an entire class of writers like Fielding, classically educated yet pauperized, who were placed at the mercy of both the booksellers and the politicians. This class of writers became the slaves of opinion, paid low wages to drive the public like mules from one side of the political divide to the other during the 1720s and 1730s. There was no question of this class of intellectuals ever becoming "counsellors," no matter how much Latin and Greek they learned, as Fielding did, at Eton. Instead, Fielding seemed to have reached all the way back to Diogenes to complain about his abject dependence upon politicians like Walpole or Dodington, or his equally demoralizing reliance upon a fickle and easily distracted audience.[64] As Fielding's early career shows, writers in this era could become the vehicles either of positive or negative publicity, but not much more than that, until they developed a following of their own. Consequently, Fielding's Diogenes became a symbol, I believe, of an impoverished class of writers who lived off of political opposition, even while they cloaked themselves in reflexive denunciations of the "vice" and "corruption" of the powerful.[65]

Neither Alexander, who is definitely not an idealized "Patriot King," nor his philosophical opposition Diogenes possesses a stable, uncontested moral authority in this *Dialogue,* in which the two sides engage in an interesting battle of tactical reason. Fielding's un-absolutist monarch can calmly listen to the Cynick's questioning of his motives, but Alexander exhibits just as much verbal aptitude as the philosopher. As we saw in Apemantus and Timon's "debate" in *Timon,* however, what results is not debate so much as a series of successive unmaskings, so that neither man can command the reflexive obedience or agreement of the other.

For this reason, in the same way that Fielding's Diogenes seems to exhibit all the losses suffered by the writing class since Erasmus, Fielding's verbally adept Alexander can be understood as a symbol of a new form of power, one that has become dependent upon the publicity it garners and the ever-wavering "support" of the public. This alteration in the nature of power has an interesting leveling effect on the dialogue between the two. For one thing, it emphasizes the provisional, functional power of those inhabiting roles, not their inherited rank and position. Thus, this kind of power-in-publicity is as recognizable in figures like Walpole or Jonathan Wild as it is in a Hanoverian monarch like George II. Not only had the sovereign been reduced into a mere locus of power, but the belief he once commanded via personal authority had lost its sacred aura as well. Consequently, the encounter of Diogenes and Alexander gave Fielding a way to talk about the manner in which both figures' power relied upon the loosely held opinions of others, a fact that Alexander characteristically acknowledged and Diogenes felt compelled to deny.

Thus, the immediate contexts for understanding this *Dialogue*, once we consider its inclusion within the politically mixed content of the *Miscellanies* of 1743, seem to be the slow collapse of one "Great Man," Walpole, and the resulting difficulties this event caused among the Opposition, which found it difficult to operate without the polarizing presence of Walpole. If this dialogue, like other works in the *Miscellanies*, reflects Fielding's disenchantment and distancing from the Opposition during this period's shifting alliances, then we might identify the hypocritical, faultfinding Diogenes with Bolingbroke himself, who had retired to Chanteloup in 1735 to write "philosophical" essays like his *Of the True Use of Retirement and Study*, while conducting his opposition from a distance.[66] Yet we need not personalize the satire to recognize the dialogue's impatience with Diogenes' reflexive criticism of Alexander's power and to see its application to the divided Opposition at this time. Not even the bungled war with Spain in 1740 had kept the Opposition together long enough to consolidate into a real alternative to Walpole. Instead, the war and the resulting realignments it caused only permitted Walpole's former enemies, who had once denounced his corruption, to switch sides and join Pulteney and Carteret in a new ministry.[67]

Though Fielding's deliberate strategies of indirection make it difficult to assign precise political allusions to this work, the dialogue provides a qualified defense of Alexander and portrays him as a verbally effective if ruthless man of action, even while it progressively discounts the railing of Diogenes. In fact, the entire *Dialogue* is an expansion of a few lines in an earlier poem, "Of True Greatness," in which a "little Cynick" hurls "Scorn and Disdain" at the "exulting Victor of the World."[68] In the earlier work, Diogenes represents a critic who despises true greatness and misanthropically shuns society, even while he is "destroy[ed]" by the carefully concealed pride that bids him to "hate and shun Men."[69]

In the years between writing "Of True Greatness" and the *Dialogue between Alexander the Great and Diogenes the Cynic*, Fielding seems to have become disillusioned enough with the Opposition, for whom he had worked nearly a decade, to have abandoned their cause sometime in 1741, just before Walpole's own downfall and their party's triumph.[70] The *Dialogue* takes away the demeaning role of the "little Cynick" from the critics of the Opposition (those who attack his patron Dodington, for example, to whom "Of True Greatness" was dedicated) and redirects it to the Opposition itself, whose hostility to those who practice power results in nothing but rancor and accusations.

When challenged by Diogenes in the *Dialogue,* Alexander sees no reason why his great "power" should not also command an equal degree of "Honor," though Alexander's notions of honor are based solely on slaughter and vainglory: "Hath then this Son of *Jupiter,* this Conqueror of the World, adored by his Followers, dreaded by his Foes, and worshipped by All, lived to hear his Power contemned"? he asks innocently.[71] Alexander cannot understand why his power has failed to win him the unanimous "worship" of inferiors like Diogenes. He steps directly into his opponent's usual trap, however, when he criticizes the self-denying philosopher for his lack of possessions. This seems designed to allow Diogenes to respond conventionally on the basis of his most obvious superiority to other men, his self-proclaimed ascetic virtue.

In a redescription worthy of Mandeville, Diogenes transforms the worshipful obedience inspired by Alexander into the involuntary "Adoration of thy servile Followers" and ridicules the emperor for his pride in the coerced opinions of mere "Slaves": "Is then the Fear or Worship of Slaves of so great Honour [asks Diogenes], when at the same time thou art the Contempt of every brave honest Man, tho', like me, an old Cloak should be his only Possession?" (228).[72]

Unlike earlier Dialogue writers like Fénelon, Fielding does not permit Diogenes' self-serving description of himself as a "brave honest Man" to go unchallenged, and Alexander asks "in what doth all Honour, Glory, and Fame consist, but in the Breath of that Multitude, whose Estimation with such ill-grounded Scorn thou dost affect to despise" (229). In other words, Alexander overturns the standard ascetic critique of worldly honor, by showing how *both* the philosopher and the ruler pursue "Honour, Glory, and Fame" and are therefore *equally* dependent upon the "Breath of that Multitude," or, in other words, upon Public Opinion. Their only difference is Diogenes' affected "scorn" of the public "Estimation" that he, like Alexander, must rely upon.

The weaknesses in Diogenes' self-proclaimed virtue, however, appear as soon as he is challenged to produce his own, positive definition of "Honour" rather than tearing down Alexander's reputation:

> *Diogenes.* Not in ravaging Countries, burning Cities, plundering and massacring Mankind.
>
> *Alexander.* No, rather in biting and snarling at them.
>
> *Diogenes.* I snarl at them because of their Vice and Folly; in a word, because there are among them many such as Thee and thy Followers.

> *Alexander.* If thou wouldst confess the Truth, Envy is the true Source of all thy Bitterness; it is that which begets thy Hatred, and from Hatred comes thy Railing: Whereas the Thirst of Glory only is my Motive. (230)

When Diogenes justifies his "snarling" at others by citing their provoking "Vice and Folly," he does not realize that his indignation could be easily recast as "Envy," an envy that rises in response to the number of Alexander's many "Followers." Accordingly, Alexander exposes the concealed will to power in the philosopher's self-denying "Bitterness." Alexander's well-known ambition is duly criticized, but the philosophic vanity, pride, and resentment of Diogenes seems more and more like an impotent and hypocritical version of Alexander's more open and forthright embrace of power. It is not ascetic virtue, but powerlessness, that sustains Diogenes' appearance of virtue.

As we saw in Davenant, Alexander critiques Diogenes' virtue by revealing its impolite or antisocial nature. Such an argument seemed unanswerable in Davenant because it aligned the sullen, snarling retired Cynic with the excluded Protestant enthusiasts and their moralizing preachers. Yet Diogenes gamely continues, unworried by Alexander's accusation:

> My Snarling is the Effect of my Love; in order, by my Invectives against Vice, to frighten Men from it, and drive them into the Road of Virtue.
>
> *Alexander.* For which Purpose thou hast forsworn Society, and art retired to preach to Trees and Stones. (231)

Diogenes disingenuously claims to "love" those whom he would frighten down the "road of virtue," but such loving words seem grossly at odds with his hostile and superior behavior toward everyone. Alexander, however, by pointing out the manifest virtues of "Society," has also pointed out the absolute uselessness of railing at "Trees and Stones."[73] In other words, Diogenes, for all his fine speech, has no audience, no followers, no listeners, and no public apart from the mute and passive trees and stones. Even while he hypocritically praises his retirement, we may recognize the carefully concealed motivation for his "Envy," "Hatred," and "Railing": his lack of power.

Fielding clinches his negative depiction of Diogenes when he has Alexander conduct an empirical experiment in ethics. The emperor suggests that he will demolish Athens, Corinth, and Lacedæmon to satisfy the philosopher's resentments against the people there. Diogenes immediately agrees to such a plan and exults, "Gods! what a Delight it will be to see the Rascals, who have so often in Derision call'd me a snarling Cur, roasting in their own Houses" (234).

Alexander compounds the temptation by offering him some portion of the loot from the ravaged city. When the philosopher agrees, the emperor exclaims in triumph: "Art not thou a true Dog? Is this thy Contempt of Wealth? This thy Abhorrence of the Vices of Mankind? To sacrifice three of the noblest Cities of the World to thy Wrath and Revenge! And hast thou the Impudence to dispute any longer the Superiority with me, who have it in my Power to punish my Enemies with Death, while thou only canst persecute with evil Wishes" (235).

Alexander has successfully revealed Diogenes' positive pleasure in the fantasy that he can roast alive the audiences that once rejected and derided him. With this final confirmation of the philosopher's affected scorn for his audience, Fielding shows that Diogenes' supposed philosophical superiority is nothing more than a ruse concealing his hatred and contempt for others, a hatred all the more malignant for never being acted upon. Alexander may not have any nobler motive for exercising power than its use, but his followers give him the power of life or death, a power that Diogenes covets but will never possess himself. In the meantime, Diogenes uses his counterfeit philosophy to rationalize his vices, spin out his useless railings, and justify his solitary inaction and impotent speech, even if he has to claim it as his "superiority." Diogenes' dishonest Cynicism has become identified with a desire to maintain his supposed superiority at all costs, reflexively discounting others' virtues, and redescribing his own moral faults so that they appear virtuous. In Fielding, these hypocritical traits are transparent enough for audiences like Alexander or the city of Corinth to see through them and reject him, but in Lyttelton the moral status of Diogenes is not so clear-cut, and his ability to draw followers far greater. This makes him a far more ambiguous figure, morally and politically.

Twenty years later, after Fielding's death, his friend George, Lord Lyttelton wrote his own Lucianic Dialogue featuring Diogenes, this time a Dialogue of the Dead between Diogenes and Plato. This *Dialogue,* when set alongside Fielding's, differs remarkably from it in tone, perhaps because it takes Diogenes more seriously as a philosopher, and because it permits a much freer dialogue to take place between the polite philosopher Plato and the rude Cynic. Nonetheless, there is some evidence to suggest that Lyttelton consciously responded to his friend Fielding's earlier treatment of the Cynic philosopher, because Lyttelton had been closely involved with Fielding during the political crisis that finally brought down Walpole in the early 1740s, and because he was a good enough friend to have a poem, "Liberty," dedicated to him in the *Miscellanies* containing the Dialogue. It is also suggestive that Lyttelton published his own Lucianic dialogue during another major period of political instability: the Wilkes crisis of the 1760s.

This was the moment when the rakish London radical John Wilkes took the political initiative away from feckless Whig magnates like Lyttelton (now Baron Lyttelton, and sitting impotently in the House of Lords) to claim his own popular following. Wilkes turned the London mobs against both the Crown and the rotten electoral system that sustained the hated Scottish favorite Lord Bute's hold over Parliament. Lyttelton had watched Wilkes take his own moderate Whiggish battle cry of "Liberty" and redirect it against Bute in the name of a broader, less polite audience.[74]

As Fielding had done in his earlier Dialogue, Lyttelton used Diogenes to represent a kind of political opposition figure (in the guise of the Cynic as "snarler" or "fault-finder"), but this time Diogenes was part of a rude, demagogic, urban opposition that explicitly derived its power from its identification with "the people." For one of the first times in the eighteenth century, Diogenes appeared not as a humourist, not as an isolated, singular, or melancholic philosopher in retirement, nor even as an enemy of "the multitude," but as someone whose natural audience *was* "the multitude." That crucial new link between the philosopher and his massified audience constituted the source of his newfound power and the cause for Lyttelton's mixed admiration and concern. It is one of our earliest glimpses of the dangerous, disbelieving modern cynic at work in a political system to which he feels no allegiance. Instead of the passive, reactive role we saw earlier in this chapter, the cynic has reassumed Certeau's calculus of "tactics," the homeless, propertyless form of reason that ruthlessly exploits whatever time, circumstance, or opportunity allow it, because "what it wins it must not keep," in the absence of any proper position of its own (*PEL* 37). The cynic's tactics represent the reason of the weak, demonstrating the kind of discredited verbal inventiveness that allows the "worse argument to seem the better" (*PEL* 38). Hence, it is significant that Lyttelton pits his Diogenes against the "polite philosopher" Plato in this dialogue.

Lyttelton in the middle of the political crises of the 1760s finds uses for Diogenes that Fielding could not. The difference seems to be that Lyttelton depicts the polite philosopher Plato delivering the conventional eighteenth-century critiques of Diogenes as misanthropic, satiric, superficially witty, impolite, and anti-social, while allowing his Cynic far more freedom to criticize in turn Plato's dominant norms of politeness and moderation. Lyttelton refuses, in other words, to reduce Diogenes to a mere burlesque Cynic. Diogenes in Lyttelton's version is a truth teller once again, though his Plato insists on labeling him, somewhat implausibly, a mere wit and scoffer.

George, Lord Lyttelton's *Dialogues of the Dead*

As I have already indicated, Lyttelton makes a number of innovations in his treatment of Diogenes and the Cynics, innovations that depart from many of the period's conventional readings of the philosopher. Lyttelton's first and foremost innovation is its assumption that the alliance of politeness and philosophy announced by Davenant's Aristophanes has ceased to function. The tyrant Dionysius, Plato's former patron who nearly had him executed, recurs several times in their conversation to remind readers of the riskiness of confronting state power. Lyttelton's second innovation is his refusal of this era's reductive reading of Diogenes as harmless burlesque philosopher or satirist, and to emphasize instead his nonsatiric, truth-telling, parrhesiast dimension. Though some traces of the rude and satirical Diogenes remain, Lyttelton also shows how the powerful can trivialize his truth telling by labeling it mere satire or wit; as Diogenes reminds Plato: "I never knew any government angry at defamation, when it fell on those who disliked or obstructed its measures. But I well remember, that the thirty tyrants at Athens called opposition to them *the destruction of order and decency*" (*Works* 391).[75]

Lyttelton's Diogenes' parrhesiastic remarks, unlike the sophisticated systems of polished philosophers like Plato or Aristotle, compel his interlocutors to speak the truth. The Cynic philosopher's self-appointed role reflects not just Lyttelton's reading but an increasingly common Enlightenment interpretation of Diogenes' real value as a philosopher. As D'Alembert remarked in 1759: "Every age, and especially our own, stands in need of a Diogenes; but the difficulty is in finding men who have the courage to be one, and men who have patience to endure one."[76] In fact, Diogenes' sharp exchanges with the other shades turn him into a metacritical surrogate for the moralizing Enlightenment historian, eager to expose the lies and impositions that sustained the rich and powerful while alive.

Lyttelton's Dialogue XXX ("Plato-Diogenes") appeared in 1765 in an expanded fourth edition of his very popular *Dialogues of the Dead* (1760), and extended his earlier, generally respectful readings of figures taken from ancient and modern history.[77] Though Lyttelton's sympathies initially seem closer to the polite philosopher Plato, Lyttelton does allow the two philosophers to disagree without predetermining the outcome. Nor does he, as Fielding had done, engineer a dramatic reversal designed to discredit the Cynic once and for all as a hypocrite. Lyttelton permits Diogenes some shrewd observations at the expense of his rival Plato, but these attacks also have unmistakable implications for his own political and philosophical attitudes and career. Since Lyttelton does not permit either side a victory in this dialogue, the debate might be regarded as a "Soliloquy" in the manner of Shaftesbury, a form of internal self-reflection staged between two conflicting impulses.

In Lyttelton's *Dialogue*, the two philosophers are first overheard discussing Plato's disastrous trip to Syracuse to visit Dionysius the younger. Diogenes' contempt for Plato's submission to tyrants becomes the pretext for a larger debate about the proper moral and political role of a philosopher in society. Should a philosopher consort with the great and powerful, and risk being turned into a sycophant or courtier, or should he maintain his intellectual independence at all costs? When Plato serenely announces that philosophy "must not be confined to a *tub* or a *cell*," and that "her sphere is in senates, or the cabinets of kings" (*Works* 383), Diogenes rudely accuses Plato of abandoning his philosophy when he went to visit the court:

> *Diogenes:* Oh! there is no flatterer half so dangerous to a prince as a fawning philosopher![78]
>
> *Plato:* If you call it fawning, that I did not treat him with such unmannerly rudeness as you did Alexander the Great when he visited you at Athens, I have nothing to say. But, in truth, I made my company agreeable to him, not for any ends which regarded only myself, but that I might be useful both to him and to his people. (*Works* 384)

We should note, first of all, how completely this Diogenes challenges the assumptions about the proper role of the "counsellor" that he had once inhabited himself. Though Davenant's or Fielding's discussion ended with the triumph of politeness and sociability over the solitary philosopher, Lyttelton begins by debating precisely those notions of politeness and philosophy that had displaced rhetoric. Do the external forms of politeness, for example, give the philosopher a greater sphere of activity than contemplation, or do they signal merely his accommodation to power?

To the eminently conventional response of Plato that he goes to court to "counsel[] those who govern nations," Diogenes directs a sarcastic remark: "Why did you not go and preach chastity to Lais [the prostitute]? A philosopher in a brothel, reading lectures on the beauty of continence and decency, is not a more ridiculous animal, than a philosopher in the cabinet, or at the table of a tyrant, descanting on liberty and publick spirit!" (*Works* 385). Notwithstanding all his respect for his model Fénelon's (or Bolingbroke's) assumption of the didactic or counseling role to the monarch, Lyttelton has allowed Diogenes to savage Plato's idealized image of the philosopher at court. Perhaps because of his troubled history with George II, the now-deceased Prince Frederick, and George III, Lyttelton never counters Diogenes' ridicule of a "philosopher in the cabinet" "descanting on liberty and publick spirit."[79] Lyttelton's philosopher cannot become a courtier without endangering his philosophy or his independence. Yet Diogenes and Plato do agree that what makes a philosopher unworthy of the name is an attitude of flattery and servility, because such attitudes cause him to neglect his duties toward the public. Yet to whom, precisely, does the philosopher owe his services? Who is a member of "the public" he addresses?

Unsurprisingly, the two philosophers cannot agree on the crucial question regarding the identity and boundaries of "the public." Plato accuses Diogenes of flattery, only flattery of a less worthy object, the despicable mob: "Your cynic railing was to [the Athenian people] the most acceptable flattery" (*Works* 386). In a gesture indicative of Lyttelton's own high-minded and conciliatory Whiggism, Plato regards his own philosophy as the only possible compromise between two unacceptable extremes and rejects both the "speculative, retired philosophers [and the] cynical revilers of princes and magistrates" (*Works* 387). Instead, Plato regards his politeness as merely strategic and instrumental for his larger philosophic aims. From Plato's own perspective, an "honest and prudent complaisance" is simply the best way for a philosopher to intervene effectively into the lives of others because it enables him to instill certain moral precepts in the monarch (*Works* 384, 386). But Diogenes questions whether Plato's complaisance has simply turned the philosopher himself into an instrument of power:

> You seem to think that the business of philosophy is *to polish men into slaves;* but I say, it is to teach them to assert, with an untamed and generous spirit, their independence and freedom. You profess to instruct those who want to *ride* their fellow-creatures, how to do it with an easy and gentle rein; but I would have them thrown off, and trampled under the feet of all their deluded or insulted equals, on whose backs they have mounted. Which of us two is the truest friend to mankind? (*Works* 387–88; Lyttelton's emphasis)

According to Diogenes, the difference between the two philosophers hinges upon their definition of their intended audience: Plato's polite, courtly philosophy serves only the rulers who wish to "ride" their fellow human beings, while Diogenes wants his philosophy to teach the people—"their deluded or insulted equals"—to throw them off. Diogenes' radical cosmopolitanism reveals itself in his loyalty to only the broadest and most general notion of community, "mankind," not to any particular ruler or nation. Intriguingly, "polishing" and politeness do not unite men into an extranational culture but actually enslave them to a series of petty and provincial masters. Though I doubt that Lyttelton himself endorsed such views, Diogenes' speech here strikingly echoes the radical positions held by Rousseau and subsequent revolutionary "Citizens of the World," with its passionate rejection of politeness for its role in fostering inequality and the subjugation of the poor.[80] At the very least, Lyttelton seems to have recognized that this is the logical consequence of views like Diogenes'. Under the pressure of this historical moment, a truly indecorous and destabilizing Diogenes, and the political contestation of politeness, have both finally become possible in the writings of the "good Lord Lyttelton."

In the end, Diogenes and Plato's debate settles upon the fundamental question of whether the philosopher is obliged by his duty to the truth to expose those deceits perpetrated by rulers.

> *Diogenes:* A philosopher cannot better display his wisdom, than by throwing contempt on that pageantry, which the ignorant multitude gaze at with a senseless veneration.
>
> *Plato:* He who tries to make the multitude *venerate nothing* is more senseless than they. Wise men have endeavoured to excite an awful reverence in the minds of the vulgar for external ceremonies and forms, in order to secure their obedience to religion and government, of which these are the symbols. Can a *philosopher* desire to defeat that good purpose?
>
> *Diogenes:* Yes, if he see it abused, to support the evil purposes of superstition and tyranny. (*Works* 389–90; Lyttelton's emphases)

As in Davenant's and Fielding's dialogues, this hostility of Diogenes toward the lightly held opinions of "the ignorant multitude" remains consistent with his previously established character, but here he is contrasted with a philosopher who wishes to teach "the vulgar" "reverence" and "veneration" "for external ceremonies and forms." To use Certeau's thematics of receding belief that I discussed earlier, Plato desires philosophy to channel and direct mass credulity toward securing "obedience to religion and government." For Plato, philosophy's proper role lies precisely in such elite management of "the vulgar" and their beliefs.

To Diogenes, however, Plato's argument for the "pageantry" required for ruling the vulgar invites abuse in the form of "superstition and tyranny," typical Whig terms of abuse for their clerical or ministerial opponents.[81] In thirty years, however, Burke would transform this debate about the need for reverence for external forms into his famous argument on the value of "prejudice."

Both of Lyttelton's philosophers recognize the revolutionary implications of Diogenes' contempt for the pageantry of state:

> *Plato:* May not the abuse be corrected, without losing the benefit? is there no difference between *reformation* and *destruction*?
>
> *Diogenes: Half-measures* do nothing. He who desires to *reform,* must not be afraid *to pull down.*
>
> *Plato:* I know that you and your sect *are for pulling down every thing that is above your own level.* Pride and envy are the motives that set you all to work. Nor can one wonder that passions, the influence of which is so general, should give you many disciples and many admirers. (*Works* 390–91; Lyttelton's emphases)

Though the identification of topical references in this dialogue can never be definitive, the polemical tone of this debate, the philosophers' wrangling over their respective definitions of "liberty" and "government" (*Works* 388), the distinctly leveling arguments of Diogenes, and the date of publication (1765) all suggest that Lyttelton has modeled Diogenes at least partly on John Wilkes and Plato on himself.[82] In doing so, Lyttelton has analyzed the motives animating the popular politician who aims to mobilize (or manipulate?) the "ignorant multitude" against the "superstition and tyranny" usually used to dominate them.[83] Surprisingly, Lyttelton does not dismiss Diogenes' opposition to tyrants and superstition as mere envy or hypocrisy. Unlike Fielding's Diogenes, who simply snarls at Alexander for his reliance upon the mob's opinions, Lyttelton's Diogenes ultimately circulates and spreads his rudeness and jeering among the multitudes by practicing a new kind of political persuasion, one based as much in "pulling down" as in "veneration," as much in de-sacralization as in sacralization, as much in the "transportation" or "reassignment" of mass credulity as in its preservation.

This new use of Diogenes, then, seems to represent an important step toward modern cynicism, which is inseparable from the process of opinion formation and the elite's rational management of others' irrational beliefs. In Lyttelton's dialogue, his postrhetorical Diogenes does not merely address rulers with the usual formulae but actually persuades "disciples and admirers" of his own to "pull down" their social superiors to their own level. In Lyttelton's Diogenes we may therefore recognize one historical origin of Alan Keenan's "insider-cynic," the disbeliever who takes an instrumental attitude toward others' beliefs, and whose existence reveals the unreal, virtual nature of "the people" he summons into being for political action. When "politeness" becomes one of several competing notions of "the social," the Cynic's disbelief seems more dangerous because it conjures up a multitude poised to imitate his "cynical reviling" of authority, or even "pulling [it] down."

FOUR

The Cynic Unveiled

Innocence, Disenchantment, and Rationalization in Rousseau

We study, we admire [Jean-Jacques Rousseau] in the closet, but we forget or slight him in the world. . . . In this age, the stoicism of a Cato would be as useless as the cynical manners of a Diogenes would be detestable. So high-strained a morality we may admire in history, but never copy in life.

—Review of *Lettre sur les spectacles* in the *Critical Review* (1759)

Excessive pride and envy have destroyed Jean-Jacques, my illustrious philosopher. . . . I will pity him if they hang him, but out of pure humanity, for personally I only consider him Diogenes's dog or rather like a dog descended from a bastard of that dog.

—Voltaire, letter to Jean le Rond d'Alembert, June 17, 1762

Rousseau has been too often extolled as a philanthropist. Mr. Burke said of him, that he loved his kind and hated his kindred. The exposure of his children, by whatever sophistry it may be excused, is an indelible blot on his humanity; and invalidates all his pretensions to philanthropy. For, can that philanthropy be genuine which is founded on the extinction of the parental affections; and which, with more than savage brutality, forsakes the poor innocents it brings into the world?

—Robert Fellowes, "Character of Rousseau," *Monthly Mirror* (1799)

By the mid-eighteenth century, with the exception of Fielding and Lyttelton's Lucianic treatments of Diogenes, the ancient and humanist versions of Cynicism in English had been reduced to garbled anecdotes tossed into the *Gentleman's Magazine,* which described such things as Diogenes trampling upon the pavement of Alexander [*sic*].[1] This English lull, however, was soon disturbed by developments on the Continent, where French and German Enlightenment writers began using Diogenes as a persona, either shameless or cosmopolitan, to talk about their hopes and fears while they played the philosophe for the public. These same writers found Diogenes to be a useful satiric device for ridiculing other philosophes when they got out of line. Jean-Jacques Rousseau became the most notorious target of this kind of projection and identification, but many of Rousseau's friends and enemies among the philosophes, including Voltaire, d'Alembert, Diderot, and others, traded in such uses of Cynicism.[2]

As we saw with Marston and his enemies in the second chapter, however, this epidemic of mutual recrimination suggests that an entire intellectual class was growing aware of its unhappy dependence and using the Cynic as a vehicle for self-reflection or polemical assaults. In this way, Diogenes and the Cynic philosophers grew into a complex trope for the aspirations of the Enlightenment as a collective movement. The "good" Diogenes served for an emblem for how this movement sought to act upon its host society, to weather its criticism or indifference, and to signify its independence in the realm of print culture and publicity (in the form of philosophe-friendly encyclopedias, journals, reviews, etc.). The rude or burlesque Diogenes served as a kind of moral caricature of the Enlightenment philosophe in all his thwarted ambitions. Thus, the rude Diogenes, with his well-known excesses and social gaffes, stood as a sardonic comment upon the official Enlightenment hope that the philosophe was the privileged agent of Enlightenment knowledge and progress, and the point at which "reflection and social action converge[d]."[3]

Concerning the Enlightenment's affinities with Cynicism, Niehues-Pröbsting's comments deserve to be quoted in full:

> In Cynicism, the Enlightenment discovers the danger of reason being perverted, reason turning into irrationality and madness, reason being frustrated because of its own far too exalted expectations. The Enlightenment becomes aware of this menace to itself through its affinity with Cynicism. The reflection on Cynicism provides a necessary piece of self-recognition and self-criticism. Consequently, the failure of the Enlightenment—or of one part of it—leads to cynicism in the modern sense of the word.[4]

Even the rude, irrational, or mad Diogenes served an ethical purpose for these writers, because he reminded them of some of the potential outcomes of their risky desire for action: ridicule, shame, isolation, even madness. Diogenes taught the Enlightenment, however, that the desire for action meant assuming this risk of failure. D'Alembert makes this very point in the comment I cited in the previous chapter: "Every age, and especially our own, stands in need of a Diogenes; but the difficulty is in finding men who have the courage to be one, and men who have patience to endure one."[5] Thus, the Enlightenment philosophes took up this philosopher knowing that he had been reinvented many times before, but now they noted how these reinventions were produced by men like themselves, trying to understand their precarious social standing.

The deepening historical analogy between the Cynics and the philosophes was therefore more than just a topical "application" of a Cynic identity upon contemporary figures and events (as we saw with Fielding and Lyttelton). It also became part of the self-understanding of Enlightenment writers as they sought to put their ideas into practice, or, as Foucault might have phrased it, to harmonize their words with their deeds. Both the reflective and polemical uses of the Cynics reopened the ethical dimension of Cynicism in a way not seen since antiquity, when the philosophes began to use the Cynic as a measure of their own and others' moral integrity and upright behavior. And whether these writers drew upon positive or negative images of Cynicism for polemical purposes, either morally inflected image was capable of measuring the target's integrity and finding him deficient. As a result, Rousseau, the era's leading candidate for modern Diogenes, could be attacked for failing to live up to the rigor of the ancient ethical models he liked to advertise, or travestied as a mountebank or buffoon passing himself off as a philosopher.[6] Voltaire managed to do both at once when he scrawled *"singe de Diogène"* (ape of Diogenes) into the margins of his copy of the *Discourse on Inequality.*[7]

Thus, the Continental reception of Diogenes exhibited two related dimensions not shared by the English response: an increasingly intimate identification with, or projection of feelings upon, the Cynic philosopher, and a set of developing print institutions that provided the philosophes with the sense that they collectively participated in what Michael Warner has termed a "counterpublic," a discrete segment of the general public that marks itself off from that general audience to show itself capable of its own autonomous actions and responses.[8] We can see how the affective and institutional dimensions were combined when we recognize how these uses often appeared in genres that appeared at the borders between the writer's public and private lives, including confession, autobiography, memoir, correspondence, personal essay, and so forth.

Though Continental writers found such uses of the Cynics appealing, their British counterparts did not imitate such approaches; perhaps the English writers, whose Enlightenment has been described as "clerical" and "polite," were less interested than their French or German counterparts in Diogenes as a model of a fully secularized ethics and philosophic reason.[9] Whatever the cause, the different institutional and political circumstances of Enlightenment in England resulted in an initial English indifference or condescension toward Diogenes as a proto-philosophe, or Rousseau as his contemporary heir.[10] This indifference disappeared, however, when the image of the Enlightenment philosophe was invested itself with all the moral ambiguity, if not outright scandal, of Rousseau's shamelessly Cynic "way of life."

In other words, the powerful dynamics of identification and projection *did* set in when British writers responded viscerally to the shameless or cosmopolitan Cynic-personae of the Continental writers, as we will see in this and the next chapter. Indeed, I shall argue in these chapters that it is precisely in these dynamics of identification, disavowal, and projection that we find the power and persuasiveness of Burke's conservative, Counter-Revolutionary reaction against Rousseau the Cynical exemplar of Enlightenment in the 1790s. The figure of Diogenes had become overdetermined, structured by its close identification with both the Enlightenment philosophe generally and the scandalous career of Jean-Jacques Rousseau.

This chapter shows why Jean-Jacques Rousseau holds a special place in the conceptual history of Cynicism, since he represents one of the few historical figures to have been labeled a "Cynic" in both the premodern and modern senses of the term during its semantic transition between, say, 1750 and 1814. These dates span the period between Rousseau's first *Discourse* and the *OED*'s first recorded modern usage of "cynical" in D'Israeli's *Quarrels of Authors.*[11]

In the first phase, which will take up the rest of this chapter, Rousseau offered his life and career to the public as an example of an authentically Stoic, manly, philosophical independence, but he was labeled instead a modern Diogenes and a "cynic"—in other words, a rude and rough-edged moralist—for his hostility toward politeness, the mixing of genders, and commercial modernity. In keeping with his self-assumed role as public moralist, Rousseau denounced politeness for fostering a feminized luxury among the great and an unseemly dependence upon everyone else, including his fellow philosophes. Rousseau's shocking attacks upon the other philosophes violated the Enlightenment paradigm of "polite philosophy," but they also linked philosophic reason with the notorious defenses of selfishness from writers like Hobbes and Mandeville.

This first phase of Rousseau the modern Diogenes ended with two damaging events, both of which Rousseau helped first to instigate and then to compound the damage inflicted upon himself. The initial event was his public turn against the theater in Geneva and his former friends d'Alembert and Voltaire in the "Letter to d'Alembert" (1762). This work, regarded as a betrayal by the rest of the philosophe party, exposed to the general public the internal disunity of the party. It also announced his suspicion of the enlightened "progress" a public theater would represent in his birthplace. The second event was far more damaging because it was not limited to the relatively self-enclosed public of the philosophes but spread to the general public that now included his English readership: the publication and translations of the *Confessions* (translated 1783). This work, with its explicit renderings of its author's most intimate and shameful thoughts and feelings, decisively altered his image from the sentimental and idealized "man of feeling" his audience had imagined from works like *Julie, or, The New Heloise* (translated 1761).

With all the permanence of print, the publication of the *Confessions* confirmed stories that supporters had long dismissed as malicious rumors, so that one reviewer could complain of the "cynical and impertinent" business of a writer unaccountably publicizing the most humiliating episodes of his life. These responses, however, were not the worst things said about Rousseau and his writings. The nadir occurred during the Anti-Jacobin assault on his reputation in the 1790s and immediately afterward and is the subject of the following chapter. But first we must turn to Rousseau in the happier moments of his philosophic life.

Rousseau's *Discourses* and the Critique of Commercial Modernity

In 1750, Jean-Jacques Rousseau won the Dijon prize with his *Discourse on the Sciences and the Arts,* a work that radically questioned the Enlightenment assumption that advances in the arts and sciences led to the moral improvement of mankind. He argued instead that these advances led to the corruption of manners and morals. With this blockbuster entry into the debate about the usefulness of the arts and sciences, Rousseau also initiated a series of attacks upon his fellow philosophes' ideal of the "polite philosopher," the reflective and socially active agent of Enlightenment modernization. To do this, he brought some familiar eighteenth-century debates about luxury to bear upon the philosophes.[12] From the start, Rousseau criticized his era's complicity between polite society and the philosophes, who had for the most part accepted Mandeville's arguments about the impossibility of defining luxury.[13] What was more distressing to Rousseau, however, was the manner in which these men seemed to applaud the dismantling of the moral traditions inherited from antiquity and Christianity. Rousseau personalized his critique when he pointed out the philosophes' financial dependence upon one of their favorite subjects, the luxury of the rich and fashionable.

When Rousseau opens the first *Discourse* with a splendidly rhetorical image of the sciences, letters, and arts spreading garlands of flowers over iron chains, we see him deliberately reversing the assumptions that had driven polite philosophy from Shaftesbury and Addison through the era of Voltaire. The "polite philosopher" announced his ability to free others through his exemplary pursuit of human reason, freedom from prejudice, and capacity for self-reflection and self-determination.[14] But had the philosophes, or politeness generally, really caused such improvements to occur, Rousseau wondered? The answer was no.

According to Rousseau, while civilization's refinement of taste certainly produces a "sweetness of character and that urbanity in mores which make relationships among [modern men] so cordial and easy," the ultimate result of all this accommodation to others' desires is only "the *appearances* of all the virtues" (my emphasis), an empty appearance that men do not bother to match in their hearts or in their lives.[15] Politeness, and the philosophy that had accommodated itself to it, had become equated with a now-universal tendency toward dissimulation, duplicity, accommodation, and the manipulation of others. We may note here how the antirhetorical critique of the aristocratic ethos of civility has been extended to a more sweeping critique of an artificial code of politeness. This is Rousseau's impatience with the stylizations and insincerity dictated by decorum.

The advancement of modern politeness, which accompanies similar advances in the arts and sciences, results in nothing more than a "retinue of vices" and a persistent uncertainty concerning the true morals of those around us. For Rousseau, vice and uncertainty are the only legacies of his era's enlightenment: "Suspicions, offenses, fears, coldness, reserve, hatred, betrayal will unceasingly hide under that uniform and deceitful veil of politeness, under that much vaunted urbanity that we owe to the enlightenment of our century" (4–5). In a striking rhetorical reversal of his contemporaries' opinions, Rousseau argues that what *appears* to be historical progress is in fact only an improvement in, and elaboration of, the verbal ruses of dissimulation and the practical techniques of immorality. The supposed improvement in morals claimed by his contemporaries was in fact strictly a rhetorical victory, unfounded in actual behavior.

Once they overcame their delight in his rhetorical skills, many of Rousseau's readers noticed the degree to which Rousseau had turned the philosophes' own arguments and methods back against them, so that he could critique the flattering self-image of intellectual independence and masculine action offered in writers like Voltaire. "Tell us, [demands Rousseau in the *Discourse on the Sciences*] famed Arouet [that is, Voltaire], how many manly and strong beauties you have sacrificed to our [era's] false delicacy, and how many great things has the spirit of gallantry, so fertile in small things, cost you?" (14). Rather than opting for inclusion within the collective movement of philosophes, Rousseau opts to distinguish himself from the others by claiming their key values of reason, unprejudiced observation, and self-reflection.

As we saw in the first epigraph to this chapter, some of those calling Rousseau a modern Diogenes, as the *Critical Review* did in 1759, did so to suggest that his writings promulgated an austere but unworkable virtue.[16] At one level, this was simply a reiteration of the trope discussed in the previous chapter, of Diogenes as a rude or burlesque philosopher. But there were other resonances, as well. The most obvious parallel was in both philosophers' dismissal of the arts and sciences in favor of practical ethics (see DL 6.24). Pairing together these two rude and disagreeable philosophers also pointed to Rousseau's anger at his dependence upon various female "patrons" in the salons. The still-active associations of Diogenes with the misogyny of the humanist tradition provided a ready analogy with Rousseau's difficult relations with the fashionable women who often worked with the philosophes and exerted their own forms of power in the salons. Associating Rousseau with the misogyny of Diogenes also made it easier to dismiss his arguments about philosophical independence with an ad hominem reference to his rudeness.[17] Finally, labeling Rousseau a modern Diogenes also implied his hostile and parodic relation to the other philosophes as a group and automatically recalled the well-known rivalry between Diogenes and Plato. This analogy between Diogenes, the "Socrates out of his senses" (DL 6.54), and Rousseau was truer than anyone suspected; the itinerant, opportunistic, improper Rousseau stood as one of the foremost opponents of the complacent, self-institutionalizing, "strategic" tendencies of the philosophes, just as Diogenes had once done in his opposition to Plato and his school.

In the *Discourse on Inequality* (1755), Rousseau extended the earlier *Discourse*'s dual critique of modern civilization and philosophic reason, to the point where civilization was redescribed as a wasteland of empty social forms and behaviors. Accordingly, the presocial world of the state of nature becomes the only way for Rousseau to wipe away the accretions to the human personality added since the advent of civilization, so that we can see a world in which ignorance and natural pity had their sway. As it turns out, one of the greatest enemies of mankind is the unfeeling philosopher, a representative of all that has corrupted human nature, and who carries within himself the reason that has silenced the voice of nature and estranged him from his fellow men. Consequently, in the *Discourse*'s final pages, we also discover Rousseau's version of Diogenes and the *quaero hominem*. Rousseau, like Erasmus, Marston, and many earlier writers, wonders where he may find a man worthy of the name in the mass of corruptions he finds in the present state of things.[18]

In the *Discourse on Inequality,* Rousseau pursues an essentially Diogenical critique of civilization, insisting that all social forms and codes are equally artificial, false, and productive of dissimulation, while conducting an equally Diogenical critique of social institutions like marriage and property for their artificiality and effeminizing effects. Yet Rousseau's Cynic critique of his contemporaries goes in historically novel directions when he argues that one of the most pernicious consequences of modernity and philosophic reason is *insensibility,* a learned indifference to such natural emotions as pity. Although Rousseau emulates the Cynics and Stoics in some respects, he attacks their cultivation of *apatheia,* their ability to resist certain so-called "womanish" or unreasonable feelings, as a mere rationalization of their selfish indifference to others' suffering.

As we shall see, Rousseau's version of the previous era's Cynic/Stoic Unmoved Man is not a philosophical hero, but a philosophic villain.[19] His two prime examples of such monsters are Hobbes and Mandeville, whose powers of reason have deformed their natural sentiment. Both Hobbes and Mandeville represent a form of philosophic reason so debased it can longer understand any motive for human behavior apart from self-interest. Their calculating and self-serving notion of human reason cannot interest itself in the plight of others, and therefore turns the philosopher into a monster of insensibility or inhumanity.

It is noteworthy that in Rousseau's secular critique of Hobbes and Mandeville, we see him attacking what will become one of the most recognizable attitudes of contemporary political cynicism: the conviction that "the ultimate motives of human action are self-interest and the quest for power."[20] This powerfully reductive understanding of human motive, and the moral denunciation of its consequences, will reappear some sixty years later in D'Israeli's epochal treatment of Hobbes's (and Mandeville's) cynicism in the *Quarrels of Authors,* where D'Israeli reiterates much of Rousseau's argument against Hobbes. It is through these repeated attacks on Hobbes's and Mandeville's egoism that modern cynicism comes to be equated with the position attributed here to Hobbes: an unabashedly low view of human reason and motivation that seeks also to rationalize, or even justify, the cynic's own self-seeking behavior.

To create his own, naturally benevolent image of mankind, Rousseau must displace Hobbes's antisocial depictions of mankind in the state of nature. Rousseau contests Hobbes's notion that the presocial, prereflective man is naturally selfish, and argues instead that the natural instinct of self-preservation is different from the artificial selfishness developed in a society that encourages the passions to proliferate.[21] Clearing away Hobbes's assumptions about the state of nature and the moral condition of precivilized man allows Rousseau to make yet another argument about the debilitating effects of men's dependence upon other men. It is not nature, but man's artificially imposed state of dependence, that has rendered man so selfish, greedy, and passionate. This condition of dependence has been reinforced by the historical development of both reason and civilization. Rousseau's summary at this point inverts the commonsense relation of knowledge and virtue, when he claims that savages are less vicious than civilized men simply because their ignorance does more to preserve them than knowledge ever could: "*So much more profitable to [savages] is the ignorance of vice than the knowledge of virtue is to [civilized men]*" (53; Rousseau's emphasis). In a paradox Mandeville would have been proud of (if it didn't originate with him in the first place), Rousseau argues the moral superiority of ignorance to Hobbes's egoistic view of human nature.

Yet Rousseau identifies another counterweight to human egoism beyond simple ignorance: "the only natural virtue" that Mandeville, "the most excessive detractor of human virtues," was able to acknowledge: pity" (53). In truth, Mandeville had only argued in the *Fable* that pity was a natural, passively felt impulse that had no inherent moral virtue. Rousseau, however, treats the existence of natural pity as evidence of mankind's fundamental goodness. Rousseau detaches pity from manners or mores and locates its source in a beneficent nature. For Rousseau, society is precisely what mankind must overcome in order to express pity. Rousseau also reworks Mandeville's opposition of pity to reason to show that reason must always be supplemented by pity in order for human society to exist (54).

Despite their similarities, Mandeville's and Rousseau's observations are brought to opposite conclusions: both men label their societies as corrupt, but Rousseau insists upon using nature as an external, ahistorical norm to criticize their unnaturalness. The general pity that one feels for members of the same species, the general, undifferentiated, cosmopolitan love that one feels for all of humankind, is for Mandeville an impossibility, for Rousseau the only hope for mankind. Rousseau therefore criticizes philosophic reason because reason individuates and isolates men from one another. At the same time, mankind's natural, untutored capacity for pity serves as the basis for any society worthy of the name. Thus, natural pity and sensibility are crucial for the foundation of society, but it is precisely these qualities of life that are threatened by the increasing complexity and social division of modernity.

In Rousseau's account, a key component of the divisive, alienating forces of modernity can be found in a false, self-seeking reason, which estranges while it individuates, and which attacks the shared sense of solidarity that unites premodern society: "Now it is evident that this identification must have been infinitely closer in the state of nature than in the state of reasoning. Reason is what engenders egocentrism, and reflection strengthens it. Reason is what turns man in upon himself" (54). Reason, reflection, and philosophy are all ultimately harmful because in their continual advancement they distance men from the suffering of fellow creatures. Rousseau's theory of history in the two *Discourses,* which stresses the moral costs of the refinements of modernity and reason, constitutes a significant advance over the simple two-stage (Ancients/Moderns) paradigms of many of his contemporaries, while making for a more historicized view of reason. Interestingly, it is Rousseau's moral critique of a historically evolving and self-seeking reason that helps to alter the paradigms of Cynicism in the eighteenth century. This view of reason helps to transform the Cynic from a Diogenical Man of Reason—a Reason whose value and effects are never questioned—into a selfish man of rationalizations.[22]

This view of philosophy also inspires Rousseau's unforgettable scene of the philosopher, another version of the Unmoved Man whose sleep is never troubled by the suffering just outside his window:

> Philosophy is what isolates him and what moves him to say in secret, at the sight of a suffering man, "Perish if you will; I am safe and sound." No longer can anything but danger to the entire society trouble the tranquil slumber of the philosopher and yank him from his bed. His fellow man can be killed with impunity underneath his window. He has merely to place his hands over his ears and argue with himself a little in order to prevent nature, which rebels within him, from identifying him with the man being assassinated. (54–55)

Rousseau offers us an unforgettable scene of a man who must rationalize his way to a calm indifference when faced by suffering. This philosopher's insensibility, along with his misuse of an unnatural reason and set of arguments, helps him render acceptable to himself his distance from his fellow human beings.

For this figure, reason has shrunk to nothing more than egoism, calculation, and self-seeking. Therein we find yet another origin for the modern, disbelieving cynic.

After these discussions of the sleeping philosopher and his impoverished notions of reason and feeling, Rousseau introduces Diogenes and the *quaero hominem*. The philosopher's emblematic appearance reopens the question broached not just by Diogenes but by Erasmus and the rest of the humanist tradition: Who deserves the name and title of "man" in this day and age? Whereas Erasmus had used this episode to demonstrate the usefulness of knowledge and eloquence for the young prince, Rousseau makes Diogenes represent his own fruitless search for a man in a society characterized by its rampant luxury and inequality.

For Rousseau, the *quaero hominem* has not just a moral but a historical meaning to teach us. Diogenes' search reveals the historical alienation of mankind from its origins. Rousseau writes: "No attentive reader can fail to be struck by the immense space that separates [the natural state of mankind from the civil state]. . . . He will realize that, since the human race of one age is not the human race of another age, the reason why Diogenes did not find his man is because he searched among his contemporaries for a man who no longer existed" (80). Rousseau thus radicalized the distinction between rude ancients and polite moderns found throughout much Enlightenment historical writing, including the Dialogues of the Dead. Rousseau's greatest historiographical achievement is to redefine his own era not in terms of its polite superiority over previous, rude eras, but in its increasing degrees of inequality. Rousseau has also, in a single gesture, historicized the human race in a way that d'Alembert, for example, was unwilling to do in "An Essay upon the Alliance betwixt Learned Men, and the Great." D'Alembert had argued against the moral primitivism of Rousseau's first *Discourse*, claiming instead the essential uniformity of mankind across time and space.[23] Instead, Rousseau emphasizes the "immense space" separating civil from natural society and the historical differences between them. Intriguingly, Rousseau renders Diogenes as a slightly pathetic and isolated figure, not unlike the Rousseau we will eventually find in the autobiographical writings, because the philosopher is never able to conclude his search for a man among his contemporaries. No man worthy of the name exists.

Hence, in the two *Discourses*, Rousseau has dissolved once and for all the Enlightenment's conventional identification of reason with sensible feeling and insists that the reason displayed by such insensible philosophers as Hobbes and Mandeville is unnatural and false. In doing so, Rousseau has essentially identified philosophic reason with egocentrism and self-seeking, while reserving a true, cosmopolitan sensibility for himself and the rest of mankind. It would not be long before Rousseau's attacks on philosophic reason encompassed not just Hobbes and Mandeville but his own former friends and allies in the philosophe party.

Apart from his polemical role in identifying and attacking one of the core attitudes of modern political cynicism, attributed here to Mandeville and Hobbes, Rousseau's polemics against philosophic reason had both theoretical implications and historical consequences for the concept of cynicism. One of the implications of Rousseau's argument against a narrowly self-seeking version of reason, barely sketched here but developed more fully in works like the *Social Contract,* is that it is the Mandevillean's myopic definition of self-interest that threatens to reduce any multiparty negotiation (or collective movement like the philosophes) to complete deadlock or fragmentation.[24] In other words, Rousseau has pinpointed one of the key factors enforcing cynicism's "ensemble effect" of stalled action: a single party's too-exclusive or narrowly defined pursuit of self-interest at the expense of other potential benefits. The sleeping philosopher, for example, cannot imagine that someone could climb through *his* window and murder him someday. And yet the fascinating thing about this episode is the way in which Rousseau and the other philosophes fell into many of the same puzzles concerning the fragmentation and deadlock of their movement, since they could not agree on what constituted progress.

At the historical level, Rousseau's assaults upon the other philosophes for their indifference to natural feelings and overreliance upon philosophic reason would serve as the model and excuse for reactionary writers like Burke and the Anti-Jacobins. Rousseau instigated many of the accusations the Counter-Enlightenment later used against the philosophes as a group (including, of course, Rousseau). By far the most damaging charge against Rousseau and the philosophes generally was their supposed failure to live up to their pronouncements, or to harmonize their words and deeds. In other words, Rousseau's effective deployment of a moral critique against the philosophes' supposed gap between appearance and reality created the rhetorical framework that allowed Burke and others to announce the public "failure of the Enlightenment" three or four decades later.

Rousseau's Open Attack on the Philosophes in the "Letter to d'Alembert"

In 1762, Rousseau's "Letter to d'Alembert" embroiled him in new controversy when he broke publicly with his former friends d'Alembert and Voltaire about opening a new theater in Geneva. Rousseau's hostility to the theater set the entire philosophe party against him. Because they came from men like Voltaire, these exchanges produced the most famous denunciations of him as a Cynic, a hypocrite, or a misanthrope playing at the moralist's role. Once defended by the philosophes, Rousseau was now treated by the same men as a fraud, in their frustration at his unwillingness to assist their cause.

The philosophe party had many good reasons to fear Rousseau and his writings. Voltaire was as worried as d'Alembert about the consequences of Rousseau's fracturing of their party, which did indeed hamper its effectiveness.[25] When Voltaire heard of these attacks from the anti-philosophe party, he complained to d'Alembert of the disloyalty of Rousseau, who had chosen not to join with the other satirized philosophes in their planned response to the anti-philosophe satirist Palissot:

> The *philosophes* are disunited. The little flock is eating at one another while wolves come and devour it. Your Jean-Jacques is the one I am most angry with. This stark madman, who could have amounted to something if he had let you be his guide, has taken it into his head to go on his own. He writes against the theater after producing a bad comedy; he writes against the France that feeds him. He finds four or five rotten staves from Diogenes's tub and gets inside to bark. He abandons his friends; he writes me the most impertinent letters ever scribbled by a fanatic. He informs me in so many words: "You have corrupted Geneva as a reward for the asylum that it gave you."[26]

Voltaire's frustration was with a member of the party who seems more interested in scoring points off his former friends than in fighting their common, traditionalist enemies. Neither Voltaire nor d'Alembert was able to understand how a philosophe, especially one who had himself written operas and comedies, could oppose an institution as civilizing as the theater. Neither had any sympathy for Rousseau's critique of civilization in the *Discourse on Inequality* or his consequent critique of theater in the "Letter." Voltaire could only understand Rousseau's behavior as a result of betrayal or vanity of their cause. Either way, how could Rousseau possibly believe the things he was writing?

In another letter to d'Alembert, from which the second epigraph to this chapter is taken, Voltaire once again diagnosed Rousseau's strange condition. Here I have included the full passage, which includes a crucial detail:

> Excessive pride and envy have destroyed Jean-Jacques, my illustrious philosopher. That monster dares speak of education! A man who refused to

> raise any of his sons and put them all in foundling homes! He abandoned his children and the tramp with whom he made them. He has only failed to write against his tramp as he has written against his friends. I will pity him if they hang him, but out of pure humanity, for personally I only consider him Diogenes's dog or rather like a dog descended from a bastard of that dog.[27]

Rousseau's attacks on his former friends drew an immediate response about his own vulnerable position, and even in this early letter Voltaire uses the information, not yet available to the general public, about Rousseau's abandonment of his children to discredit his philosophy.[28] The implication is clear: anyone capable of abandoning his children is disqualified from any reflective discussion of ethics because he failed the first and most consequential test, caring for the human beings most dependent upon him. Almost thirty years later, Edmund Burke would be making similar accusations against Rousseau, but this time to discredit the entire Enlightenment movement as frauds and atheists, d'Alembert and Voltaire along with Rousseau.

Especially after the break with d'Alembert and Voltaire, Rousseau's reputation as a modern Diogenes began increasingly to emphasize his pathetic self-delusion and insincerity, in contrast with the more genuine Cynicism of his ancient model Diogenes. He was an ape or mimic of Diogenes, Diogenes' dog, or a performing mountebank or charlatan, a mere buffoon whose philosophizing could only impress the gullible. Such a view is echoed in d'Alembert's 4 August 1770 letter to Voltaire: "Jean Jacques is a nasty fool, and a plain charlatan, but this fool and this charlatan has zealous partisans. . . . Thus I would not have, either near or far, for better or for worse, any relations at all with this Diogenes."[29] As the image of Rousseau as a charlatan or mountebank indicates, however, philosophes like Voltaire or d'Alembert worried about Rousseau not simply because he was a fool, but because he was a fool with a following. As we saw in the last chapter, this devoted following brings with it a certain power that the other philosophes had to respect. He has "zealous partisans," and his opinions, no matter how bizarre or unfounded, have consequences outside himself. Rousseau was not simply a mean and crazy misanthrope but a charlatan who nevertheless possessed an undoubted power to shape public opinion. This is how Rousseau, like Lyttelton's Diogenes, anticipated the disbelieving modern cynic: he becomes a complex symbol uniting elite disbelief with mass credulity. His views, no matter how false or paradoxical, had the power to spread through a susceptible general public in ways that remained outside the control of the other philosophes and their more restricted audience. Rousseau's more general readership reminded the philosophes of the limits to their own "counterpublic" and threatened their ability to claim the attention or legitimacy conferred by the widest possible audience.

In this sense, Rousseau's accusations against the philosophes reawakened the great scandal of Cynic philosophy by calling attention to the luxury and superfluity that sustained aristocrats and philosophes alike. This scandalous attack had destructive personal consequences for Rousseau, but it also helped to provoke debate about the philosophes' claims that they stood apart from the society they observed. Rousseau, however, insisted—as so many of his contemporaries did not—on the scandal of property ownership as the root source of the luxury that they denounced or celebrated in the abstract, without recognizing their conditioning by the very same forces. When Rousseau accused the philosophes as a class of heartlessly encouraging a destructive process of social division, and continued to insist upon his own unbounded, selfless sensibility, he made himself vulnerable to Voltaire's rejoinder about his abandoned children. Rousseau's moralistic accusations of others invited his enemies to puncture his public image as a moralist, by (cynically, reductively, in bad faith) uncovering the degree to which he failed to live up to his own professed standards of sensibility, selflessness, and rectitude.

Rousseau's habit of accusing others of failings while eagerly confessing his own turned him into an object of intense curiosity. Many people probed his life for signs of weaknesses and failings, in order to contrast these with his famously eloquent language. In this respect, Rousseau became well known not just as a sentimentalist but as a man whose sentiment seemed to be flagrantly, shamelessly contradicted by most of the details of his life. This is another way that Rousseau's life story, or rather, its dramatically different reception from one moment to the next, encouraged people just after his death to view him as a cynical manipulator of appearances, someone who put on the appearance of virtue without bothering to follow its dictates. Rousseau spent his life opposing this split between appearance and reality, negating it with his own concepts of sincerity and authenticity, and ended up being identified with it himself.

Some Versions of Rousseau (1758–79)

After his break with the philosophes, Rousseau complained in his "Letter to Christophe de Beaumont" (1763) of the degree to which his reputation was now at the mercy of a fickle and undiscerning public: "Thus fluctuating is the public opinion concerning me; those who adopt it being as ignorant why they detest me now, as why they once respected me. As to myself, however, I have always remained the same."[30]

And yet his polarized public reception exhibited none of the unity he felt while writing his works, a disparity that to him only demonstrated the falsity of others' partial views:

> I had always the same system of morals, the same faith, the same maxims, and, if you will, the same opinions. Very different, however, have been the opinions that have passed on my books. . . . After the publication of my first Discourse, I was said to be a Writer fond of paradoxes, who amused himself in proving things he did not believe. . . . After my Discourse on the Inequality of Mankind, I was deemed an Atheist and Misanthrope: after my Letter to Mr. d'Alembert, on the Theatres, I was celebrated as the Defender of Christian Morals: after Eloisa, I was supposed to be passionate and tender: at present I am a monster of impiety; and shall, probably, by and by, be a miracle of devotion.[31]

Rousseau's "Letter to Beaumont" argues that it is not any protean quality in himself but rather the fluctuations in public opinion that have generated these multiple, contradictory images of him, whether "Atheist and Misanthrope," or "passionate and tender." For Rousseau, however, these confused opinions had grave consequences because they helped foster an increasingly polarized and incoherent response to his writings outside France. And yet because such statements, however sincere, could not interrupt the public's ongoing discussion of him but were merely reprinted and recirculated along with all the other "opinions" (as this one was by the sympathetic *Monthly Review* in 1763), Rousseau's only ability to control discussion of his image was to keep writing and hope that the public took the cue. Henceforth, however, the reception of Rousseau only grew more fractured with his subsequent publications in the 1760s and 1770s.

I think it safe to say that after 1762, a split developed and grew among cosmopolitan Rousseau's widespread publics, so that many English and German readers and writers were content to value him for his sensibility and had too little personal information otherwise to question the self-image offered in works like the "Letter" or *Julie, or, The New Heloise.*[32] Writers like Kant[33] and Wieland, for example, attracted to the earnest and idealized image of the philosophe promulgated by Rousseau, were happy to draw upon the Diogenes-Rousseau parallel by praising the Genevan as "that subtle Diogenes" or by writing an entire novel about Diogenes as a sentimental Citizen of the World misunderstood by an uncomprehending reading public.[34]

The majority of the comparisons of Rousseau to Diogenes, however, were intended to discredit Rousseau, attributing to the modern philosopher all the worst aspects of his supposed ancient model. According to his energetic enemies in the philosophe camp (including many second-tier writers like Grimm and Marmontel), among the anti-philosophes like Palissot, and throughout the rest of Europe, Rousseau was not a true citizen of the world, but a misanthropic, rude, and plebeian Cynic, and an enemy not just to society, commerce, or the advancement of the arts and sciences, but to morality itself.[35] For his enemies, the best evidence for this charge lay in the inconsistent public image of which Rousseau had complained, but for his detractors this inconsistency only demonstrated Rousseau's lack of integrity, not the falsity of the images.

The classic accusation in this manner was the remark of Voltaire's recorded in Marmontel's *Memoirs* (1804/translated 1805). Upon being told that the initial hint for the first *Discourse*'s rejection of the arts and sciences came from Diderot, Voltaire exclaims: "You do not at all surprise me . . . this man is artificial from head to foot; his mind and soul are wholly artificial. But it is in vain for him to act the stoic and cynic alternately; he will constantly betray himself, and will be suffocated by his own mask."[36] This passage demonstrates how deeply the Enlightenment suspicion of rhetoric attached itself to Rousseau, even portraying this eloquence as a "mask" threatening to "suffocate" him. For all of Rousseau's claims of sincerity, his contemporaries among the philosophes took these claims as a ruse designed to fool those who were not aware of how easily he could argue either side of the case. In their view, Rousseau simply opted for the showier, more ostentatious approach to the question, whatever his personal views might have been, just to gain public attention and applause for his *Discourse on the Sciences and the Arts.* As Marmontel told Voltaire: "His writings appeared to me to be only those of an eloquent sophist, and his character that of a pretended cynic, who would burst with pride and rage in his tub if people gave up looking at him."[37]

In Britain, however, Rousseau's reception remained favorable enough through the 1770s to win him respect, if not necessarily favor, from British readers and journals like the *Monthly Review.*[38] As late as 1779, the *Monthly Review* was still defending Rousseau against his old enemy Palissot, who had published a preemptive *Éloge* upon his death in 1778. Palissot's equivocal *Éloge* for his former enemy provoked this defense from the reviewer:

> The Public have always perceived something excentric and extravagant in the citizen of Geneva, and could not but discern those offensive effusions of pride and self-applause which he was perpetually throwing out, without any kind of disguise, in his writings and conduct:—but the same Public beheld, with no small degree of toleration and indulgence, those failings, which were compensated by the most splendid marks of integrity, sentiment, and genius.[39]

This review shows that English public opinion owed whatever favorable judgment it had of Rousseau to two intimately linked aspects of his writing and personality: his presumed honesty and sensibility. Even when English readers recognized his emotional excesses or lapses in judgment, these they held less important than the intensity with which he experienced what the *Monthly Review* terms "the *great,* the *good,* the *beautiful,* and the *affecting,*" and the imaginative force with which he was able to communicate these feelings to others.

The presumed honesty and sensibility of Rousseau inspired both adulation and ambivalence among his English admirers during this phase of his career. Here we may still find examples of the "identification" or "projection" earlier described by Niehues-Pröbsting, but directed toward the sentimental hero Rousseau, and blocked now by the "cynical" appearance of his self-isolation and misanthropy. One example also interestingly documents how a particular member of Rousseau's public made private use of his writings, but in a manner that reveals some of the paradoxes inherent in their relation; the letter shows an interesting mix of the personal and impersonal and treats Rousseau as both an intimate friend and an unknowable stranger.[40]

In an undated document written sometime in the 1760s or 1770s, the writer William Combe, best known as the author of *Dr. Syntax,* and a possible translator of Rousseau himself, wrote the following "Letter to Jean-Jacques Rousseau":

> Railing does no good to any cause, especially to that of virtue. Again I repeat, Rousseau, love mankind and be happy! To prove this assertion more fully, I must have recourse to an unpleasing subject—I must speak of myself. I have neither fortune nor friends; I have neither father nor mother, nor brother nor sister. . . . I pity every one's infirmities; I laugh with those who laugh, and weep with those who weep. I adore Virtue wherever I find her, and pray that she may soon take up her dwelling where I find her not. . . . [I ask myself?] why is [Rousseau] cynically retreating from the world, and copying music in a garret? Why does he give up the duties of a Chris-

> tian for those of a machine? These are questions, my dear Rousseau—but it is time for me to draw to a conclusion. . . . Cease to act unworthy of your nature as a man, and your character as a Christian. O Rousseau, I bid you once more adieu! My last valediction is—love mankind and be happy!"[41]

This rhapsody consists of equal parts self-exhortation and fan mail. It defends Rousseau from some presumed sin of misanthropy, meaning man-hating and railing. Combe's identification with Rousseau is complete, and this identification spurs him on to urge his idol to recover his former love of mankind. Yet even Combe, as uncritical as he is, refuses to accept the idea of his hero "cynically . . . copying music in a garret." Here, "cynically" seems to imply not just misanthropy but a meanness of soul that Combe cannot accept in the writer who serves as an ethical model. For all his presumed honesty and sensibility, Rousseau's equally presumptive misanthropy makes his fans feel cheated, as if they themselves were included in the hatred that Rousseau offered to all but the most dedicated supporters. Combe's conviction, however, that he himself could never be included in Rousseau's misanthropy gives him the courage to mention his own disappointments and to attempt to move his hero in the same way he himself was moved by Rousseau's writings.

Because of Rousseau's supporters' faith in his superlative honesty, his sensibility was attributed peculiar powers. Once those assumptions were reversed, however, Rousseau seemed a very different figure: a monster of pride and vanity, a dangerously duplicitous hypocrite who paraded his false sensibility to impress others, and a selfish man who insisted on presenting himself as a paragon of unselfishness. This was Voltaire's position for most of Rousseau's career, and the other French philosophes, annoyed by Rousseau's division of their party, eventually held similar views. In England, however, opinions remained divided through the 1770s between the advocates of his sensibility and those threatened by his religious and political heterodoxy.

The part of the English public most likely to charge him with misanthropy and cynicism were those who perceived a moral inconsistency between the "Atheist and Misanthrope" visible in the *Discourses* and the "passionate and tender" author of *Julie, or, The New Heloise,* as Rousseau recognized in the "Letter to Beaumont." It is noteworthy, then, that John Wesley records in his *Journal* of 1776:

> I read with much expectation a celebrated book—Rousseau upon Education [*Émile*]. But how was I disappointed! Sure a more consummate coxcomb never saw the sun! How amazingly full of himself! . . . But I object to

> his temper more than to his judgement: he is a mere misanthrope; a cynic all over. So indeed is his brother-infidel, Voltaire; and wellnigh as great a coxcomb. But he [Voltaire] hides both his doggedness and vanity a little better; whereas here [in Rousseau] it stares us in the face continually.[42]

Wesley's pious horror of Rousseau is suggestive in its equally severe judgment upon Voltaire, who is called a "brother-infidel" who only hides better his "doggedness and vanity." Wesley is not concerned with their well-known antagonism to one another but only treats them as similarly effeminate "coxcombs" and unbelievers who offer commonplaces "disguised under new expressions." "Such discoveries," harrumphs Wesley, "I always expect from those who are too wise to believe their Bibles." Though Rousseau divided the philosophe party with a religiosity that Voltaire detested, Wesley's Methodist view collapses the two together into an infidel party of philosophes eager to destroy belief wherever they go.

This kind of reading of Rousseau as a disbeliever and threat to religious faith anticipates by two decades the party line of Burke and the Counter-Enlightenment opponents of Rousseau and the French Revolution. As Burke famously declared in the *Reflections,* "We are not the converts of Rousseau; we are not the disciples of Voltaire; Helvetius has made no progress amongst us. Atheists are not our preachers; madmen are not our lawgivers."[43] What Wesley and Burke share in these two passages separated by twenty years is an awareness of the philosophes as an intellectual class, whatever their personal jealousies and differences. Burke has specifically targeted these philosophes as would-be "preachers" and "lawgivers" ready to usurp these roles for an unsuspecting British populace.

Rousseau the Parrhesiast: *The Dialogues* and *Confessions*

In the decade before his death in 1778, Rousseau produced two autobiographical works that meditated upon truth telling and the philosopher's life, and assessed how well his practices coincided with those of his ethical models. Naturally Diogenes and Cynic philosophy loom over both these works, as a moral-historical parallel whose meaning Rousseau cannot quite control when he compares himself to the ancient philosopher.

Because of Rousseau's increasingly unhinged state in the 1770s, it is unsurprising that between 1772 and 1774, in the midst of persecutions real and imagined, he produced a work as aggrieved and defensive as *Rousseau Judge of Jean-Jacques.*[44] Otherwise known as the *Dialogues,* this work reflects upon the myriad ways that an indifferent or hostile public opinion has distorted his life story. Against these distortions, he reiterates his own truth-claims, while alerting his readers to the (imagined?) conspiracies and cabals working against him. For those unfamiliar with the form of this remarkable work, I should also mention that it is a dialogue of sorts, conducted between "Rousseau" and "The Frenchman" about the true character of "Jean-Jacques," a man who has had the most terrible things said about him. "Rousseau" and "The Frenchman" examine as objectively as they can the evidence about "Jean-Jacques" to determine the final truth about him.

In his recounting of the sad story of "Jean-Jacques," "Rousseau" depicts a pathetic "Jean-Jacques" who has been abandoned to the belatedness and isolation of the Diogenes alluded to in the *Discourse on Inequality.*[45] "Rousseau" reports that he learned that "Jean-Jacques" was not the misanthrope of other people's reports but only a man unable to find another man, let alone a man worthy to be his friend:

> After many useless efforts, [Jean-Jacques] had not found anything even among the most decent people except betrayal, duplicity, lying, and that while they all hastened to welcome him, to warn him, to attract him, they appeared so happy about his defamation, contributed to it so willingly, gave him such false caresses, praised him in a tone so insensitive to his heart, showered him with extreme admiration with so little respect and consideration, that tired of these mocking and deceitful displays, and indignant at being thus the plaything of his supposed friends, he stopped seeing them, withdrew without hiding his disdain from them, and after seeking a man without success for a long time, he extinguished his lantern and shut himself up completely within himself.[46]

This is Rousseau as the pathetic Diogenes, the man who is unable to find a man and who therefore extinguishes his lantern and shuts himself up completely within himself. Rousseau makes this composite of himself and Diogenes into a figure of disillusioned sensibility, unable to bear the duplicity or attentions of his false, insensible friends.

Yet Rousseau was also reflective enough to resist any easy identification with Diogenes, and to show—truthfully, once again—how he failed to measure up to the high standard of his philosophic models Diogenes and Epictetus. "Rousseau" describes to "The Frenchman" the results of the attempt by "Jean-

Jacques" to break free of the influence of the fashionable world by taking up music copying:

> I told you that I had found [Jean-Jacques] copying music at ten sols a page, an occupation ill-suited to the dignity of an Author and scarcely resembling those which gave him such a reputation as much for good as for ill. This first item already provided me with two topics of research to be done: first, whether he devoted himself to this work sincerely, or just to mislead the public about his true occupations; the other whether he really needed this trade to live, or whether it was an affectation of simplicity or poverty to copy an Epictetus or Diogenes as your Gentlemen claim. (132)[47]

In this elaborate staging of self-assessment and internal debate, the author's surrogates remain remarkably ambivalent toward the ethical models they nonetheless deploy: "Rousseau" asks himself, Is "Jean-Jacques" truly an austere Epictetus or a Diogenes, or merely performing that role to impress onlookers? To use the Cynic distinction, Is "Jean-Jacques" copying music from strict economic *need* or from a more insidious *desire* to be seen as needy, and therefore virtuous? As the author Rousseau was well aware, such questions had once been as persistently applied to the Stoics and Cynics as they were to himself. His surrogate investigator "Rousseau" therefore probed the feelings of "Jean-Jacques" further: Was this simplicity and poverty true and sincere or merely an affectation put on for the sake of influencing public opinion? Which is more shameful, poverty or an affectation of poverty designed to convince others of his virtue?

This is another example of how, in Niehues-Pröbsting's words, Rousseau's reflections on Cynicism led him toward an act of "self-recognition and self-criticism" about his philosophic independence, his desire to be more independent than the other philosophes. "Rousseau" must continually question "Jean-Jacques" to make sure his motives are sincerely and truthfully reported, while keeping the stern example of Diogenes before him to inspire him to further acts of self-exposure.

But why compare himself to Diogenes, a famously unpleasant, proud, and misanthropic philosopher according to this period's opinion, when so many of his enemies had already, and humiliatingly, dismissed him a modern Diogenes? The answer, I believe, lies in Rousseau's daring embrace of two aspects of Cynic philosophy that his more decorous colleagues could not afford to imitate: poverty and truth telling. Unlike almost every other contemporary writer who discusses Cynicism in this period, Rousseau lived and wrote and celebrated these values, as Foucault would put it, "to the point of *scandal.*" For these qualities of risky truth telling, Rousseau well deserves Foucault's label for this type of philosopher, the parrhesiast.[48]

In his *Discourses* especially, but throughout his writings, Rousseau reactivates the long-dormant ancient Cynic notion of an *ethical* and *exemplary* poverty, a (secular) poverty designed to signal a certain ascetic virtue in its "possessor" and to point its onlookers to "an other life," in Foucault's phrase. For this purpose, Rousseau had before him the singular example of the ancient philosophical hero Diogenes, a man capable of embracing hardship as a form of training, as an education in self-sufficiency. Like Diogenes, Rousseau's embrace of poverty was not merely ascetic but performative, the most forceful way to remind others of their dependence upon a thoroughly corrupt and unnatural social order. To the majority of his contemporaries, however, Rousseau's Diogenical decision to embrace poverty rather than patronage was treated as singular in the extreme, a sign of his misanthropy and perhaps madness. Such behavior was literally incomprehensible to his contemporaries. Yet Rousseau remained consistent on this point and seemed constitutionally incapable of accepting any form of help or dependence on others for any length of time.

Jean Starobinski is the critic who has written most persuasively on this issue of Rousseau's choice of self-deprivation, or what we might call poverty, suspicion, and ingratitude as a philosophical "way of life." According to Starobinski, Rousseau presented himself as a Cynic philosopher whose impudence and ingratitude allowed him to beg without falling into an unseemly dependence:

> Jean-Jacques proclaims his ingratitude. The equality he wants—the reciprocity of free minds—excludes dependence of any kind, and in the first place the dependence created by the kindness of the benevolent. . . . His decision was firm: accept nothing in order to owe nothing. Poor, dignified, and on display to an astonished public, Rousseau made *visible*—and even enviable—the previously unnoticed existence of the frugal artisan. When Diogenes renounces everything he owns down to his soup bowl, the rich can no longer look unashamed upon the superfluous luxury in which they live. Entangled in a gilded web of boredom, they feel unhappy. They want to cross the divide.[49]

As the history of Rousseau's reception shows, Rousseau's contemporaries often interpreted his "Cynical" stance uncharitably and treated his "ingratitude" as mere misanthropy, madness, or hypocrisy. Moreover, Rousseau leaves open the *Dialogue*'s question of whether the music-copying career of "Jean-

Jacques" is a mere affectation to impress others or a gambit designed to gain the sympathy of the despised rich. Rousseau's only solution is to alienate everyone equally, particularly his friends and supporters, so that he can avoid feeling dependent upon anyone.

Yet these passages of Rousseau, and Starobinski's commentary, also raise the issue of Rousseau and Diogenes' shared strategies of what I have been calling moral redescription. In other words, Starobinski has beautifully shown how Rousseau has taken the conventionally negative term "poverty" to align it with the morally inflected language of "simplicity" and honesty. With Starobinski's assistance, however, even Rousseau's "ingratitude" suddenly stands revealed not as rudeness but as an upright "independence." To use Skinner's suggestive formulation, the force of this kind of "new and favourable" redescription, when successful, "entails the *defeat* of the original and unfavourable description, or at least to argue that the new description, even if it does not defeat the original one, can at least be seen to *override* its unfavourable evaluation by providing a more powerfully favourable evaluation" (Skinner's emphasis).[50] And yet as the parrhesiast is well aware, the victories or defeats provided by such redescriptions are never total, and so the other, unfavorable meanings may very well hang in the background to shadow the redescribed object, just as "ingratitude" hangs in the background of our perceptions of Rousseau, no matter how eloquently defended by Starobinski.

The uncharitable or hostile reception that Rousseau received from his peers and public showed the unending risks he ran as a truth teller or parrhesiast. As we saw in the first chapter, however, the parrhesiast in antiquity had certain prior conditions to meet, which do seem fitting for Rousseau's case: first, "he had to speak the truth, but this truth could not merely be . . . a mere coincidence of speech with fact"; second, "he had to really believe it himself and to manifest that belief"; third, "in speaking the truth, the parrhesiast had to run a personal risk before the other to whom he spoke" (*FP* 103). The largest single difference lay in the third condition, which emphasizes the orality of the parrhesiastic exchange between, say, ruler and philosopher, which can only be imperfectly emulated by the philosophe in a world of print publicity. Yet there can be no denying that Rousseau, who was chased all over Europe because of his printed works, ran significant risks of violence or arrest throughout his career, no matter how large and worshipful his reading public.

What we are finding in Rousseau's career, particularly in the final phase featuring his most scandalous autobiographical writings, is the self-conscious parrhesiast who must live and embody the truth that he announces to his audience, at whatever cost. I think that the self-exposure, even self-humiliation inherent in works like *Rousseau Judge of Jean-Jacques* or the *Confessions* is better explained as part of this philosophic "other life" than as some masochistic or delusional impulse. The Rousseau who was chased around Europe during this time understood the potentially violent responses his writings could inspire. Ironically, despite the philosophes' more playful identifications with Diogenes, it was Rousseau who most closely approximated the scandalous independence of the Cynics.

In Rousseau's *Confessions,* first translated into English in 1783, five years after his death in 1778, we see a less attractive side of parrhesia and redescription, where these Cynic practices are used un-Cynically, as it were, to deflect shame from himself and evade the self-testing and accurate self-assessment demanded by Cynic discipline. Here again Rousseau becomes a symptomatic example of "enlightened false consciousness" and "the failure of the Enlightenment."

Nonetheless, it is in this work that Rousseau completed the lifelong exploration of the possibilities of intellectual independence that he had initiated with the *Discourse on the Sciences and the Arts* almost forty years earlier. Yet the *Confessions'* descriptions of his numerous attempts to win independence exhibit a pathos that his more philosophical or political writings do not share. For one thing, the autobiographical writings make it possible to see for the first time the costs of Rousseau's pursuit of independence for those around him. These include some of the most notorious aspects of the *Confessions:* Rousseau's own suspicious nature; his panicked desertion of his friend Le Maitre; his infatuation with aristocratic women; his strange relation with his pseudo-spouse, Thérèse; and most notoriously, his abandonment of his and Thérèse's children at the Foundling Hospital.

It is striking how the philosophical independence demanded in works like the first *Discourse* came to be translated into a very specific style of masculine independence in the *Confessions,* an independence that cannot be assimilated easily into the legitimizing social institutions of marriage or family. To use Flynn/Foucault's words again, Rousseau is attempting to show in the *Confessions* how he has lived "an 'other life,' the truly philosophical life, the 'true life'" (*FP* 110). Yet this attempt gained him very little applause.

In the *Confessions,* it is Rousseau's versions of "courage" and "truth"—or is it willingness to expose himself to public shame?—that reveal most clearly his affinities with Diogenes and Cynic philosophy. Book 8 of the *Confessions* rehearses a variety of themes strongly associated with Diogenes since antiquity: the suspected fraudulence of the philosopher as a mere philosophizer; the luxury and corruption that render polite society insubstantial and unreal; the philosopher's resulting need to remain independent of society, meaning free of all attachments below that of "citizen"; the grounding of the philosopher's masculinity in his ability to offer an ethical example to others, not in the socially imposed roles of husband or father. While narrating the events that he revisits in the music-copying scenes of *Rousseau Judge of Jean-Jacques,* book 8 of the *Confessions* shows how his early literary successes in the 1750s panicked him into a poor impersonation of a Cynic and misanthrope.

While he "was philosophising upon the duties of man," Rousseau was faced with an event "which made [him] better reflect on [his] own [duties]": Thérèse's third pregnancy.[51] How, then, to become fully independent? Rousseau's decision was to deposit this child like all the others with the Foundling Hospital. Rather than feeling shame at such an act, Rousseau claims that "in destining them to become workmen and peasants, rather than adventurers and fortune hunters, I thought I acted like an honest citizen, and a good father, and considered myself as a member of the republic of Plato" (183).

As Edward Malkin has pointed out, the model for this astonishing rationalization is perhaps not Plato's *Republic* but Epictetus's *On the Calling of the Cynic,* which argues that a married Cynic would be better off exposing his children than rearing them conventionally, especially if he is married to a less-than-philosophical woman.[52] Rousseau, of course, does not report Thérèse's role in these deliberations. Unlike the rakes and libertines who taught him this practice, Rousseau depicts his own decision as the result of conscious, philosophical choice. He portrays his rational deliberations in the matter as unaffected by any outside prejudices of his social circle, or by any feelings of Thérèse whatsoever, and ignores any opinion that might proscribe such an act from careful consideration. In his account, the decision to abandon a child becomes a victory for masculine philosophy, fatherhood, and country over unenlightened prejudice or feminized shame. For performing this supposedly unselfish deed, for publishing it to the world, and then for justifying it philosophically in a grotesque piece of redescription, Rousseau sustained a lifetime of attacks against both his morality and his masculinity, attacks waged by the antiphilosophical and philosophical parties alike.[53]

It is worth reflecting for a moment about this episode, which shows the genuine limits of the ancient ethical models Rousseau deploys. Rousseau's temporizing passages show how he has travestied his own philosophy, first by reducing it to the self-seeking reason he critiqued in Hobbes and Mandeville, and second by using these rationalizations to compound his moral errors with a false, self-serving version of fraudulent moral reflection, a form of self-reflection devoid of introspection or self-criticism. In this respect, the Rousseau on display here fully exemplifies Sloterdijk's notion of Cynicism as "enlightened false consciousness," a "modernized, unhappy consciousness, on which enlightenment has labored both successfully and in vain. It has learned its lessons in enlightenment, but it has not, and probably was not able to, put them into practice."[54] In other words, Rousseau's own behavior, in spite of his attacks on Mandeville and Hobbes, has become the best, most symptomatic argument possible for modern cynicism's core assumption in the twentieth century that "human conduct is directed, either consciously or unconsciously, wholly by self-interest or self-indulgence, and that appearances to the contrary are superficial and untrustworthy."[55]

Having made this confession about abandoning his children, Rousseau proceeds as if no one could question this decision and complains about the disruptions caused by his literary celebrity. Henceforward, he began a process of self-estrangement from polite society that made him take on the appearance of an unregenerate Cynic. As he described the next step in the process of renouncing his attachments: "My foolish timidity, which I could not conquer, having for principle the fear of being wanting in the common forms, I took, by way of encouraging myself, a resolution to tread them underfoot. I became sour and a cynic from shame, and affected to despise the politeness which I knew not how to practice" (210).

In this remarkable string of admissions, Rousseau has inverted the long-standing associations of Cynic shamelessness in order to describe his own extraordinary case: the man whose Cynicism is merely an appearance, a sham, and a device for existing unmolested by society. This makes him a fraud like all the others, only one whose fraud makes him a better human being. Rousseau's cynical contempt for both politeness and fashion is itself merely a performance, and a bad one at that. Rousseau's desire to unmask himself, and to expose the gracelessness that he had originally concealed under the cover of philosophic austerity, results in a paradoxical form of self-justification:

> This austerity, conformable to my new principles, I must confess seemed to enoble [*sic*] itself in my mind; it assumed in my eyes the form of the intrepidity of virtue, and I dare assert it to be upon this noble basis, that it supported itself longer and better than could have been expected from any thing so contrary to my nature. Yet, notwithstanding, I had the name of a

> misanthrope, which my exterior appearance and some happy expressions had given me in the world; it is certain I did not support the character well in private, that my friends and my acquaintance led this untractable bear about like a lamb, and that confining my sarcasms to severe but general truths, I was never capable of saying an uncivil thing to any person whatsoever. (210–11)

This passage shows how Rousseau never even approximated the churlish integrity of Diogenes, who would never stoop to such dissimulation. In fairness, however, we can also see that here and in the child-abandonment scenes of the *Confessions* Rousseau has chosen a mode of self-exposure far riskier than anything that his contemporaries ever attempted. Anyone can be praised for honesty; only Rousseau wishes to be congratulated for his poor job at dissimulation.

It is here, however, that we encounter one of the paradoxes inherent in the practice of parrhesiastic self-examination: the disclosure of one's former acts of dissimulation. Rousseau has just told us—truthfully, we assume—of his attempt to appear misanthropic rather than overtly tender toward his well-wishers. He wishes to appear before others as a "bear" rather than a "lamb," while (truthfully) admitting that the imposture was never particularly successful. Yet such behavior violates one of the first principles of Cynicism, the "absence of dissemblance to the point of dramatization" (*FP* 110), the deliberate rudeness being designed to shake others out of their conventional values. It is an odd admission for a would-be Cynic to make.

Moreover, such admissions of dissimulation threaten the contract between readers and author in autobiography, the contract that holds that everything contained within the autobiography is (as far as the author believes) truthful. Since the younger Rousseau depicted by the autobiographer Rousseau seems so ready to lie or dissimulate to others, why should we believe him now? Rousseau's habit of rationalizing his former behavior to reassert his virtue, as he does so unconvincingly in episodes like the child-abandonment passages, throws further doubts upon the truthfulness of his *Confessions.* It is the peculiar vulnerability of moments like these in his autobiographical texts that began to invert his reputation for truthfulness and gave him the reputation for lies and rationalizations that haunts him to this day. The subsequent hostility engendered by his lies and rationalizations indicates just how important his *parrhesia,* his absolute truthfulness, had been to his literary reputation at an earlier stage of his career.

Rousseau's task of self-definition in the *Confessions* is almost completely negative, demonstrating how he lacks the most commonplace masculine attributes, and how he flouts the most minimal masculine duties. Rousseau shows himself rejecting the duties of either husband or father that would define him as an adult man in relation to women or children. He fails to take full moral responsibility for his own acts, and he openly depicts his almost shameful eagerness to influence others' opinions of himself. Rousseau's negation of conventional, adult, superordinate masculinity creates a mixture of traits that can appear oddly childish.[56] He refuses to surrender to what Judith Butler would term the "regimes of intelligibility" governing the adult male of his own era.[57] Rousseau has chosen one form of Cynic independence, the inversion of conventional values of masculinity, over another form, the traditional masculine self-mastery represented Diogenes.

This choice has provoked the intense hostility, tempered with admiration, of readers ever since the *Confessions* were first printed. Rousseau, even when he pretends to be cynically indifferent, consistently violates the norms of masculinity that demand that a real man take his lumps without tears, complaints, or recriminations. Rousseau's affectations, his embarrassing lapses into erotic fantasy or perverse sexual practices, his feigned indifference, his emotionalism, his inadvertent cruelty, all these qualities reveal the contradictions and difficulties in the more conventional definitions of masculinity found in his own period. Because the *Confessions* show a flesh-and-blood Rousseau actively attempting to put his values into effect in the midst of a hostile and uncomprehending society, it is an invaluable document of what happens to a philosophical concept like independence when situated in a particular historical time and place. In this respect, the *Confessions,* even as they show Rousseau falling far below Diogenes' ascetic standard, represent a distinguished eighteenth-century example of the "lives and opinions" genre of philosophical history pioneered by Laertius.

The Disintegration of Rousseau's Public Image

Though Rousseau had been threatening to publish the *Confessions* for years, the consequences of publication had been very different from what he had intended. In the famous phrase of the opening paragraphs, Rousseau had vowed to bare all his depravities and misdeeds, warning, "Let any man who dares, say 'I was a better man than he.'" This is fully in keeping with his desired public image as a truth teller. Rousseau's public readings from the *Confessions* had certainly garnered him the attention that he desired in the 1770s, when he was otherwise unable to print his own works. He had not anticipated, however, the extent to which his recorded misdeeds would overshadow the rest of the *Confessions.* Readers in both France and England found the work distasteful for a variety of reasons: old enemies, whether orthodox or philosophical, found them as vain and self-obsessed as ever.

As demonstrated by the quotation from "Character of Rousseau" (1799) that stands as the chapter's third epigraph, the now-confirmed and fully publicized story of his abandoned children made it impossible for his once-loyal English followers in England to accept "his pretensions to philanthropy."[58] After such revelations, his audience, no matter how loyal, could no longer accept at face value Rousseau's own description of himself as a model of honesty and integrity, let alone "philanthropy." For one thing, Rousseau seemed capable of accusing himself of actions pettier, more ungenerous, and yet more shameless or even monstrous in the aggregate than anything his worst enemies could have invented. This was as true of the child abandonment as it was of his rather awkward history of infatuations and love affairs.

A still more serious difficulty for his once-loyal readers lay in the compulsive tendency to rationalization that accompanied the most scandalous materials. Though Rousseau confessed to many shameful acts, he refused to admit how these acts cumulatively affected his readers' notions of his moral character, which he stubbornly insisted remained fully and completely virtuous. In short, his resistance to the most obvious meanings suggested by those acts seemed less than honest. Finally, the very openness with which Rousseau discussed his lapses into dissimulation opened the possibility that his much-publicized sensibility and honesty had been false and artificial all along. Rousseau's parrhesiastic role was therefore not simply undone, but inverted, so that he became a symbol of the falsity, hypocrisy, and lies of the Enlightenment.

Under the pressure of the scandals and the rationalizations offered by the *Confessions,* even the supporters of Rousseau had to admit that he increasingly resembled the monster, madman, or compulsive liar that his enemies had long accused him of being since his break with the philosophes. In Niehues-Pröbsting's terms, the Rousseau on display in the *Confessions* embodied better than any other philosophe the "failure of the Enlightenment" and "the danger of reason being perverted, reason turning into irrationality and madness, reason being frustrated because of its own far too exalted expectations."[59] Niehues-Pröbsting maintains that the *combination* of Rousseau's life and writings, and the way that the life helped to ironize the self-descriptions contained in the writings, helped make him into a symbol of "reason being perverted" and therefore a symbol of a broader "failure of the Enlightenment."

The *Monthly Review,* which had always been among his staunchest supporters, reflected this change in its review of the first installment of the *Confessions.*[60] The Monthly Reviewer can scarcely believe that Rousseau would have wished to publish these kinds of stories about himself, preferring instead to blame "some greedy French bookseller, or some tool of the Parisian philosophers" for the circulation of "this strange mixture of secret, personal history, with the wild but sometimes ingenious effusions of an over-heated brain."[61]

The Monthly Reviewer allows that "this honest man laboured . . . under a certain *touch* of insanity," an insanity that formed "rather a useful ally than an enemy to his genius."[62] Nonetheless, he still values Rousseau's sensibility to the extent that it avoided the "insipid, ridiculous, trivial, and indecent."[63] Yet he cannot understand why an "honest man" would insist on exposing not merely himself, but his former lovers, to the public's derision:

> —Another circumstance will greatly contribute to hurt the reputation of this strange man, and that is, the freedom he uses in exposing to censure and contempt the reputation of others: for while we allow him to dishonour *himself,* and to cover himself with dirt before the eyes of the Public (which however we think a cynical and impertinent business), we find no pretext that can diminish the atrocity of his exhibiting the Countess of *Warens* to public view in the manner he has done. She was his benefactress, as we have seen;—she was a woman of quality;—he thought her an *angel,* but he *must* have known that the stories he has told of her would inevitably make her pass for a *wh[or]e;* and he *might* have known, that he himself would pass for a cynical fool in the judgment of those who should read the following sentence: *Her constitution* (speaking of Madame Warens) *was as cold as ice: she would have admitted* (to express the matter much more modestly than our Author has done) *twenty suitors every day, with a safe conscience; for she could have no moral scruples, as she had no lascivious desires.* —All this is out of nature and probability; and were it not so, our Author had no decent or honest vocation to reveal *his* amours with this lady, nor *hers* with her preceptor, her servant, &c.[64]

As a document in the history of the concept of cynicism, this passage is illuminating because it shows not a cynically misanthropic Rousseau but a "cynical and impertinent" Rousseau covering himself with dirt before the eyes of the public. In other words, "cynicism" here means something closer to "shamelessly indifferent to public outrage." The Monthly Reviewer has criticized Rousseau for violating precisely the kinds of decorum that the parrhesiast must challenge. The Reviewer, however, has another problem with Rousseau: his excessive sensibility, which has become associated with his shameful excesses, not his more socially acceptable moments.

Note also that the seductive sentiments found in *Julie, or, The New Heloise,* and so beloved by his English readers, become threatening at the point when Rousseau, now the "cynical and impertinent" writer soiling his own reputation, demonstrates how sensibility can lead to sexual contact between servants and mistresses. The Monthly Reviewer can comprehend Rousseau's desire to expose himself, except that this desire also reveals the existence of sexual desires crossing class lines. Such an act of Cynic self-exposure makes Rousseau into a "cynical fool" and Madam Warens into nothing more than his "wh—e." It is precisely this nightmare vision of a shameless, excessive, cynically transgressive sensibility that will haunt Burke and the Anti-Jacobins in just nine years, because Rousseau's seductive sensibility leads not to some form of social harmony but to a total collapse of social hierarchies.

Following the publication of the *Confessions,* critics used Rousseau's own parrhesiastic disclosures to note the gap between Rousseau's sentimental professions and his unsentimental, self-interested actions. This opened the way to regard Rousseau not as a philosophical hero or tender Man of Feeling, but as a liar and dissimulator. The *Confessions* also provided his readers a thoroughly plausible psychological account of his own extraordinary powers of verbal rationalization. Rousseau, in the words of one critic, had decided that "Having examined himself and producing no evidence of an *inner feeling* of wishing to do harm, he moved inexorably to the conclusion that he was naturally good, prior to word or deed. . . . His own actions, since they were performed by him, were axiomatically good or, alternatively, lacked any moral significance."[65] Even supporters like the *Monthly Review* became disillusioned with Rousseau's inability to square his insolent behavior with his eloquent words.

Having done away with Rousseau's reputation for honesty and sensibility, the *Confessions* also made it possible to dismiss even his philosophical writing as a fraud or symptom of madness. Rousseau's entire career could now be dismissed as a product of uncontrolled misanthropy, and his writings regarded as "the wild but sometimes ingenious effusions of an over-heated brain." By reducing Rousseau to a mere misanthrope or hypocrite, the post-*Confessions* discussion of Rousseau treated his now-sordid public image as a simple inversion of the sentimental idealism elaborated in his writings.

In this inversion of the would-be philosophical hero into Lucianic sham and philosophizer, Rousseau's public image split along the conventional lines of ancient Cynicism. Rousseau was both Diogenes *and* Peregrinus Proteus, as Wieland realized when he wrote novels about both historical figures using Rousseau as their basis. Yet Rousseau's contradictory role as figurehead and enemy of the Enlightenment philosophes helped to transform him into one of the first models of modern, lowercase cynicism, because he represented not only philosophic reason, but also the historical forces that defeated the ideals of philosophic reason. Rousseau, or at least the Rousseau of his enemies' vengeful caricatures, represented the modernity that the philosophes did not anticipate, but helped to bring about: not Reason but rationalization; not tolerance but indifference; not skepticism but disbelief; not independence but distrust; not sensibility but empty professions of feeling. The wreckage of Rousseau's aspirations and ideals became a potent partisan symbol of Enlightenment reason's historical failure.

FIVE

Edmund Burke and the Counter-Enlightenment Attack on the "Philosopher of Vanity"

I beg leave to subscribe my assent to Mr Burke's creed on the Revolution of France. I admire his eloquence, I approve his politics, I adore his Chivalry, and I can almost excuse his reverence for Church establishments. I have sometimes thought of writing a dialogue of the dead, in which Lucian, Erasmus, and Voltaire should mutually acknowledge the danger of exposing an old *superstition to the contempt of the blind and fanatic multitude.*

—Edward Gibbon, *Memoirs of My Life* (ca. 1791)

With horrified satisfaction, conservatives saw the French Revolution degenerate into terror and war. Nothing since then has nourished the conservative image of humanity more strongly. It thinks it knows that human nature, set loose here and now, deserves no optimism or glowing phrases.

—Peter Sloterdijk, *Critique of Cynical Reason*

THOUGH ONE OF THE LAST PHILOSOPHERS to attempt imitating Diogenes' parrhesiastic "way of life," Jean-Jacques Rousseau helped anchor the concept of cynicism in the contemporary world of moral and political argument. This reorientation of Cynicism occurred when Rousseau was mocked and vilified by British conservative writers.[1] While events unfolded in Revolutionary France, these writers ridiculed the deceased Rousseau, the one-time Citizen of the World and modern Diogenes, for being an unregenerate Cynic and disillusioned misanthrope. They jeered and belittled the defenseless Rousseau, the better to note the irony that it was *this* man—a man incapable of either trust or human attachment—who had the nerve to offer himself as a philosopher of universal benevolence. In their polemical reading of Rousseau, his sentimental philosophy was merely a pose, a hypocritical sleight of hand designed to conceal his selfishness and pass off his churlish faultfinding as the righteous indignation of an honest man.[2]

Yet these writers, as contemptuous as they were about Rousseau's clumsy attempts to manipulate his audience, worried that the less sophisticated part of the public could still be taken in. Consequently, they labored to reach the broader, less determinate, more popular audience whose opinions had suddenly assumed real political importance in the wake of Rousseau and the Revolution.[3] Hence, the need for what soon became a regular manufacture of governmentally approved and -subsidized opinion in the press: first in a pair of dependable daily newspapers in 1793, then in the "Anti-Jacobin" journal with a host of other journals from 1798 onward. All were devoted largely to "Church and King" propaganda and seasoned with copious amounts of ridicule targeting Rousseau and his "Jacobin" followers at home and abroad.[4] In the early years of the Revolution, Pitt's government spent £5000 a year just to keep these presses running, and distributed its money generously enough that at least nine or ten newspapers pelted Londoners with such stories and images on a daily or tri-weekly basis.[5] So this polemical battle over Rousseau and the Revolution was not simply a matter of debate or persuasion, but a highly coordinated publicity war, initiated or steered by lesser versions of Burke or Pitt in the presses centered in London, and responded to by Wollstonecraft, Paine, Godwin, and their own followers in the press and in the radical political clubs and societies throughout the countryside.[6]

In disseminating this highly effective caricature of Rousseau as a fraudulent philosophizer, Burke and the British conservative press reduced Rousseau over and over again to the most humiliating episodes in the *Confessions*, while drawing a convincing causal connection between his shameless Cynicism and his self-interested rationalizations. Through this unceasing vilification of Rousseau, the post-Enlightenment Cynic was not merely linked with established Cynic traits like misanthropy and shamelessness, but increasingly joined with emerging traits like hypocritical dissimulation and self-interested verbal manipulation.[7] Of course, in this convergence of Cynic and misanthrope, we still see the outlines of the early modern snarling Cynic, still present in Johnson's oft-reprinted 1755 *Dictionary* definition of "Cynick" ("philosopher of the snarling or currish sort; a follower of Diogenes; a rude man; a snarler; a misanthrope").[8] Rousseau, however, as an idiosyncratic modern Diogenes, had begun to fill the concept of Cynicism with new content, which included the failed Enlightenment philosophe along with the sometimes misanthropic disillusionment of the superannuated "man of feeling," an eighteenth-century character type sometimes termed a "benevolent misanthrope" or "sentimental cynic."[9]

Burke and his followers' travesty of Rousseau constituted one of the most successful and enduring acts of political redescription in British history, to the extent that Burke's interpretation still influences contemporary liberal and conservative views of Rousseau and the Revolution.[10] Nonetheless, Burke's writings upon Rousseau display qualities of projection, identification, and disavowal that resemble earlier ambivalent treatments of the Cynics, suggesting that we could fruitfully explore Burke's responses to Rousseau's cynicism, to see what it exposes to view in Burke. Such a view pushes to the foreground two striking resemblances of the two: their ambiguous class status and their heavy reliance upon their gifts of redescription and rationalization, two qualities that help us recognize Burke's own affinities with modern cynicism. As Pocock has observed, "[Burke's] theory of revolution . . . stressed not the independent power of men of wealth, but the uncontrolled energy of men of talent; he feared the rise of a revolutionary intelligentsia, made up of the kind of men he might easily have been himself."[11]

Thus, in the same way that the popular disturbances of the seventeenth and eighteenth centuries inspired the antipopulist and populist images of Cynicism explored in chapter 3, the Revolutionary era's recentering of Cynicism offered yet another prescriptive definition of who "the people" were and how "they" should behave. In this instance, Rousseau's ambiguous social status, bad morals, and cosmopolitan identity helped Burke define the boundaries of "the people," not on the bases of geography, lineage, or creed, but on the bases of history, institutions, and beliefs, to which he gave the polemical name "prejudices."[12] Thus, by virtue of the *Reflections'* addresses to a public willing to identify itself by its fundamental "prejudices," Burke summoned into existence a virtual public of loyal Britons, devoted to the institutions of "Church and King," contemptuous of the French, and proudly chauvinistic and class-stratified. For Burke, it was this segment of the public who were the genuine "lovers of freedom" and who therefore represented the truest form of "patriotism," not the philosophical radicals who had inherited those terms from the Wilkites and Opposition.[13]

Over and against this virtual public, however, stood Rousseau's monstrous creation "Jacobinism," which represented both the cosmopolitan Enlightenment and the rapid radicalization and militarization of the Revolution. Rousseau's Jacobinism represented a more alien and unpredictable version of the public, because it comprehended all the potential violence of a fully active and mobilized "people," whose new political role was being adumbrated by Rousseau's admirer Robespierre. Unlike earlier forms of popular political mobilization (including the American Revolution), Jacobinism terrified Burke because it attacked not individual politicians but entire cultural institutions wholesale, tearing apart the historical guarantors of stability and continuity—religion, family, and the nation—that gave the British "people" their fundamental meaning and unity. To those who would tax him with his former political ties to the American Revolution and the Opposition, Burke defended himself by saying that his "whole politics" were devoted to defeating the cause of Jacobinism, which he defined as "an attempt (hitherto but too successful) to eradicate prejudice out of the minds of men, for the purpose of putting all power and authority into the hands of the persons capable of occasionally enlightening the minds of the people. For this purpose the Jacobins have resolved to destroy the whole frame and fabric of the old societies of the world and to regenerate them after their fashion."[14]

In their nationalistic hostility to Rousseau, Edmund Burke and the British conservative writers helped to assemble some of the most important terms in the semantic cluster that helped create a modern, disillusioned and disillusioning cynicism. To denounce Rousseau's supposed irreligion, some labeled him a cynical disbeliever, atheist, or (in Wesley's words) "brother infidel" along with his one-time enemies Voltaire and Hume.[15] To call attention to his failings as a husband and father, others like the *Monthly Review* denounced him as a "cynical fool," shamelessly indifferent to his own honor or his family's needs. To criticize his false sensibility, some labeled him a selfish hypocrite more attached to his international literary reputation than to his own children.

Consequently, when taken as an ensemble of traits, Rousseau's posthumous image helped define some of the leading attributes of the modern, lowercase cynic. All these new meanings were the result of the activities of the "Counter-Enlightenment" in Britain from 1790 to 1815, from the rise of Robespierre and the Jacobins through the surrender of Napoléon.[16] Moreover, through the miserable fate of Rousseau, conservative writers were able to denounce the dangerous vanity of the Enlightenment philosophes in claiming to direct both reflection and social action for society at large.[17] Developing a conservative trope that remains potent to this day, Burke mocked the philosophes for their belief that an entity as complex as society, which is the result of untold individuals' blind actions and their incremental refinements to institutions over time, could be rationally planned and directed in this manner.[18] Yet the new meanings for "cynicism" produced during this period survived its specifically reactionary political-historical context and have endured to this day, so that "cynicism" has become one of our most important contemporary terms for the forms of persuasion and resistance generated by the political workings of power and publicity. Modern cynicism refers to *both* the manipulative practices of politicians and publicists, and the popular resistance to such practices.

I should note, however, that cynicism's emergence as part of the modern political lexicon occurred not in any theoretical discussion of the concept on its own, but rather during a series of polemics devoted to other topics, especially Hobbes's and Mandeville's deprecatory treatment of human nature, motivation, and reason. Here we may find the origin of Keenan's cynical "doctrine" that "the ultimate motives of human action are self-interest and the quest for power."[19] This degrading picture of human nature, and the self-seeking reason it entailed, was eventually termed by D'Israeli—who closely followed Rousseau's earlier arguments against egoistic reason—as "cynical," but this was never the whole story regarding the concept.

The other semantic dimension of Cynicism that Rousseau opened up in the course of his career was the concept's *rhetorical* dimension of persuasion and self-interested quasi-deliberation, which we refer to nowadays as "cynical manipulation": we find this rhetorical dimension in the *Discourse on Inequality*'s sleeping philosopher, who "argue[d] with himself a little" to ignore the noises that would disturb his sleep, or in Rousseau's fellow philosophes arguing with him over their right to the pleasures of the theater in Geneva, or indeed in Rousseau's account of the deliberations that led him to abandon his children and rename his action a victory for philosophy.

In other words, the manipulative Cynic exerts his reason to accommodate his words and deeds to the dictates of his desires, not the other way around. It is this habit of verbal accommodation that I have termed Rousseau's self-interested "rationalization," which imitates the forms of open argument, but only to evade more honest forms of (self-)assessment or deliberation. In the words of Adorno, "Reason in the service of unreason—in Freud's language, "rationalization,"—rushes to the aid of opinion and so hardens it that nothing more can affect it or reveal its absurdity.".[20] It is this self-enclosed, rationalizing quality of Rousseau's that flagrantly contradicts his claim to being a free and unprejudiced observer of his own actions, after denying similar claims by his fellow philosophes.[21] As odd or idiosyncratic as Rousseau was as a man, however, this trait of rationalization featured in the *Confessions* would have a spectacular future, in the form of "opinion." In effect, Rousseau's and the philosophes' political scapegoating in the 1790s helped identify a historically emergent class of intellectuals—the professional shapers of public opinion whose job it is to channel, consolidate, and direct the public's beliefs and opinions. As they go about their business, the members of this class label one another, and find themselves labeled in turn, cynics. Rousseau's vilification as a morally compromised, rationalizing philosophe suggests the genealogical link between the philosophes and modern cynicism, changes driven by the nationalism and popular mobilizations of the early nineteenth century.[22] It becomes this class's function to publicize power and rationalize its dictates as best it can, though it also takes on the moral onus of the public's contempt when its verbal rationalizations and redescriptions strain the public's credulity. That is when the mutual accusations of "cynicism" really begin to fly.

To get some sense of the professionalization of the management of public opinion since Walpole or the Wilkes crisis, we should recognize how the Diogenes featured in Fielding's *Dialogue* suggests that an Opposition writer could never transcend his hireling status in comparison with the grandees and great men who wielded real power, while Lyttelton's Diogenes only exposes his creator's uncertainties regarding his proper political role during the Wilkite disturbances.[23] In contrast, the very public careers of Burke, Southey, Cobbett, Canning, Croker, and others indicate at the very least the high stakes for those directing public opinion between the 1790s and the 1820s. Consequently, the modern cynic elaborated in the Revolutionary and Regency period is a symptomatic figure, inseparable from the elaboration, measurement, and manipulation of political communications in the modern nation-state, and especially revealing of the tensions between the competing notions of the "public" and its "opinions" during this period.

This chapter begins by showing how Diogenes and Rousseau together helped Burke to formulate the *Reflections*' epochal defense of "prejudice," by representing an elite cosmopolitan philosophy consistently hostile to the claims of popular prejudice, superstition, and ceremony. In other words, Burke has characteristically aligned "the people" and their cherished prejudices and traditions against the philosophes' ahistorical views of reason while vowing to defend the people against such depredations. In this respect, Burke's fundamental gesture was to side himself with the unenlightened, who now represented the "less enquiring . . . whom Providence dooms to live on trust" (195–96). This realignment of reason with a rather passive, loyal, and above all, *trusting* multitude allowed Burke to discover a form of popular reason hitherto neglected by the Enlightenment, which inhered in the slow, blind processes governing societies over long periods of time.[24]

The following section analyzes Godwin's post-Revolutionary treatment of the Rousseauean misanthrope Fleetwood in his 1805 novel of the same name. Rousseau's name and legacy pervades Godwin's novel, which is devoted to showing how its lead character's misanthropic and prejudiced cynicism eventually becomes a form of derangement that isolates and imprisons him, a loss of reason from which only his devoted wife, Mary, can rescue him. The final section describes how D'Israeli's portrait of Hobbes retrospectively inserts the seventeenth-century philosopher into the emerging Cynic themes of selfishness, power, and rationalization that Rousseau helped to introduce into the concept during his critique of the earlier egoistic philosophers. The hallmark of D'Israeli's Hobbes, along with the other "polished Cynics" described in this biographical essay, is a dismissive view of the human race that only rationalizes his selfish accommodations with power and helps him to cloak his unsavory attitudes and behavior (65). These cynical qualities of rationalization and dissimulation, writ large in all its institutions of power and publicity, are what help to create Adorno's vision of the "Opinion Delusion Society," a society in which publicity has preemptively fortified it against the most basic questioning or debate of its conventional opinions, no matter how pathological, irrational, or toxic their effects.

Burke's Defense of Prejudice against Philosophic Reason

Diogenes in Burke's *Note-Book*

Burke's project of defending the vulgar and their prejudices from philosophic scrutiny extended throughout his life and had a variety of targets over the years. One of Burke's earliest discussions of this topic occurred in his "Several Scattered Hints concerning Philosophy and Learning," written in his *Note-Book* some thirty or forty years before the *Reflections*. Unsurprisingly, considering his educational background and training, Burke's initial meditation of these topics occurred in a commonplace book amplification of a Diogenes anecdote.[25]

While reflecting upon one of Cicero's most famous stories concerning Diogenes (Cicero, *Tusc. Disp.* 1.43, 104–5; DL 6.79), Burke defends certain vulgar "forms and ceremonies" from the "refinement" of "reason" (90): "When Diogenes was dying, his friends desired to know how he would have his Body disposed of. 'Throw it into the fields,' says he. They objected that it might be liable to be devoured by wild Beasts. 'Then set my Staff by me to drive them off.' One answered, 'You will then be insensible and unable to do it.' 'So shall I be' (sayd he) 'of their injuries'" (91). Burke reads this story as a tale of a philosopher who has gone too far "in the road of refinement" (90) to understand the popular customs he would ridicule.[26] "I like the vivacity of the Turn in this Story" (91), writes Burke. Yet he still finds the philosophic reason depicted there to be seriously faulty, and goes on to discover the real reasoning behind such funeral ceremonies: "[Diogenes'] philosophy is shewy [continues Burke] but has no substance; for to what would he persuade us by this odd example? Why, that our Bodies being after Death neither capable of pain nor pleasure, we should not trouble our heads about them. But let this pass into a general principle, and thence into a general practice, and the ill consequence is obvious" (91).

In his eagerness to demonstrate his superiority over the rude or the popular, Burke's Diogenes has neglected the most important function of funeral ceremonies, their usefulness for the living. And the prejudices surrounding death lead Burke to consider those surrounding birth and the relations of the sexes. Burke, however, treats these issues with an unmistakable note of religious mystery. Burke therefore criticizes Diogenes in terms that anticipate his later critique of the "converts of Rousseau" (75) in the *Reflections:*

> It is not easily conceived [continues Burke in his *Note-book*] what use funeral ceremonies (for my story led me to think) are to mankind. Triffling [*sic*] as they may seem, they nourish humanity, they soften in some measure the rigour of Death, and they inspire humble, sober and becoming thoughts. They throw a decent Veil over the weak and dishonourable circumstances of our Nature. What shall we say to that philosophy, that would strip it naked? Of such sort is the wisdom of those who talk of the Love, the sentiment, and the thousand little dalliances that pass between the Sexes, in the gross way of mere procreation. . . . I have read some authors who talk of the Generation of mankind as getting rid of an excrement; who lament bitterly their being subject to such a weakness. They think they are being extremely witty in saying it is a dishonourable action and we are obliged to hide it in the obscurity of night. It is hid it's true, not because it is dishonourable, but because it is mysterious. (91–92)

Burke has paired funeral ceremonies with the mutual attachment of the sexes, while investing both practices with a religiosity and emotion foreign to the skeptical Hume's earlier treatment of the topic, which simply uses the tale to demonstrate the "Liveliness and Ferocity of [Diogenes'] Temper."[27] In fact,

Burke has portrayed these ceremonies and institutions as specifically venerable and sacrosanct in ways that the skeptical Hume chose not to.

In Burke's more overtly antiphilosophical treatment, both the mysteries of Love and those of generation are the common targets of a demystifying philosophy that would metaphorically strip away any value for which it could not account. Emblematic of such a rude and dismissive attitude are the would-be wits criticized in Burke for treating the "Generation of mankind as getting rid of an excrement," unable to conceive of the productions of their bodies as anything more than waste.[28] The philosophic reason represented by Diogenes and his like-minded authors is false because it is reductive and incapable of recognizing the wider, social purposes behind ceremonies, and by extension, the prejudices that would "throw a decent Veil over the weak and dishonourable circumstances of our Nature."

What Burke has brought to this allegory of philosophic reason impotently challenging vulgar prejudice is the eminently *political* awareness of the symbolic importance of "forms and ceremonies," an insight missing from Hume's more disengaged treatment. "Let this [philosophical contempt for the now useless dead body] pass into a general principle," Burke writes, "and thence into a general practice, and the ill consequence is obvious." These ceremonies are not conducted for the sake of the individuals placed on the funeral bier, but for the community that survives them. As we will see in the *Reflections,* an unthinking prejudice throws a veil over something precious to the community, and Burke would protect both the prejudice and the mysteries it hides from a philosophic reason "that would strip it naked."

Prejudice in the *Reflections*

By the time of the fall of the Bastille, the march of the Parisians to the Versailles, and Richard Price's 1790 sermon urging his audience in the Revolution Society "to consider ourselves as citizens of the world," Burke's public defense of prejudice had taken on the status of a fundamental gesture of political transvaluation.[29] Burke was by this time consciously overturning the meanings of a key term in a half-century's worth of Enlightenment polemics against the forces of unthinking superstition and unreason.[30] Moreover, Burke's celebration of prejudice was a double assault, attacking both the philosophes' claim that their observations were free and unblinkered, and the authority they derived from such powers of observation.[31] Burke's most important rhetorical move, however, was to transform prejudice into something belonging to "us" and not to "them."[32] He had recaptured a key piece of his opponents' vocabulary and used it to define both himself and his potential following. Consequently, prejudices—and those who held them—no longer involved the "interested error" propounded by a small group of men to thwart humanity's progress but instead reflected the unarticulated yet powerful views of the unphilosophical public.[33]

In one of the most notorious passages in the *Reflections*, Burke asserts: "You see, Sir, that in this enlightened age I am bold enough to confess, that we are generally men of untaught feelings; that instead of casting away all our old prejudices, we cherish them to a very considerable degree" (183). For the "we" that Burke identifies himself with, the "men of untaught feelings," have abandoned any notion that political authority proceeds from secure possession of Truth, either religious or Enlightened. Instead, political authority resides at the rhetorical level of prejudice and opinion and feeling, in the zone of partial knowledge and the benefit of the doubt. For Burke, prejudices, no matter how fantastic or objectively untrue, remain more politically effective than the operations of reason because their subjectively felt "truth" can be cherished in ways that scientifically confirmed observations cannot, while enlisting both feeling and reason on behalf of some salutary belief.[34] Despite the cavils of philosophers, it is only prejudice, in its powerfully prerational and affective influence over individuals, that can assemble a public together to act as a nation.

Consequently, Burke's overtly prejudiced public inhabited a broad range of historical, national, social, and domestic relationships and identities that the Enlightenment's "Citizens of the World" had ignored, including the plebeian, the nationalistic, the pious, and the feminine. Burke's celebration of everyday attachments, matched with his critique of the philosophes' artificial isolation, undid the traditional elitism of the philosopher as "Man of Reason" that had been part of Western philosophy's self-image from Socrates and Diogenes onward.[35] Now the philosophe's apparent *lack* of such attachments resembled vanity, hypocrisy, isolation, or outright pathology, not the male philosopher's conventional superiority to his fellow men. Hence, Burke, with his overt gendering of the cosmopolitan philosopher's detached "way of life," helped reduce him to either a harmlessly celibate bachelor or shameless libertine. Thus, Rousseau's abject version of cosmopolitan philosophy, along with such mannish female Jacobins as Mary Wollstonecraft or Mary Hays, represented famous examples of the Revolutionary "gender trouble" that provoked the "gender panic" of conservative female writers like Hannah More or Elizabeth Hamilton.[36]

Nonetheless, to distinguish his and his public's "prejudices" from the philosophes' heartless rationalism, Burke works up a consistent linkage between national and domestic attachments throughout the *Reflections*, a strategy that reaches its climax in the famously chivalric descriptions of Marie Antoinette. In this emblematic episode, Burke reverently offers up Marie Antoinette as a beautiful artifact, one whose pathos has been magnified by subsequent threats of exposure, disrobing, and rape. Burke then announces his alarm that "the pleasing illusions, which made power gentle, and obedience liberal . . . are to be dissolved by this new conquering empire of light and reason" (171).[37] Burke's allegory of Enlightenment and prejudice transforms Marie Antoinette into a sacred object of "pleasing illusions" that must not be violated by "this new conquering empire of light and reason." In other words, Marie Antoinette becomes Burke's symbol of prejudice and its mysterious operations upon a receptive audience. Prejudices are beautiful, pleasing, and powerful, even when threatened, and invested with all the allure and authority of the young dauphiness on display at Versailles.

With this image of Marie Antoinette hovering in the background, Burke repeatedly personifies prejudice as a beautiful, partially dressed woman threatened with exposure by a crudely masculine philosophy:

> All the decent drapery of life is to be rudely torn off. All the super-added ideas, furnished from the wardrobe of a moral imagination, which the heart owns, and the understanding ratifies, as necessary to cover the defects of our naked shivering nature, and to raise it to dignity in our own estimation, are to be exploded as a ridiculous, absurd, and antiquated fashion. (171)

Prejudice is what attaches us to our nation and makes us love it as part of ourselves. Prejudice is the "decent drapery of life," the "super-added ideas," the "pleasing illusions" that clothe nations and cover "our naked shivering nature." Unlike the superficial philosophy that would ridicule the most venerable prejudices for being out-of-date, prejudices derive from a nation's "antient opinions and rules of life" and make us value it precisely for its antiquity (172).

In contrast to these "pleasing illusions," including the comfort, stability, and protection afforded by such unreflective prejudices, Burke offers a brutal series of redescriptions, indeed a full-scale lecture on rhetorical *paradiastole*, designed to demystify the demystifying language of "this barbarous philosophy" (171) and where it will lead:

> On this scheme of things, a king is but a man; a queen is but a woman; a woman is but an animal; and an animal not of the highest order. All hom-

> age paid to the sex in general as such, and without distinct views, is to be regarded as romance and folly. Regicide and parricide, and sacrilege, are but fictions of superstition, corrupting jurisprudence by destroying its simplicity. The murder of a king, or a queen, or a bishop, or a father, are only common homicide; and if the people are by any chance, or in any way gainers by it, a sort of homicide much the most pardonable, and into which we ought not to make too severe a scrutiny. (171)

Prejudice, then, is all that shields us from the fearsome, almost Cynic leveling of existing social ranks and hierarchies into a "natural" state of animal existence and mutual predation. This state resembles Timon's misanthropic vision of the world as ruled by beasts (4.3.394), except that now these violent acts of desacralization ("animal" for "queen," etc.) have been assigned to a corporate agent not visible in *Timon:* "the people," on whose behalf the philosophes warn us against "too severe a scrutiny." (An interesting echo of what Burke himself is doing with his own version of the British "people.")

Yet Burke counters that such rhetorical acts can serve only as preemptive rationalizations for more physical acts of spoliation. More ominously, he warns that the chivalrous respect for feminine rank, along with the entire "mixed system of opinion and sentiment" (170) that sustained "manners" and deference for inherited rank throughout Europe (172), were no more than "prejudices" in the eyes of the revolutionaries at home and abroad.[38] Every historical institution that sustained European "civilization" (173) will be discarded with the disappearance of rank and religion, the "spirit of a gentleman and the spirit of religion" (173); even learning, the proudest possession of the philosophes, "will be cast into the mire, and trodden down under the hoofs of a swinish multitude" (173). The single, carefully delineated phrase "a swinish multitude," with its indefinite article as a protective fig leaf, nonetheless set off at least one burning of "an effigy of 'Burke riding a swine'" in Sheffield in 1792, along with countless other rejoinders to the phrase "swinish multitude."[39]

Nonetheless, Burke distinguishes between English and French philosophers by their willingness to think seriously about prejudice, which is ultimately the ability to think rationally about the irrationalities of history: "Many [British] men of speculation, instead of exploding general prejudices, employ their sagacity to discover the latent wisdom which prevails in them. If they find what they seek, and they seldom fail, they think it more wise to continue the prejudice, with the reason involved, than to cast away the coat of prejudice, and to leave nothing but the naked reason" (183). Thus, Burke's historicist, "conservative" critique of Enlightenment rationalism led him to treasure the "coat of prejudice" that protected our "naked reason." In so doing, he effectively redefined the social function of the intellectual class represented by the French philosophes, while charging British intellectuals with the job of protecting rather than exposing popular prejudices.[40] British prejudices must be protected against any hint of violation, especially from the "converts of Rousseau." Instead of violating prejudices with analysis or critique, British "men of speculation" have learned—or should learn—how to "employ their sagacity to discover the latent wisdom" in prejudices. In the *Reflections'* polemic against French rationalist philosophy, prejudice does not represent the inequalities that destroy societies, but the "latent wisdom" that holds them together, despite the conscious efforts of their members.

Yet we should never forget, as Burke's twentieth-century commentators occasionally do, that prejudice in Burke still retains some vestigial sense of *half* truth, an all-too-potent modification of the truth that lends it all its rhetorical power and political force.[41] It is to Burke's *Reflections* that we may apply part of Sloterdijk's memorable description of Nietzsche's "cynicism": it "offers a modified approach to 'saying the truth': [His approach to truth telling] is one of strategy and tactics, suspicion and disinhibition, pragmatics and instrumentalism."[42] Burke's one-time ally Philip Francis discovered this when he warned Burke from publishing the *Reflections,* both because of its potential damage to his reputation as a Whig and for its unaccountable "foppery" in defending Marie Antoinette, a woman with the bad reputation of an unchaste "Messalina."[43]

Burke reasonably begins by countering that it was not merely the historical individual Marie Antoinette with whom he was commiserating, but the extinction of that "chivalrous spirit" that had been the "great source of those manners which have been the pride and ornament of Europe for so many ages."[44] Yet Burke attains another, weirdly Rousseauean register when he reiterates the "truth" of his feelings, whatever their empirical basis:

> I tell you again, that the recollection of the manner in which I saw the queen of France, in the year 1774, and the contrast between that brilliancy, splendour, and beauty, with the prostrate homage of a nation to her, and the abominable scene of 1789, which I was describing, *did* draw tears from me and wetted my paper. These tears came again into my eyes, almost as often as I looked at the description; they may again. You do not believe this fact, nor that these are my real feelings; but that the whole is affected, or, as you express it, downright foppery. My friend, I tell you it is truth; and that

it is true, and will be truth, when you and I are no more; and will exist as long as men with their natural feelings shall exist.[45]

At the very moment where Burke asserts again and again his own certainty, the modern reader must wonder if Burke will allow any understanding of these things outside his own. This is Burke in Rousseau's own mode of self-asserted virtue and transparent feeling, the mode that allows him to ignore every other perspective and rationalize in an undisturbed fashion. Similarly, it is striking how some of the most compelling details of Burke's historical narratives in the *Reflections* turned out to be fictitious, and that he declined to correct them in subsequent editions: the character of Marie Antoinette, the identity of the loyal "centinel" who supposedly sacrificed himself for the royal family (164), and who turned up, very much alive, to converse with Richard Burke in 1791, as well as the actual occasions of the speakers and committees whom Burke criticizes for an impious glee over the king's downfall.[46] It was this kind of prejudice as half truth, and this kind of emotional argumentation, that respondents like Paine and Wollstonecraft fruitlessly tried to correct in their pamphlets; ultimately, the violent course of events in France made it impossible for the radicals to resist Burke's pessimistic reading of the revolutionaries, or the inveterate anti-French prejudices he had aligned with it.[47]

Burke's notion of prejudice, then, plays two roles in the formation of modern, political cynicism: in his influential attack upon the philosophes for cynically spreading disbelief in the guise of attacking prejudice but also in his own notion of prejudice as "latent wisdom." Burke's instrumental attitude toward prejudice positions British "men of speculation" in the crucial role of communicating and explicating its "latent wisdom" to a largely passive, unconscious mass audience incapable of recognizing it for themselves. In Burke's prescient model of the intellectual's role in a society of mass communications, it is Burke's "men of speculation" who will become Keenan's "insider-cynics" who mediate between the powerful and the powerless in the imperfectly democratic politics of public opinion. If, as the maxim tells us, states rest on nothing more than public opinion, then we can understand Burke to extend the maxim so that the state rests on nothing more substantial than prejudice.

Rousseau and Diogenes in the "Letter to a Member of the National Assembly"

Burke's next stage in his defense of prejudices against a Jacobin Enlightenment occurs in the "Letter to a Member of the National Assembly" (1791), in which he attacks Rousseau for his vanity in affecting the role of moralist and philosophizer. Burke echoes the philosophes' longtime complaints about Rousseau as a rude and vain modern Diogenes, and adds to those familiar accusations the newer charges of sentimental hypocrisy and fraudulence. Burke brands Rousseau, now the revolutionaries' and legislators' favorite model for their new Republic, the "insane *Socrates* of the National Assembly," echoing Plato, Laertius, and Wieland, when they in turn labeled Diogenes as a "Socrates out of his Senses"; Burke also recalls the time when the English had seen the "great professor and founder of the philosophy of vanity" in their own country.[48] Burke identifies a single overriding passion for this man, vanity: "It is from the same deranged eccentric vanity, that this, the insane *Socrates* of the National Assembly, was impelled to publish a mad Confession of his mad faults, and to attempt a new sort of glory, from bringing hardily to light the obscure and vulgar vices which we know may sometimes be blended with eminent talents" (48). It is fitting that Burke's own attack upon cosmopolitan, French models of philosophy should revert to this phrase of Laertius. In his adoption of "insane Socrates," Burke makes Rousseau into a representative of Enlightenment philosophy's excesses of reason, not reason itself.

Edward Duffy has argued that the immediate impetus of Burke's "Letter" was the French National Assembly's resolution to erect a commemorative statue to Rousseau, which was designed to "illustrate the enlightened and virtuous policy of the new regime as well as to repair in some measure the contumely that the old order had heaped upon the person and works of 'l'Homme de la nature et de la Vérité.'"[49] As Duffy points out, the National Assembly's gesture gives Rousseau a symbolic centrality for the new regime that Burke could readily exploit for his own purposes. Thus, Burke warns again and again that the Rousseauean Citizen of the World is in danger of becoming a literary, cultural, and even legislative model for British subjects.

As far as Burke is concerned, Rousseau's personal errors and vices, however pathetic or destructive they may have been in his own life, had nonetheless become *politically* problematic the moment when Rousseau was taken up as a public model by the National Assembly. As he had once commented on Diogenes' "shewy" philosophic stunts, "let this pass into a general principle, and thence into a general practice, and the ill consequence is obvious." Any society modeled upon Rousseau would treat virtue as mere abstract benevolence and produce whole armies of "Citizens of the World." According to Burke, citizens literally conceived as cosmopolitans suffused with a generalized, universal benevolence, however, would lack any of the immediate feelings of parental love or domestic ties so important to society. In other words, Rousseauean citizens would lack the local attachments—that is, the unthinking prejudices—that form the basis for national as well as domestic ties:

> It is that new-invented virtue which your masters [i.e., the French statesmen imitating Rousseau] canonize, that led their moral hero [Rousseau] constantly to exhaust the stores of his powerful rhetoric in the expression of universal benevolence; whilst his heart was incapable of harboring one spark of common parental affection. Benevolence to the whole species, and want of feeling for every individual with whom the professors come in contact, form the character of the new philosophy. . . . [Rousseau] melts with tenderness for those only who touch him by the remotest relation, and then, without one natural pang, casts away, as a sort of offal and excrement, the spawn of his disgustful amours, and sends his children to the hospital of foundlings. The bear loves, licks, and forms her young; but bears are not philosophers. Vanity, however, finds its account in reversing the train of our natural feelings. Thousands admire the sentimental writer; the affectionate father is hardly known in his parish. (49)

Burke's labeling of his antagonist as an "insane Socrates" condenses the old charges of pride, shamelessness, and vanity made against the earlier Cynics with the new, politicized accusations of effeminacy and unnatural hatred of his own offspring directed at the Rousseauean Citizen of the World. Rousseau, the "philosopher of Vanity," insists upon denying or neglecting his closest ties and duties to pursue a specious connection to the entire world. As a cosmopolitan, Rousseau predictably chooses a "universal benevolence" at the expense of his own offspring. Like the ancient Socrates out of his Senses, this philosopher is driven only by vanity masked by his philosophical enterprise. Most devastatingly, however, Burke points to the gap between Rousseau's public professions and private actions, crystallized in the contrast between the "sentimental writer" and the "affectionate father." For Burke and many others, Rousseau's inability to function as a father completely undermines any moral claim he wishes to make as a philosopher.

Echoing his earlier discussion in the *Note-Book* about the sacred prejudices surrounding the generation of children, Burke makes Rousseau into a monstrous figure incapable of even the most minimal attachments or domestic love. Burke's famous image of the bear that "loves, licks, and forms her young" provides an appropriate counterweight to this most flimsy and insubstantial of moralists. It is not the savage bear but the philosopher who is capable of abandoning his young. Instead, this philosopher, like the unnamed wits who ridicule the miracle of generation, simply discards his own offspring as so much "offal and excrement."

We should also note that Burke's famous image of the "bear [that] loves, licks, and forms her young" rewrites Rousseau's description in the *Confessions* of his bearish cynicism and harshness in polite circles. For Burke, Rousseau's philosophy has rendered him morally inferior to the bear, which after all is simply a product of nature, not the philosophy that has formed Rousseau in this monstrous fashion. Bears are not philosophers; nor should they be, when philosophers like Rousseau were unable or unwilling to follow the "train of our natural feelings" and raise their own young.

Finally, Burke seemed particularly disturbed by the theatricality and openness of Rousseau's self-portrait in the *Confessions* ("a mad Confession of his mad faults"), qualities that rendered him brutally indifferent toward his own children, yet also effeminate and hypocritical in his relations with other men. Rousseau the philosophizer is simply too "spurious, fictitious, and false" (50) to acknowledge his offspring the way that other men would. The French "Statesmen," however, do not wish to denounce him, but erect statues to him: "As the relation between parents and children is the first among the elements of vulgar, natural morality, they erect statues to a wild, ferocious, low-minded, hard-hearted father, of fine general feelings; a lover of his kind, but a hater of his kindred" (50). Rousseau, who once moralized against the hypocritical gap between verbal professions and outward behavior in works like the *Discourses* or the "Letter to d'Alembert," now represented to the highest degree this hypocritical quality for Burke and the Anti-Jacobins. In sum, the "philosophic gallantry" of Rousseau's *Julie, or, The New Heloise* (52) threatened to introduce an element of French falsity into the foundational British institutions of marriage and family.

From the point of view of the history of cynicism, one of the most interesting things about Burke's treatment of Rousseau the "insane *Socrates* of the National Assembly" is its palpable fear that the vain, mad, and misanthropic Rousseau could somehow transfer all his susceptibilities to the body politic as a whole. Rousseau's singularity, his mad individualism, serves as no defense from his influence, when he insists upon publishing his "mad Confession" and statesmen erect statues to him anyway. Misanthropy and distrust, oddly enough, somehow threaten to become universally imitated. With Rousseau now present to the British public as a dangerously foreign political and ethical model, such "philosophers of vanity" could be viewed as bearers of a form of distrust that seemed dangerously communicable to others; they represented a moral and political sickness that weakened the ideals of societies. In its compounding of Rousseauean misanthropy with a dangerously alien cosmopolitanism, Cynicism could be treated as a form of moral and political corruption, along with the traditional metaphorical associations of the "decay, degeneration, disintegration, and debasement" of the body politic as a whole.[50] Once again, the Cynic had become equated with what he had once tried to oppose, in this case, corruption, falsity, artificiality, hypocrisy, and vice.

Coda: Exit Diogenes in "An Appeal from the New to the Old Whigs"

When Burke was forced to retire from the Whig party in 1791, he reflected upon Diogenes one last time but chose to value him finally for his philosophical independence of opinion. Burke presented Diogenes as a man who announced his manhood by consciously choosing certain attachments and abandoning others, and who was able to accept his forced exile only because he had turned it into the basis of his philosophy (DL 6.49). I would also argue that this change in attitude toward Sinope's most famous exile suggests that Burke's writing was more indebted to Enlightenment cosmopolitanism than his own rhetoric in the *Reflections* or the "Appeal" might indicate.

In what is perhaps one of the last serious, rhetorically based humanist reflections upon Diogenes, Burke announces his separation from his old associates in the following manner:

> Whether Diogenes the Cynic was a true philosopher, cannot easily be determined. He has written down nothing. But the sayings of his which are handed down by others, are lively; and may be easily and aptly applied on many occasions by those whose wit is not so perfect as their memory. This Diogenes (as everyone will recollect) was citizen of a little bleak town situated on the coast of the Euxine, and exposed to all the buffets of that unhospitable sea. He lived at a great distance from those weather-beaten walls, in ease and indolence, and in the midst of literary leisure, when he was informed that his townsmen had condemned him to be banished from Sinope; he answered coolly, "And I condemn them to live in Sinope."
>
> The gentlemen of the party in which Mr. Burke has always acted, in passing upon him the sentence of retirement, have done nothing more than to confirm the sentence which he had long before passed upon himself.[51]

Burke's use of Diogenes is particularly striking because it reveals new dimensions of vulnerability and aggression on Burke's part, and a new willingness to identify with the earlier philosopher's wit and self-sufficiency, even when they appear at the expense of his former "townsmen," the Whigs. Now that even his former friends accuse him of deserting his attachment to the Whig party, Burke begins to appear again in the guise with which he began his career, an itinerant Irish adventurer. Emulating the performance of Diogenes before the gaping Sinopean crowd (see DL 6.49), Burke presents himself as being systematically stripped of his dearest attachments, even while his writings and sayings are being digested and collated by hostile editors, to have their inconsistencies exposed to the public (100).

These hostile digests, Burke claims, are responsible for the accusation that he is inconsistent. Yet Burke claims for himself a much grander "consistency" (100) than what his opponents will recognize and asserts that any sympathetic reader should be able to discern its outlines in his writing. Burke's consistency, like that of Diogenes, lies not in any specific writing or saying attributed to him but in an ethos that has guided him throughout his career: his defense of vulgar prejudices. "Strip him [that is, Burke] of this [consistency], and you leave him naked indeed," he announces (100). Thus, the imagery of shivering, exposed nakedness that we have seen running from the *Note-book* through the *Reflections* and the Anti-Jacobin writings is finally brought back to Burke himself, in an attempt to shield himself from the derision of his former friends.

As with many of the earlier depictions of Diogenes, Burke's description of Diogenes in the "Appeal" also represents a strategic self-description, another act of projection and identification: like Diogenes, the newly unattached Burke is beyond his enemies' reproaches and only appears inconsistent because of their ignorance of his central, animating ethos. Moreover, in light of all his other statements about prejudices, the episode of Diogenes and the Sinopeans' mutual condemnation is noteworthy because it shows that Burke finally does acknowledge that political affiliations, at least at the level of party affiliations, can legitimately arise from individual choice. This departure from his usual position on prejudice might have occurred because his exclusion from the Whig party had forced him to consider not just national loyalties but also the question of how party loyalties were to be regarded in the context of national conflict.[52]

In a rare moment of openness in Burke's post-Revolutionary writings, the local views of a community and its settled prejudices do not trump those of its outsiders and excluded. Burke was ready to claim exile as his own. In his moment of crisis, Burke was glad to have the example of Diogenes before him, in order to remind his former friends and allies of the pettiness and provinciality of their exclusions, and to inform them of what lay outside the "weather-beaten walls of Sinope." Prejudice had indeed triumphed, and Edmund Burke was forced to embark upon a new career as a cosmopolitan and exile, even as he was reluctantly embraced by those in power. Though Burke had spent much of his career fighting against those, like Rousseau, who would call for an "other life" (*FP* 110) led apart from communal prejudices, Burke had to learn a new way to live when public opinion had moved beyond him.

Godwin's Rousseauean Misanthrope in *Fleetwood*: Cynicism and Disillusionment

In 1805, Godwin offered a Rousseauean Cynic as the protagonist of his novel *Fleetwood,* a novel that forced readers to reexamine the hopes and ideals that had animated the previous century's most heightened expressions of feeling, whether radical or conservative.[53] Unlike the earlier, polemical treatments of sensibility, Godwin's novel took a historical rather than a moralizing view of its sentimental Cynic. Accordingly, it did not present its "man of feeling" as a dissimulating villain but as the product of a specific set of experiences and influences.[54] The result was a historical critique of eighteenth-century sensibility that showed it leading to the cynic's reflexive habits of disillusionment, which took the form of "prejudice" and "prejudging" others.

Hence, as a specifically post-Enlightenment, post-Revolutionary Cynic, Fleetwood represents the historical convergence of Rousseau's "sentiment" with Burke's "prejudice." The fact that Godwin was able to write and publish such a book in 1805 suggests that the ideological battles that had once overtaken the reputation of Rousseau were over—for Godwin at any rate—and that Godwin was now able to write about the previous decade's controversies from a new perspective, informed as much by Burke's historicism as by his and his old allies' philosophic idealism. The former strength and appeal of sentimental discourse had been dissipated in the polemics of the 1790s, and now readers and writers were becoming interested in explanations about how such a movement could have ever arisen.

From the outset, Godwin signals the historical contexts of his character and plot. Fleetwood, identified on the title page as the "New Man of Feeling," consistently betrays the deep-rooted selfishness motivating his supposed sensibility. In this way, Godwin's skepticism about sentimentalism resembled that of the Anti-Jacobin satirists. Instead of attributing this camouflaged egoism to some fundamental hypocrisy, Godwin sought to discover the specific causes for Fleetwood's selfishness as well as his sensibility. To accomplish this, the novel takes its cues from Rousseau's later autobiographical writings, despite Godwin's considerable ambivalence about Rousseau.[55]

Once again with recognizable debts to the Anti-Jacobins' version of Rousseau, Godwin used the philosopher's life story to reflect upon the personal consequences of both sensibility and reflexive cynicism, but here he treated Rousseau as a morally mixed historical figure rather than a satirical target. At the same time, Godwin allowed an extensive group of Rousseauean traits, tropes, and devices to infiltrate the entire novel, so that they became part of the pervasive atmosphere of the book and helped to set its mood of unrelieved melancholy and paranoid self-delusion.[56] Such dark and uncertain moods made the novel seem all the more Rousseauean in 1805. In fact, Fleetwood's entire characterization derived from the compromised image that Rousseau put forth in the *Confessions.* Godwin's most important comment upon Rousseau, however, was his decision to tell the story through a first-person narrator whose egoism has made his observations of himself and the world around him completely unreliable.

Imitating Rousseau's first-person mode of narration allows Godwin to examine Rousseau's habits of rationalization without falling into debates over his truth-claims or taking Rousseau's account at face value. Instead, Godwin redirects his readers toward correcting the narrator's prejudices and supplying the insights so obviously lacking in the narrator. This narrative strategy moves readers away from the previous era's models of polemical reading and self-assertion, though without losing sight of the deceptions and self-deceptions successfully perpetrated during that era.

Godwin's mode of first-person narration helps to highlight the novel's crucial distinctions between conscious acts of deception and unconscious states of self-deception. Godwin demonstrates how Fleetwood's cynicism is a reflex he developed to see through the deceptions of others, even while he deceives himself and is readily manipulated by the novel's real villains. In fact, Fleetwood, like Rousseau before him, has been led by his imagination to suspect everyone around him, but this self-confirming suspicion grows to the point that he also invents the "betrayals" that would justify his eventual, lunatic abandonment of his wife and family. By allowing this character to expose his own claims of wounded sensibility as both self-serving *and* unconscious, Godwin can critique Rousseau's habits of self-exculpation with some degree of sympathy. These Rousseauean habits, however, are also given a social and historical context that allows Godwin to assume the Burkean project of revealing the "latent wisdom" and genuine value in even transparently misleading or prejudiced accounts of figures like Fleetwood, Rousseau, or even Burke.

Fleetwood's plot takes up the love-triangle first elaborated in Rousseau's *Julie, or, The New Heloise,* but it also reflects the influence of Burke's attacks upon this work. In the "Letter to a Member of the National Assembly," for example, Burke had warned that Rousseau's idealized notions of marriage and male-female friendship had the potential to corrupt marriages everywhere. Like Rousseau's paranoid suspicions of the world around him, Burke's equally paranoid denunciations of Rousseau have been assigned to the fearful Cynic Fleetwood. Burke's fears are tacitly equated with the unfounded fears of a misogynist husband who struggles to distinguish fantasy from reality in his unhappy marriage.

Fleetwood's plot, which includes hints from *Othello* and other seventeenth-century English tragedies, is devoted largely to the narrator's baseless jealousy and estrangement from his wife, Mary. Oblivious to the feelings or needs of others, this egocentric "New Man of Feeling" cannot be trusted with himself, let alone with a helpless wife and family.[57] At the same time, Godwin is careful to stress how Fleetwood's self-pity and suspicion have left him helpless against the emotional manipulations of his evil young relation, the Iago-like Gifford, who pursues a relentless campaign of insinuation against Mary for her supposed affair with his hated half-brother, Kenrick.[58] These doubts, and Fleetwood's abandonment of his family, lead finally to his complete nervous collapse near the novel's end. After Gifford's evildoing is exposed and his prejudices corrected, however, Fleetwood begs his wife to forgive him and reconcile.

But how did Fleetwood ever become a misanthrope in the first place? Early on, Fleetwood's quiet temperament, romantic rural upbringing, and unhappy experiences at the university and in his love affairs have turned him into a "worthy successor of Diogenes" (104), as his first lover, the coquettish Marchioness, terms him.[59] The disillusioning experiences of his education and love affairs, however, do not seem adequate for explaining the depth and the rigidity of his disenchantment at this point in his life. He simply has not experienced enough to make these attitudes seem more than playacting.

This gap between Fleetwood's experiences and his self-described misanthropy shows Godwin psychologizing the Cynic and eschewing the usual fixity and repetition of older humours-style characterization. Instead, we get a psychologically plausible narrative of misanthropy as a persona assumed, a little incongruously, by a young man. In the hopes of impressing the Marchioness, Fleetwood has adopted a misanthropy that is as conventional as his rival Sir Charles Gleed's empty though amiable politeness; this role-playing allows

Gleed, like Fleetwood himself, to "speciously imitate qualities, to the reality of which he was a stranger" (98). Accordingly, the wandering attentions of the Marchioness make no distinction between the two young men, much to the irritation of Fleetwood. Here, then, we learn the origin of the young Fleetwood's Cynical misogyny: in his disappointed anger that the fickle Marchioness had not singled him out at all: "[though he] thought [he] possessed her whole, [he learned from Gleed that he] really divided her favours with every comer—a music-master—an artisan—a valet," a discovery that produced a "sudden" and "terrible" "revolution" within him (109). Thus, Fleetwood suffers exactly the kind of cuckolding that Burke had predicted in the "Letter to a Member of the National Assembly" and spends the rest of his life imagining its repetition with new women.[60] It is this incident that causes his lifelong prejudice against all women and leads him to suspect even Mary of duplicity, against all evidence and appearances to the contrary.[61]

Yet even before this incident, Godwin offers an otherwise odd and unconnected episode from Fleetwood's university experiences that resonates with this novel's deep concern with deception and impostures. Fleetwood describes his schoolmate Withers's exemplary humiliation when he was taken in by a crude prank of his classmates. Withers is a schoolboy poet devoted to tasteless imitations of classical epic, and the pranksters persuade him to share his work with more and more people, each group pretending to praise his poetry in order to keep the joke going and expose him to further half-concealed ridicule and contempt. Finally some older students lead Withers into a darkened room, where they have dressed up a ventriloquist's puppet in the master's robes to berate and chastise him for the previous night's disturbances. When the figure raised up its hand, as if to strike him,

> this indignity put Withers beyond all patience, and worked him into a momentary insanity: he flew at the master, and positively began to cuff at the image with violence: the machine was unable to resist this species of rudeness, and actually fell in pieces about the ears of its assailant. The candles were extinguished, and the room left in utter darkness; and at the same moment a long, obstreperous, and deafening peal of laughter burst out from every person in the assembly. (88)

When Withers realizes how badly he has been fooled, he flees, grows depressed, then finally drowns himself in the Isis.

The odd detachment of this episode's narration from the rest of Fleetwood's narrative (Fleetwood is not involved with the incident and does little besides recite the narrative), and its mixtures of sadism and masochism bring to mind Freud's analysis of the masochistic dream, "A child is being beaten." With its dreamlike disconnection from the rest of the novel and its strange displacements of agency and victimhood, I suspect that it is best explained as a sudden, barely fictionalized eruption of Godwin's memories of the public derision that he and Wollstonecraft shared in the 1790s. The "long, obstreperous, and deafening peal of laughter" in the dark represents the gothic cruelty of the public, delivered through a shared set of deceptions that prey upon those too weak to contest them, even when they are able to see through them.

Nonetheless, at the intellectual and thematic level, this episode also resonates with Godwin's earlier criticisms about Rousseau's and Burke's overreliance upon deceptions and impostures to manipulate their audiences. For example, we suspect the master-puppet's presence in *Fleetwood* functions as a comment upon Rousseau's *Émile,* with its notorious little wax duck that both deceives and educates Émile. This suspicion is confirmed when we recall that Godwin had once criticized Rousseau's "whole system of education" for being nothing more than "a series of tricks, a puppet-show exhibition, of which the master holds the wires, and the scholar is never to suspect in what manner they are moved."[62] Clearly, the result of Withers's experience was not an education at all, but humiliation and death, and for Fleetwood, nothing more than a lifelong fear of being deceived.

Consequently, Withers witnesses a puppet show but learns nothing but betrayal when the master-puppet (not puppet-master) is exposed. The outcome of the episode suggests perhaps a Burkean skepticism about the wisdom of philosophically exposing prejudices. But Godwin's 1798 edition of *Political Justice* explicitly links Burke with Rousseau for their shared reliance on political imposture:

> [Arguments like Rousseau's and Burke's form a] system of political imposture [that] divides men into two classes, one of which is to think and reason for the whole, and the other to take the conclusions of their superiors on trust. . . . Consider what sort of discourse must be held, or book written, by him who should make himself champion of political imposture? He cannot avoid secretly wishing that the occasion had never existed. What he undertakes is to lengthen the reign of "salutary prejudices." For this end, he must propose to himself the two opposite purposes, of prolonging the deception, and proving that it is necessary to deceive. . . . But at the same time that he tells us, we should cherish the mistake as mistake, and the prejudice as prejudice, he is himself lifting the veil, and destroying his own system.[63]

Godwin has noted how the entire polemical thrust of Burke's "prejudice" is to divide men into two classes, the deceivers and the deceived. One tells the other that they must take what they are told by their superiors "on trust." And yet attempting to justify his own post-Enlightenment version of the "double thought" lays bare the contradiction at the heart of Burke's rhetoric, which is that it cannot simultaneously function as persuasion and imposture at the same time. You cannot persuade an audience by telling them that you must, of necessity, deceive them about your real intentions. Thus, the seeming power and stability of "prejudice" functions only as imposture, not persuasion, and is ready to fall about the ears of its assailants if treated with sufficient "rudeness," though with not so enlightening consequences as we might hope.

Like the little wax duck that teaches Émile, the ventriloquist's puppet offers Withers and Fleetwood together their first lesson about the potentially dangerous consequences of demystifying prejudices. As Withers learns, destroying the illusion to see through its mechanics is far more humiliating than accepting it at face value, because its force lies not simply in the imposture itself but in the group that is willing to enforce an imposture upon others. Withers's iconoclastic gesture of knocking the dummy over (an eminently Enlightened moment of demystification) only leaves him exposed to his schoolmates' open and collective derision, rendered all the more mysterious and terrifying in its gothic form of dislocated, collective laughter. Godwin's pessimism about the benefits of stripping the veils from such illusions seems learned from Burke, but we should also note how the thing revealed is not our "shivering nature," as Burke would put it, but yet one more layer of artifice and imposture—in other words, another puppet.

Such an experience of another's failed attempts at demystification helps transform Fleetwood into a Cynic who wishes never to be fooled and publicly humiliated in a similar fashion, and who therefore reflexively assumes that everyone around him is false. Needless to say, it is his capacity for unreflective prepossession—prejudice—that causes him to suffer exactly such a humiliation at the hands of another group of malicious puppets endowed with horrible life by his own imagination.

Godwin further emphasizes the delusional, self-enclosed qualities of Fleetwood's misanthropic Cynicism when he introduces the figure of Mr. Macneil, a friend of Fleetwood's and one-time confidant of Rousseau. Macneil, a friendly Scotsman, advises Fleetwood to surround himself with friends and family. At the same time, he makes some observations about the aged Rousseau that predict Fleetwood's own eventual jealousy and madness:

> I could see [says Macneil] that one of [Rousseau's] great misfortunes had been, that almost all his intimates were chosen from among the French, that nation of egotists! Rousseau was a man of exquisite sensibility, and that sensibility had been insulted and trifled with in innumerable instances, sometimes by the intolerance of priestcraft and power, sometimes by the wanton and ungenerous sports of men of letters. He lived, however, toward the close of his life in a world of his own, and saw nothing as it really was; nor were his mistakes less gross, than if he had asserted that his little cottage was menaced by a besieging army, and assailed with a battery of cannon. (191)

Rather than treating the "exquisite sensibility" of a Rousseau or a Fleetwood as a persecuted virtue, Macneil shrewdly identifies it as a symptom of an extremely powerful egotism, which as a Scotsman he can blandly regard as a constitutional weakness of the French. Rousseau's sensibility, alternately petted or irritated by the actions of others, ultimately leads him into gross errors about the motives of others, mistakes that leave him in a perpetual state of worry. Yet this excessive suspicion and failure of trust left Rousseau with no effective way to respond to his genuine enemies, as Macneil points out.

Characteristically, Fleetwood ignores these strategically dropped hints about sensibility and selfishness, just as he rejects every other potential lesson given him throughout this book. Instead, he marries Macneil's daughter Mary, after Macneil and the rest of the family have perished at sea. Both Mary and Fleetwood know that this circumstance will give him an uncommon degree of power over her, but they proceed with the marriage anyway.

It is in his marriage that Fleetwood's prejudices become most apparent and expand his already excessive self-love into full-blown madness. After Fleetwood weds Mary, he grows predictably gloomy, despotic, and harsh toward his wife, though still aware enough of her merits to feel guilty at his treatment of her. Following the machinations of his evil relation Gifford, however, Fleetwood begins to imagine that she is having an affair, in the manner of the *Julie, or, The New Heloise,* with Gifford's naïve half-brother, Kenrick. Fleetwood's behavior toward the now-pregnant Mary grows so outrageous that he drives her away, then flees to Europe with his false friend Gifford.[64] In the final stages of his insanity, Fleetwood stages a bizarre anniversary ceremony featuring a tableau of wax dummies dressed as Kenrick and Mary, complete with an empty crib and bedclothes.[65] He dresses them up and speaks in a babylike way to the dummies as his toys and playthings: "I locked myself in, and drew them forth one after another. At each interval of the ceremony, I seated myself in a chair, my arms folded, my eyes fixed, and gazed on the object before me in all the luxury of despair" (334). Godwin makes Fleetwood's surrender to the "luxury of despair" a grotesque spectacle, since the misanthrope's losses are not merely self-created but entirely the product of his imagination. There is nothing to stop Fleetwood from reuniting with his own family except his own misanthropic delusions of injury. Fleetwood's pleasure in assuming the masochistic role of abandoned child seems all the more powerful for its fantasmic basis: he is literally playing at being abandoned, while his real family remains poor and neglected at home. Fleetwood has sacrificed his entire family for a childish fantasy that he refuses to submit to rational critique.

When Fleetwood begins to chide and cajole the puppet dressed as Mary, however, she comes horribly to life, and finally talks back to him. Fleetwood finally passes over from a consciously maintained state of self-deception to a state of madness reminiscent of the hapless Withers:

> But, while I was still speaking, I saw her move—if I live, I saw it. She turned her eyes this way and that; she grinned and chattered at me. I looked from her to the other figure; that grinned and chattered too. Instantly a full and proper madness seized me; I grinned and chattered, in turn, to the figures before me. It was not words that I heard or uttered; it was murmurs, and hissings, and lowings, and howls. I became furious. I dashed the organ into a thousand fragments. I rent the child-bed linen, and tore it with my teeth. I dragged the clothes which Mary had worn, from off the figure that represented her, and rent them into long strips and shreds. (335)

Fleetwood expends his most violent emotions on a woman now literally become an object, attacking a dumb, lifeless, woman-thing whose insensibility frustrates his desires, violent or otherwise, to manipulate her. Whether Fleetwood wishes to hurt or converse with her, "Mary" cannot respond. In this state of mental and social deterioration, Fleetwood and his imagined family can produce no expression more articulate than "murmurs, and hissings, and lowings, and howls." Is such a state of absolute self-isolation and nondialogue the unintended consequence of the philosopher's naïve faith in the virtues of self-sufficiency? Godwin's ludicrous reconciliation and happy ending suggests that this is so, because it provides Fleetwood, the text's surrogate-Rousseau, with precisely what the real Rousseau was never able to manage in his own life, a real wife and family capable of dispelling his fantasies of such things.

Godwin's character Fleetwood constitutes an important moment in the history of the concept of cynicism because he confirms the absolute centrality of

Rousseau for the concept's semantic evolution in the late eighteenth century. Fleetwood shares many of the misanthropic characteristics of the Rousseau found in the late autobiographical writings and in the polemics of the Anti-Jacobin, including a persistent partiality of vision and a perennial distrust of others. Yet this novel is also important because it reflects upon the broader function of Rousseau as part of a cultural myth in Britain, the myth of the failure of the Enlightenment. It is this myth, with its ad hominem dismissal of Rousseau and consequently of the entire Enlightenment's aspirations to the collective improvement of humanity through the correction of popular prejudices, that feeds into the concept of cynicism as political disenchantment in the early nineteenth century. The unreflective, psychically well-armored distrust of Godwin's Fleetwood only helps to reinforce his selfishness and irrationality, not rectify it. Godwin therefore reveals the biggest danger of modern cynicism, which does not reside in its disbelief so much as its complacency regarding its own partial—meaning prejudiced and collectively enforced—opinions.

D'Israeli's Psychological Portrait of Hobbes

After so much discussion of Rousseau's contributions to the formation of the modern meanings of "cynicism," it may surprise the reader to learn that the *OED*'s first recorded instance of "cynic" in its modern sense involves not Rousseau but his recurring philosophic target, Thomas Hobbes. A few reflections, however, can account for that gap. First of all, modern cynicism is a product not so much of Rousseau's own writings and career as the long-term reaction to his public image in a post-1789 British culture that defined itself defensively against a cosmopolitan, Jacobin Enlightenment with violent political ambitions. So, as Godwin's *Fleetwood* shows, modern cynicism was not really elaborated as a political threat until the Napoleonic wars made clear the importance of intellectuals in shaping and directing a nationalist public opinion conceived along the lines of Burke's "just prejudice," which makes a man's duty into "a part of his nature" (183).

Isaac D'Israeli's *Quarrels of Authors* (1814) repeatedly labeled the philosopher Thomas Hobbes a "Cynic," but not a Cynic in the manner of Diogenes or even Rousseau. D'Israeli's switching of historical referents for the cynic from Rousseau to Hobbes shows just how central the notions of power and self-interest had become to cynicism. Significantly, D'Israeli's discussion of Hobbes (and, by extension, Mandeville) echoes Rousseau's earlier critique of them in the *Discourse on Inequality*. Rousseau blames Hobbes and Mandeville's philosophic reason for their qualities of selfishness, coldness, and indifference to others, qualities that become in turn hallmarks of Hobbes's cynical philosophy in D'Israeli's discussion. Thus, despite its occasional uppercase spelling, the term "Cynic" in D'Israeli retained almost nothing of its historical links to ancient Cynicism, having become a byword instead for a selfish misanthropy or timid indifference toward others. The modern cynic, as represented by Hobbes, has grown far too passive and accommodating toward the powerful. D'Israeli displaces the older, more positive and philosophical meanings of Cynicism to emphasize the modern cynic's distrust, disbelief, indifference to moral norms, and his conviction that "the ultimate motives of human action are self-interest and the quest for power." Unlike the misanthropic and isolated figure of Fleetwood, however, the Hobbesian cynic is dangerous to the extent that he serves power and finds an audience for his destructive notions.

As in Godwin's treatment of this figure, D'Israeli insisted upon the misanthropic selfishness of Hobbes's philosophical stance, but he drastically departed from earlier versions when he also stressed Hobbes's timidity and trimming of his own beliefs to suit the powerful:

> [The vesting of power in either the sovereign or the people] was, I believe, a matter perfectly indifferent to our Philosopher, provided that whatever might be the government, absolute power could somewhere be lodged in it, to force men to act in strict conformity. It happened that our cynical Hobbes had no respect for his species; and this sovereign remedy of arbitrary power was always unworthy of a great spirit to endure, though convenient for a timid one, like his own. Hobbes, considering men merely as animals of prey, living in a state of perpetual hostility, had for his solitary principle of action, Self-preservation at any price.[66]

As D'Israeli portrayed him, Hobbes lacked the "great spirit" and intellectual autonomy that D'Israeli expected of a philosopher, and appeared instead as timid, dependent, and physically afraid, a passive and effeminate captive of the state power that he so abjectly served. For example, D'Israeli's emphasis upon the philosopher's timidity and passivity echoes aspects of Rousseau's autobiographical writings. If we recall Diogenes' "Cynical" rejection of Alexander, the encounter of the "cynical Hobbes" with state power is depressingly familiar and reveals the extent to which we in the twentieth century assume that cynics will accommodate themselves to the powers that be. As Adorno notes: "What is deemed true and what mere opinion—that is, chance and caprice—is not decided according to the evidence, as the ideology would have it, but rather by societal power, which denounces as mere caprice whatever does not agree with its own caprice. The border between healthy and pathogenic opinion is drawn *in praxi* by the prevailing authority, not by informed judgment" (234). In D'Israeli's portrait, Hobbes does not represent the "informed judgment" of the Man of Reason but the Freudian definition of rationalization taken up by Adorno, "reason in the service of unreason" (108).

D'Israeli's psychologized portrait of Hobbes, however, did take up other features of the satirized Cynic philosopher—his excessive pride, his well-developed vanity—and assigned them to a man who does not bother to conceal his low opinion of the human race and who therefore feels no shame in accommodating himself and his philosophy to political circumstances he has no intention of challenging. In Adorno's words: "What parades as the incorruptible skepsis of someone who will have no dust thrown in his eyes is the citizen shrugging his shoulders . . . the complacent announcement of the subjective relativity of all knowledge. It amounts to the view that stubborn and blind subjective self-interest is and should remain the measure of all things" (234).

D'Israeli's historical frame of reference for Cynicism has shrunk down to the most notorious immoralists of modernity and the biggest defenders of egoism and dissimulation, instead of the historical Cynics of Greece or Rome. D'Israeli has essentially taken his genealogy of cynicism away from the long-standing discussion of luxury and morality culminating in Rousseau and substituted the major exponents of a political theory of interests, self-interest, and the state running from Machiavelli through Hobbes, Mandeville, and Helvetius. During his attack on Hobbes, for example, D'Israeli claimed that Hobbes's philosophic system has simply projected his own singular, abject experience of selfishness, fear, and dependence onto the psychology of the entire human species: "This simple error has produced all the dogmas of Cynicism; for the Cynic is one whose insulated feelings, being all of the selfish kind, can imagine no other stirrers of even our best affections, and strains even our loftiest virtues into pitiful motives" (8). And a little later, we learn that these supposed Cynic "dogmas," a "philosophy true only for the wretched and the criminal," are the property of such *modern* writers such as Mandeville, Swift, and Chesterfield, Helvetius, Rochefoucauld, and, especially, Machiavelli (65). As D'Israeli observed: "[These writers] only degrade us: they are polished Cynics!" (65). D'Israeli's description of this rather courtly group of writers as "polished" may or may not have been meant to sound paradoxical. Nonetheless, his description of these eighteenth-century figures as Cynics made a temporizing selfishness, self-preservation, and moral degradation into the primary meanings of "Cynic" and abandoned most of the term's historical links to the rude, impoverished, and emphatically masculine and independent philosopher Diogenes. "Every thing was seen in a little way by this great man; who, having reasoned himself into an abject being, 'licked the dust' through life" (64). Not coincidentally, Hobbes's fellow cynics represent the major exponents of a politics of self-interest running from Machiavelli onward.

What D'Israeli has substituted for Cynicism's former historical content was Rousseau's earlier complaint about his fellow philosophes; in Rousseau's view, they were all far too willing to fall into a dependence that led them into inhumanely narrow or selfish conclusions. In a recognizably modern use of the term, D'Israeli makes Hobbes "cynical" to the extent that he has produced not a genuinely independent philosophy, but a quasi-philosophic rationale designed to protect and justify his pursuit of self-interest. D'Israeli's elevation of selfishness into the core meaning for "cynicism," and his corresponding deemphasis of the Cynic's rudeness, has established the definitive features of the modern "cynic."

Modern cynicism, in fact, can be recognized as such because it has incorporated into its meanings Rousseau's own critique of his era's intellectuals in their pursuit of politeness: intellectuals are regarded as cynical, meaning false, intellectuals when they disregard the truth for the sake of a polite accommodation with the rich and powerful. The only trace of Rousseau and the philosophes' formative role in the creation of modern, post-Enlightenment notions of cynicism is the persistent association of "cynicism" with the professional manipulation of public opinion. Though Voltaire, Rousseau, Diderot, and the other cosmopolitan philosophes did not anticipate this legacy of their work, Edmund Burke's conservative attack upon the Enlightenment appropriated Enlightenment techniques in its understanding and manipulation of public opinion.[67]

The mass opinion that had been weakly and ambivalently addressed by the philosophes was eventually captured and mobilized by a new class of conservative intellectuals who resided in the media. Thus, the Anti-Jacobin period of reaction against Enlightenment helped to spawn that most recognizable and noxious aspect of contemporary politics, the cynical media insider. Alan Keenan and William Chaloupka have both written about the role of such cynical insiders in destroying the hope and effectiveness of democratic politics, largely by filling up the precious public spaces of discussion with insider-talk or empty chatter that effectively excludes all but the most determined or politically connected citizens from participating.[68] What neither of these political theorists has noticed, however, is the historical origin of this figure in the political dynamics of the eighteenth and early nineteenth centuries, the period when public opinion first becomes a source of legitimacy and authority in its own right. Neither have they observed how the modern cynic embodies all the contradictions and ambiguities of an unstable and potentially delusional public opinion as described by Adorno—"the view that stubborn and blind subjective self-interest is and should remain the measure of all things" (234).

The emergence of this figure at the beginning of the nineteenth century deserves historical notice. The modern cynic—whose attributes include distrust, disbelief, shameless indifference, and contempt for all motives besides self-interest and the pursuit of power—appears in a society in which opinions circulate, but in ways that ensure that they have no particular force or effect upon its political direction. This implies, of course, an already disenchanted view of democratic politics and its notions of popular political participation. Before the end of the eighteenth century, cynicism had long been recognized as an attribute of both the powerful (Alexander admitting in the Dialogues of the Dead that he needed illusions to rule) and the plebeian (Diogenes calling the rhetoricians and politicians of his day lackeys of the mob). After 1800, the modern cynic takes up the position of what Keenan calls the "disempowered insider," the intellectual whose job is to accommodate himself to the "caprice" fostered by Adorno's "prevailing authority" (234) while managing the public or publics on its behalf.

As I have noted, Niehues-Pröbsting has suggested that modern cynicism was created by a "failure of the Enlightenment," which was represented on the one hand by the final stages of Rousseau's life and career and on the other hand by the emergence and triumph of Burkean conservatism in Britain.[69] What these two sets of events helped to make visible was a new intellectual class professionally devoted, like D'Israeli's Hobbes, to the manipulation of what Adorno terms "pathological opinion, the deformations due to prejudice, superstition, rumor, and collective delusion," that they themselves never believed (106). This is the new political rationality that Adorno identifies with the "history of mass movements" (106), a rationality that coolly exploits the irrationality of others for personal or political gain. Hence, we see the increasing use of cynicism as a term to describe those who disbelieve themselves, but who would persuade others to believe, for the sake of their own or others' power. The lowercase, modern cynic is able to make a living off of public opinion because he remains cynically indifferent toward the specific content of the toxic attitudes he peddles to others. After Rousseau and Burke, this post-Enlightenment figure is not a philosopher but a media intellectual, and he helps to degrade conditions of communication from the communicative promise of Habermas's "public sphere" to the pathological self-enclosure of Adorno's "Opinion Delusion Society."[70]

SIX Cynicism and Dandyism

An analysis of the situation is not tantamount to conformity to that situation. In reflecting upon the situation, analysis emphasizes the aspects that might be able to lead beyond the given constraints of the situation.

—Theodor Adorno, "Marginalia to Theory and Praxis"

When Isaac D'Israeli made Hobbes the paradigmatic philosopher of cynicism in 1814, he offered one of the first cynics reflecting the term's new constellation of meanings in the nineteenth century: D'Israeli's Hobbes was sneering rather than snarling, politely dissimulating rather than rude and rough-edged, and accommodating to the powerful rather than resistant to them. Most important, Hobbes, along with Mandeville, had been notorious for well over a century for his supposed defenses of egoism. These debates over egoism and the nature of reason were eventually imported into the term's definitions in the twentieth century, so that cynicism was defined in 1913 as the fundamental assumption that "human conduct is directed, either consciously or unconsciously, wholly by self-interest or self-indulgence, and that appearances to the contrary are superficial and untrustworthy."[1] For D'Israeli, it was Hobbes's shockingly reductive view of human nature, his insistence on the uniformly base motives for human conduct, and his assumption about the universality of dissimulation in human affairs that rendered his works a "philosophy true only for the wretched and the criminal."

D'Israeli's account of Hobbes signaled the end of an entire Enlightenment debate about the role played by the philosophe movement in European societies. The tacit elitism of Enlightenment thought regarding the "people," which Burke's *Reflections* had only exaggerated with its notion of the "less enquiring . . . whom Providence dooms to live on trust" (195–96) made further conflations of the philosophes and the "people" impossible after 1789. The Revolutionary and Counter-Revolutionary era's nationalism and mass mobilizations also made it difficult for intellectuals to remain aloof from this period's political debates. Instead, post-1789 intellectuals placed themselves at the disposal of power derived from one version or another of "the people." In the context of this period's nationalism, however, the "people's will" could now encompass authoritarian figures like Napoléon or Pitt. In this rethinking of the relation of philosophical reason to power, Hobbes, along with his fellow writers Machiavelli, La Rochefoucauld, Mandeville, Helvetius, Swift, and Chesterfield, were now dubbed "polished cynics"—politely dissimulating cynics whose cynicism inverted the rude, truth-telling philosophy of Diogenes—or Rousseau. Yet Hobbes's fellow cynics also shared a rhetorical or persuasive ability that would become a defining characteristic of an emerging class of intellectuals that Alan Keenan has labeled "cynical insiders."[2]

Like earlier, more independent Cynics, cynical insiders redescribe people and events in order to change their moral valuations, just as Burke had shown that prejudices were to be cherished rather than discarded. Unlike those earlier philosophers, the unreflective and amoral "polished cynics" performed their acts of persuasion at the behest of the powerful, without worrying themselves about the moral or social consequences. While ancient and early modern oratory had treated such acts of persuasion as one of the chief duties of the eloquent man in leading his community, the Enlightenment demise of rhetorical culture swept away the political, social, and communicative structures that had once underwritten such notions of linguistic action. Instead, the postrhetorical, post-Enlightenment intellectual's acts of persuasion could be stigmatized as "cynical" in the sense of manipulating the feelings of a mass audience in a calculated and self-serving way. The cynic manipulated his audience emotionally, bypassing its capacities for reason, inquiry, or intelligent debate. Like Burke's Providence, the cynical insider "doom[ed]" his audience to "live on trust." This was "rationalization" in Adorno's sense of "reason in the service of unreason."

D'Israeli's description of the overly accommodating Hobbes, equally happy serving both the Commonwealth and Charles II, is suggestive of an entire series of historical displacements and negations that associated cynics with power and publicity rather than philosophy and truth telling in the early nineteenth century. In other words, D'Israeli's Hobbes represents an increasingly potent strain of cynicism because he personifies the insider-cynic's knack for persuasive moral redescription, the ability to redescribe a situation so persuasively that audiences become willing to abandon their own views and change sides. Through these practices of interested transvaluation, we find ancient Cynicism's genealogical link to the modern political practices of redescription. As Skinner pointed out in relation to Bolingbroke's Opposition, such political "debate" is conducted largely through competing descriptions of reality offered to the general public. By recruiting from this public, each side strives to assemble the larger and more active following. Interestingly, some of the first traces of this strand of meanings turned up in Fielding's disgruntled treatment of Diogenes and his nonfollowers, which was the by-product of Fielding's early career working for the Opposition press.

Hence, the passage from premodern to modern cynicism announced by D'Israeli's portrait of Hobbes entailed not just a historical shift from rude to polished cynics but also the appearance of meanings for the term that eventually constituted William Chaloupka's "ensemble" of mutually reinforcing attitudes. These semantic changes came about piecemeal, as the cynic's attributes of sneering, faultfinding, and so on were increasingly conceptualized in relation to an anonymous mass public figured as the cynic's natural audience and target.[3] By the end of the nineteenth century, "cynicism" did not simply refer to the ancient philosophic sect; instead it elaborated three distinct positions relative to power and publicity, positions that all functioned within the nexus of interests created by cynicism's "ensemble effect." This was the version of cynicism that we still confront today.

This chapter describes the final set of developments that brought the Cynic out of the nineteenth century and into the twentieth. I begin with some Cynics contemporaneous with D'Israeli who exemplify Keenan's roles of master-cynic, outsider-cynic, and cynical insider. All these cynics are suggestive of this era's recentering of cynicism around power and publicity. Then I examine the genealogical link between D'Israeli's "polished Cynics" to the dandies of the Regency era who exemplified their own version of the life lived apart from social convention. Afterward, we spend some uncomfortable hours with the dangerous cynics of the mid-nineteenth century, who, when united with the most decadent moments of dandyism, make a smooth transition into the varieties of cynicism found in Oscar Wilde's *Dorian Gray.* All these examples allow us to reflect upon the larger cultural and political stakes of cynics and dandies in the writings of both Wilde and Foucault, who gave us hints about how to pursue the Enlightenment philosophe's convergence of reflection and action, along with the philosophical "way of life," in a new way.

Three Versions of Cynicism, with Some Definitions

Around the time of D'Israeli's *Quarrels of Authors,* we can begin to find instances of "cynics" that fall in line with Keenan's tripartite scheme of cynicism as master-cynicism, insider-cynicism, and the disillusioned cynical public. One of the earliest, though ambiguous, instances of "master-cynicism" seems to be Byron's address to the recently defeated Napoléon in *Childe Harold* (1817):

> But men's thoughts were the steps which paved thy throne,
> *Their* admiration thy best weapon shone;
> The part of Philip's son was thine, not then
> (Unless aside thy purple had been thrown)
> Like stern Diogenes to mock at men;
> For sceptred cynics earth were too wide a den.[4]

Byron's comparison reworks the commonplace contrasting of Alexander (Philip's son) with the "stern Diogenes," but he also refers to Napoléon's mastery of public opinion as his "best weapon." The emperor's defeat—the ruler brought down to the level of the impoverished philosopher—is registered in the paradox of "sceptred cynics," while also suggesting that this master-cynic, even while in power, treated the entire world as nothing more than his "den." Byron's note to this passage explains that Napoléon's "great error" lay in revealing his "want of all community of feeling for or with [mankind]."[5] Such contempt accords with Keenan's description of the calculating, self-seeking master-cynicism that rules on the assumption that "the ultimate motives of human action are self-interest and the quest for power." Nonetheless, Byron blames Napoléon's downfall precisely on his *lack* of dissimulation, his inability to maintain a politically useful dissimulation that would have otherwise kept him in power. As we saw with D'Israeli's Hobbes, Byron's application of the term "cynic" to Napoleon reveals how cynicism was now being viewed as allied to power rather than opposing it.

Keenan's ideal-type of the disillusioned outsider-cynic appears in an 1815 poem addressed by William Drennan to an anonymous libelist, for whom the poet prophesies a terrible fate in old age:

> The bile, tho' *splendid,* by degrees
> Becomes the cynic's sore disease.
> Works to the heart, corrodes unseen.

And makes [the cynic's] breast the cave of spleen;
Till, by a sort of moral trope,
The coxcomb turns a misanthrope;
His ruling maxim, and his fate,
Hated by all, and all to hate.[6]

The anonymous cynic, labeled "the *virus* . . . in age," has become a punishment to himself and others, a social disease. The venom and gall once produced to stir others' malice works upon him instead, transforming him by stages from coxcomb to misanthrope to social outcast. The cynic's pose of disenchantment is soon pursued in earnest, and his attitude toward others quickly produces like results: "Where'er he comes, his atmosphere / Turns the sweet smile into a sneer" (lines 69–70). Poetic justice—"by a sort of moral trope"—will overtake the coxcomb-satirist when he learns that such squibs will only leave him shunned by those whom he once wished to impress. This example shows how the social effects of the cynic's disillusionment follow from his psychology, figuring the cynic as a walking "virus" that others must flee. The poem's recurrent metaphor of cynicism as a sickness afflicting both the cynic and the social body will continue to be elaborated over the next century and a half. Though Drennan treats lightly the trope of the cynic-libelist as a walking virus, we find the trope pursued in earnest by the time we reach the moralists of the mid-nineteenth century.

Nonetheless, it is D'Israeli's "polished cynics" who connect most clearly with previous notions of cynicism, if only by negation, and whose successive transformations will provide the main narrative thread for the remainder of this chapter. These early insider-cynics' verbal inventiveness provides the clearest link between ancient Cynicism and its degraded modern counterpart. D'Israeli's "polished cynics" had all at one time or another been attacked for abandoning traditional moral and religious categories in their worldly descriptions of human behavior. To the conventional moralists opposing them, intellectuals like Machiavelli or Hobbes represented all the dangers of rhetorical slipperiness in a postrhetorical world. At the same time, D'Israeli's group of "polished cynics" had, in their indiscreet descriptions of human behavior, anticipated one of Oscar Wilde's most famous aphorisms on the topic of cynicism: "Cynicism," says Wilde, "is merely the art of seeing things as they are instead of as they ought to be."[7] D'Israeli's "polished cynics" had been labeled cynics for "seeing things as they are" and, worst of all, for telling others what they had seen.

Wilde's aphorism ironically pretends that cynics like Hobbes, Mandeville, or Machiavelli were simply seeing what others could not. Yet an analysis of their rhetoric shows that they were in fact refusing to take conventional names or descriptions of things at face value, while digging beneath conventional meanings and valuations to discover the hidden rationality underneath: this is what gave this group's redescriptions the force of Cynic or "cynical" transvaluation.[8] It is also important that these writers' rejection of conventional values did not alienate them from the powerful, largely because they often used notions like *raison d'état* or moral realism to shield the powerful from moral criticism. Machiavelli celebrated the lies and dishonorable behavior of rulers for their political effectiveness. La Rouchefoucauld praised dissimulation and insincerity for the advantages they gave the ambitious at court. Mandeville analyzed the pursuit of luxury, and Helvetius that of self-interest, for their beneficial effects on society as a whole. Chesterfield became a symbol of aristocratic duplicity that consciously cultivated insincerity and dissimulation. Each of these figures grew notorious for his eloquence on behalf of what seemed to be an amoral, worldly, and powerfully entrenched perspective, and each writer was blamed for the confusion of moral categories that seemed to result from his writing.

One of the greatest accomplishments of Burke's political redescription of the French philosophes was to rework what had once been an Enlightenment critique of ancién regime moral realism into an accusation against the French Enlightenment for its destabilization of moral distinctions. D'Israeli's subsequent discussion condensed into a single set of "polished cynics" two distinct through related historical and cultural movements of the eighteenth century, the Enlightenment and the discourse of politeness, so that together they became a modern, circumspect cynicism characterized by verbal accommodation of an amoral reality. The "polished cynic" was only Voltaire's "polite philosopher" viewed from the post-Burkean, historical perspective of D'Israeli. Nonetheless, with a figure like Hobbes in the foreground, the fashionable cynic modeled upon Chesterfield assumed the historical defeat of the Enlightenment master-narrative of historical and intellectual progress directed by the reflective philosophe, so that subsequent cynics could represent the most *un*-reflective aspects of Mandeville's vision of "commercial modernity": fashion and dissimulation.[9] This widespread acceptance and normalization of Mandeville's views about luxury, commerce, and modernity helped to recast the nineteenth-century cynic—a little surprisingly, if we consider his role in the previous epoch—into a representative of all the thoughtless, morally questionable aspects of fashionable life.[10]

Though the terms of Samuel Johnson's original 1755 definition of "cynic" were still being echoed as late as 1791 in Walker's *Critical Pronouncing Dictionary* (for example, "a philosopher of the snarling or currish sort"), some elements in Johnson's initial semantic cluster had undergone significant alterations between 1755 and 1814, notably that of "misanthrope" and "rude man."[11] The best explanation for these semantic changes was the rise and fall of the "benevolent misanthrope" type between Goldsmith and Rousseau, a change that coincided with the defeat of both politeness and Enlightenment reason as dominant cultural ideals in the Counter-Revolutionary era.[12] The changes to the rude or misanthropic terms in the cynic-cluster created a split in the concept of cynicism, separating rude "snarlers" from nominally polite "sneerers" sometime in the nineteenth century.

The *OED* confirms this important shift from snarling to sneering cynics. Alongside the traditional railing cynic "disposed to rail or find fault," we begin to see around the time of D'Israeli a more compromised cynic who "shows a disposition to disbelieve in the sincerity or goodness of human motives and actions, and is wont to express this by sneers and sarcasms; a sneering faultfinder."[13] As Drennan's poem on the would-be libelist showed, however, the sneering cynic is as likely to suffer from disillusion as to communicate it to others: "Where'er he comes, [says Drennan] his atmosphere / Turns the sweet smile into a sneer." Cynicism becomes more than an attitude; it is a social "atmosphere" that the cynic carries around with him.

The nineteenth-century shift from snarling to sneering cynics, or from cynical railing to cynical disbelieving, is crucial to understanding the difference between D'Israeli's and Wilde's modern cynics and the earlier premodern Cynics modeled in one way or another on Diogenes or Timon. At this pivotal moment in the history of the term, the uninhibited incivility or rudeness of the cynical railer had become internalized in the form of cynical detachment or disbelief, hostile attitudes now expressed indirectly with the modern cynic's "sneers," "censures," and "sarcasms," though this faultfinding now had little relation to even the pretense of moralizing or reflection.

The "cynic sneer" soon became a verbal formula as fixed and as popular in the nineteenth century as the "snarling cynic" had been in the seventeenth and eighteenth centuries. The term was applied to figures like the famously introspective poet Cowper, whom Anna Seward had chided in a posthumously published poem of 1810 for his "sarcasms levelled at national gratitude" in his poem *The Task:* "'Tis not to check, / With cynic sneer, that fervour of the soul, / Which, grateful for the transport Genius gives, / Praises the unwearied culture of its powers" (lines 128–30).[14] What Seward's poem reveals especially well is the new role of the modern disempowered cynic as an undeclared enemy and silent censurer of others' actively held, publicly acknowledged feelings and beliefs.[15] This poem remains one of the earliest cases in which a cynic is criticized not for his tactless freedom of speech but for an obliquity that shades into hypocrisy and dissimulation. Such sneering, censuring behavior may be an expression of misanthropy, as Seward portrays Cowper's reactions. These examples also suggest that cynicism and misanthropy were both taking on new meanings during this period. Even when cynicism and misanthropy were linked, they increasingly depicted a cold, dispassionate, and selfish personality. In a word, the cynic is increasingly being defined as "morose" as well as "churlish."[16] This "morose" quality harked back to the early modern Cynic's melancholic or retired gentleman, but it also looks ahead to the disenchantment or disillusion of the insider-cynic or the cynical public. Nonetheless, despite their shared basis in the cynic's misanthropy, the "churlish" and "morose" modes of cynicism developed in increasingly separate directions during the nineteenth century.

It took some time, however, for the semantic shifts identified retrospectively by the *OED* to turn up in the period's own dictionaries and reference books. One of the earliest appears in Hester Lynch Piozzi's *British Synonymy* (1794), which classes "cynical" along with "snappish, snarling, taunting, sarcastick," as terms "very near if not exactly synonymous." Though Piozzi allows "cynical" to derive etymologically from the "*cur*rish qualities" of the ill-bred dog, she also observes that the "SARCASTIC gentleman who when at club lies close to give his neighbour a *biting* answer if he can, will not confess himself a CYNIC; which in common and corrupt use seems to imply misanthropy and distance from mankind, rather than ill-humour when among them."[17] While Piozzi associates the "CYNIC" with his traditional currish and "snarling" qualities, she also acknowledges that in at least some users' minds the cynic's misanthropy is expressed by a restrained "distance from mankind" rather than "ill-humour" or outright rudeness. Piozzi's identification of the emergent meanings (significantly denigrated as "common and corrupt use") of the term "cynic" remains one of the few pieces of contemporary evidence showing how the term's meaning was changing between the 1790s and the mid-nineteenth century.

Webster and other dictionary writers, both British and American, continued to produce variants of Johnson's 1755 definition throughout the nineteenth century. The "common and corrupt use" distinguishing between snarling and sneering cynics does not seem to have entered the dictionaries until the early twentieth century, when we find Webster's (1913) definition, which adds to the standard etymological definition ("1. having the qualities of a surly dog; snarling; captious; currish") this final subheading: "4. given to sneering at rectitude and the conduct of life by moral principles; disbelieving in the reality of any human purposes which are not suggested or directed by self-interest or self-indulgence."[18] By the time we reach the twentieth century, the modern senses of "cynicism" as distrust or disbelief have detached themselves from its earlier suggestions of misanthropy. Modern cynicism has taken on all the cold, calculating, and selfish meanings once assigned to nineteenth-century misanthropy and detached itself from its earlier snarling and misanthropic modes. Not only does Webster (1913) distinguish between the snarling and sneering modes of cynical faultfinding, but its definition also stresses how the sneering cynic, in his contemptuous disregard of the views of others, disbelieves in the existence of any human motive or purpose beyond "self-interest or self-indulgence."[19]

Despite the persistence of old-style snarling, currish, or crabbed cynics, it was the modern, fashionable, sneering, disbelieving cynics and their reductive views of human motivation and self-interest that would be developed in twentieth-century political discourse. Cynicism named an attitude that functioned as a morally and socially defined "atmosphere" (to quote Drennan's description of the Cynic-libelist once again), an "atmosphere" equally applicable to how one ruled, how one persuaded, and how one allowed oneself to be ruled or persuaded.

Beau Brummell, Dandyism, and the Fashionable Cynic

In the same way that the once solid distinction between Diogenes and Alexander collapsed in Byron's phrase "sceptred cynics," we find that D'Israeli's phrase "polished cynics" collapsed the former opposition between fashionable society and traditional Cynic notions of masculinity, austerity, and asceticism. The tacit acceptance of Mandeville's defense of luxury meant that cynics could now be seen as defenders of a feminized luxury and fashion. Emblematic of this new alliance of cynicism and fashion was D'Israeli's inclusion of Chesterfield in his pantheon of "polished Cynics." Chesterfield could only have been included for his blunt advocacy of polite, aristocratic dissimulation as the indispensable means to courtly self-advancement and power.

As far as Chesterfield was concerned, such behavior was recommended by the specifically aristocratic value of decorum, which he once defined as "a general *exterior* decency, fitness, and propriety of conduct in the common intercourse of life" (my emphasis).[20] Citing Cicero's *De officiis,* Chesterfield argued that decorum was to be strictly observed by the "most sensible and informed part of mankind, I mean the people of fashion," because it "does not extend to religious or moral duties, does not prohibit the solid enjoyments of vice, but only throws a veil of decency between it and the vulgar, conceals part of its native deformity, and prevents scandal, and bad example." Chesterfield's amoral notions of decorum, which were heavily attacked when they appeared in his famous *Letters* to his son, happen to coincide perfectly with our notions of the master-cynicism of the powerful, and the master-cynic's hypocritical reliance on the moral codes of "the vulgar." Yet this example also shows how dramatically cynicism's meanings changed when it was aligned with, and not against, politeness, decorum, and fashion. Once politeness had lost its function as a dominant cultural discourse, the term "polished cynic" suggested that it was aristocratic decorum that had become "cynical," in the sense that it represented empty social forms practiced without feeling, belief, commitment, or sincerity.[21]

In D'Israeli's terms, both Hobbes's distrust and Chesterfield's dissimulation stemmed from the "cynical dogmas" that justified the pursuit of self-interest simply because of its ubiquity in human affairs. When exemplified by the discredited Chesterfield, or Wilde's middle-aged dandy Lord Henry Wotton, the "polished cynic" no longer opposed the corrupting influences of fashion and politeness but has actually merged with that world to become its best advocate.

Yet the collapse of the opposition between cynicism and fashion had another consequence at the level of gender relations. When cynics became aligned with fashion, they also lost the Diogenical qualities traits long coded as masculine, such as activity, agency, or resistance to the social. Instead, cynics acquired a host of sexually equivocal qualities such as physical delicacy, passivity, effeminacy, or homoeroticism. Thus, when Cynicism lost its grounding in the philosophy of Diogenes, it also lost its remaining associations of moral rectitude along with its heavily gendered claims of physical and intellectual independence. As we shall see, it was only after cynicism lost its specifically gendered qualities in the mid-nineteenth century that it became possible to label female writers as cynics in its emerging sense of "disbelieving."

For example, in a character sketch written just before his essay on Hobbes, D'Israeli produced another portrait of a polished cynic: Horace Walpole, in the significantly titled "Pains of Fastidious Egotism," who was portrayed as an aristocratic cynic modeled forthrightly on the dissimulating example of Chesterfield. D'Israeli wished to understand why Walpole "pretended to shun authors, and to slight the honours of authorship."[22] When D'Israeli analyzed his subject's talents, he decided that despite Walpole's high social position, "highly polished" taste, and brilliant "vivacity," he simply lacked the "genius" of a "great author" (43). At least part of the problem was the fact that Walpole's undeniably high rank interfered with his appreciation of other writers' genius: "he was so imbued with the petty elegancies of society that every impression of grandeur in the human character was deadened in the breast of the polished cynic" (43). D'Israeli seems to be modeling his account of Walpole on Chesterfield's negligent treatment of Samuel Johnson, which concluded with Johnson's famous letter rejecting his claims to patronage.

Walpole's aristocratically cynical indifference to the more rugged genius of Sir Philip Sidney, for instance, was not only "heartless" (45), but it also reflected his "sickly delicacy" (46) and his inability to contemplate the merits of others.[23] These unmistakably effeminate qualities of professional jealousy and defensive egotism made him the worst kind of critic (presumably in contrast with the generous D'Israeli, who remained on good terms with writers of the first rank like Byron). Walpole was "as willing to vilify the truly great, as to beautify deformity; when he imagined that the fame he was destroying or conferring, reflected back on himself" (46). In other words, Walpole's willingness to "vilify" or "beautify" his subjects whichever way would please him most made him yet another "polished cynic" rationalizing his own preferences with an "artificial" critical practice. Yet D'Israeli's insistence on Walpole's artificiality and sickly delicacy in comparison with such "GREAT M[E]N" as Sidney, Goldsmith, and Johnson shows that these nineteenth-century transformations of the cynic involved not just this period's assumptions about genius but also its assumptions about masculinity.

These nineteenth-century shifts in masculinity and their effects on the meanings of cynicism become most apparent in this period's labeling of its ultrafashionable dandies as "cynics." Men like Beau Brummell, the originator and foremost representative of dandyism, belonged to a distinctive new phase in the history of manners, one in which the former tokens of masculine rank (marriage, family, and land) had lost much of their former fixed value in the "fast" new fashionable world of Regency high society.[24] Instead, the dandy represented a new and more ephemeral form of status, one that was signaled by the dandy's selective violation of certain conventions of masculine dress and conduct. These very public violations of social codes, and their courting of accusations of singularity, were intended to distinguish the dandy from those who slavishly followed such social forms.[25] The highest compliment for such a performance was to be universally imitated as an "original."

Though the ancient Cynics and the dandies shared little else, we can recognize a commonalty in the manner of their founding, which was accomplished by a charismatic and witty figure who influenced others simply by his mode of life and remarks to others—what Michel Foucault would call a distinctive "stylistic of life," or "aesthetic of existence" in relation to the ancient Cynics (*FP* 109–10). Like Diogenes, what Beau Brummell offered his contemporary "audience" or "public" (an interesting notion for a man who wrote nothing and whose accomplishments consisted of careful attention to dress, facial expressions, and a gift for impromptu remarks) was not a doctrine or body of writings but a distinctive "way of life" conducted in public and recorded in countless anecdotes and stories. It seems absurd and heavy-handed to turn such a man, no matter how fascinating, into a full-fledged "philosophical hero," but at least part of his notoriety came from his mixture of tact and effrontery, his ability to offer up in himself a carefully modulated parody of the "forms and habits of common life" with only the barest hint of his distinction from his contemporaries (*FP* 110). It is the dandy's hostile parodies of the common or conventional values of his contemporaries that give his lifestyle a flavor of cynical transvaluation. It is this tacitly aggressive, parodic dimension of the dandy's pose that linked the Regency-era Beau Brummell with his Victorian imitator Oscar Wilde.

Around the same time that Isaac D'Israeli was writing his biographical sketches of Hobbes and Walpole, Beau Brummell was approaching the end of his career as the self-appointed judge of the entire fashionable world of Regency London. Brummell's fine masculine style of dress, independent manner, and wit took the place of conventional values of work, marriage, and family. They also brought him a form of authority, that of taste and fashion, that seemed distinct from more traditional forms of cultural authority, whether moral, political, or aesthetic. It also seems important that Brummell's reign as arbiter of taste coincided with the Regency period, the moment when the bad domestic relations in the royal household were matters of regular public scandal, and when the mutual hatred between the bloated, dandyish Regent and "the people" was particularly blatant.[26] Brummell's example suggested that a man need not be a husband or provider to be interesting, but only a striking figure worthy to be looked at and admired by others.

The dandy reduced the figure of the nineteenth-century fashionable gentleman to its essentials, stripping away anything that would diminish the aesthetic impact of the dandiacal self. As Hazlitt noted, Brummell's genius, if it could even be called genius, lay in his arriving "at the very *minimum* of wit, and reduc[ing] it, 'by happiness or pains,' to an almost invisible point."[27] As Ellen Moers comments: "The dandy, as Brummell made him, stands on an isolated pedestal of self. He has no coat of arms on his carriage (indeed, Brummell kept no carriage), no ancestral portraits along his halls (and no ancestral halls), no decorations on his uniform (he had rejected the uniform), and no title but Mr Brummell, *arbiter elegantiarum* or, in the language of Brummell's day, 'top of the male *ton*.'"[28] Like the Cynics and misanthropes we have earlier surveyed, the Brummellian dandy has disavowed all attachments in order to maintain a certain splendid independence from the commonplace. Moers comments upon the usefulness of Brummell's distance, for example, from conventional notions of family pride:

> The dandy has neither obligations nor attachments: wife or child would be unthinkable, and other relatives are unfortunate accidents. When Brummell first came up to London he disposed of his brother and sister by cutting them, and disowned his ancestors by alluding to his origins as baser than they were. "Who ever heard of George B.'s father," he would say, "and who would ever have heard of George B. himself, if he had been anything but what he is?"[29]

After Brummell's well-publicized flight to Calais in 1816 to escape his debts, writers began introducing fictionalized versions of him into the fashionable novels of the 1820s. These novels only reminded readers of the historical distance between the dandies of their own era and the now-absent progenitor of the movement. One of the first of the dandy novels was Thomas Henry Lister's popular *Granby* (1826), which satirized the manners of the *Ton* and contained a vivid depiction of Brummell in the cynically detached, indifferent Trebeck.[30] Here is Trebeck viewed through the sympathetic though critical perspective of Caroline, Lister's heroine, after he announces that he will stay on at the country house where Caroline is also visiting:

> Caroline was not vain enough to imagine that she was instrumental in influencing his stay; but she was rather glad to find that she should see more of him; for he was an useful ally, and an entertaining companion, and the little vanity which she did possess was gratified by his notice. Yet she did not like him, and often wondered by what fatality it should have

> come to pass that a sort of confidence should exist between them; as he was decidedly the last person to whom she would voluntarily entrust a secret, and whom she would dare to rely on as a friend. There was a heartlessness in his character, a spirit of gay misanthropy, a cynical, depreciating view of society, an absence of high-minded generous sentiment, a treacherous versatility, and deep powers of deceit, to which not all his agreeable qualities and fashionable fame could effectually blind her.[31]

Caroline's ambivalence centers upon Trebeck's ultrafashionable politeness, which however entertaining also seems insincere and ultimately treacherous and deceitful; his cynicism encompasses not just his fashionable tastes but his mastery of social forms for the purposes of self-indulgence or self-advancement.

In other words, Trebeck's politeness has become equated with his cynicism, now rendered as the dandy's "gay misanthropy." This is Rousseau's critique of the man of fashion brought to life, in which a man who essentially lives for and within fashionable society is equally incapable of friendship, trust, or any other form of attachment. The cynical dandy's self-absorption is indeed entertaining in the protected spaces of mixed company, where the witty and composed Trebeck shines in comparison with the dimwitted or pretentious members of the *Ton.* There his "gay misanthropy" and "cynical, depreciating view of society" hit exactly the right note and help to reassure Caroline that her perceptions of others are accurate.

While Caroline finds Trebeck "useful" (a significant word) as an "ally," his "treacherous versatility" as well as his capacity for deceit make him a dangerous and unpredictable partner. Most disturbingly, his delight in exposing the defects of his favorite "originals" does not recall the moralist so much as the showman anxious to display his puppets to maximum effect. His "gay misanthropy" is thus better described as "heartlessness" or indifference toward others rather than a Timon-style passionate rage. He has mastered the social forms of his fashionable set, but his cynical aptitude for dissimulation, his "treacherous versatility" in words and appearances, his selfishly instrumental attitude toward other human beings, all these eminently cynical qualities have made him unsuitable for any sincere communication or friendship.

Between the success of *Granby* in 1826 and the decade of Brummell's death in the 1840s, a number of other novels and memoirs also emphasized this dandy's well-known "cynicism," adding new tonalities to the term's former suggestions of snarling misanthropy. These, however, differed from *Granby* by focusing on the pathetic spectacle of an aging and disillusioned Brummell exiled in Calais, unwillingly detached from the glamour and authority of his former life. For those who saw or read about Brummell's remarkable decline into early senility and decrepitude, the lesson taken from the cynical dandy's rise and fall was less about the splendid powers and independence of his youth as it was the remarkable downfall of a once-powerful judge of the fashionable world. Brummell's broken-down and exhausted condition in exile revealed how precarious his position had been all along, how insubstantial the approval of the fashionable world had been, and how ephemeral the power that this group had granted him. Though Brummell had always posed as an absolutely self-sufficient and arbitrary judge to his social set, his humiliation and exile proved him nothing more than a disempowered insider-cynic, in Keenan's terms. His power had lasted only as long as his sponsorship by the king.

In the same year as *Granby,* for example, Edward Bulwer-Lytton's *Pelham: or The Adventures of a Gentleman* (1826) provided a darker fictionalized portrait of Brummell that stressed the bitterness of his exile and his disillusioned contempt for those whose opinions he once led. Brummell appears as Russelton, a slightly tarnished if still impressive character whom the dandy-hero Pelham patronizes on his foreign travels. Pelham describes him "as a soured and disappointed man; his remarks on people were all sarcasms—his mind was overflowed with a suffusion of ill-nature—he bit as well as growled."[32] Russelton wastes his days regretting the trifles of his former life. He is also malicious and filled with what Pelham calls a "ladylike languour" and a strangely cold disposition metaphorically confirmed by his need for a roaring fire throughout the day. Lytton's Russelton does exhibit the traditional doggish, misanthropic qualities of the uppercase Cynic, but he also supplements these qualities with the un-Diogenical attributes of effeminacy, passivity, and calculation, qualities redolent of modern cynicism.

When Russelton describes his early accession to social power, he discloses the kind of reductive, cynical calculation he made of the fashionable people he intended to dominate: "I saw that the character of the English was servile to rank, and yielding to pretension—they admire you for your acquaintance, and cringe to you for your conceit" (131). What Russelton had grasped was that the opinions of the English *Ton* are most easily manipulated by turning oneself into an advocate of exclusivism, pronouncing social doom on others, and facing down the objections of those much better qualified to judge. As he announced earlier: "The great secrets of being courted are, to shun others, and seem delighted with yourself. The latter is obvious enough; who the deuce *should* be pleased with you, if you yourself are not?" (130). And yet even those who once courted him have now rejected him, a rejection no less painful when he recalls how easily he had once led them. Russelton/Brummell's cynicism therefore suggests the disillusionment of the con artist or "insider-cynic," the man who once knew how to manipulate his targets but has now lost his touch.

Captain Jesse's *Memoirs* of Beau Brummell ([1844?]) extended this image of the aging cynical dandy in exile and treated his cynical misanthropy or indifference toward humanity as the direct result of disillusioning experience with the weak minds of his fashionable set. Jesse's *Memoirs* are filled with scenes of the lonely cynic-dandy meditating upon his losses in Calais, but he also introduces a new note of soured hedonism into the portrait that looks forward to Oscar Wilde's fusion of cynicism with decadence:

> The cynical beau, satiated with every pleasure, and callous to almost every species of excitement, could weep over the untimely death of a mouse, and grieve at the loss of his favourite dog, while the death of some of the companions of his early life would possibly have created little emotion in his mind; for with the remembrance of them would be associated recollections of the insincere and trifling character of their friendship and career and bitter reflections on his past and present position, —disease reminding him of the brilliant revels of the palace, and penury, the sums that he had squandered in wanton and unmeaning extravagance.[33]

Jesse's Brummell, "satiated with every pleasure, and callous to almost every species of excitement," betrays here a Baudelairean spleen, an indolence that verges on physical exhaustion. Brummell's cynical indifference, however, derives not just from his former devotion to physical pleasures, but also from his "bitter reflections on his past and present position." This state of continual remorse is indeed a kind of misanthropy, but one produced by his awareness of the insubstantiality of his former life. Jesse's dandy has become as deeply identified with excesses of physical pleasure as with fashion and the social forms of decorum. These excesses, however, now contribute to a cynicism based on disillusion rather than physical self-control, or what Hartley Coleridge called in a contemporaneous poem the "garb uncouth / And Cynic sneer of o'er experienced Sin."[34]

When Jesse stated that "Brummell's occasional fits of cynicism for his own species surpassed even those of Diogenes himself," the operative term here is "surpassed." Brummell's "cynicism" far outdoes that of Diogenes in the term's *modern* sense of "a morose contempt of the pleasures and arts of life" (as one contemporary dictionary defined it), though of course Brummell's contempt for pleasure also savored of sour grapes.[35]

Hence, Jesse's [1844?] application of "cynicism" to Brummell ascribed a number of new qualities to the cynic that would become important to Wilde and the subsequent development of the term: dandyism, naturally, but also the concern with fashion, social form, and pleasure that the dandiacal lifestyle entailed; selfishness and coldness; and finally, disillusionment. None of these terms could be considered part of the original semantic cluster of terms surrounding Diogenes or the early modern Cynics, though each term related in one way or another to the development of cynicism across the nineteenth century.

Underlying these transformations in the "cynic" between D'Israeli and Jesse, however, lay the notion of cynical indifference as an effective defensive strategy for the man of privilege caught up in an increasingly democratic, undifferentiated, mass society. The modern cynic, like Brummell, responded to this status confusion by acting unilaterally, exploiting the eagerness of others for approval while pretending not to care about their opinions. Because of the persistence of the misanthropic strand of cynicism through much of the nineteenth century, many writers interpreted Brummell's cynical indifference as a barely concealed misanthropy, but this misanthropy had a somewhat different flavor than earlier misanthropies—this was a cynical contempt for the species caused by long experience of its susceptibility, a susceptibility, however, he tacitly shared with those he manipulated. Unlike Diogenes or the singular early modern Cynic, the dandiacal cynic is not "cynical" because he pursues virtue or delusively believes himself more virtuous than others, but simply because he enjoys revealing the weaknesses of others. Casting cynicism in this light removes its specifically gendered links to the history of morality or philosophy, and so it is only at this phase of its semantic development that the term can be applied to women.

Margaret Oliphant demonstrates an awareness of the problems surrounding this concept in her *Blackwood's Magazine* review of Austen-Leigh's *Memoirs* of Jane Austen in 1870. Oliphant's criticism focuses on what she calls Austen's "feminine cynicism," a perverse enjoyment in identifying the weaknesses of others that has become detached from the rigors of moral judgment. Even if we do not share the explicitly Christian and didactic grounds of her criticism, Oliphant's rationale deserves close attention for her justifications for using such a term to describe Austen:

> Mr Austen-Leigh [author of the posthumous Austen *Memoir* that Oliphant is reviewing], without meaning it, throws out of his dim little lantern a

> passing gleam of light upon the fine vein of feminine cynicism which pervades his aunt's mind. It is something altogether different from the rude and brutal male quality that bears the same name. It is the soft and silent disbelief of a spectator who has to look at a great many things without showing any outward discomposure, and who has learned to give up any moral classification of social sins, and to place them instead on the level of absurdities.[36]

What we learn, first of all, from this passage is that by 1870 a writer and reviewer as sensitive as Oliphant had begun to feel a new sense of "feminine" cynicism emerging from the "rude and brutal male quality that bears the same name." In applying this new sense to Austen, she emphasizes how its discreetly feminized "disbelief" is far too accepting of "social sins," and how such cynicism is ready to treat social sins as "absurdities" for its own and others' enjoyment. In other words, Oliphant's reaction to Austen exhibits the same discomfort that Lister's Caroline had felt over Trebeck's "gay misanthropy" in exposing other people's weaknesses. Austen has in effect refused the traditional moralist's role of chastising those whose weaknesses she detects, a decision Oliphant regards as an abandonment of morality and activity together:

> —such are the foundations upon which the feminine cynicism which we attribute to Miss Austen is built [writes Oliphant]. . . . It is not absolute contempt . . . , but only a softened tone of general disbelief—amusement, nay enjoyment, of all those humours of humanity which are so quaint to look at as soon as you dissociate them from any rigid standard of right or wrong.[37]

It is the cynic's use of such materials for the sake of "amusement, nay enjoyment" that Oliphant remains most uneasy about, because it constitutes a perverse form of pleasure in the weaknesses of others. Though we are unused to hearing Austen described in this manner, this accusation opens up a surprising affinity between Austen's writing and Wilde's Lord Henry Wotton, who considers morality only to the extent that it spurs on his own pleasures. This is the zone in which we find the dangerous and decadent cynics of the second half of the nineteenth century.

Dangerous Cynics

When Jesse stressed the pathos of Brummell's final years, he simply retold in a different key the sad fate of Drennan's Regency-era "coxcomb turned misanthrope" who aspired to become a libelist. Drennan's pathologizing treatment of the cynic as a walking "virus" became increasingly important as the century wore on. The double trope of the diseased cynic/cynic as disease accompanied the loss of the cynic's specific class-character in a system of aristocratic decorum. The cynic was becoming a figure suggestive of both democratization *and* decadence, of cultural pathology spreading indiscriminately throughout an undifferentiated mass society.

The snarling yet isolated Cynic, though by no means absent from the scene, was gradually losing his dominance to a new figure, the ultrafashionable, sneering disbeliever and corrupter of youth. In some respects, this modern disbelieving cynic was modeled upon the Regency era's cynical dandy because he represented the tyrannical authority of fashion and novelty over traditional social and moral categories. But the fashionable cynic by the midcentury could be inserted, like the dandy, into much more alarming theories of cultural decadence, theories that hinged on the loss or recovery of masculine activity and strength.[38] Like a walking virus, the dangerous cynic spread disbelief and disillusion wherever he went.

For example, in the popular American preacher/lecturer Henry Ward Beecher's antebellum character study "The Cynic," Beecher called the Cynic "one who never sees a good quality in a man, and never fails to see a bad one" (115).[39] Beecher's set piece offers yet another example of the Cynic as embodiment of the worst moral possibilities of persuasion, a personality type who personifies bad influence, opportunistic use of language, and moral instability. Beecher's Cynic, however, wrenches language and morality out of joint not to excuse himself but to blacken others' motives and behavior. He does this because he has calculated, not without reason, that his own depraved character will be less visible if he focuses upon other people's moral failings. Because Beecher's Cynic interprets the ambiguities of human behavior and motive as uncharitably as possible, he has lost his welcome in human society. For Beecher, banishing the Cynic is a matter of civic hygiene, eliminating a source of doubt and disbelief from community life.

Beecher's Cynic is therefore "the human owl, vigilant in darkness and blind to light, mousing for vermin, and never seeing noble game. The Cynic puts all human action into only two classes—openly bad, and secretly bad. All virtue and generosity and disinterestedness are merely the appearance of good, but selfish at the bottom. He holds that no man does a good thing except for profit" (115). Beecher's Cynic can always discover selfishness in others because he discerns it in himself and needs to justify its presence in his thoughts.

But Beecher wishes to analyze the Cynic primarily for the damage he does to others with his language: "Thus his eye strains out every good quality and takes in only the bad. To him religion is hypocrisy, honesty a preparation for fraud, virtue only want of opportunity, and undeniable purity, asceticism. The live-long day he will coolly sit with sneering lip, uttering sharp speeches in the quietest manner, and in polished phrase, transfixing every character which is presented: *His words are softer than oil, yet are they drawn swords*" (116). The Cynic has mastered an art, not Wilde's art of "seeing things as they are," but of moral and verbal redescription that "strains out every good quality and takes in only the bad," turning virtue, for example, into mere "want of opportunity." His chronic disbelief in goodness damps and depresses all he encounters and makes those around him more like himself, "sore and morose." Yet this is done in the quietest, most polite manner possible. Because he assumes that some evil always resides in those outwardly good, he reduces everything beautiful and good about humanity into something mixed and unpleasant.

Beecher's Cynic is in fact a "polished cynic" along the lines of D'Israeli's Chesterfield and Walpole, a man whose hypocritical words are dangerous to the extent that their softness conceals their true malignity. Beecher points out the seductive appeal of such a figure for the young, when the Cynic's polite indifference to conventional morality teaches an equally ironic distance toward social authority. His effect upon the young is unmistakable: "They begin to indulge themselves in flippant sneers; and with supercilious brow, and impudent tongue, wagging to an empty brain, call to naught the wise, the long tried, and the venerable" (118). The imitation of the Cynic's unreflective "sneers" is dangerous chiefly for inexperienced youth, or for anyone still forming their beliefs.

Beecher concludes by warning readers against the Cynic's indifference to virtue, asserting that the Cynic's disbelief is a deliberate choice and therefore subject to blame. At the same time, the Cynic's disbelief and indifference are also symptoms of a morally compromised nature:

> Although experience should correct the indiscriminate confidence of the young, no experience should render them callous to goodness wherever seen. . . . Let it be remembered, that no man, who is not himself mortally diseased, will have a relish for disease in others. A swoln [*sic*] wretch, blotched all over with leprosy, may grin hideously at every wart or excrescence upon beauty. A wholesome man will be pained at it, and seek not to notice it. Reject, then, the morbid ambition of the Cynic, or cease to call yourself a man! (118–19)

Beecher's Cynic ultimately raises the question of experience in the moral formation of the young because this figure exhibits Coleridge's "Cynic sneer of o'er experienced Sin," a degree of experience that has rendered him ultimately "callous to goodness." Beecher's final image of the diseased cynic, blotched all over with leprosy and culpably enjoying whatever defects he can find, offers a complicated allegory of the Cynic's enjoyment of others' failings, because it assumes that only a perverse pleasure could make the Cynic "relish" others' "warts or excrescences."

To Beecher's diseased cynic we may add a metaphorical counterpart, the cynical public of Charles Mackay, which we may regard as an entire population vulnerable to an epidemic of stupidity and degradation. The audience affected by the cynic has graduated from face-to-face encounters (that is, the coxcomb-misanthrope able to witness the "sweet smile [turning] into a sneer") to an anonymous mass audience defined as passive and undiscriminating. This transformation of the insider-cynic's audience from an individual to an entire disillusioned public takes us one step further toward the ensemble effect described earlier in this chapter.

Charles Mackay (1814–89), editor, journalist, songwriter, and author of the famous *Extraordinary Popular Delusions* (1841), knew the public well enough from fifty years as a man of letters to announce his contempt for their judgment in an angry poem, "Cynical Ode to an Ultra Cynical Public" (1884). In his preface to the 1852 edition of the *Delusions,* Mackay had written, "We find that whole communities suddenly fix their minds upon one object, and go mad in its pursuit; that millions of people become simultaneously impressed with one delusion, and run after it, till their attention is caught by some new folly more captivating than the first."[40] Accordingly, Mackay's "Cynical Ode" depicts *cynics* (the plural is important, because it indicates the acknowledgment of an entire class of cynics) as dangerous because they can easily sway an equally degraded "Ultra Cynical Public."

According to Mackay, the cynics and the "Ultra Cynical Public" resemble one another in their shared willingness to sneer at anything good. Mackay's title, however, shows the author as a would-be moralist immoderately angry at a particular abuse, and lapsing into the cynical, meaning reductive, attitude of his target, the public. Mackay writes:

> You [the "Ultra Cynical Public"] prefer a buffoon to a scholar,
> A harlequin to a teacher,
> A jester to a statesman,

An Anonyma flaring on horseback
To a modest and spotless woman—
Brute of a public!
You think that to sneer shows wisdom,
That a gibe outvalues a reason.
That slang, such as thieves delight in,
Is fit for the lips of the gentle,
And rather a grace than a blemish,
Thick-headed public!
You think that if merit's exalted
'Tis excellent sport to decry it,
And trail its good name in the gutter;
And that cynics, white-gloved and cravatted,
Are the cream and quintessence of all things,
Ass of a public!
You think that success must be merit,
That honour and virtue and courage
Are all very well in their places,
But that money's a thousand times better;
Detestable, stupid, degraded
Pig of a public![41]

Mackay's first two stanzas follow the line of attack seen in Beecher, in which the "Ultra Cynical Public," when confronted with a better and worse alternative, consistently prefers the worse. The final two stanzas complain about the public's desire to decry and degrade merit wherever it finds it. In such an atmosphere, the "ass of a public" has decided that "cynics, white-gloved and cravatted, / Are the cream and quintessence of all things." The "Ultra Cynical Public" is more interested in the opinions of the ultrapolite, ultrarich and ultrafashionable cynics than in those of anyone else. The force driving all these upside-down assessments is money, the universal and conventional value that wipes out any competing values in its wake.

Coming near the end of a genealogy that began with Brummell's dandyish cynic, Mackay's poem suggests that the nineteenth-century shift to a comfortable, well-dressed, fashionable cynic coincides with the recognition of the cynic's intimate relationship with a powerful though frustratingly indifferent and manipulated public. The concept of cynicism develops, therefore, alongside the notion of the public participating legitimately in a democratic polity, but whose mode of participation remains disappointingly passive and spectatorial.

As a result, "the people" have been degraded into an "Ultra Cynical Public," or what one political theorist has termed "an undifferentiated mass of political consumers."[42] Nonetheless, we should remember that these are interested representations of the public and its passivity, the product of the desires and frustrations of the intellectual class whose professional role is to move them in a particular direction. This relation of the cynic to the disillusioned target of his persuasion becomes particularly clear in Wilde's *Dorian Gray,* when he takes up the question of Lord Henry's strange influence over the once-innocent Dorian.

Oscar Wilde's *Picture of Dorian Gray*

Oscar Wilde stands at the end of the genealogy of the cynic-dandy, an all-male "lineage" that stretches even further back to the aphoristic tradition of self-sufficient, itinerant wit represented by Diogenes. Wilde's incorporation of aphorisms into the preface to *Dorian Gray* also pushes the lightly disguised fiction or anecdotal compilations about nineteenth-century dandies into a more reflective, aestheticizing direction.[43] Yet it is no accident that Wilde's writings and remarks should also constitute some of the most powerful reflections we have upon the meaning of cynicism in the nineteenth century. Like Nietzsche, Chamfort, or La Rochefoucauld, Wilde discovered that a cynical wit is best conveyed in the abbreviated space of the aphorism.

It is doubly fitting, then, to conclude this chapter's genealogy with Wilde's *Picture of Dorian Gray,* to show how the previous trajectory of the cynical dandy, with its associations of publicity, fashion, decadence, and disillusion, has been folded into the characterization of Lord Henry and his verbal seduction of the youthful Dorian. Wilde expands the dandy's deliberate transgressions of socially defined masculinity into an "atmosphere" of unmistakable though closeted homoeroticism, by showing how Henry's cynicism entails a playful inversion of commonplace values like marriage and decorum, values associated in this text with a feminized institutional morality.

At the same time, Wilde exploits the earlier writers' emphasis upon the disillusioned experience of the cynical ex-hedonist, in order to hint at the strictly physical pleasures that have ceased to give Henry enjoyment. Instead, the disenchanted cynic-aesthete Henry contents himself by treating others' moral transgressions as a combination of joke, aesthetic spectacle, and scientific experiment. Wilde, however, does not share Henry's openly instrumental attitude toward other people's suffering and distinguishes between the verbal consequences of Henry's "cynical jesting" and the far more destructive results of Dorian's earnest, believing imitation of his mentor's philosophy.

Dorian Gray makes at least three important contributions to the concept of cynicism in its post-1814, modern phase. The first is its narrative demonstration of how the entire "ensemble effect" is produced and maintained by the interaction of the three distinct cynicisms described by Keenan, cynicisms that are part of a system of power and publicity that helps to disenchant the public. Not only is Henry readily understandable as a disempowered insider-cynic, but we can also find instances of a cynically disenchanted public (Sibyl's outraged theatrical audience, leading to Dorian's disillusionment) and the master-cynic's exercise of power (Dorian's blackmail of Alan Campbell) running throughout the book. The important thing to remember is that the notion of power operating throughout this book is akin to Michel Foucault's famous analysis of a "power network" in which "power is exercised through innumerable points, in the interplay of nonegalitarian and mobile relations."[44] In other words, Henry may be perfectly able to exercise power as a master-cynic in his relations with servants and actresses, but in his relations with Dorian his power is limited to the persuasive force of his words. That is the plight of the insider-cynic.

The second contribution of this book to the concept of cynicism is Wilde's epochal transvaluation/redescription of the fashionable or dangerous cynic in his ambiguous characterization of Lord Henry. Wilde takes an ironic attitude toward those like Beecher who would be horrified at Henry's unscrupulous desire to influence youth, his opportunistic use of language, and the moral instability he introduces into society. Instead, Wilde works hard to make Henry's cynicism and dandyism as attractive as possible. He accomplishes this first of all by pointing out the artificiality and dissimulation of the conventional people around Dorian, to show that Henry's dandyish attitude is not a departure from his society's values but a parodic intensification that renders such values visible for the first time. Then Wilde acknowledges the genuine social appeal of cynics like Henry, whose jokes offer others a chance to share and publicly acknowledge their disenchantment.

The book's third contribution to the concept is Wilde's reworking of the earlier narratives of decadence and degeneration that focused on the dangers faced by the public if large numbers tried to imitate the cynic. These narratives includes the double notion of diseased cynic/cynic as social disease, as well as the melodramatic narratives of improper influence, all of which Wilde heightened into scenes of verbal homoerotic seduction. Wilde departs from these scenarios by exploring Henry's influence upon Dorian as a series of superb verbal performances that somehow inspire the young man to pursue his own dreadful actions. To the extent that we blame Henry for Dorian's behavior, we acknowledge the force of his words. Yet no one could equate Henry's destabilizing words with the ultimately selfish and destructive acts of Dorian. Cynicism, therefore, raises profound ethical questions about language's social implications: how language functions in this book not just as description but as verbal action, impelling actors in particular directions, and for which we hold language users like Henry accountable to some extent. Most important, Wilde has invited us in any number of ways to make the comparison between Henry and his own modes of (cynical) verbal invention.

To make sure that I am not misunderstood, I should say at the outset that I do not read Wilde as a cynic in any simple or unreflective sense. To the contrary, I treat him as a writer who uses this term as a vehicle for self-reflection and as a tool to analyze his ambivalent relation to an audience that he wished to please but also persuade, perhaps even change in some important way. When we think about Wilde's socialist writings, for example, we can safely say that Wilde did believe that political, social, and economic changes on a wide scale were both possible and desirable. In this respect, we should not read back into his cynicism an attitude of quietism or defeatism.[45]

In the case of *Dorian Gray,* the concept of cynicism clearly suffused Wilde's characterization of Lord Henry and enabled Wilde to extract and place onto the page a specific, and specifically social, dimension of his personality—the dandy, performer, and wit—to see how much tension he could introduce between his audience's most deeply held beliefs and their enjoyment of his brilliantly inverted commonplaces. Henry's compulsive philosophizing therefore reflects the intellectually dominating part of Wilde, the self-assured wit able to keep his audiences at a remove.

At the same time, Lord Henry's cynical detachment is tested by his ambiguous friendship with Dorian, so that his superior wit does not gain him much more happiness than the shorter-lived Basil. Henry's self-announced superiority to the commonplace is not as complete as he would like, and his habitual irony leads him into a state of disenchantment that finally resembles stoic resignation. Henry's cynicism therefore becomes a reflective mode that is essentially conducted in public, in front of an audience. Consequently, Wilde explores the full reach and range of the modern concept of cynicism further than any other nineteenth- or twentieth-century writer in English, because he renders it in a way that make its social as well as moral dimensions visible.

The *Picture of Dorian Gray* captures both the aphoristic and the dandiacal modes of cynicism in its presentation of Lord Henry, whose remarks probe the weaknesses of both the gorgeous boy-thing Dorian and the artist Basil.[46] Lord Henry is a full-fledged society wit, a fashionable favorite who produces paradoxes on demand and represents an attitude of intellectual playfulness that both delights and repulses the other characters. Yet Lord Henry is also a dandy and a do-nothing, a man whose leisure allows him to set aside social and moral constraints for the sake of his own pleasures. Lord Henry is a surrogate for Wilde in his aphoristic dandy mode, but with more economic security and a better lineage than Wilde himself; he also exhibits enough faults and blind spots that readers should beware of imitating his paradoxes too closely or literally. That is one of the many lessons that Dorian fails to learn.

It is also significant that Lord Henry's cynicism, like Wilde's, is most powerfully conveyed in aphorisms, which like Diogenes' apothegms or Nietzsche's aphorisms enforce reflection but do not congeal into settled philosophic doctrine. Best of all, they invite readers to compare the "philosophizer's" life with the substance of his sayings, to see whether the life reflects the "opinions." We wish to see how a man who says such wicked things manages to live with his wife and friends, and Henry's private life looks both unremarkable and strangely uninhabited, a place that he rarely visits. Like Brummell, he seems scarcely to exist when he is not in company. We cannot imagine him sitting at home alone. Yet give him an audience, and he will say splendid things.

Fittingly, Wilde's own remarks about cynicism neither agree with themselves nor fully endorse Lord Henry's stance. The first one comes from Wilde's play *Lady Windermere's Fan*, when Lord Darlington defines the cynic as one who "knows the price of everything and the value of nothing."[47] Darlington offers a definition reminiscent of Beecher's and Mackay's conventional cynics, who have substituted the polite and fashionable values of money and status for older notions of virtue. These conventional cynics are also unconcerned about any values not reducible to money and status. Hence, Darlington's version of the cynic is dismissive about others' feelings, aspirations, and motivations and disbelieves them when they give their reasons for their conduct. As I pointed out in the introduction, this version of the cynic is so confident that he has unmasked interlocutors, and so dismissive of their stated arguments and reasons, that he makes anything like real dialogue or debate impossible. In his defensive stance, this conventional cynic has rendered himself unpersuadable. So why is Wilde so eager to study this figure, or to present a more complex version in Lord Henry?

Wilde answers this question in a second aphorism, where he notes the particular value of the cynic's perspective. This is the aphorism I quoted at the outset of this chapter: "Cynicism," says Wilde, "is merely the art of seeing things as they are instead of as they ought to be." Under this definition, cynicism can be described as moral realism, the ability to observe "things as they are" without allowing one's own values, prejudices, or interests, to distort the account. This "art of seeing things as they are" might seem to require only a correction of one's perceptions, simply separating facts from values, values from facts. But is it really so easy to "see things as they are"? Wilde's phrase "the *art* of seeing things" suggests that such demystification does not come naturally to the would-be cynic. Instead, cynicism represents an ethos that must be cultivated and a form of knowledge that can only be drawn from experience. The cynic can only become what he is after some time and effort spent distinguishing "things as they are" from "things as they ought to be."

For his struggle to distinguish between moral description and moral prescription, however, the cynic draws heavy, continuous fire from civic moralists like Beecher, who call him a "burnished adder, whose life is mischief, and whose errand is death" (118).[48] It is clear, nonetheless, that the difference between the first and second remark on cynicism hinges on the conventionality of the cynic's judgments. A conventional cynic who judges others solely and reductively on their "price" is not as valuable as the cynic who sees "things as they are," without the help of conventional values and ideals. And the distinction between conventional and unconventional cynics is harder to draw than it initially seems, as we shall find with Lord Henry.

Unsurprisingly, Lord Henry receives widely divergent responses from the other characters, though even his friends recognize that he is "cynical" largely because he is indifferent to others' moral qualities. He always notes the shortfall between their moral professions and their actual performance, though he does so ironically, without blaming his targets for their failures. It is his indifference to matters of morality that makes him both attractive and unsettling. As Lord Henry says: "I never approve, or disapprove, of anything now. It is an absurd attitude to take towards life. We are not sent into the world to air our moral prejudices. I never take any notice of what common people say, and I never interfere with what charming people do. If a personality fascinates me, whatever mode of expression that personality selects is absolutely delightful to me" (111). Lord Henry disregards moral questions because he wishes to enjoy people's sins and foibles as if they were works of art. Moral judgments are simply "what common people say," and he never needs to "interfere" or act upon "what charming people do." This quality of cynical detachment carries an undeniable air of class privilege in its aesthetic enjoyment of others' lives.

The five uses of "cynic" or "cynicism" in *Dorian Gray* reflect Henry's irony toward the conventional values represented by women, marriage, or other moralizing institutions. In spite of his marriage, Lord Henry boasts of a dandyish indifference to women, an indifference equally suggestive either of the conventionally homosocial world of all-male Victorian private clubs or the homoerotic world of 1890s bohemian life. For all of Wilde's careful equivocation about the relation between Dorian and Henry, it is obvious that this story is at some level a seduction tale along the lines of Beecher's hysterical scenario of young boys and dangerous cynics. We could even call it a love story conducted via quotation. Wilde, of course, lovingly quotes from himself throughout Henry's dialogues and speeches, but we should also note how the only evidence of Dorian's attachment to the older man lies in his habit of referring back to Henry. Henry, of course, is much quieter about his attachments, choosing simply to project a pose of indifference about marriage and women that seems unaltered by the presence of Dorian, Basil, his wife, or his mistress.

Henry's indifference appears in the very first chapter, when he tells Basil that "the one charm of marriage is that it makes a life of deception absolutely necessary for both parties" (46). Basil refuses to believe, however, that Henry is as bad a husband as his jokes would suggest: "I hate the way you talk about your married life, Harry. . . . You never say a moral thing, and you never do a wrong thing. Your cynicism is simply a pose" (46). Basil, in other words, is accusing his friend of (cynically) failing to make his pose a reality. Henry's pose, however, is conducted not for the sake of actions but for the verbal reflections it provides, verbal reflections shared with an audience always intent on overhearing his bons mots. This kind of behavior, then, is not half-hearted participation in society but a redirection of his energies toward a verbal invention continually shared with others. This dandyish delight in rhetorical display is confirmed, however, with the pleasure he takes in one of the more realistic by-products of married life, the lies told by couples intent on following social forms. Henry actually enjoys these lies because of the verbal inventiveness they inspire. Even marriage can be seen as a source of Art rather than Life when viewed this way.

Basil's ironic accusation of Henry's "hypocritical" pose as a bad husband takes the usual form of such accusations, but accusing a cynic of a cynically false pose of cynicism leaves us wondering what portion of Henry is *not* pose, grimace, or artifice? Henry, for all his aesthetic, distanced enjoyment of sin

("Sin is the only real colour-element left in modern life," he observes), never aspires to the more physical or literal-minded libertinism of his moral/psychological "experiment" and protégé Dorian Gray. This is the superbly Brummellesque note to his character: his quality of self-restraint. Henry talks a great deal about pleasure and sin but is rarely seen engaging in it, once we discount the strawberry smoothie he consumes in the first chapter. Unlike Dorian, Henry's reputation never prevents him from mixing in the finest circles of London society. Henry's tacit conformity to the demands of aristocratic society make him that much more cynical than Dorian, because Dorian suffers and worries over his numerous transgressions, while Henry's transgressions remain at the level of verbal paradox and dinner-table wit.

In another scene, Wilde explores the pleasing social exchanges instigated by Henry's cynicism, even while the inwardly transformed Dorian sits close by in self-enclosed agony. For all their mutual attraction, these two have been set on very different paths. Dorian, who has caused Sybil's death and murdered Basil, silently suffers from thoughts that his beautiful appearance never betrays. Henry is as blithe as ever and puts in one of his best performances. The clueless Lady Narborough asks Henry for his assistance in marrying off Dorian to an eligible young woman. She wishes Dorian to have "what *The Morning Post* calls a suitable alliance, and I want you both to be happy" (209).

> "What nonsense people talk about happy marriages!" exclaimed Lord Henry. "A man can be happy with any woman, as long as he does not love her."
>
> "Ah! what a cynic you are!" cried the old lady [Narborough], pushing back her chair, and nodding to Lady Ruxton. "You must come and dine with me soon again. You are really an admirable tonic, much better than what Sir Andrew prescribes for me. You must tell me what people you would like to meet, though. I want it to be a delightful gathering." (209–10)

Lady Narborough's enthusiasm for Henry's talk stems from her own disillusioned experience of marriage: "'Narborough wasn't perfect' cried the old lady" (208). Yet Wilde has juxtaposed this kind of social comedy with much more melodramatic material, something worthy of even Beecher's sermonizing. While Henry impresses Lady Narborough with his "wickedness," the seemingly innocent Dorian sits calmly with the rest of the dinner party, grimly conscious that his now sneering portrait hangs in a locked room.

Yet Wilde is interested in presenting something that a moralist like Beecher cannot fathom, the genuine social appeal of a cynic like Lord Henry:

> Lady Narborough hit him with her fan. "Lord Henry, I am not at all surprised that the world says that you are extremely wicked."
>
> "But what world says that?" asked Lord Henry, elevating his eyebrows. "It can only be the next world. This world and I are on excellent terms." (208)

Here we might see something of Henry's secret appeal: he voices the doubts of others about the proprieties they follow simply for the sake of form. His irony does not drive away the respectable the way it might in Beecher but actually draws them closer to him. Listeners like Lady Narborough eagerly follow his fun at the expense of the moral life, and he brings his audience together in a sense of shared discontent and disenchantment. As Freud explained of "cynical jokes," when the cynic voices his discontent with the institutionally imposed sacrifices of moral and social life, others may very well take pleasure in his jokes because they confirm what everyone has sacrificed for the sake of civilization: spontaneous physical pleasures.[49] The fact that Henry is so clearly a product of the refinement that he protests against somehow makes him more appealing as a dinner guest. This social dimension of cynicism, the pleasures it gives to people by voicing their complaints about the unpleasures of moral and social life, seems crucial to understanding its appeal and its persistence.

Moralists like Beecher may blame the cynic for voicing dissatisfactions about social life, but these common dissatisfactions are precisely what cynics allow us to exchange with one another. For Beecher, such complaints would either not exist, or perhaps would never get exposed, were it not for the cynic. Yet Wilde, for all his supposed cynicism, seems by the respective fates of Dorian and Lord Henry to suggest that it is Dorian's fate, not Henry's, to become the grotesque monster. As the true believer in Henry's "poisonous theories," Dorian experiences sins and consequences that Henry never imagines. Which is worse, Wilde tacitly asks, Dorian's quality of belief, or Henry's cynical disbelief?

The final instance of "cynical" emphasizes the estrangement between Henry and Dorian, cynic and sinner, while making it clear that cynicism often reveals the weaknesses of others without comprehending what it reveals. The word appears after Sybil Vane's brother, intent on murdering Dorian in revenge for her suicide, is accidentally shot during a hunting party at the Duke and Duchess of Monmouth's. When Dorian regrets bringing the subject up to the Duchess as a "hideous subject," Henry returns that it is a mere accidental killing, and unworthy of notice:

> "It is an annoying subject," broke in Lord Henry. "It has no psychological value at all. Now if Geoffrey [the one who shot the man] had done the

thing on purpose, how interesting he would be! I should like to know some one who had committed a real murder."

"How horrid of you, Harry!" cried the Duchess. "Isn't it, Mr Gray? Harry, Mr Gray is ill again. He is going to faint." (234)

While Henry and the Duchess trade remarks, Dorian hides in his room, overcome by the consciousness of guilt that Henry's remark had reactivated: "Upstairs, in his own room, Dorian Gray was lying on a sofa, with terror in every tingling fibre of his body. Life had suddenly become too hideous a burden for him to bear. The dreadful death of the unlucky beater, shot in the thicket like a wild animal, had seemed to him to prefigure death for himself also. He had nearly swooned at what Lord Henry had said in a chance mood of cynical jesting" (235).

This scene reasserts the relative innocence of Henry, whose "cynical jesting" strikes at his friend Dorian only by "chance." Henry's curiosity about the psychological implications of murder is as mannered as ever, but it only distances him from Dorian's far more tormenting experience of guilt. This is one of the few moments in the novel where Henry sounds genuinely naïve, especially when compared with his supposed protégé. As a cynic, Henry only toys with the emotions and actions that Dorian has experienced as a real murderer. Unlike Henry, Dorian has acted upon his friend's seductive words about good and evil. Dorian's indifference, like the "high indifference of joy" he felt just before the man (his would-be avenger Jim Vane) was shot, is swept away by every reminder of his guilt, while Henry's indifference remains secure in its purely verbal and reflective form.

In the same way that Shakespeare's *Timon* rigorously dismantled the conventional equation of Cynic philosopher and misanthrope, Wilde's *Dorian Gray* performs a similar dismantling of the moralistic equation of cynic and sinner. Wilde takes Beecher's conventional narrative of an older cynic influencing (or seducing) the young man but goes on to make the cynic a mere commentator upon sinfulness rather than a sinner himself. Henry's doctrine of Individualism appears in his refusal of everyday moral language, but Wilde also shows that Dorian is at some level incapable of understanding Henry's ironies, no matter how much he loves to repeat them. One hint of Henry's superiority comes from Dorian's inability to produce any wit of his own. He can only quote Henry, and even that in ways that seem lame compared to Henry's delivery.

Once *Dorian Gray* was published, however, the public ignored the irony of its treatment of the philosophic seduction narrative. Instead, *Dorian Gray*'s conclusion provided the moral pattern that structured the public shaming and punishment that Wilde himself would personally undergo during his very public trial. Wilde's sympathetic portrayal of the all-male, fashionable world of Dorian, Henry, and Basil cemented his reputation for immorality, an immorality made worse somehow by his public pose of dandyish flippancy. The *Daily Chronicle* reviewed *Dorian Gray* upon its first appearance in *Lippincott's*, and called it a

> tale spawned from the leprous literature of the French Decadents—a poisonous book, the atmosphere of which is heavy with the mephitic odours of moral and spiritual putrefaction—a gloating study of the mental and physical corruption of a fresh, fair, and golden youth, which might be horrible and fascinating but for its effeminate frivolity, its studied insincerity, its theatrical cynicism, its tawdry mysticism, its flippant philosophizings, and the contaminating trail of garish vulgarity which is over all Mr Wilde's elaborate Wardour Street aestheticism and obtrusively cheap scholarship.[50]

Note that the description echoes the terms of Beecher's warnings against the cynic's deformed and corrupting enjoyment of disease. Note also that the reviewer has in effect read *Dorian Gray* as if it were centered on Lord Henry, and endorsed his view alone as the truth. Yet Henry is a sad and irrelevant character by the end of the novel, has no awareness of Dorian's agony, and plays no role at all in the final catastrophe. By the end of the book, Henry's "cynical jesting" can only reach Dorian by chance.

Julian Hawthorne, in a *Lippincott's* review of 1890, takes more care to distinguish between the cynicism of Lord Henry and the more ambiguous attitude of Wilde:

> [Wilde's epigrams'] wit is generally cynical; but they are put into the mouth of one of the characters, Lord Harry, and Mr Wilde himself refrains from definitely committing himself to them; though one cannot help suspecting that Mr Wilde regards Lord Harry as being an uncommonly able fellow. Be that as it may, Lord Harry plays the part of Old Harry in the story, and lives to witness the destruction of every other person in it. He may be taken as an imaginative type of all that is most evil and most refined in modern civilization,—a charming, gentle, witty, euphemistic Mephistopheles, who deprecates the vulgarity of goodness, and muses aloud about "those renun-

ciations that men have unwisely called virtue, and those natural rebellions that wise men still call sin."[51]

Hawthorne and other contemporaries receptive to *Dorian Gray* have noted that Wilde does not commit himself fully to any character's perspective in this fiction, despite his affinity for the cynicism of Lord Harry.[52] Hawthorne's review does, however, suggest one possible reason for the anxiety of the *Daily Chronicle* review: the role of Lord Harry as Old Harry, the Mephistophelean tempter who represents "all that is most evil and most refined in modern civilization."[53] Wilde's most daring gesture is to make the cynic—and in this case, the barely disguised, effeminate, and morally indifferent unheterosexual Lord Henry—the representative of both the refinement and moral corruption of modern civilization. No wonder that Henry, and by extension, Wilde, invite violent denunciations from the press, as self-styled protectors of popular piety.

By 1895, during Wilde's trial against the Marquess of Queensberry for libel, the *London Star* carried this headline: "OSCAR WILDE/DEFENDS HIMSELF AT THE OLD BAILEY/CHARGES BROUGHT AGAINST HIM BY LORD QUEENSBERRY/The Aesthete Gives Characteristically Cynical Evidence, Replete with Pointed Epigrams and Startling Paradox, and Explains his Views on Morality in Art."[54] The tendency to read Wilde as another version of Lord Harry led to his arrest and disgrace, with every bit of evidence of Wilde's irony or ambiguity soundly punished by the newspapers and the court as further evidence of his guilt. Wilde's refusal of shame, and his continued insistence on paradox, made his offenses the more aggravating to both press and public desiring an unequivocal confession of guilt and remorse. Wilde became an emblem of immorality, of unhealthy sexual desires, of modern civilization gone wrong. To his accusers he seemed the embodiment of lowercase, sneering and disbelieving cynicism. Yet it was Wilde's willingness to undergo a process of public shaming for the sake of his paradoxes that placed him in the same genealogical line of uppercase Cynics and parrhesiasts like Diogenes or Jean-Jacques Rousseau.

From Oscar Wilde to Michel Foucault: The Cultural Politics of Cynicism

In the Regency period and afterward, the cynical dandy scandalized the intellectuals competing with him for the public's attention because he protested against modernity's conventional values of work and utility through strategies of public self-display. Because the dandy's protest, in its deliberate uselessness, was not intelligible as "protest" in its conventionally intellectual and literary modes, the dandy was treated dismissively as a passive and effeminate personality. Carlyle's *Sartor Resartus* is a classic example of this kind of antidandiacal writing in the earlier period. Antidandiacal writers, however, remained oblivious to the fact that dandyism—at least at the level practiced by Brummell or D'Orsay—constitutes a mode of lived criticism of utility and productivity that showed their ethical emptiness as normative ideals; more important, their lives demonstrated that a man need not be useful or productive to be recognized as a man.[55]

Following Wilde's trial, the antidandiacal writing of the earlier period fed into an emerging anticynical discourse, which criticized the cynic's passivity, conformity, and surrender by upholding the conventional masculine values of activity, independence, and self-possession. Wilde, however, anticipated and foiled this kind of reductive reading of Lord Henry by redescribing his dandyism, and therefore his cynicism, as a superior form of masculine self-possession.

There is no fitter representative of the lowercase, modern cynic and philosophizer than Wilde's Lord Henry, with his languid eyes and his bad habits of lounging on sofas and smoking opium-laced cigarettes. The numerous critical attacks on Wilde's *Dorian Gray* show the anxieties raised by the dangerously seductive Lord Henry, who preaches surrender to the senses but is never seen in a disordered state. Is he feminized in his surrender to temptation, or self-possessed like a true gentleman? Wilde throws out contradictory hints and gives no definitive answer. Henry threatens the moral boundaries of the social order to the extent that he drops critical epigrams on marriage, yet remains married, and retains his membership in the same social circles that closed ranks against Dorian Gray. Henry's example shows not only the minimal levels of belief needed for marriage to work, but also how little belief is needed in general for societies to work. He represents a scandal to the notion that societies rest on some coherent set of communal beliefs rather than some configuration of interests, opinions, institutions, and power.

The hostile nineteenth-century reception to *Dorian Gray* can also provide us with some insight into more recent denunciations of present-day cynicism. For example, Timothy Bewes's left-wing critique of cynicism and postmodernity uses the same passages I have just quoted about Dorian's supine terrors and Lord Henry's cynical jest.[56] Bewes makes an extended analogy between Lord Henry's cynical jesting and the political and moral irresponsibility of postmodern cynicism. Oddly enough, Bewes regards Tony Blair's New Labour Party, postmodernism, and Lord Henry as equivalent manifestations of the same "cynicism."[57] As I have already argued, treating cynicism as if it functioned the same way coming from the powerful, their publicists, or from the disillusioned public is a serious error. I would suggest therefore that Bewes's notions of cynicism are reductive when not incoherent, and that his entire critique is based on a significant misreading of Wilde's and Henry's dandyism. Bewes simply fails to understand how the dandy questions conventional values and puts his own into effect: through carefully gauged acts of ironic self-display.

In his hatred of postmodern dandyism, Bewes unwittingly recapitulates the terms of the antidandiacal writing of the nineteenth century and makes clear its extension into the critiques of cynicism still popular in the twentieth century. In his hostility toward all things dandyish, ironic, and self-consciously playful, Bewes unaccountably forgets the homoerotic dimension to Henry's dandyism and neglects its critical charge in a society given over to compulsory heterosexuality and Christianity. According to Bewes, Lord Henry's "blasé attitude in no way challenges mundane reality but appear[s] rather as a defeatist accommodation with it, an abnegation of responsibility that Hegel describes as 'fleeing from the universal,' a form of self-satisfaction that exercises wilful blindness as a psychic strategy, that declares 'All is vanity,' and resorts instead to the superficial pleasures of personality." (37). This reading of Henry seems wrong on several counts, since it overlooks the criminalized status of homosexual behavior during Wilde's time, including the prosecutions and disgrace that Wilde suffered, not least from the notoriety caused by *Dorian Gray*'s representations of homoerotic love. Henry's aphorisms on behalf of a homoerotically charged pleasure, uselessness, and wit were designed to confound the commonplace understandings of "mundane reality" of the heterosexual portion of the reading audience, as the scandalized contemporary reviews of *Dorian Gray* attest. Bewes's reading of the cynical dandy as a mere passive observer of reality does not do justice to Henry's function in the book as an "influence" upon Dorian, or as a spokesman for the moral superiority of "experience" and "Individualism" over more commonplace notions of morality. We may or may not wish to quarrel with Lord Henry over his peculiar notions of morality, but he cannot be dismissed that easily as superficial or willfully blind. In this respect, the reference to Hegel is a giveaway because indeed Henry in his Nietzschean, aphoristic moments is utterly uninterested in the earnest notions of progress he hears about in fashionable drawing rooms. But this is not to agree with Bewes that Henry therefore fails to act.

What Bewes seems not to understand about nineteenth-century dandyism, and therefore about Henry's characterization, is his *parodic* relation to his period's notions of gentlemanliness, an aggressive form of imitation that dares others to notice the difference between a green and a white buttonhole carnation (Wilde's sole extravagance in dress after his U.S. tour, and a tacit signal of his closeted identity). When a dandy deliberately conforms to gentlemanly canons of behavior and dress (with infinitesimal variations, of course), he becomes threatening to the extent that he can pass as a gentleman to the stupid and undiscerning part of that class. In other words, it is not the self-display of the dandy that signals his contempt for the upper classes but his carefully modulated conformity, which signifies participation without belief. Regenia Gagnier and others have convincingly read Wilde's all-male trial as a form of symbolic exclusion of the homosexual man, in which the unacknowledged homosocial ties of the Public School and the Gentlemanly class were forced to distance themselves from the more open, bohemian style of homoerotic attraction found in Wilde's artistic circles.[58] Because Wilde's attachments to other men so closely resembled the Public School ties of more conventional gentleman, he was attacked for his dandyish cynicism and sent into exile. In the character of Lord Henry, where Bewes sees "defeatist accommodation" and superficial, apolitical pleasure, I would find an aggressively parodic attitude to his own era's moral and gender norms, and an insistence upon the value of his own pleasures.

Unsurprisingly, we must look to a different kind of commentary, with far more flexible definitions of politics and gender, to recognize the historical significance of cynicism and dandyism. When we look into the works of Michel Foucault, we discover that Foucault once linked together nineteenth-century dandies, Enlightenment philosophes, and the ancient Cynics into a genealogy of men attempting to extend their freedom by closely examining the philosophical and political opportunities afforded them by modernity. There is nothing passive or spectatorial about Foucault's triad of dandy-philosophe-Cynic: each of these types is interested in a form of self-cultivation that does not end with the self. Each man must cultivate himself in public, perform himself in public, and communicate with others, to fulfill his mission.

Foucault's essay "What Is Enlightenment?" cites Baudelaire's treatment of the dandy in "The Painter of Modern Life" as a particularly acute discussion of the dandy's peculiar relation to modernity:

> Modernity for Baudelaire is not simply a form of relationship to the present; it is also a mode of relationship that has to be established with oneself.

> The deliberate attitude of modernity is tied to an indispensable asceticism. To be modern is not to accept oneself as one is in the flux of the passing moments; it is to take oneself as object of a complex and difficult elaboration: what Baudelaire, in the vocabulary of his day, calls *dandysme*.[59]

We may briefly note how Baudelaire, and by extension, Foucault, remain within the implicit gendering of asceticism, so that Baudelaire's dandy and Foucault's "Modern man" are the most fully active, ascetic, independent, free, and, self-possessed men imaginable, simply because they have mastered their own pleasures.

Nonetheless, Baudelaire's misogyny, joined with Wilde's and Foucault's indifference to women's fates, raises the question of whether Foucault's heavily gendered ideal of self-sufficiency is even available to women.[60] My response would be that a dandiacal discipline like Henry's makes visible the institutionalized moralities that affect both men and women. I also suspect that women may make use of this kind of cynicism, however limiting, in the way that Lady Narborough made use of Henry's smart remarks: as an opportunity to voice their own discontents. In this respect, Wilde's version of the philosophical life may be more open and useful to feminist readers than Foucault's dandyism.

We find in the dandy's ethos of unceasing self-invention another version of Foucault's preferred vision of the "philosophical life" made possible by the Enlightenment. In the final paragraphs of the essay, the philosophical life, as it is elaborated in the Enlightenment, is one "in which the critique of what we are is at one and the same time the historical analysis of the limits that are imposed on us and an experiment with the possibility of going beyond them (50). According to Foucault, the ethos shared by dandies and the Enlightenment is this stress on the philosophical life, the life of critique of what we are and historical analysis of the limits imposed on us. As Foucault announced in a 1983 interview: "The key to the personal poetic attitude of a philosopher is not to be sought in his ideas, as if it could be deduced from them, but rather in his philosophy-as-life, in his philosophical life, his ethos."[61] Even Gagnier, who is skeptical of Foucault's final movement into a "care of the self" modeled on ancient philosophy, proposes Wilde's "Soul of Man under Socialism" as a reminder of "what a really radical aesthetic, a socialist aesthetic, looks like: it is an aesthetic not reduced to artworks, an aesthetic of the everyday rather than the extraordinary, of the many rather than the few."[62]

In these respects, Foucault's final lectures on the Cynics anticipate some of Gagnier's demands for a "really radical aesthetic": in his emphasis on the Cynics' philosophical "way of life," their harmonization of word and deed through self-testing, and their parrhesiastic mission to shock the maximum number of people out of their false opinions. Yet Foucault clearly diverges from Gagnier when he theorizes political action apart from an overarching master-narrative of historical progress.

Foucault's refusal is implicit in the *History of Sexuality*'s post-Marxist elaboration of concepts like "power networks" and "discourse," but it is also consistent with his other critiques of modernity and modernization narratives, especially with regard to emerging scientific rationalities. In contrast with those more conventional modernization narratives, Foucault's compound of the dandy and philosophe represents an ascetic, self-conscious form of modernity that takes itself "as object of a complex and difficult elaboration," not as an instance of completed historical progress.[63]

Hence, in the absence of a worldwide socialist movement he wished to join or a millennial revolution or utopia he could participate in, Foucault became interested in the historic standoff between the Cynic and the Platonic traditions: "For the Socratic 'other world' [the Cynics] substituted an 'other life,' the truly philosophical life, the 'true life'" (*FP* 110). Rather than hoping for an "other world," Foucault—in the familiar dynamics of projection and identification we have seen throughout this book—characteristically chose the Cynic route of pursuing an "other life," a Cynic assertion of ethical agency over the one thing we have some knowledge of, and control over: our own "style of existence," even while this existence encompasses other people.

There is one final point to be made about the significance of the "other life" demanded by the Cynics, and its relation to the "other world" promised by the Platonic tradition. The Platonic tradition's denigration of Cynics and cynics alike stems from its inability to recognize an intelligible "other life" that does not entail an absolute break with the past. This attitude is visible in Bewes's Hegelian dismissal of Lord Henry, so that Henry's dandyish cynicism becomes merely a "blase attitude [which] in no way challenges mundane reality but appear[s] rather as a defeatist accommodation with it." Bewes seems to assume that any attempt at "politics" that doesn't begin on radically new ground, with brand-new assumptions in place, is in some way "defeatist." This, I would argue, is an idealist's misunderstanding of the uses of language in political action. If Skinner and his school of historians are correct, even the most radical ideological innovators, if they wish to accomplish their purposes, must assume the risk of drawing upon existing terms and concepts, in order to deploy them in new contexts for new purposes. Such uses of existing language are no more "defeatist" than the invention of brand-new terms that have no discernible impact on existing political discussion.

Foucault's reading of the Cynics, which I would extend to modern, degraded forms of cynicism, takes this entire debate about the relation of philosophical language to action and redirects it in an interesting way. He argues that both ancient and modern cynicism demand a rejection of metaphysics (indeed, this is how ancient Cynicism came to be downgraded into modern cynicism). The rejection of metaphysics, however, is the least important aspect of cynicism, because the real interest should remain *what kind of life one leads as a consequence of one's philosophy.* This is the ethical concern that remains unaddressed by elaborate descriptions of an "other world" in which philosophies ought to be staged but rarely are. Where else can they be staged but in this world, and in the lives of those who pursue them?

Both forms of cynicism ask questions like, "How can we anticipate the ways in which we routinely invert our principles in our actions? How can we avoid becoming liars, dupes, and hypocrites every time we speak?" Even the most degraded forms of disillusioned cynicism work as comic relief from the self-serving idealizations that are offered up to the public. No wonder that politicians, advertisers, and journalists so often denounce cynicism for its pernicious effects. They, too, promise an "other world."

EPILOGUE How Not to Talk about Cynicism

A Conclusion, and Request for Further Discussion

NOW THAT WE HAVE EXAMINED the full historical trajectory of Cynicism from its ancient origins to the present, I may offer a fuller explanation of how the various elements of the modern concept of cynicism descended from specific moments in its past history. This should enable us to answer the central question with which we began in the introduction: How does the prehistory of cynicism as an important moral concept—uppercase Cynicism prior to 1800—illuminate its subsequent evolution into an important, though underanalyzed term in our modern moral and political lexicon?

As I outlined in the first chapter, Foucault's last course at the Collège de France discussed *parrhesia,* or truth telling, in the ancient Greek and Roman worlds (*FP* 108). Foucault's observations on the Cynics and the historical fate of their distinctive style of truth telling, however, help throw light on the entire trajectory of Cynicism, from its ancient to modern forms. This is because Cynicism, even after it ceased to be a viable philosophical "way of life," remained a vehicle for a succession of writers and orators contemplating its distinctive "aesthetic of existence" for their own reflections, identifications, projections, and disavowals.

Thus, the first major context for understanding contemporary cynicism is the Cynic movement's emphasis upon the philosopher's public life as the truest expression of the *consequences* of one's philosophy, and the place where one's doctrines could be examined by the public for their truth or fraudulence. This admirably ascetic and egalitarian ethos, however, had the interesting historical effect of incorporating philosophical failure, fraud, and vanity into Cynicism's own self-images and traditions. The Cynics used these images of failure and fraudulence as a form of ascetic self-regulation, to ensure their own discipline and to harness the considerable collective energies of public scandal on behalf of its philosophic mission.

Certeau's contrast between "tactical" and "strategic" rationalities should remind us that this standoff between Diogenes and Plato involved not simply the difference between two distinct philosophical styles but the question of how philosophical reason could and should be reproduced. Diogenes and the Cynics built into their practice a suspicion of any philosophy, including Cynic philosophy, that could harden into a set of social conventions unthinkingly transmitted by a philosophical elite and passively accepted by the would-be philosopher or his followers. In opposition to such limiting notions of philosophy's relation to the world, the Cynics held that the philosopher's service was always to the broadest possible grouping of humanity, and always began with the discipline of ethical self-transformation and self-testing, to ensure the continual harmonization of doctrine and practice.

According to Flynn: "Foucault sees at the core of [the Cynic] movement the theme of life as the scandal of truth. It is in this 'moral' guise that it penetrated Western thought" (*FP* 110). The Cynics accomplished this core aspect of their philosophic mission by "defacing the currency" of conventional language and thought. The Cynics' challenge to communally held norms was never merely verbal or personal, but occurred in the same public arena that the Cynic shared with his nonphilosophical spectators and his philosophical competitors, in the form of the philosopher's life.

This emphasis upon one's life as the prime testing ground of philosophical truth dictated the anecdotal, fragmentary, or antitheoretical forms and genres in which Cynicism is best transmitted. What we are interested in is not so much the doctrine itself but the visible *effect* that the doctrine has upon whoever enunciates it. As Flynn notes: "The Cynics' scheme of life . . . is expressed and transmitted by stories, paradigmatic figures like Hercules, and case histories. Because what is to be communicated is a way of life more than a doctrine, the philosophic hero becomes of prime importance and philosophic legend is common coin" (*FP* 110). The result was that Cynicism, as a mode of philosophical writing, always maintained a strong connection to anecdote, oral narrative, and storytelling rather than system building, in order to show how its heroes and villains did or did not live up to their reputations.

In each chapter of this book, we have seen examples of how the Cynics' "scheme of life" penetrated a variety of writings in English between the sixteenth and twentieth centuries. We have also seen how its corpus of "stories," "paradigmatic figures," and "case histories" made its way into the literary, philosophical, and historical writings of a wide range of male authors who found some aspect of themselves reflected in Diogenes. We have also seen how the Cynic as "philosophical hero" offered in Diogenes Laertius and travestied in Lucian was eventually transformed, after the celebrity and disgrace of Rousseau, and Burke's publicity campaign against Rousseau, the French Enlightenment, and the French Revolution, into the fashionable, outwardly conformist, selfish, disbelieving cynic represented by D'Israeli's Hobbes or Lord Henry Wotton. Thus the philosophical hero of antiquity was gradually transformed, through one negation after another, into the unreflective, or seemingly unreflective, cynical insider.

The Cynic as philosophical hero offers himself as an example of a "true life," while the modern insider-cynic is one who exemplifies, in Sloterdijk's terms, nothing more than "enlightened false consciousness." The modern cynic offers the outward appearance of reason or ideals, but there is always a gap between his fine pronouncements and his less impressive actions, as Rousseau taught his readers to recognize. Lord Henry therefore represents one of the last in a series of inversions of the Cynic "philosophical hero." Even in his inversion, however, we can still recognize Lord Henry's mastery of the recognizably Cynic impulse of upending existing moral conventions. The degraded cynic's inversion of Cynic ideals is a joke as old as Lucian and can find plenty of precedents in the absurd or mocking anecdotes of Laertius. Such inversions, moreover, seem an inevitable feature of the genre of the "life of the philosopher," at least whenever life is shown to be more powerful than the philosopher's will.

Thus, we learn more about Cynicism's fate in the postclassical world by analyzing the negative rather than the positive images of the Cynics. We can see this in the succession of "bad Cynics" offered in this book, which features a lively group of polemically enhanced philosophizers ready to demonstrate their dangerously bad faith to the reader: Peregrinus Proteus, Apemantus, Lyttelton's Diogenes, Jean-Jacques Rousseau, D'Israeli's Hobbes, and Lord Henry Wotton. Each of these figures belongs to a different social order, however, and takes his protective covering of fraudulence and the misuse of reason from his surroundings.

Yet the thematics of truth telling, philosophy, the philosophical hero, and the scandalous inversion of communal values do not exhaust the meanings of Cynicism as it passed from antiquity into the modern era. The next major context contributing to modern cynicism came from rhetoric and involved the models of reasoned persuasion that helped to preserve and transmit classical Cynicism to the early modern era. Ironically, the increasing identification of

Cynicism with rhetoric began when the Cynics were used by rhetorical pedagogues as tropes for the courtly philosopher's—or "counsellor's"—*opposition* to rhetoric's potentially flattering or instrumental abuses of language in the service of power. As I have argued at length, all these morally destabilizing possibilities existed within the rhetorical practice of redescription, one of the riskiest outgrowths of rhetoric's theory of verbal action. By the mid-seventeenth century, however, the early modern rhetoricians' embrace of the Cynics was itself negated during the Enlightenment's turn against the rhetorical culture that preceded it.[1] The result was the uncannily rhetorical appearance of the modern insider-cynic, whose emergence coincided with the demise of rhetorical culture in the early nineteenth century. It is the strongly rhetorical cast of the postclassical, vernacular cynic, whose descent from Diogenes' model had already marked him a fraud, which ultimately severed cynicism's links with truth telling and philosophy.

In fact, the modern insider-cynic strongly resembles the figure Stanley Fish has called "Rhetorical Man," the straw-man version of rhetoric set up by those who wish to denounce it. These opponents insist that "Rhetorical Man" suffers from deficiencies "epistemological" (because he is "sundered from truth and fact), "moral" (having been "sundered from true knowledge and sincerity"), and "social" (pandering to "the worst in people and mov[ing] them to base actions").[2] Through these successive negations and displacements, Cynicism became intimately linked with the problematics of language, persuasion, collective action, and power in ways quite foreign to its philosophic origins.

The next contribution to the concept came from the Enlightenment-era discovery of a political and economic rationality, powerful though indirect, capable of managing large-scale, aggregated social and historical forces, as these were represented by "the people" and "commercial modernity." The political and normative chaos of the Civil Wars and Interregnum made the task of developing such a rationality urgent for governing elites, who had discovered that rhetorical culture's former models of authority, social hierarchy, and reasoned persuasion had collapsed during the earlier period. Instead, both enlightened and governing elites began to elaborate theories of modern sociability and commerce that demonstrated how such human interactions and effects in the aggregate could be understood apart from inherited traditions of morality and religion. In this historical scheme, a moralist like Diogenes rudely rejected luxury and dissimulation along with Mandeville's calculus of "private vice, public benefits." Consequently, the rude Cynic exemplified an outmoded notion of personal virtue that refused the undeniable historical, collective, and material improvements produced by modern politeness and commerce. In other words, Diogenes is precisely the opposite of Mandeville's heroic agent of modernization, the dissimulating "skillful politician" who exploits the blind vanity, hypocrisy, appetite, or acquisitiveness of every social class to build his grumbling hive.

By the mid-eighteenth century, however, this isolated, "humorous" Diogenes had been transformed, in two Lucianic dialogues, into a representative of an emerging political rationality. The Cynic had shifted from being a reflexive opponent of "the multitude" to one of its most effective leaders. This shift coincided with two periods when popular political disturbances were matched with divisions among political elites and seems linked with Bolingbroke's establishment of the routine institutional functions of a standing Opposition press. These functions were to serve as a publicity- and communications wing for the party, and to provide the public with a steady stream of moralizing redescriptions designed to win supporters over to its side. The Diogenes featured in both these dialogues, written by two disillusioned veterans of Bolingbroke's long-standing Opposition press campaign, reflects the emergence of an entire class of writers devoted to this kind of political work. The Diogenes presented in these dialogues maintains an interesting ambivalence toward the mob whose beliefs mobilize them into blind followers. Accordingly, Lyttelton's Diogenes represents one of the first instances in which Diogenes is depicted not as a humorous or isolated misanthrope, but as a dangerously influential questioner of the most fundamental beliefs of society, with the persuasive power to inspire imitators and reshape politics in an entirely new direction.

The next major contribution to the concept of Cynicism came from Jean-Jacques Rousseau's peculiarly vulnerable yet aggressive rendition of the rationality of the Enlightenment philosophe. More than any other philosophe, Rousseau attempted to live a fully conscious philosophical existence in which reflection and action might converge, but he instead watched his life transformed into a public example of the excesses of reason, of reason turned into irrationality and madness, of the failure of the Enlightenment. In this respect, he helped to discredit the philosophes' self-image of an unprejudiced Enlightenment reason and persecuted virtue, first of all in his memorable attacks on the self-interested behavior of his fellow philosophes, and then more damagingly in the impulsive and self-deluded behavior he rationalized in his autobiographical writings. In the profoundly unhappy contours of his life story, Rousseau seemed to represent a providential example of the terrible consequences of questioning conventional values and codes of behavior in one's writings and one's life.

The entire arc of Rousseau's long-term involvement with Cynicism helped to redefine the concept because he began his career as a Diogenical moralist whose radical critique of luxury opened out into a more sweeping and paradoxical critique of civilization, "commercial modernity," and its institutions that helped to support his fellow philosophes in their activities. One of his greatest accusations against this modernity and its civilization was its elaboration of a calculating, self-seeking, egoistic reason at the expense of natural feeling. And yet as Rousseau published his sentimental works to an ever wider and more popular public, these works encouraged readers to imagine him as a hero of sentimentality and plain, natural feeling. In his final works, however, his desire to absolve himself of wrongdoing, even in his conscious decision to abandon his children, helped to destroy this reputation for honesty and feeling and give him the reputation of being a monster of egotism, hypocrisy, and affectation, one who used his claims of innocence to attract public sympathy and to conceal or mitigate his bad behavior. What had seemed to be at least an assertion of virtue was in fact the purest dissimulation and egoism. And this was the pattern followed by Cynicism as it was degraded into modern, disillusioned cynicism.

The pivotal context for the shift toward a degraded cynicism was Burke's conservative publicity campaign against Rousseau, the philosophes, the Revolution, and reform generally at home in Britain. Burke accomplished this not by stressing the sheer irrationality and intractable violence of "the people," as reactionaries and the propertied had often done following popular disturbances. Instead, Burke rhetorically addressed a different version of "the people" than that addressed by the Jacobins at home or abroad. Moreover, by defending British institutions as long-cherished "prejudices" that required protection from philosophic questioning, Burke successfully caricatured Rousseau and the other philosophes for their supposed attacks upon religion and other useful beliefs. After Burke's successful assault upon Enlightenment philosophy, however, modern cynicism becomes inextricably linked with historical disillusionment, the blighted hopes of the Enlightenment philosophes in the power of Reason and benevolence to vanquish prejudice and cruelty.

It is for this reason that the first philosopher to be called a "cynic" in the modern sense is Hobbes, that patron saint of realpolitik, in Isaac D'Israeli's post-Revolutionary psychological and political portrait of the philosopher in his *Quarrels of Authors* (1814). As with Lyttelton's Diogenes, D'Israeli's Hobbes is "cynical" to the extent that he is also political, a philosopher capable of influencing others' opinions. Moreover, D'Israeli's Hobbes is neither rude nor resistant to power ; instead, he is physically fearful and eager to submit his intellect to whatever sovereign power is willing to pay him and to use his intellectual powers to rationalize this surrender to self-interest. Ironically, D'Israeli has taken Rousseau's rather paranoid assessment of his fellow philosophes and applied it to Hobbes in his analysis of Hobbes's "selfish dogmas." D'Israeli's cynic is excessively accommodating, thoroughly selfish, and jealous of his perquisites as a member of a new class of intellectuals who will eventually be called "opinion-makers." This portrait is the earliest depiction of Keenan's "insider-cynic," the man whose moral redescriptions assist those in power.

Readers who have followed me this far may well wonder how the history of the concept of cynicism can provide answers about our deadlocks in contemporary political discussion, problems centering upon the deeply complicitous, mutually reinforcing relations between power and publicity in the workings of contemporary political discussion. How might historical knowledge interrupt this cycle of disenchantment?

My response is that cynicism is a good example of a concept that developed almost inadvertently over long periods of time, as a remote portion of philosophical history that became isolated from the live part of the Western philosophical tradition, but that absorbed and retained meaning from various epochs while it was being preserved and transmitted. As such, it gradually and imperceptibly grew into one of what Empson called the "vague rich intimate words" that ultimately form a more decisive part of our moral vocabulary "than in the clear words of [our] official language."[3]

Empson goes on to note that the official moral and religious formulae of a society also help create "a kind of shrubbery of smaller ideas, [the formation of which] may be the most important part of [the formulae's] influence, yet which may [also] be a half-conscious protest against the formulae, a means of keeping them at bay."[4] "Cynicism" therefore became part of this "shrubbery" surrounding the official language and doctrines of participatory politics, helping to preserve the official values by "keeping them at bay," while mitigating the official doctrine's most fatal tendencies with a joking, half-conscious opposition. This "odd little class of joke phrases," he adds later, "carry doctrines more complex than the whole structure of [our] official view of the world."[5] Such unexamined "complex words" therefore contain doctrines that are not only surprisingly intricate but also largely unspoken and therefore hidden from view. Empson remarks, "If our language is continually thrusting doctrines at us, perhaps very ill-considered ones, the sooner we understand the process the better."[6]

Viewed as a "complex word," cynicism has become a symptomatic term in political discussion because it points to complexities that our official political doctrines have been otherwise unwilling to acknowledge. Just how much popular participation, for example, or extended discussion, is possible in our political system? This means that the most common denunciations of cynicism systematically exclude certain dimensions of the concept that careful historical and semantic study could reintroduce into the discussion.

To name only the most important contexts that have informed the concept since its inception, Niehues-Pröbsting provides a long list of themes linking ancient to modern cynicism: "sexuality and satire, misanthropy, the social exclusion of outsiders and extreme individualism, the critique of culture and the advocacy of natural conditions free of civilization. In the modern period, shameless sexual speech as well as biting satire and insulting sarcasm were perceived as being decisively Cynic; and not surprisingly, the roots of the modern concept of cynicism are to be found there."[7] In addition to these "sexual and comical" dimensions of the concept, we could add the verbal, performative, and rhetorical aspects of cynicism, which heighten the paradox of the itinerant philosopher whose lack of ordinary possessions or attachments actually increases his persuasive powers. What is most instructive historically is that the vast majority of these contexts cluster as paradoxes around Keenan's shameless insider-cynic, while the power associated with the master-cynic and the disenchantment of the disillusioned cynic are relative latecomers to the concept. Nonetheless, each of the three contemporary polarities of power, publicity, and disenchantment must be addressed if we wish to make political discussion more fruitful and its potential for change more real. Unlike the psychological approach, the historical and genealogical approaches to cynicism allow us to separate out the various doctrines of the "complex word" so that we may understand its full meaning.

I have stressed how misleading the psychological views of cynicism are, because these tend to collapse and equate the various positions, blaming each equally for the shared atmosphere of disenchantment, without accounting for the disparate roles and actions that helped to create these beliefs in the first place. Treating modern cynicism as simply a psychological state of dismissiveness, skepticism, or passivity therefore misses the point. The real interest of cynicism lies not in any individual cynic's distance from conventional beliefs but in the process by which Keenan's disempowered, verbally inventive insider-cynic often becomes the scapegoat for a system driven by the self-seeking of the powerful. Insider-cynics try to avoid this fate by scapegoating other intellectuals or the public as a whole for their refusal to believe. The cycle of mutual accusations and recriminations crowds out more substantive discussion, heightening the feelings of disenchantment and futility for those outside the political system, while allowing the powerful to continue their self-seeking behavior in secret, without political cost. Thus, singling out the insider-cynic while neglecting the master-cynicism of the powerful or the disillusioned cynicism of the powerless leaves their structural complicities untouched.

At this juncture, it might help to consider the peculiar vulnerabilities faced by Lord Henry Wotton as Wilde's exemplary insider-cynic. Henry's rhetorical gifts are impressive, and usually winning, but they also lead him to justify Dorian's callous abandonment of Sibyl, which is only one of a series of brutal expressions of master-cynicism that Dorian commits in this story, acts that lead to the death or destruction of virtually everyone around him. In the few instances where we are allowed to glimpse Dorian exercising power, he simply tells his victim what he wants, plainly and without ambiguity. As he tells the unfortunate Alan Campbell when he blackmails him into disposing of Basil's murdered corpse: "The thing has to be done. Face it, and do it." There is no trace of persuasion in this statement, only a promise of terrible consequences if his request is denied.

This blunt, instrumental attitude about language could not be more different than Henry's insinuating "murmur" and love of paradoxes. Watching Henry abuse his superb linguistic gifts by stretching his aesthetic theories to suit Dorian's selfishness reminds us of how degraded he becomes when he serves Dorian in this abject manner. And yet if we transpose this model to the contemporary political realm, the word-spinning of degraded insider-cynics is oftentimes the only trace we have of the self-seeking behavior of the powerful, who prefer either to keep those moments secret, or to accomplish such things through proxies, as Dorian forces Alan to become. The insecurity or self-hatred of this particular class of intellectuals should not go unvalued, because without these qualities we would never discover the shameful secrets of those in power. As Nietzsche famously wrote: "Cynicism is the only form in which base souls approach honesty; and the higher man must listen closely to every coarse or subtle cynicism, and congratulate himself when a clown without shame or a scientific satyr speaks out precisely in front of him."[8] Such "base souls," once discontented or out of employment, may very well have valuable information about the real workings of power, and help us to see "things as they are instead of as they ought to be."

Cynicism therefore takes its dynamism from this morally compromised class of functionaries whose home institutions serve the interests of the powerful. These insider-cynics must constantly scramble to readjust their descriptions in the right direction, but their work leaves plenty of openings for others to attack. For one thing, their legitimating efforts can easily backfire and create widespread disenchantment if their role becomes too obvious. Any time the insider-cynics' mediation grows too blatant to be effective, the institutional defenders of the powerful will respond by blaming the disbelieving "cynicism" of those who point out the gap between official representations and the public's experience of reality. It is the insider-cynics' chronic powerlessness and institutional dependence—and not some epidemic of distrust or disbelief in the public at large—that multiplies the ubiquitous charges of cynicism in contemporary discussion. As Leslie Stephen wrote a long time ago: "When institutions have nothing better to say for themselves than that they still occupy the ground, the respect for them becomes snobbishness. The times are ripe for satire and the satirist will be denounced as a cynic."[9] Thus, the most vociferous attacks upon cynicism come from the defenders of the same institutions that helped to create the public's disenchantment in the first place.

My final point is about the implicit role of political language in contemporary debates about cynicism. Many of the attacks on cynicism, whether from the political right or left, are based on an untenable distinction between political action and political language.[10] These attacks betray their impatience with the vagaries of free discussion, which they figure as an empty delaying tactic designed to forestall genuine action or change. In such attacks, the cynical disbeliever passively toys with words, while the committed and active believer insists that discussion cease and the real action begin with his own words. As Keenan admits, there is some justification for this general impatience with protracted discussion: every modern democratic state must live with the fundamental tension between the polity's need to air and resolve conflicting views and the welfare state's imperative to provide timely and continuous care for its citizens.[11] Yet the public's impatience or disenchantment with the messiness of genuine discussion can only lead them to embrace the one political actor able to act unilaterally in this system, the master-cynic untroubled by others' scruples. This may be one reason why popular discontent and cynicism often do not lead in the direction of progressive reforms, as one might expect, but toward a still more conservative embrace of those who already project power and authority.

Nonetheless, those who denounce cynicism often find little use for the exchange of views in politics because they feel that the ultimate goals of politics have already been settled and any further discussion is not just useless but obstructive. Consequently, certain kinds of doubts may not be admitted into political discussion, or certain kinds of discussion may not even take place, because they hinder "our" ability to act decisively, as if political discussion existed solely to debate the means used to accomplish goals and not the desirability of those goals. "It's time for the critics to exchange their cynicism for a tough-minded, yet hopeful realism," reads the tough-minded, yet hopeful press release from the William E. Simon Fellow in Religion and a Free Society at the Heritage Foundation.[12] Well, why should we?

NOTES

Introduction

1. Fournier, "Dick Gephardt Says Dean Can't Be Trusted."

2. Lerner, *Politics of Meaning*, 3.

3. Jamieson and Cappella, *Spiral of Cynicism*, 17.

4. Goldfarb, *Cynical Society*, 1.

5. Arthur H. Miller, "Political Issues and Trust in Government"; Citrin, "Comment: The Political Relevance of Trust in Government."

6. Litt, "Political Cynicism and Political Futility," 314.

7. Quoted in Agger, Goldstein, and Pearl, "Political Cynicism," 478.

8. Hoffman, *Snarl of a Cynic*, 30.

9. Henry Ward Beecher, "The Cynic," in "Portrait Gallery," in *Lectures to Young Men, on Various Important Subjects* (New York, 1853), 115. All subsequent citations will be to this edition and will appear parenthetically in the text.

10. The studies that I have found most useful have been Sloterdijk, Chaloupka, and Keenan, which I discuss below. These rise above the symptomatic level of discussion found in Lerner, Goldfarb, and to some extent Jamieson and Cappella. For cynicism and modernity, see Sloterdijk's *Critique of Cynical Reason*. For a thoughtful discussion of Sloterdijk, see Niehues-Pröbsting, "The Modern Reception of Cynicism," 331–32 n. 3; and 363–65. For a leftist political critique of Sloterdijk, see, for example, Bewes, *Cynicism and Postmodernity*.

11. For reasons that I will make clear later in this chapter, cynics have been consistently gendered as male for most of the history of the term because of their historical connections to Cynic philosophy and the "Man of Reason," Diogenes the Cynic.

12. For the cynic's rueful recognition that an organization's fixable problems will not be fixed for reasons outside the cynic's control, see, for example, Dean, Brandes, and Dharwadkar, "Organizational Cynicism," 344.

13. The *OED* defines "cynic" as one who is predisposed "to disbelieve in the sincerity or goodness of human motives and actions, and [who is] wont to express this by sneers and sarcasms" (*OED*, s.vv. "cynic," cynical," "cynicism"). As I shall explain shortly, however, this emphasis on "belief" and "disbelief" in the current definitions needs to be supplemented with the semantic history of the concept, which encompasses other notions like philosophic asceticism and misanthropy.

14. For the antidemocratic, conservative dimensions of the feelings of futility directed against proposed political changes, see Hirschman's *Rhetoric of Reaction*, 43–80.

15. See Beer, "Two Models of Public Opinion," 164.

16. In a paradox that demonstrates Chaloupka's important observation that cynicism feeds upon its remedies, the political idealism that discounts widely shared feelings of cynicism only confirms and reinforces the cynical belief that popular feelings have no effect on the workings of the political system. See William Chaloupka, *Everybody Knows* (Minneapolis: University of Minnesota Press, 1999), xv. All subsequent citations will be to this edition and will appear parenthetically in the text.

17. For moralism as a symptomatic, and counterproductive, rejection of politics, see Brown, *Politics out of History,* 18–44.

18. For an attempt to work through the political implications of a historiography no longer bound up with modern assumptions of progress, see, Brown, *Politics out of History,* 3–17, esp. 5–10.

19. For the rhetoric of reaction and perverse or futile outcomes, see Hirschman, *Rhetoric of Reaction,* 11–80. Chaloupka also devotes a chapter to the "uses of backlash," in which contemporary conservatives organize against symbols of political progress in order to generate perverse or futile outcomes. See Chaloupka, *Everybody Knows,* 129–54.

20. See Michel de Certeau, *The Practice of Everyday Life,* trans. Steven Rendall (Berkeley and Los Angeles: University of California Press, 1984), 178. All subsequent citations will be to this edition and will appear parenthetically in the text using the abbreviation *PEL* followed by the page number.

21. For this phrase, see Certeau 177. Certeau, following Foucault and Bourdieu, associates "practices" with the study of the making (*poiesis*) or "use" of materials that takes place in popular culture or among marginal groups, where "consumption" is anything but passive and impoverished but is often hidden or scattered across areas that "belong," to others. See, for example, the following statement: [In the study of practices,] "'popular culture,' as well as a whole literature called 'popular,' take on a different aspect: they present themselves essentially as 'arts of making' this or that, i.e., as combinatory or utilizing modes of consumption. These practices bring into play a *ratio,* a way of thinking invested in a way of acting, an art of combination which cannot be dissociated from an art of using" (*PEL* xv).

22. On institutions and collective action, see Douglas, *How Institutions Think,* 21–30. For the effects of scale on collective action, see also Olson, *Logic of Collective Action,* 53–65.

23. For this reason, cynicism should not be confused with notions of individualism, which rely upon robust notions of the modern subject. For a reading of Diderot's *Rameau's Nephew* as an example of abject cynicism and failed autonomy, see Bernstein, *Bitter Carnival,* 59–83.

24. See Chaloupka, *Everybody Knows,* xv.

25. For this taxonony, see Keenan, "Twilight of the Political," #4. For the conceptual underpinnings to the notion of "the public" in modernity, see Warner, *Publics and Counterpublics,* 65–124.

26. Keenan, "Twilight of the Political?" #4.

27. What Keenan, following Sloterdijk, calls "master-cynicism" has been identified

with Machiavellian political rationality since D'Israeli's famous description of him as a "polished cynic" (see *Democracy in Question*, chapter 5). For Machiavelli's treatment of public opinion as a force to be managed, see, for example, Minar, "Public Opinion in the Perspective of Political Theory," 33–34.

28. Keenan, "Twilight of the Political," 4.

29. For polemics and legitimation, see Foucault, "Polemics, Politics, and Problemizations."

30. See Ankersmit, "Representational Democracy," 39–46, which contains Ankersmit's discussion of Rawls's arguments on toleration in *Political Liberalism* (Rawls 134). Thanks to my UH colleague William Nelson for his helpful comments on Rawls, though this reading of Ankersmit and Rawls is my own. See also the volume of essays edited by Pennock and Chapman, *Compromise in Ethics, Law, and Politics.*

31. My method in this book derives from Foucault, "Nietzsche, Genealogy, and History." My project of closely studying the semantic history of a single concept—in this case, cynicism—is also deeply indebted to Empson's *Structure of Complex Words.*

32. Brown, *Politics out of History*, 16, 91–120. Brown also makes the point that genealogies are a mixed genre.

33. See Michel Foucault, "What is Enlightenment?" in *The Foucault Reader*, ed. Paul Rabinow (New York: Pantheon, 1984), 38. All subsequent citations are to this edition and will appear parenthetically in the text.

34. For "conceptual history" generally, see Gumbrecht, "A History of the Concept 'Modern,'" 80–81.

35. See Koselleck, "Begriffsgeschichte and Social History": "Social and political conflicts of the past must be interpreted and opened up via the medium of their contemporary conceptual limits and in terms of the mutually understood, past linguistic usage of the participating agents" (79). See also his "The Historical-Political Semantics of Asymmetric Counterconcepts": "History can only be written if the correspondence between material that was once comprehended conceptually and the actual material (methodologically derived from the first) is made the subject of investigation. This correspondence is infinitely variable and must not be mistaken as an identity; otherwise, every source that was conceptually unambiguous would already be the history that was sought within it. In general, *language and politico-social content coincide in a manner different from that available or comprehensible to the speaking agents themselves*" (161–62; my emphasis).

36. See Chaloupka, *Everybody Knows*, xv.

37. The best recent source in English on the ancient Cynics and their reception history is the collection of critical essays edited and introduced by Bracht Branham and Marie-Odile Goulet-Cazé, *The Cynics: The Cynic Movement in Antiquity and Its Legacy.* In addition to this volume's introduction by Branham and Goulet-Cazé, Heinrich Niehues-Pröbsting's essay "The Modern Reception of Cynicism" has proved invaluable for my reading of Cynic philosophy and its relation to modern cynicism. For the history of ancient Cynicism, I have also relied upon the standard account in Dudley's *History*

of Cynicism, as well as Sayre, *The Greek Cynics,* and Navia, *Philosophy of Cynicism.* For Diogenes' biography, I have relied upon the accounts of Branham/Goulet-Cazé and Dudley. For the conflicting scholarship on the equally conflicting accounts of the etymologies and origins of the term "Cynicism," see Branham/Goulet-Cazé's introduction to *The Cynics.*

38. William Baldwin, *Treatise of Morall Philosophie,* 38.

39. Contemporary discussions of modern cynicism converge intriguingly with some recent treatments of the ambiguities of compromise in politics and ethics. For the "moral chameleon" in ethics and politics, see Benjamin, *Splitting the Difference,* 8–10, 46–52.

40. For Certeau's "strategic" and "tactical" reason distinction, see *PEL* 29–42.

41. See also MacIntyre: "The link [between Diogenes and] the English word *cynicism* lies in the Cynic claim to see through all conventional values." *Short History of Ethics,* 101.

42. Wilde, *Lady Windermere's Fan,* act 3, 418.

43. From Johnson, *A Dictionary of the English Language* (1755), s.v. "Cynick." See also Johnson's definition of "Cynical": "Having the qualities of a dog; currish; brutal; snarling; satirical."

44. For the notion of vernacularization as one of the processes underlying the production of modernity, I am indebted to a talk by S. Shankar, "Translating Modernity," given at the University of Houston on December 5, 2003.

45. Genevieve Lloyd's work on the "maleness of the Man of Reason" deserves mention at this point because the ancient Cynic is so emphatically (I could say, anatomically) male that he disarms the most paradoxically gendered feature of the "Man of Reason," a "sexless soul," as adumbrated in more canonical philosophers like Plato or Aristotle (xi). For all her interest in philosophy's historical origins and exclusions, Lloyd does not discuss the Cynics. The Cynic's ideal of reason, and his consequent practice of ascetic self-government, "excludes the feminine" in one sense, but the movement's openness to the female philosopher Hipparchia and its quarrels with hegemonic philosophers like Plato make its relation to dominant notions of masculinity more complicated.

46. Thomas Flynn, "Foucault as Parrhesiast: His Last Course at the Collège de France," in *Final Foucault,* ed. James Bernauer and David Rasmussen (Cambridge: MIT Press, 1991), 110. Since much of Flynn's article transcribes or summarizes otherwise unpublished or inaccessible lectures of Foucault's, I am treating them as coauthors and referring to the corporate author as "Foucault/Flynn." All subsequent citations to this article will appear parenthetically in the text using the abbreviation *FP* followed by the page number.

47. Phillips, *Society and Sentiment,* 13.

48. Niehues-Pröbsting, "Modern Reception of Cynicism," 330–31.

49. For Mencken and others as exemplary early twentieth-century cynics, see Chaloupka, *Everybody Knows,* 101–6, 113–14.

1. Diogenes of Sinope and Philosophy as a Way of Life

1. See Branham/Goulet-Cazé, introduction; Long, "Socratic Tradition"; and Niehues-Pröbsting, "Modern Reception of Cynicism"—all in Branham/Goulet-Cazé, *The Cynics*. For the dating of Diogenes and the Cynic movement, see Dorandi, "Chronology," 47–48.

2. For the historical value as well as the peculiarities of Laertius, see Mansfeld, "Sources," in Agra, 11–12, 16–30.

3. Dudley describes Sinope in Pontus as "a city of commercial importance but on the outer rim of the Greek world" (20), while Sayre makes the interesting suggestion that Diogenes may have developed some of Cynicism's most distinctive ascetic practices through the expansion of the Macedonian empire, which might have placed him in contact with Indian philosophical sects like the Gymnosophists. See Sayre, *The Greek Cynics*, 39–49.

4. All citations to Diogenes Laertius will be to the standard Loeb translation, unless otherwise noted. See *Lives of Eminent Philosophers*, trans. R. D. Hicks (Cambridge: Harvard University Press, 1979). Citations to this translation will be appear parenthetically in the text using the abbreviation "DL" followed by book and section number. To avoid confusion between Diogenes the Cynic and his biographer, I will refer to the biographer simply as "Laertius" for the remainder of this book.

5. See Long, "Socratic Tradition," 34, 45.

6. Long, following Dudley, argues that if the numismatic evidence of coins bearing Hicesias's name is correct, then Diogenes' exile and arrival in Greece occurred sometime between 350 and 340 BC, while Antisthenes' death has been dated some twenty years earlier, around 366 BC. If these dates are correct, then both Plato and Antisthenes were dead by the time Diogenes reached Greece, and the ancient traditions about their personal encounters and relationships were fabrications. See Long, "Socratic Tradition," 32, 45; Dudley, *History of Cynicism*, 54–55.

7. For the importance of this notion for ancient philosophy generally, see Hadot, *Philosophy as a Way of Life*.

8. For this principle, see Moles, "Cynic Cosmopolitanism," 108; and "Cynics and Politics," 137–38.

9. *Nomisma*, derived from *nomos*, meaning things sanctioned by usage or custom, or literally, the state coinage. My thanks to Richard Armstrong for help with this passage.

10. See Long, "Socratic Tradition," 39–40; Moles, "Cynics and Politics," 140–43, and "Honestius Quam Ambitiosius?" 108.

11. See Foucault, *Hermeneutics of the Subject*, xiii–xvii, 381–91, 403–7, 529. For the 1983 seminars, see Foucault, "Discourse and Truth," esp. "Parrhesia and Public Life," 43–51.

12. See, for example, Foucault, *Hermeneutics of the Subject*, 62 n. 6, 417, 518.

13. See also Niehues-Pröbsting, "Modern Reception of Cynicism," 329–32; and Long, "Socratic Tradition," 31.

14. See also Foucault, "Socratic Parrhesia," in "Discourse and Truth," 38.

15. Foucault, "Parrhesia and Danger," in "Discourse and Truth," 4.

16. See Branham, *Unruly Eloquence,* 26–28.

17. Long, "Socratic Tradition," 34–35.

18. Ibid., 36.

19. I should reiterate here Moles's point that the ancient Cynics, insofar as they accepted female Cynics like Hipparchia into their movement and preached a Cosmopolitan openness to non-Greek peoples and practices, were "non-sexist" (*Honestius Quam Ambitiosius?* 111). Indeed, this indifference to conventional social distinctions and hierarchies was probably what helped them become one of antiquity's most popular philosophical movements and provoked the disgust or unease of later writers like Cicero or Lucian (Branham/Goulet-Cazé, introduction to *The Cynics,* 15–16). Yet this cosmopolitan openness to women and other outsiders was effectively reversed when Diogenes' apothegms, either chosen or invented for their misogynist or racist humor, were incorporated into the lower-level grammar curriculum in antiquity to train non-Greek boys in the Greek language. See Morgan, *Literate Education in the Hellenistic and Roman Worlds,* 185–89.

20. Long, "Socratic Tradition," 34–35; Branham, "Defacing the Currency," 83–84.

21. Dudley, *History of Cynicism,* 1, 14.

22. Luhmann, "Work of Art and the Self-Reproduction of Art," 200.

23. Foucault, *Hermeneutics of the Subject,* 385

24. Foucault, "Parrhesia and Danger," and "Parrhesia and Rhetoric," in "Discourse and Truth," 4, 6, respectively. See also Foucault, *Hermeneutics of the Subject,* 381–86.

25. For "doctor of souls," see the introduction to Branham/Goulet-Cazé, *The Cynics,* 27; for the centrality of the didactic, missionary role of Cynic philosophers, see Moles, "Cynic Cosmopolitanism," 114–15.

26. From "Parrhesia and Criticism," in "Discourse and Truth," 4–5.

27. Foucault, *Hermeneutics of the Subject,* 379–81.

28. Ibid., 381–86.

29. This occurs in Foucault's discussion of Dio Chrysostom's treatment of the Alexander-Diogenes anecdote in the Fourth Discourse. See "Parrhesia and Public Life," in "Discourse and Truth," 51.

30. For the gradual transition of *parrhesia* from democratic political practices in fifth-century Athens to a "philosopher's virtue" in late antiquity, see Colclough, "*Parrhesia,* 182; and Momigliano, "Freedom of Speech in Antiquity," 260.

31. Moles, "Cynic Cosmopolitanism," 114–20.

32. Dudley, *History of Cynicism,* 27.

33. Niehues-Pröbsting, "Modern Reception of Cynicism," 333.

34. Hadot, *Philosophy as a Way of Life,* 265–66, and *What Is Ancient Philosophy?;* Mansfeld, "Sources," in Long, 34. See also Long, "Scope of Early Greek Philosophy," 14; and Marrou, *History of Education in Antiquity,* 206–16.

35. Antisthenes was reputedly one of the companions of Socrates at his death in 399 BC. Though earlier histories of philosophy once identified Antisthenes as the first

Cynic philosopher, scholarly opinion now designates Diogenes as its founding figure. See Dudley, *History of Cynicism*, 1–15; Branham/Goulet-Cazé, introduction to *The Cynics*, 6–7.

36. Hadot, *What Is Ancient Philosophy?* 109.

37. See, for example, Marrou, *History*, 36–45, 116–32.

38. Laertius, *Lives, Opinions, and Remarkable Sayings of the Most Famous Ancient Philosophers. Written in Greek by Diogenes Laertius. Made English by Several Hands*, [trans. William Baxter], 430.

39. Hadot, *What Is Ancient Philosophy?* 3–4.

40. Cf. Freud, *Jokes and Their Relation to the Unconscious:* "The technique of the nonsensical jokes which we have so far considered really consists, therefore, in presenting something that is stupid and nonsensical, the sense of which lies in the revelation and demonstration of something else that is stupid and nonsensical" (67).

41. See Moles, "Cynic Cosmopolitanism," 106.

42. For language and its role in institutionalizations, see Weber, *Institution and Interpretation*, 3–17. For the disparity between personal beliefs and institutional practices—or even the betrayal of beliefs by practices—see Certeau, *PEL* 177–89, which can be read as extensions or revisions to Max Weber's theories of modernization. For an anthropological critique of Max Weber's overemphasis upon bureaucratic rationality in his studies of institutionalization and the "disenchantment of the world," see Douglas, *How Institutions Think*, 93–96.

43. Branham/Goulet-Cazé, introduction to *The Cynics*, 7.

44. Lievsay, "Some Renaissance Views of Diogenes the Cynic," 450.

45. For Lucian's relation to the so-called Menippean traditions of satire (named for the lost works of the Cynic Menippus), see Relihan, "Menippus in Antiquity and the Renaissance," 265–80; and his *Ancient Menippean Satire*, 39–48, 103–18; as well as Weinbrot, *Menippean Satire Reconsidered*, 62–69. For the complex relation of Menippean satire to Cynic philosophy generally, see Relihan, *Ancient Menippean Satire*, 42–44. Because my focus remains Lucian's very specific transformation of the Cynic philosophical hero into a philosophic fraud, I will pursue the narrower story of Lucianic influences and imitations rather than the more difficult questions of the definition and long-term trajectory of the entire Menippean genre of satire (which contains much non-Diogenical material, and which is ably documented in Relihan's and Weinbrot's books).

46. Niehues-Pröbsting, "Modern Reception of Cynicism," 331.

47. Robinson, *Lucian and His Influence in Europe*, 14–15.

48. Dudley, *History of Cynicism*, 171.

49. Lucian, "The Passing of Peregrinus," 5:18.

59. Dudley, *History of Cynicism*, 179–81.

51. Foucault, "*Parrhesia* and Public Life" in "Discourse and Truth," 51.

52. Branham/Goulet-Cazé, introduction to *The Cynics*, 18.

53. Lucian, "The Passing of Peregrinus," 5:33.

2. Diogenes the Cynic as "Counsellor" and Malcontent in Early Modern England

1. Niehues-Pröbsting, "Modern Reception of Cynicism," 331.

2. See, for example, Branham, "Defacing the Currency," 83; Krueger, "Bawdy and Society," 223–24. For the dynamic interplay of oral, scribal, and printed media in early modern England, see also Fox, *Oral and Literate Culture in England.*

3. For Diogenes in the gnomic schooltexts of ancient Greece, see Morgan, *Literate Education in the Hellenistic and Roman Worlds,* 123, 185–89.

4. From the very beginnings of formal rhetorical instruction in antiquity, Diogenes lore had always been prominently featured in the Greek *chreiai,* or sayings, collected and used by rhetoricians for teaching young boys proper grammar and the construction of arguments. Such collections remained in use to the end of the seventeenth century. According to Hock and O'Neil, the figure of Diogenes dominated "the chreia[, which had] existed as a literary form long before it became a subject for rhetorical analysis and instruction in those beginners' textbooks on composition, or *Progymnasmata*" (1). For the endurance of the *Progymnasmata* within European rhetorical instruction, see Hock and O'Neil, 10–22. The *Progymnasmata* of Apthonius of Antioch (fourth century AD), for example, which took up a Diogenes *chreia* to define and demonstrate the rhetorical uses of the *chreia* form, remained an important textbook for teaching rhetoric until at least the beginning of the eighteenth century; for this example, see Hock and O'Neil, 215. For the invention and function of the progymnasmata within the rhetorical curriculum of the Hellenistic period, see also Conley, *Rhetoric in the European Tradition,* 31–32; and Kennedy, *New History of Classical Rhetoric,* 83–84, 202–7.

5. For the popularity of such compilations and commonplace collections, see, for example, Ong, "Tudor Writings on Rhetoric," 58–61.

6. For Cicero's recommendation of philosophic collections of "opinions" for learning the construction of arguments on either side of the case, see Seigel, *Rhetoric and Philosophy in Renaissance Humanism,* 17–18. For the centrality of arguments *in utramque partem* in rhetorical training and practice since Cicero, see Skinner, *Reason and Rhetoric in the Philosophy of Hobbes,* 9–10, 15–16, 27–30, 97–99, 103, 116–17, as well as Altman, *Tudor Play of Mind,* 31–63.

7. For some of the important sources of Diogeniana in the Renaissance, see Lievsay, "Some Renaissance Views of Diogenes the Cynic," 447.

8. For the metaphor of historical frames, see Phillips, *Society and Sentiment,* 13.

9. See Colclough, "*Parrhesia*"; Foucault, *Hermeneutics of the Subject,* 381–86; Parkin-Speer, "Freedom of Speech in Sixteenth-Century English Rhetorics."

10. For the *ars rhetorica,* see Skinner, *Reason and Rhetoric in the Philosophy of Hobbes,* 19–65. For early modern theories of "counsel" and "counsellors," see Guy, "The Henrician Age," 13–20; and "The Rhetoric of Counsel in Early Modern England."

11. Lievsay, "Some Renaissance Views of Diogenes the Cynic," 450. See also Krueger, "Bawdy and Society," 225; and Robinson, *Lucian and His Influence in Europe,* 15.

12. For the close connection between the commonplace tradition and teaching of virtue and vice, see Lechner, *Renaissance Concepts of the Commonplaces,* 201–25.

13. See Spencer, "The Elizabethan Malcontent"; Konstan, "A Dramatic History of Misanthropes"; Babb, *Elizabethan Malady,* 73–101.

14. For suggestive links between vernacularization and modernity, see, in addition to the talk by Shankar already cited, Bender and Wellbery, "Rhetoricality," 21; and Copeland, *Rhetoric, Hermeneutics, and Translation in the Middle Ages.* For historical accounts of the emergence of literary and scholarly writings in the English vernacular, see Barber, *Early Modern English;* Jones, *The Triumph of the English Language;* Blank, *Broken English.* For a comparative account of classical imitation in the European vernaculars, see Bolgar, *Classical Heritage,* 317–29.

15. See Blank, "Languages of Early Modern Literature in Britain," 145–48, 160–61; and *Broken English,* 1–32.

16. See, for example, Cawdrey, *A Table Alphabeticall of Hard Usual English Words* (1604), t.p., or the extended title of Cockeram's *English Dictionarie: or an Interpreter of hard English Words. Enabling as well Ladies and Gentlewomen, young Schollers, Clarkes, Merchants, as also Strangers of any Nation, to the understanding of the more difficult Authors already printed in our Language, and the more speedy attaining of an elegant perfection of the English tongue, both in reading, speaking, and writing* (1623), t.p. For the grammar school curriculum of Tudor England, see Simon, *Education and Society in Tudor England,* as well as Abbott, "Rhetoric and Writing in Renaissance Europe and England."

17. For "proverbial wisdom," "sayings of the philosophers," and their entanglements with oral, scribal, and print forms of education and communications in the early modern period, see Fox, *Oral and Literate Culture,* 112–72. For gnomologies in the ancient world, see Morgan, *Literate Education in the Hellenistic and Roman Worlds,* 120–51. For Diogenes in two such texts, see, for example, *Dicts and Sayings of the Philosophers* (1477), 62–72; and Baldwin, *Treatise of Morall Philosophie* (1547–64), 42–45.

18. Fox, *Oral and Literate Culture,* 117. For the role of Erasmus in helping to establish the rhetorical curriculum for English schools and universities, see, for example, McConica, *English Humanists and Reformation Politics,* 13–43; Grafton and Jardine, *From Humanism to the Humanities,* 122–60; Skinner, *Reason and Rhetoric in the Philosophy of Hobbes,* 19–40.

19. For the history of classical scholarship and the humanist recovery, reconstitution, and recirculation of Greek authors through Latin translations and Greek editions, see, for example, Pfeiffer, *History of Classical Scholarship.* For the development and institutionalization of Greek studies in England, see Clarke, *Classical Education in Britain: 1500–1900;* and *Greek Studies in England: 1700–1830.* For a survey of the various approaches to reading and "misreading" Plato during the humanist revival, see Hankins, *Plato in the Italian Renaissance,* 1:3–26. For the impact of this "rediscovery" on views of the Cynics, see Lievsay, "Some Renaissance Views of Diogenes the Cynic," 447.

20. Grafton, *Defenders of the Text,* 23–73.

21. If we credit the *OED*'s examples, the meaning of the cynic as railer dates back only as far back as 1596 ("Age is a cynic, not a flatterer" [*Edward III*]), or perhaps 1588, if we include the earliest example for "cynical," in the important new sense of "Resembling the Cynic philosophers in contempt of pleasure, churlishness, or disposition to find fault" ("Canst thou not love? Commeth this Cynicall passion of prone desires, or peevish frowardness?" [Greene, *Pandosto*]).

22. The most extensive study of a rhetorical education's impact upon an eminently vernacular, non-university-trained writer is T. W. Baldwin, *Shakespeare's Small Latine.*

23. Bullokar, *An English Expositor: Teaching the Interpretation of the hardest words used in our Language* (1616), s.v. "Cynike."

24. For the classical background to Diogenes' misogyny, see DL 6.52; and Lievsay, "Some Renaissance Views of Diogenes the Cynic," 447–55. For additional examples, see Goddard, *A mastif whelp with other ruff-Island-like Currs fetcht from amongst the Antipedes. Which bite and barke at the fantasticall humorists and abusers of the time* [1598?] and *A Satirycall dialogve; or, A sharplye-invectiue conference betweene Allexander the Great and that truly woman-hater Diogynes by William Goddard. Imprinted in the Lowcountryes for all such gentlewomen as are not altogeather idle nor yet well ocvpyed* [1615]. See also Swetnam, *Arraignment of Lewd, Idle, Froward, and Vnconstant Women* (1615) with at least seven reprints and expansions, as well as the feminist replies: Speght's *A Mouzell for Melastomus, the Cynicall Bayter of, and foule mouthed Barker against Evahs Sex. Or an Apologeticall Answere to that Irreligious and Illiterate Pamphlet made by Io. Swetnam by him Intituled, The Arraignment of Women* (1617); and Constantia Munda's *The Worming of a mad Dogge: Or, A Soppe for Cerberus the Iaylor of Hell. No Confutation but a sharpe Redargution of the bayter of Women* (1617).

25. Erasmus, *Apophthegmes of Erasmus,* trans. Nicolas Udall (Boston: Roberts, 1877), 76. All subsequent citations will be to this edition and will appear parenthetically in the text. See also Elyot's definition: "a sect of phylosophers, whych lived in poverte without shame, like doggis" (*The Dictionary of Syr Thomas Eliot Knyght* [1538], s.v. "Cynici").

26. Lievsay, "Some Renaissance Views of Diogenes the Cynic," 450, 452.

27. Saccio, *Court Comedies of John Lyly,* 34. See, for example, Bartolus, S.J., in *The Learned Man Defended and Reform'd* (1660), who celebrates Diogenes' self-denial in spite of his mean appearance in a discussion of the "Wise Poor Man" but later attacks the philosopher as a drunkard and madman in "Detraction," 36–37; 215–16.

28. Thomas, *Dictionarium linguae Latinae et Anglicanae* [1587], s.v. "Cynicus."

29. Rider, *Bibliotheca scholastica* (1589), s.v. "A Dogge."

30. Cockeram, *The English Dictionarie* (1623), s.v. "Doggish": "cynicall, canine."

31. Cawdrey, *A Table Alphabeticall of Hard Usual English Words* (1604), s.v., "cynicall.": "doggish, froward."

32. *Riders Dictionarie, Corrected and Augmented* (1640), s.v. "*Cynicus.*": "Cynicall, clownish, or doggish."

33. For a virtuoso treatment of the social implications of "dog," "rogue," etc., see Empson, *Structure of Complex Words,* 175–84.

34. For the early modern concept of "civility," see, for example, Bryson, *From Cour-*

tesy to Civility, 1–74. For the centrality of "decorum" for understanding courtly writing as well as conduct, see Javitch's reading of Puttenham in *Poetry and Courtliness in Renaissance England,* 50–75.

35. See, for example, Gainsford's entry for "Singularity" in his conduct book *The Rich Cabinet* (1616): "Singularity discovered the pride of Diogines even in his poverty: for he not onely despised the other sect of Phylosophers, but contested with the great Alexander himself, who yet commended his humour, and made him more proud in saying; that if hee were not Alexander, he would be Diogines: but all others traduced him for his singularity, and the common people called him Cinicke, or dogge" (138). See also Lodge, *Catharos: Diogenes in his Singularitie* (1591).

36. See Bryson, *From Courtesy to Civility,* 75–106; 151–92.

37. See Colclough, "*Parrhesia,*" 182, 196.

38. See Jardine and Grafton, "Studied for Action," 31.

39. For these genres' role in formulating and documenting early modern manners, see Bryson, *From Courtesy to Civility,* 26–42.

40. For the centrality of the orator and rhetorical models of eloquence to Renaissance conceptions of knowledge and power, see, for example, Gray, "Renaissance Humanism"; Vickers, "The Power of Persuasion," 411–35. For Cicero's *De officiis* and the relation of "*decorum*" ("seemliness" or, as Richards translates it, "propriety") to "*honestas*" ("honorableness" or "moral goodness"), see Richards, *Rhetoric and Courtliness,* 26–27. For an extensive discussion of *decorum,* see *De officiis,* 1.27.

41. Bender and Wellbery, "Rhetoricality," 6. For Cicero's role in the institutionalization of rhetoric, see also Copeland, *Rhetoric, Hermeneutics, and Translation,* 9–36; Kennedy, *Art of Rhetoric in the Roman World,* 103–300.

42. For the "two logics of action [tactical and strategic] that arise from these two facets of practicing language," see Certeau, *PEL,* xx, 37–39.

43. From Copeland, *Rhetoric, Hermeneutics, and Translation,* 32. For two empirical case histories of such purpose-driven readings of the classics, see Jardine and Grafton, "Studied for Action"; and Sharpe, *Reading Revolutions.*

44. See Seigel, *Rhetoric and Philosophy,* xiii. Cf. Cicero, *De oratore,* 1.8.

45. For the political implications of classical humanism, the *vita activa,* and Cicero in the 1570s and 1580s, see Peltonen, *Classical Humanism and Republicanism in English Political Thought,* 18–53. For the claim that Diogenes was a philosopher "improfitable" for potential "counsellors" because he "estranged" himself from the "conversation and actions of men," see, for example, Goslicius [Laurentius Grimaldus], *The Counsellor* (1598), 2:82–83. Peltonen discusses Goslicius in *Classical Humanism,* 105–11.

46. Richards, *Rhetoric and Courtliness in Early Modern Literature,* 26.

47. For the Ciceronian origins and contexts of "civil conversation," see Richards, *Rhetoric and Courtliness in Early Modern Literature,* 24–29.

48. For "dominant" and "residual," see Williams, *Marxism and Literature,* 123.

49. Rich, *My Ladies Looking Glasse* (1616), 53.

50. On this topic, see, for example, Kristeller, "The Active and the Contemplative Life in Renaissance Humanism."

51. For an extensive list and discussion of early modern comparisons of Timon and Diogenes, see Farnham, *Shakespeare's Tragic Frontier,* 39–77; Pauls, "Shakespeare's *Timon of Athens* and Renaissance Diogeniana"; Tambling, "Hating Man in *Timon of Athens.*"

52. See Empson, *Structure of Complex Words,* 185–201.

53. According to Lievsay, many of the discussions of Diogenes from this period's English pamphleteers, including Samuel Rowlands's *Diogines Lanthorne,* Barnabe Rich's remarks in various pamphlets, and the pamphlet wars surrounding Joseph Swetnam's misogynist pamphlets, evidently derived from Pettie's Guazzo (in the original and in translation) rather than any direct classical source. For Guazzo's importance to the period, along with his writings' subterranean influence as a repository of wit for numerous unacknowledged borrowings, see Lievsay, *Stefano Guazzo and the English Renaissance;* Richards, *Rhetoric and Courtliness in Early Modern Literature,* 42.

54. Stefano Guazzo, *The Civile Conversation of M. Steeven Guazzo,* ed. Edward Sullivan (London: Constable, 1925), 21. All subsequent citations will be to this edition and will appear parenthetically in the text.

55. Rowlands, *Diogenes Lanthorne* (1608), t.p. For an extensive list of Rowlands's borrowings from Guazzo in *Diogenes Lanthorne,* see Lievsay, *Stefano Guazzo,* 133–38.

56. Colclough, "*Parrhesia,*" 177–86.

57. Ibid., 184–85.

58. For rhetoric as "an art of positionality in address," see Bender and Wellbery, "Rhetoricality," 7; for the practice of deference and accommodation in civil speech and writing, see Bryson, *From Courtesy to Civility,* 151–92.

59. For the strong gendering of a rhetorical training he dubs a "Renaissance puberty rite," see Ong, "Tudor Writings on Rhetoric," 50–51, and "Latin Language Study as a Renaissance Puberty Rite," 114–18.

60. See, for example, *The Dicts and Sayings of the Philosophers* (1477), 62; Baldwin, *Treatise of Morall Philosophie* (1547–64), 43; Goddard, *A Satyricall dialogue* (1615); Whitney, *A Choice of Emblemes* (1586), 198–99.

61. From Bacon, "The Proficience and Advancement of Learning Divine and Humane" (1605), 250. See also Monsarrat, *Light from the Porch,* 123. Monsarrat describes the Stoic significance of Anthony Stafford's treatment of this anecdote in *Staffords Heavenly Dogge* (1615) in *Light from the Porch,* 122–25, as does Peltonen, *Classical Humanism,* 131. For another Stoicized version of this anecdote, see du Vair, *The Moral Philosophie of the Stoicks* (trans. 1598), 78.

62. See Grafton and Jardine, *From Humanism to the Humanities,* xiii–xiv.

63. Guy, "The Henrician Age," 14.

64. See, for example, Laertius: "Being asked what sort of Beast bit worst, [Diogenes] said of Wild Beasts, a Detractor, and of tame Beasts, a Flatterer" [DL 6.51]. For these objections to the culture of civility, see Bryson, *From Courtesy to Civility,* 193–242.

65. See, for example, the praise of Diogenes for "Freenesse of speache" and the criticism for "flatters, fawners, and southers of mennes saiynges" in Wilson, *Arte of Rheto-*

rique, 396–97. More examples can be found in Parkin-Speer, "Freedom of Speech," and Colclough, "*Parrhesia,*" 186–212.

66. Ulpian Fulwell, *Ars adulandi, or The Arte of Flattery* (1579), 118, lines 10 and 12–13.

67. For the unresolved tension between the rhetorical and antirhetorical uses of *parrhesia,* see Colclough, "*Parrhesia,*" 185–86. For the complex relation of Lyly's Diogenes to Erasmus's and More's rhetorical humanism, see Hunter's introduction to *Campaspe,* by John Lyly, 10–12; as well as Kinney, "Heirs of the Dog," 304.

68. For the semantic "overlap" between the early modern senses of "wit" as "great mental capacity" and as "apt, agile, or entertaining use of language," see Barber, *Early Modern English,* 145–47.

69. For the background to this joint translation, see Thompson's "Introduction" in More's *Works,* xvii–lxxii. All subsequent citations will be to page and line numbers from this edition and will appear parenthetically in the text.

70. *Preface,* 3, lines 1–13. See Robinson, *Lucian and His Influence in Europe,* 165–97; Branham, "Utopian Laughter."

71. For a more detailed examination of Erasmus and More's complex identification with the Cynics, see Kinney, "Heirs of the Dog," 321–28.

72. For the literary significance of Erasmus's *Apophthegmes,* see Riggs, *Shakespeare's Heroical Histories,* 50–52; T. W. Baldwin, *Shakespeare's Small Latine,* 1:308–310.

73. For the controversy over Lucian's appropriateness for a grammar-school text, see Rummel, *Erasmus as a Translator,* 50, 122–23. See also Thompson, "Introduction", xliv–xlv.

74. From Erasmus, *Modus conscribendi epistolas,* quoted in T. W. Baldwin, *Shakespeare's Small Latine,* 1:307.

75. For the commonplaces as rhetorical "colours" used for amplifying arguments, see Skinner, *Reason and Rhetoric in the Philosophy of Hobbes,* 111–19.

76. For the popularity of Guazzo at Gabriel Harvey's Oxford in 1580, a year before his appearance in English, and evidence of his influence on Lyly, Harvey, Spenser, and Tuvill, among others, see Lievsay, *Stefano Guazzo,* 48–49, 78–113.

77. For the reading of Lyly as a (would-be) "humanist courtier," see Hunter, *John Lyly,* 1–35, esp. 34. This interpretation is contested, but not, in my opinion, significantly revised by Pincombe, *Plays of John Lyly,* 1–51. See also Bevington, *Tudor Drama and Politics,* 156–86, esp. 171–75. The classic study of Lyly's deeply rhetorical prose style remains Barish, "Prose Style of John Lyly."

78. Ong, "Tudor Writings on Rhetoric," 49–50.

79. Hunter, introduction to *Campaspe,* by John Lyly, 16, citing Saccio's *Court Comedies* along with other commentators upon its distinctively rhetorical, antinarrative form.

80. Ibid., 24. See also Altman, *Tudor Play of Mind,* 196–206.

81. See Bevington, *Tudor Drama and Politics,* 173.

82. Scholars in William Lily's generation could use their linguistic and rhetorical

training to attain high diplomatic posts (Elyot), to participate in the highest councils of state (More), or gain access to the royal household as tutors and confidential advisors to the children of the great (Cheke and Ascham). See Hunter, *John Lyly,* 15; Skinner, *Reason and Rhetoric in the Philosophy of Hobbes,* 71. For the suggestion about the role of humanist intellectuals as royal tutors, I am indebted to Wyman Herendeen.

83. Hunter, *John Lyly,* 34.

84. Pincombe emphasizes the uncourtly, specifically commercial and genteel audiences of the Blackfriars boys' troupe that Lyly ran (*Plays of John Lyly,* 18–19), but McCarthy argues that the boy companies, in their literal diminution of courtly male honor and competition, were well-suited for Elizabeth's staging of royal power before male courtiers. See her "Elizabeth I's 'picture in little,'" 450–56, 459.

85. From John Lyly, *Campaspe,* ed. G. K. Hunter (Manchester: Manchester University Press, 1991), 2.2.168–70. All subsequent citations to this play will be to act, scene, and line number from this edition and will appear parenthetically in the text.

86. See *OED,* s.v. "sweetness."

87. Guy, "Rhetoric of Counsel," 294.

88. See Scragg, "*Campaspe* and the Construction of Monarchical Power," 70–78; Pincombe, *Plays of John Lyly,* 29–30.

89. For the diatribe as a specifically Cynic genre, see Branham, "Defacing the Currency," 85.

90. From Laertius, see, for example, Diogenes' abuse of the crowds he has gathered around himself (DL 6.27) or his definition of man as a featherless biped (DL 6.40). For a jest-book analogue to this scene, see Pincombe, "Lyly's *Campaspe* and the Tudor 'Owlglass,'" 30–31. Gabriel Harvey, mentioned by Pincombe as the most likely source of the "Owlglass" to his one-time friend Lyly (31), was also, as we have seen, a devoted reader of Guazzo during this period (Lievsay, *Stefano Guazzo,* 48–49). Consequently, Harvey was as likely to have supplied Lyly with Guazzo as the "Owlglass," though Lyly was probably familiar with both. For the crowd's "rough music," see Ingram, "Ridings, Rough Music and Mocking Rhymes in Early Modern England."

91. Hunter suggests that Lyly is treating the philosopher as an early example of "stage puritan" type found later in Shakespeare's Malvolio, for example. See Hunter, ed., *Campaspe,* 42, n. 48. For the "Martin Marprelate" controversy and its role in the polemical construction of the "stage puritan" in 1588 and 1589, see also Collinson, "Ecclesiastical Vitriol," though see also Clegg, *Press Censorship in Elizabethan England,* 170–97. Whether this scene represents a darkening of Lyly's otherwise positive view of Diogenes or an incursion of anti-Puritan satire into Lyly's comedy, I cannot determine. The play's apophthegmatic mode of presentation makes it difficult to resolve such inconsistencies.

92. For redescription (*paradiastole*) and its moral risks, see Skinner, *Reason and Rhetoric in the Philosophy of Hobbes,* 138–80.

93. For an analogy between rhetorical "colours" (inventive redescription) and painting, see Campaspe's speech to Apelles: "If you begin to tip your tongue with cunning, I pray dip your pencil in colours and fall to that you must do, not that you would do"

(3.3.53–55). Lyly's treatment constantly plays on the analogies between Apelles's "counterfeiting" of Campaspe's image as an artist, the persuasive "colours" of rhetorical language, and the courtly dissimulation of emotion. For Lyly and *paradiastole,* see Skinner, *Reason and Rhetoric in the Philosophy of Hobbes,* 168.

94. See Peacham, *Garden of Eloquence* (1577): "Paradiastole . . . is when by a mannerly interpretation, we doe excuse our own vices, or other mens whom we doe defend, by calling them vertues, as when we call him that is craftye, wyse: a covetuous man, a good husband: murder a manly deede: deepe dissimulation, singuler wisedome . . . whoredome, youthful delight & dalyance: idolatry, pure religion: glotony and dronkennesse, good fellowship" (sig. N, iiii[v]).

95. Wilson, *Arte of Rhetorique,* 396–97.

96. For the identification of "Kinsayder" with Cynic, see Horne, "Voices of Alienation," and Hardin, "Marston's Kinsayder." For Marston's social origins and their impact on his satire, see Finkelpearl, *John Marston of the Middle Temple,* 1–18. Kernan treats Marston's embattled, hypocrite-moralist Kinsayder as emblematic of the contradictions of post-1590s English satire; see Kernan, *Cankered Muse,* 96–97.

97. For satiric depictions of Marston, see *The Second Part* of the *Return from Parnassus* (ca. 1600) in *Three Parnassus Plays (1598–1601),* ed. J. B. Leishman, 241, lines 267–84; along with works such as W.I., *The Whippinge of the Satyre* (1601). For the background to the 1599 Bishops' Ban, which ordered the burning of personal satires by Marston, Guilpin, Middleton, Davies, and Hall (later reprieved), along with works of an erotic or at least misogynist nature, see Clegg, *Press Censorship in Elizabethan England,* 198–217. Clegg, however, has little to say about satire's *generic* role in the ban apart from these writers' allusions to the Earl of Essex.

98. For the relation of the satirical to the sexual and political content in the banned materials, see Boose, "The 1599 Bishops' Ban, Elizabethan Pornography, and the Sexualization of the Jacobean Stage." See also Kernan, *Cankered Muse,* 81–140.

99. See, for example, Goddard, *A mastif whelp* (1598). For the political uses of Diogenes as a moralist (Rowlands) or satirist (Goddard) in the Jacobean era, see McRae, *Literature, Satire, and the Early Stuart State,* 101–2, and more generally of satire, 85–113.

100. See Patterson on the deliberate ambiguity involved in using historical commonplace figures like Diogenes under conditions of censorship: "Censorship encouraged the use of historical or other uninvented texts, such as translations from the classics, which both allowed an author to limit his authorial responsibility for the text ('Tacitus wrote this, not I') and, paradoxically, provided an interpretive mechanism. That is, the reader was invited to consider not only the timeliness of the retelling of another man's story, but the implications of the model, and the methods of selection, transmission, and adaptation" (*Censorship and Interpretation,* 65).

101. For a reading of the *Scourge* as incoherent in its attitude toward the satirist, see Finkelpearl, *John Marston of the Middle Temple,* 83–124; for a stoicized reading of Marston's satirist, see Caputi, *John Marston, Satirist,* 52–79. See also Monsarrat, *Light from the Porch,* 152–87.

102. John Marston, *The Poems of John Marston,* ed. Arnold Davenport (Liverpool:

Liverpool University Press, 1961), line 171. All subsequent citations will be to this edition and will appear parenthetically in the text with title and line number.

103. Sharpe, *More Fooles yet* (1610), E2.

104. For the diminished cultural capital of the classically educated gentry and clergy during Elizabeth's reign, and the increasing presence of the aristocracy in the grammar schools and universities, see Hexter, "Education of the Aristocracy in the Renaissance," 45–70, esp. 50–56. For the "cultural capital" that academic institutions bestow upon their students, see Bourdieu, *Distinction,* 23–26.

105. Marston, *The Malcontent,* ed. G. K. Hunter, 1.3.161–65.

106. For Marston's "neo-Stoic" contempt of "Opinion," see Caputi, *John Marston, Satirist,* 63.

107. For the "Cynick Dad," see also Sat. III: "*Redde, age, quae deinceps risiti,*" *Scourge,* lines 33–40, 47–52.

108. For the purposes of this argument, I will refer to "Shakespeare" as the sole author of *Timon,* though evidence has been building for some time that this play resulted from some collaboration between Shakespeare and the poet/playwright Thomas Middleton, the T.M. of the *Micro-Cynicon* already discussed. Since this collaboration brings Shakespeare even closer to the Cynics and malcontents of the verse satires of the 1590s as well as Middleton's city comedies, I find this a promising line of interpretation. Nonetheless, because I do not wish for my argument about cynicism to await the resolution of debates that have been raging for at least three hundred years, I invite readers to examine Vickers's convincing (and exhaustive) treatment of the evidence in *Shakespeare, Co-Author,* 244–90, 473–80, as well as Jowett, "Middleton and Debt in *Timon of Athens,*" in *Money and the Age of Shakespeare.*

109. See, for example, Warburton's gloss on Apemantus in his 1747 edition: "See this character of a Cynick finely drawn by Lucian, in his *Auction of the Philosophers;* and how well Shakespere has copied it" (*Annotations by Sam. Johnson & Geo. Steevens,* 15).

110. In addition to the Farnham, Pauls, and Tambling essays already cited, see Wright, *Authorship of "Timon of Athens,"* 8–9. When I was completing this study, an unpublished conference paper also came to my attention, Blissett's "Cynics, Canadians, and *Timon of Athens*" (presented at IAMPE 2004).

111. Copeland, *Rhetoric, Hermeneutics, and Translation,* 7.

112. See Vickers, "The Power of Persuasion," 413–15.

113. For "ensemble effect" as a hallmark of modern cynical deadlock in political discussion, see Chaloupka, *Everybody Knows,* xiv–xv.

114. See Skinner, *Reason and Rhetoric in the Philosophy of Hobbes,* 119, which also cites Jonson's joke in *Epicoene* (1609) discounting Aristotle as a "mere commonplace fellow."

115. For the flattery/dogs imagery cluster in *Timon,* see also Skura, *Shakespeare the Actor,* 195–202.

116. For *Timon*'s link to the economic irrationalities of James I's extravagant borrowing and gift-giving, see Kahn, "Magic of Bounty"; Bevington and Smith, "James I and *Timon of Athens,*" 62, 77.

117. William Shakespeare, *Timon of Athens,* ed. H. J. Oliver, Arden edition (Cambridge: Harvard University Press, 1959), 1.1.60–62. All subsequent citations will be to act, scene, and line number from this edition and will appear parenthetically in the text.

118. Colclough, "*Parrhesia,*" 184–85.

119. Empson, *Structure of Complex Words,* 176.

120. Since Vickers and other dual-author critics have identified this scene (1.2) as Middleton's, this aside might represent a coarsening of Apemantus's misanthropy into sheer malice, but it certainly reinforces the play's overall conception of Apemantus as a fraudulent philosopher. For inconsistencies in Apemantus's characterization, see Vickers, *Shakespeare, Co-Author,* 247, 479.

121. For this reconstruction, see Oliver's annotation to this passage in *Timon,* 35 n. 249.

122. For the thematic importance of gold in *Timon,* see Chorost, "Biological Finance in Shakespeare's *Timon of Athens.*" See also Konstan, "A Dramatic History of Misanthropes," 111.

123. See Jowett, "Middleton and Debt in *Timon of Athens,*" 221, 225–27.

124. For Marx's interest in the play's anticapitalism, see O'Dair, *Class, Critics, and Shakespeare,* 43–66.

125. See Peacham, *Garden of Eloquence,* sig. N, iiii[v.] For the gendering of rhetoric, see Skinner, *Reason and Rhetoric in the Philosophy of Hobbes,* 158 n. 127; for the pervasive misogyny of this play, see Kahn, "Magic of Bounty," 35–41; 50–54; Tambling, "Hating Man in *Timon of Athens,*" 155–57.

126. Sloterdijk, *Critique of Cynical Reason,* 14.

127. Ibid., 15.

128. See Knight, *Wheel of Fire,* 225. Rather than adjudicate the debate in favor of Timon, as Knight does, or in favor of Apemantus, as Wyndham Lewis does, I would prefer to see this encounter as a mutually destructive flyting session that in some sense expands Altman's notion of the rhetorical drama of moral ambivalence to include Shakespeare's dynamic presentation of character. See Wyndham Lewis, *Lion and the Fox,* 249–56, and Altman, *Tudor Play of Mind,* 31–63.

129. Empson, *Structure of Complex Words,* 182.

130. *Annotations by Sam. Johnson & Geo. Steevens,* 63.

131. C. S. Lewis, *English Literature in the Sixteenth Century Excluding Drama,* 54.

3. From Rude Cynics to "Cynical Revilers"

1. For the Enlightenment critique of rhetoric's meta-discursive role, see Bender and Wellbery, "Rhetoricality," 4, 8–13. See also Copeland, *Rhetoric, Hermeneutics, and Translation,* 14; and Struever, *Language of History in the Renaissance,* 15. For the post-1750 decline of rhetoric, see Vickers, *In Defence of Rhetoric,* 196–213; and Potkay, *Fate of Eloquence in the Age of Hume.* For a detailed examination of the state of classical studies in the public school curriculum at Eton (Fielding's and Lyttelton's school) from 1701 to

1750, see Nancy Mace's very useful *Henry Fielding's Novels and the Classical Tradition,* 17–38, which documents the persistence of the Latin-based rhetorical education in the public schools during the century, though English lectures replaced Latin ones in such schools by midcentury (19), and nonelite schools like the dissenting academies increasingly turned to an entirely vernacular curriculum around the same time (25–28).

2. For Cynicism's gradual exclusion from histories of philosophy, see Niehues-Pröbsting, "Modern Reception of Cynicism," 330. For rhetoricians' responses to the new science, see Howell, *Eighteenth-Century British Logic and Rhetoric,* 5, 441–47. See also Conley, *Rhetoric in the European Tradition,* 151–234.

3. For the discontinuity introduced into political thought by the regicide, see Pocock and Schochet, "Interregnum and Restoration," 146–50.

4. For the combined political effects of the interactions of print culture and rhetoric during the lead-up to the Civil Wars, see, for example, Smith, *Literature and Revolution in England,* 23–35. Also relevant are Hobbes's far-reaching responses to this tradition detailed in Skinner, *Reason and Rhetoric in the Philosophy of Hobbes,* 307–437. Thanks to Jeffery Barnouw for pointing me to some of his own work on Hobbes and rhetoric.

5. For more seventeenth- and eighteenth-century English references to Diogenes, see Henry Knight Miller, *Essays on Fielding's "Miscellanies,"* 386–409, esp. 404.

6. Butler, "Fragment of an intended Second Part of the foregoing Satyr [the "Satyr upon the . . . abuse of Human Learning"]," in *Satires and Miscellaneous Poetry and Prose,* 2:74, lines 55–56.

7. Ibid., 2:73–74, lines 29–32.

8. For "commercial modernity," see Hundert, *Enlightenment's Fable;* for "politeness," see Klein, *Shaftesbury and the Culture of Politeness;* and for vernacularization and the Enlightenment critique of rhetoric, see Bender and Wellbery, "Rhetoricality," 17–19.

9. Stanley, *History of Philosophy, Life.*

10. For the significance of the *Querelle des anciens et des modernes,* see Gumbrecht, "A History of the Concept 'Modern,'" 84–89.

11. Diogenes and the Cynics, along with the Lucianic/rhetorical tradition that contained them, moved from "dominant" to "residual" status after 1660. See Williams, *Marxism and Literature,* 123.

12. See T.B. [Thomas Blount], *Glossographia: or A Dictionary Interpreting all such Hard Words* (1656): "There was in *Greece* an old Sect of Philosophers, called *Cynicks,* first instituted by *Antisthenes;* and were so called, because they did ever bark at, and rebuke mens vices, and were not so respective in their behavior as civility required. *Diogenes* was so famous in this kind of Philosophy, that he was surnamed the *Cynick.*" (s.v. "Cynick").

13. From E.P. [Edward Phillips], *New World of English Words* (1658), (s.v. "Cynical"). See also the entry for "Diogenes": "he was for his churlish disposition and clownish conversation called the Cynic."

14. Pocock, "Cambridge Paradigms and Scotch Philosophers," 243.

15. "Sensibility" is a key concept for eighteenth-century culture generally, but those new to the period may begin with the following sources: for sensibility's complex

though implicit meanings, see Empson, *Structure of Complex Words,* 250–305; for sensibility as an episode in literary history, see Mullan, *Sentiment and Sociability.*

16. For a genealogy of "the people" and their uses in early modern political thought, see, for example, Schochet, "Why Should History Matter?" For two recent historical studies of the "people" in eighteenth-century English politics, see Kathleen Wilson, *Sense of the People*, and Rogers, *Whigs and Cities.*

17. For the background to this performance, see Smith, *Literature and Revolution in England,* 87–88; Edmond, *Rare Sir William Davenant,* 121–36; and Nethercot, *Sir William D'Avenant,* 295–309. For the ideological slipperiness of Davenant, see Wiseman, "History Digested"; and Wilcher, *Writing of Royalism,* 317–20.

18. Sir William Davenant, *The First Day's Entertainment at Rutland House,* in *Dramatic Works,* ed. James Maidment and W. H. Logan, 5 vols. (Edinburgh, 1873), 3:199. All subsequent citations will be to page numbers from volume 3 of this edition and will appear parenthetically in the text.

19. See Cope, "Rhetorical Genres in Davenant's *First Day's Entertainment at Rutland House*"; Jacob and Raylor, "Opera and Obedience."

20. For the strategies of "indirection" made possible by "uncreated texts" like historical commonplaces, see Patterson, *Censorship and Interpretation,* 65.

21. In his choice of Diogenes the Cynic as a designated declaimer against spectacles and pleasures, Davenant could be alluding to the analogous theatrical role of a rudely dressed Cynic in Thomas Campion's *Entertainment at Cawsome House* (1613) who argued for the moral benefits of theatrical entertainments. The generic resemblance between the two "entertainments" and the similar metacritical function of both "Cynics" argue for some intertextual relation between the two.

22. For the Enlightenment discourse of luxury, see Berg and Eger, "The Rise and Fall of the Luxury Debates," 7–27; Berry, *Idea of Luxury,* 101–76; Hundert, *Enlightenment's Fable;* as well as Sekora, *Luxury.* For a typical reference to Diogenes in such moral critiques of luxury, see Mackenzie, *The Moral History of Frugality* (1691), 10.

23. For Davenant's removal of the monarch, see Wiseman, "History Digested," 191. For the tension between those seeking legitimate governance by "the people" and those seeking governance by "the Saints," see Sanderson, *"But the People's Creatures,"* 178.

24. For the pre–Civil War consensus among the propertied classes about the political dangers of "the multitude," see Hill, "The Many-Headed Monster."

25. For the loaded religio-political associations of "assembly" see, for example, Berkenhead's *The Assembly-man,* 17; and Wilcher, *Writing of Royalism,* 262.

26. Jacob and Raylor, "Opera and Obedience," 227–31.

27. From Rich, *Opinion Diefied. Discouering the Ingins, Traps, and Traynes, that are set in this Age, whereby to catch Opinion* (1613), 43.

28. Hobbes, *Leviathan,* 140–41.

29. For Hobbes's distrust of oratory and eloquence for fostering "diversity of opinion," see Dykstal, *Luxury of Skepticism,* 3, 25–33.

30. Bryson, *From Courtesy to Civility,* 151–92

31. See Bender and Wellbery, "Rhetoricality," 7.

32. Warner, *Publics and Counterpublics,* 74.

33. See ibid., 65–87, 159–86.

34. For Protestant "enthusiasm," see, for example, Pocock, "Enthusiasm."

35. For the comparable aesthetic and political critique of the "sullen" puritans/"Jews" in Davenant's preface to *Gondibert,* see Zwicker, *Lines of Authority,* 9–36.

36. Mandeville, *Fable of the Bees,* Remark (O.), 157.

37. Hundert, "Mandeville, Rousseau and the Political Economy of Fantasy," 33.

38. For the "serio-comic," see Branham, *Unruly Eloquence,* 26–28.

39. Because the Citizen of the World synthesized the dominant discourses of modernization in this period—politeness, sensibility, cosmopolitanism—the Citizen has been understood since the eighteenth century as a self-image of the Enlightenment philosophe. For two views of eighteenth-century cosmopolitanism, see Schlereth, *Cosmopolitan Ideal in Enlightenment Thought;* and McKillop, "Local Attachment and Cosmopolitanism—The Eighteenth-Century Pattern." For the close relation of "philosophe," "cosmopolite," and "Citizen of the World" in Enlightenment writing, see Schlereth, *Cosmopolitan Ideal in Enlightenment Thought,* 47.

40. These were the private philosophical notebooks he maintained during his retreats in Holland in 1698 and 1703–4.

41. From Third Earl of Shaftesbury, ["Maxims"], in the *Philosophical Regimen,* in *The Life, Unpublished Letters, and Philosophical Regimen,* ed. Benjamin Rand (New York: Macmillan, 1900), 225. All subsequent citations will be to page numbers from this edition and will appear parenthetically in the text. Ms. Lori Branch has been kind enough to share some of her own transcriptions from the unpublished Shaftesbury papers, to help correct my quotations from Rand's sometimes garbled transcriptions.

42. Demonax, who appears in Francklin's 1770 translation of Lucian as a proto-Samuel Johnson, was a widely respected philosopher in his city, and Shaftesbury considers Lucian's unsatirical praise for him the greatest possible tribute to this philosopher's good nature.

43. From "Soliloquy," in the *Characteristics,* 165. For Klein's discussion of this passage and the philosophical succession offered here, see his *Shaftesbury,* 42–43; for Shaftesbury's central role in popularizing this aristocratic, Whiggish model of "polite philosophy," see *Shaftesbury and the Culture of Politeness,* 21. The Polite Philosopher was often identified with Aristippus and contrasted with the rude Diogenes. See, for example, Forrester's *The Polite Philosopher: Or, An Essay on that Art Which Makes a Man Happy in Himself and Agreeable to Others:* "In a word, [Aristippus] had the Integrity of DIOGENES, without his Churlishness; and as his Wisdom was useful to himself, so it rendered him agreeable to the rest of the World" (2–3).

44. From "Soliloquy," in the *Characteristics,* 167. For the significance of these passages of Shaftesbury for the Continental reception of the Cynics, esp. Diderot, see Niehues-Pröbsting, "Modern Reception of Cynicism," 350.

45. For the sentimental cynic or benevolent misanthrope, see Preston, *Not in Timon's Manner.*

46. Flecknoe, *Sir Wm. Davenant's Voyage to the Other World: With his Adventures in the Poets Elizium* (1668), 7.

47. Ibid., 13.

48. For "desacralization" and the eroding of the sacred aura around the body royal, see, for example, Zaller, "Breaking the Vessels."

49. For "secularization" as the resetting of the discursive boundaries of religion and politics (which I term "desacralization," following Zaller and other historians), see McKeon, "Politics of Discourses and the Rise of the Aesthetic in Seventeenth-Century England."

50. For this genre, see Robinson, *Lucian and His Influence in Europe,* 16–17, 37–41,

51. As Weinbrot points out (63), many late seventeenth-century writers continued to regard Lucian as an anti-Christian "scoffer." This essentially personal judgment against Lucian, however, did not prevent Christian writers from appropriating the Dialogues of the Dead in a polite, anti-Menippean fashion, especially after the influential successes of Fontenelle and Fénelon (see below). See Weinbrot, *Menippean Satire Reconsidered,* 69–77.

51. For English translations and imitations of Lucian during this period, see Keener, *English Dialogues of the Dead,* 11–13; Craig, "Dryden's Lucian."

52. For the paradigmatic movement from rhetoric to literature, see Bender and Wellbery, "Rhetoricality", 7–13. For the emergence of history as a separate discipline after the demise of rhetoric, see Nadel, "Philosophy of History before Historicism."

53. *Letters from the Westminster Journal,* 96.

54. For this phrase, see Boyce, "News from Hell," 404.

55. See, for example, Gunn, *Beyond Liberty and Property,* 260–315.

56. Hobbes, *Leviathan,* 132. See Koselleck, *Critique and Crisis,* 23–40; Habermas, *Structural Transformation of the Public Sphere,* 90.

57. Hobbes, *Leviathan,* 134.

58. Ibid. As Certeau comments, "Through this link [between authority and belief], politics [in the English tradition of political philosophy] made its relationship of difference and continuity with religion explicit" (*PEL* 178).

59. See, for example, Kramnick, *Bolingbroke and His Circle,* 8–38.

60. For the important role of temporalization and circulation in the formation of publics, see Warner, *Publics and Counterpublics,* 96–114.

61. For Bolingbroke's role in establishing and institutionalizing the functions of an Opposition press, see Skinner, "Principles and Practice of Opposition," 95–96. See also Dickinson, *Bolingbroke,* 154–83, 212–46.

62. See Keenan, "Twilight of the Political?" #4.

63. For Fielding's lifelong interest in Lucian, which included a proposed translation of his Works, see Henry Knight Miller, *Essays on Fielding's "Miscellanies,"* 365–86. Though Mace, arguing against Miller, denies the centrality of Lucian to Fielding as a stylistic model (54–57), she nonetheless admits Fielding's close imitation of Lucian in at least this work and a few others in the *Miscellanies*, and acknowledges the persistence of

Lucian in the Eton curriculum (22) and classical literary canon of this period (150–51). See *Henry Fielding's Novels and the Classical Tradition*, 56. For the un-Menippean dialogues of Fielding and Lyttelton, see also Weinbrot, *Menippean Satire Reconsidered*, 79–85.

64. Battestin's biography contains two episodes that suggest some contemporary associations of Fielding with Cynicism. The first was Garrick's unflattering anecdote, as recalled by Helfrich Sturz: "Fielding [Sturz recalls Garrick saying] was a complete cynic, who would not be inferior to the old dog in the barrel in anything and chewed tobacco, wine, and epigrams together in a very unappetizing way. Once, at his home, when Garrick and a few friends were dining with him, a disagreeable smell tickled their noses; Fielding soon helped them out of their bewilderment when, as he stood up laughing, the company became aware that he was sitting at table on his chamber pot" (364). The second is the letter Fielding wrote to his friend James Harris just after his wife's death in 1744: "This is in good earnest the present Situation of my Mind, which you will find at our next meeting neither soured nor depress; neither snarling like a Cynic nor blubbering like a Woman" (386).

65. For the heavy reliance of the Bolingbroke wing of the Opposition, including Lyttelton and Fielding, upon a discourse of ministry corruption and vice to criticize Walpole, see Kramnick, *Bolingbroke and His Circle*, 30–35; Skinner, "Principles and Practice of Opposition," 120–21.

66. See Dickinson, *Bolingbroke*, 247–76, esp. 248–49. One of Bolingbroke's earliest "philosophical" essays, his "Reflections upon Exile" (1716), which dated from one of his first periods of enforced retirement, exhibits Bolingbroke imitating, a little implausibly, the Stoic meditations of Seneca, and therefore consoling himself with the example of Diogenes: "Diogenes was driven out of the kingdom of Pontus for counterfeiting the coin. . . . But you have obtained your liberty by doing your duty" (196). *Of the True Use of Retirement*, the product of a later period of enforced exile, goes on in a similarly rationalizing vein, with Bolingbroke reassuring himself that it was the voice of his Socratic "genius," and not the Ministry's threats of prosecution, which led him to study philosophy in France (345).

67. For the background to the Spanish War and its role in bringing down Walpole's Ministry, see Woodfine, *Britannia's Glories*. In his essay "Government Harassment of the Press in the late 1730s," Woodfine describes the interesting case of an impoverished French Jacobite physician and hack writer, Denis de Coetlogon, who had once written, like Fielding, for the *Craftsman*, and who later published a pamphlet, *Diogenes's Rambles* (1743), which similarly used Diogenes as a mouthpiece to critique both Walpole and his reflexive Opposition during the Spanish War; Fielding's treatment is much more critical of the philosopher, but both writers criticize the great man and his reflexive opposition. Woodfine's article points out that Coetlogon's resentment was understandably directed at the Walpole Ministry, which had once detained and threatened to imprison him (25), but that Coetlogon was also irritated by the Opposition journals' concealed backers like Bolingbroke or Pulteney, who never troubled themselves about the writers who were prosecuted for doing their dirty work (26–27). The closeness

in timing, sentiments, and Diogenical personae of these two writers provides further circumstantial evidence for my reading of Fielding's dialogue as a disavowal of Opposition hack-writing. My thanks to Philip Woodfine for bringing Coetlogon and this article to my attention. For Fielding during this period, and an analysis of *Jonathan Wild* and other works for signs of Fielding's shifting political attitudes, see Goldsmith, "Faction Detected," 9–12. Miller finds no evidence to date the dialogue, beyond the fact that it expands a topic originally included in "Of True Greatness," published in 1741, and described there as "writ several Years ago" ("General Introduction," xlv). In my view, however, the dramatically increased psychological interest of Fielding's treatment of the Diogenes-Alexander commonplace suggests a later date and some external event to provoke Fielding's revisiting of the commonplace.

68. From "Of True Greatness," in Fielding, *Miscellanies by Henry Fielding, Esq.*, 21, lines 55–58.

69. Ibid., line 63.

70. Fielding's exact political affiliations during the period 1741–43 are still being debated, since he seems to have published both pro- and antiministerial works during this period. What we do incontrovertibly know is that 1742 brought both the success of *Joseph Andrews* and the downfall of Walpole, but Fielding kept his distance from the public fray that brought down Walpole. In 1743, Fielding was finally able to bring out the pieces contained in the long-delayed *Miscellanies,* which seems to have been conceived while he was still writing for the Opposition, but which ended up as a far less partisan document. Viewed as a record of its author's political affiliations, the *Miscellanies* live up to their title and give mixed messages to those who would seek evidence of Fielding's own political beliefs. As the collected work of someone who had written for years on behalf of the Opposition, the *Miscellanies* exhibit both pro- and anti-Walpole pieces, a similarly mixed subscription list, and a denial of personal satire in *Jonathan Wild,* its most powerful writing. See, for example Miller's general introduction to the *Miscellanies,* xi–xv; Coley's general introduction and notes to the "Opposition," in *Contributions to "The Champion" and Related Writings,* lxxxiv–cvi; Battestin's *Henry Fielding,* 317–43, 369–73.

71. "A Dialogue between Alexander the Great and Diogenes the Cynic," in Henry Fielding, *Miscellanies by Henry Fielding, Esq.*, vol. 1, ed. Henry Knight Miller (Middletown, Ct.: Wesleyan University Press, 1972), 228. All subsequent citations will be to this edition and will appear parenthetically in the text. For the Dialogue, see Miller, *Essays on Fielding's "Miscellanies,"* esp. 386–93, 405–9; and Robinson, *Lucian and His Influence,* 198–235.

72. Diogenes' complaints about the slavish credulity of Alexander's followers, who consented even to Alexander's absurd claims of divinity, may be based on Fénelon's "Dialogue of Alexander and Diogenes," which makes similar charges. Fénelon's Alexander admits that while he "despised" the "fables" concerning his divinity, he nevertheless "made use of them, because they gave [him] an absolute power over men." From Fénelon, "Alexander and Diogenes," in *Dialogues of the Dead* (1770), 1:111–12.

73. The contrast between the retired and active life could still inspire such references to Diogenes, even in the late seventeenth and eighteenth centuries. See, for example,

Evelyn's *Publick Employment and an Active Life . . . Prefer'd to Solitude* (1666), 32. If this dialogue is indeed targeting Bolingbroke, the irony of identifying the libertine, would-be philosopher Bolingbroke with the churlish, impoverished Diogenes would be delicious and would take further satiric charge in the context of Walpole's previously labeling him an "anti-minister" incapable of exercising real power. See Dickinson, *Bolingbroke,* 243–44.

74. For John Wilkes and his movement, see Rudé, *Wilkes and Liberty.* For the notion of a crisis in Whig/Tory party structures precipitated by George III and exploited by Wilkes, see Brewer, *Party Ideology and Popular Politics at the Accession of George III.* See also Kathleen Wilson, *Sense of the People,* 206–36.

75. Because Lyttelton only printed this Dialogue in his expanded 1765 edition of the *Dialogues,* my text for this work will be taken from Lyttelton's *Works,* ed. George Edward Ayscough, 3 vols. (London 1776), 383–93. All subsequent citations to this Dialogue will be to page numbers of the Ayscough edition and will appear parenthetically in the text.

76. From d'Alembert, "An Essay upon the Alliance betwixt Learned Men, and the Great," 153–54.

77. For the historical and biographical background to Lyttelton's *Dialogues,* see Keener, *English Dialogues of the Dead,* 75–103; Davis, *Good Lord Lyttelton,* 310–25.

78. Here again we might find a personal allusion in Lyttelton's treatment of Diogenes' debates with his rival, this time in Lord Bute's unpopular mentorship of the young George III.

79. See Pocock's suggestive remarks about the myth of Bute the evil counsellor as a symptom of the ambivalence of the British public toward George III as a personal monarch or would-be "Patriot King." See Pocock, "The Imperial Crisis," 253–54.

80. Another possible identification for the shamelessly plebeian and demagogic version of Diogenes here could be Rousseau, whose *Discourse on Inequality* appeared in 1755 and whose controversial "Letter to d'Alembert" appeared in 1762.

81. All three terms taken together (pageantry, superstition, tyranny) would resonate with the reflexive anti-Catholicism of the period. See also Certeau's observation that "superstition" represents the aspects of inherited beliefs that have not yet been transported or redirected into new areas of progress (*PEL* 178–79).

82. It is tempting to see this Dialogue's Plato as enacting Lyttelton's own Whiggish ambivalence between an unsatisfactory court (George III and Bute) allied with an equally unsatisfactory ministry (Grenville) and a frighteningly demagogic popular politics represented by Wilkes. In the time between the publication of Lyttelton's first edition of the *Dialogues* in 1760 and the expanded fourth edition of 1765, Wilkes began publication of the *North Briton* (1762); published and was arrested for his famous no. 45 attack on Bute in the *North Briton,* only to be released on bail (1763); and was expelled from the Commons and outlawed for his failure to appear for his pornographic *Essay on Woman* (1764). There are parallels between Plato's statements on liberty and government (Works 388) and Lyttelton's own position against Wilkes's reliance on parliamen-

tary privilege in his 1763 speech to the House of Lords collected in the *Works,* 3:39. For Lyttelton's ambivalence regarding Wilkes, see Davis, *Good Lord Lyttelton,* 273–80.

83. Diogenes here helps to enact Brewer's "'alternative' political nation" described in Brewer's *Party Ideology and Popular Politics,* 160, and more generally, 139–269. In this respect, the views ascribed to Diogenes reflect Goldsmith's summary of Brewer's "alternative structure of politics" thesis: "radical ideology, extra-parliamentary organization, and popular protest" ("Faction Detected" 7).

4. The Cynic Unveiled

1. "Humility and Pride," *Gentleman's Magazine* 18 (August 1748): 352.

2. See Niehues-Pröbsting, "Modern Reception of Cynicism," 331–53. See also Starobinski, "Diogène dans *Le Neveu De Rameau,*" 152. Thanks to Louisa Shea and Sharon Stanley for sharing with me their works in progress on Sade, Diderot, and the French Enlightenment's relation to ancient Cynicism.

3. Gumbrecht, "Who Were the *Philosophes*?" 134. For the gendering of the "Man of Reason" in the Enlightenment, see Lloyd, *Man of Reason,* 57–64.

4. Niehues-Pröbsting, "Modern Reception of Cynicism," 333.

5. From Jean d'Alembert, "An Essay upon the Alliance betwixt Learned Men, and the Great," in *Miscellaneous Pieces in Literature, History and Philosophy by Mr.* D'Alembert (London, 1764), 154. All subsequent citations will be to this edition and will appear parenthetically in the text. See Goodman, *Republic of Letters,* 35–40; see also Grimsley, *Jean d'Alembert,* 108–56, esp. 144, 153.

6. For Rousseau's reputation, and the repeated labeling of him as a Diogenes, Cynic, or misanthrope, see, for example, Roddier, *J.-J. Rousseau en Angleterre au XVIII*[E] *siècle,* 58–63, Voisine, *J.-J. Rousseau en Angleterre a L'Epoque Romantique.* For the "rude dignity" represented by Diogenes and Rousseau in eighteenth-century France, see France, *Politeness and Its Discontents,* 4, 62, 127–28.

7. For Voltaire's impatience with Rousseau, see Havens, *Voltaire's Marginalia on the Pages of Rousseau,* 21. For other writers' comparisons of Diogenes to Rousseau, see also Ambrus, "La figure du philosophe," 218.

8. See Warner, *Publics and Counterpublics,* 96–124.

9. For the clerical, polite character of the English Enlightenment, see Pocock, "Clergy and Commerce."

10. For the English reception generally, I am indebted to James H. Warner's unpublished dissertation, "The Reputation of Jean Jacques Rousseau in England, 1750–98" (Duke, 1933), which provides a wealth of examples; as well as Edward Duffy, *Rousseau in England.*

11. See *OED,* s.v. "cynical": "disposed to disbelieve in human sincerity or goodness," and the D'Israeli example, which will be discussed extensively in chapter 5.

12. For Rousseau's debts to the Enlightenment debates over Mandeville's *Fable,* see Hundert, "Mandeville, Rousseau and the Political Economy of Fantasy," 33–37.

13. For Voltaire's and Montesquieu's acceptance of Mandeville, see Hundert, *Enlightenment's Fable,* 16–23.

14. Gumbrecht, "Who Were the *Philosophes*?" 135.

15. From *Discourse on the Sciences and the Arts* in Jean-Jacques Rousseau, *Basic Political Writings,* trans. Donald A. Cress (Indianapolis: Hackett, 1987), 4. All subsequent citations will be to this edition and will appear parenthetically in the text.

16. In addition to Niehues-Pröbsting, see Payne, *Philosophes and the People,* 172–74.

17. Goodman, *Republic of Letters,* 35–36.

18. See Starobinski, *Jean-Jacques Rousseau,* 284–86.

19. Lewis, *English Literature,* 53.

20. Keenan, "Twilight of the Political?" #4.

21. From Rousseau, *Discourse on the Origin and Foundations of Inequality Among Men,* in Jean-Jacques Rousseau, *Basic Political Writings,* trans. Donald A. Cress (Indianapolis: Hackett, 1987), 53. All subsequent citations will be to this edition and will appear parenthetically in the text.

22. For this use of "rationalization," see Adorno, "Opinion Delusion Society" (discussed at length in chapter 5), for a definition of Freudian rationalization as "reason in the service of unreason" (108), along with the translator's helpful definition: "a process through which the subject attempts to provide a logically coherent or morally acceptable explanation for behavior, actions, thoughts, feelings, etc., whose real motives are unknown" (344 n. 3).

23. "The wise man [says d'Alembert], who calmly contemplates all ages as well as his own, discerns among all mankind a pretty near resemblance" (d'Alembert, "An Essay upon the Alliance betwixt Learned Men, and the Great," 115).

24. See Keenan, *Democracy in Question,* 41–70; for a comparative analysis of this problem in small vs. large groups, see Olson, *Logic of Collective Action,* 53–65.

25. The philosophes were now drawing hostile publicity in works like Palissot's satire *The Philosophes* (1760), which depicted a group of sham philosophes manipulating their patrons; Rousseau himself was turned into Crispin, a ranting philosophe who walked on all fours and ate lettuce (as Diogenes had once recommended to Aristippus) in order to reject the corruptions of civilization. See Duffy, *Rousseau in England,* 12.

26. Voltaire, *Selected Letters,* "To Jean le Rond d'Alembert. March 19, 1761," 219

27. Ibid., June 17, 1762, 230.

28. For information about the child-abandonment story, which seems to have begun circulating around the time of Rousseau's first celebrity (ca. 1751), see Cranston, who argues that Rousseau justified the practice in a variety of unconvincing ways to his confidantes, including the grotesque claim that the Foundling Hospitals reared children in the vigorous, unluxurious manner of peasants and workers. This claim ignored the massive numbers of infants and young children who immediately died from disease or neglect while under the charge of these institutions. Nonetheless, there were also plenty of rumors that Rousseau's anatomical difficulties and Thérèse's infidelity also made it unlikely that any of the children were his own. See Cranston, *Jean-Jacques,* 244–46.

29. Quoted in Goodman, "Pigalle's Voltaire nu," 108 n. 28.

30. Reprinted in *Monthly Review* (March 1763): 226.

31. Ibid., 225–26.

32. For these phases in Rousseau's English reception, see Duffy, *Rousseau in England,* 9–53.

33. See, for example, Kant's effusive praise of both Diogenes and Rousseau in his early *Lectures on Ethics:* "The Cynic sect said the highest good would be a thing of nature and not art: For Diogenes the means of happiness were negative. He said that man is by nature content with little; because man, by nature, has no needs, he also does not feel the want of means, and under this want he enjoys his happiness. Diogenes has much in his favor, for the provision of means and gifts of nature increases our needs, since the more means we have, the more our needs are augmented, and the thoughts of man turn to greater satisfactions, so that the mind is always uneasy. Rousseau, that subtle Diogenes, also maintained that our will would be good by nature, only we always become corrupted; that nature would have provided us with everything, if we did not create new needs." See *Lectures on Ethics,* 45. For more discussion of Kant's reading of the Cynics, see also Niehues-Pröbsting, "Modern Reception of Cynicism," 340.

34. Wieland's novel, *Socrates out of his Senses: Or, Dialogues of Diogenes of Sinope,* which narrates the picaresque adventures of Diogenes the philosopher among his fellow "citizens of the world," thoroughly sentimentalizes both Rousseau and Diogenes. For example, Wieland's teasing "Preface of the Publisher" argues that the readers of his *Dialogues* should not be misled by the absurd images of Diogenes offered by the "injudicious compiler" Laertius or the "prating author [Athenaeus] [of the] *Deipnosophisticis,*" just as we must be able to distinguish between the "humourous, but good-mannered and delicate satyrist of human follies [that is, the Diogenes presented by Wieland] from a greasy and unpolite misanthrope" (1:xv). The "Publisher's" chief argument for discounting the prejudiced testimonies of envious contemporaries is "the famous John James Rousseau of Geneva, a man, who is perhaps really but half so singular, as he seems to be" (1:xxiii). For the significance of Wieland's idealized Diogenes, see also Niehues-Pröbsting, "Modern Reception of Cynicism," 334–39.

35. For the difficulties in Rousseau's reputation following the break with Voltaire, d'Alembert, and Diderot, and the repeated labeling of him as a Diogenes, Cynic, or misanthrope, see, for example, Malkin, "Rousseau and Epictetus," 117. See also the discussion of Rousseau and Diogenes in Niehues-Pröbsting, "Modern Reception of Cynicism," esp. 339–45. Very full documentation of Rousseau's treatment in the French press may be found in Sean Campbell Goodlett's doctoral dissertation "The Origins of Celebrity: The Eighteenth-Century Anglo-French Press Reception of Jean-Jacques Rousseau" (University of Oregon, 2000). I am grateful to Mr. Goodlett for making this research available to me.

36. Marmontel, *Memoirs of Marmontel,* 1:322.

37. Ibid., 1:320; see also 1:359.

38. See Duffy, *Rousseau in England,* 30, for this review and the continued English support of Rousseau immediately following his death.

39. *Monthly Review* 60 (February 1779): 137.

40. Warner, *Publics and Counterpublics,* 74–87.

41. From Combe, "Letter to Jean-Jacques Rousseau," 570, reprinted from *Ackermann's Repository of Arts* (1824). The undated text is said to have been written sometime between 1766, when Rousseau was in England, and 1776, when Combe himself took up railing satire in his *Diaboliad.* The lack of evidence regarding the letter's dating makes it hard to determine how or where Combe learned of Rousseau's music copying. In the words of the editor of *Ackermann's Repository of the Arts,* "[This letter] is addressed to Rousseau, whose aversion to society, we might almost say misanthropy, is well known, evidently with a view to awaken in his bosom more kindly feelings, and to reconcile him with his species" (*Ackermann's Repository* 205). For Combe's role as a translator and possible imitator of Rousseau, see Barbier, "Letters of an Italian Nun and an English Gentleman (1781)."

42. Wesley, *Journal,* 352–53. Quoted by Voisine, *J. -J. Rousseau,* 70.

43. Edmund Burke, *Reflections on the Revolution in France,* ed. Conor Cruise O'Brien (New York: Penguin, 1968), 75. All subsequent citations will be to page numbers from this edition and will appear parenthetically in the text.

44. Because my discussion focuses upon the history of English responses to Rousseau, I have decided to examine the works in the order of their appearance in English, not in the order of their composition. Hence, I address *Rousseau Judge of Jean-Jacques,* written between 1772 and 1774 and published in 1780, before the *Confessions,* which were begun around 1765, though they did not appear in English until 1783 (pt. 1) and 1790 (pt. 2).

45. In other words, a "Diogenes [who] did not find his man . . . because he searched among his contemporaries for a man who no longer existed" (*Discourse of Inequality,* 80).

46. From the "Second Dialogue" in Rousseau, *Rousseau, Judge of Jean-Jacques: Dialogues,* vol. 1, ed. Roger D. Masters and Christopher Kelly, trans. Judith R. Bush, Christopher Kelly, and Roger D. Masters (Hanover: University Press of New England, 1990), 102. All subsequent citations will be to this edition and will appear parenthetically in the text. For this passage and additional instances of Rousseau's discussions of Diogenes, see Scanlan, "Jean-Jacques Rousseau and Diogenes the Cynic."

47. See also Niehues-Pröbsting, "Modern Reception of Cynicism," 341–42.

48. For Cynic *parrhesia,* see Flynn/Foucault, *FP* 102–18.

49. Starobinski, *Jean-Jacques Rousseau,* 286.

50. Skinner, "The Principles and Practice of Opposition," 111.

51. Jean-Jacques Rousseau, *The Confessions of J.J. Rousseau, Citizen of Geneva. Part the Second,* trans. anon., 3 vols., 1:181. All subsequent citations will be to volume and page numbers from this edition and will appear parenthetically in the text.

52. See Malkin, "Rousseau and Epictetus," 121–27.

53. For Rousseau and masculinity, see, for example, Lloyd, *Man of Reason,* 57–64; Blum, in *Rousseau and the Republic of Virtue,* 37–56; and Starobinski, *Jean-Jacques Rousseau,* 365–77.

54. Sloterdijk, *Critique of Cynical Reason,* 5.

55. See *Webster's Revised Unabridged Dictionary* (Springfield: G&C Merriam, 1913), s.v. "Cynic": "a person who believes that human conduct is directed, either consciously or unconsciously, wholly by self-interest or self-indulgence, and that appearances to the contrary are superficial and untrustworthy." Found at ARTFL Project: Webster Dictionary, 1913.

56. See Tosh, "What Should Historians Do with Masculinity?"

57. See Judith Butler, *Gender Trouble,* 16–17. For the "man of feeling" and his implication in the "gender panic" of the late eighteenth century, see also Wahrman, "*Percy's* Prologue," 123.

58. Fellowes, "Character of Rousseau," *Monthly Mirror* 8 (August 1799): 71.

59. Niehues-Pröbsting, "Modern Reception of Cynicism," 333. In other words, Rousseau's failures both as a man and as a "man of reason" become symbols of a larger failure of Enlightenment Reason and help to connect cynicism permanently with a false or failed reason rather than its supposedly true, authentically philosophical counterpart.

60. See *Monthly Review* 67 (September 1782): "Upon the whole, it is certain, that this publication will diminish considerably the high idea, which has been formed of M. ROUSSEAU, and will perhaps lower him in the esteem of the Public more than he deserves to be" (232).

61. *Monthly Review* 66 (June 7, 1782): 530.

62. See ibid. 67 (September 1782): 229.

63. See ibid., 232.

64. See ibid., 232–33.

65. Blum, *Rousseau and the Republic of Virtue,* 79.

5. Edmund Burke and the Counter-Enlightenment Attack on the Philosopher of Vanity

1. For the provenance of "conservative" in the nineteenth-century "Tory" appropriation of Burke, see Sack, *From Jacobite to Conservative,* 4–6.

2. For Burke's influential reading of Rousseau as a sentimental fraud, see Johnson, *Equivocal Beings,* 1–19. For the Anti-Jacobins, see Marilyn Butler, *Jane Austen and the War of Ideas,* 88–123. For the political reaction to sentimentality, see Barker-Benfield, *Culture of Sensibility,* 351–95.

3. See Philp, "Vulgar Conservatism," 43.

4. According to Sack, these subsidies commenced in earnest in 1792 with the radicalization of the French Revolution, were augmented by the Irish Rebellion (1798), and helped to foster an "exponential" growth in the "national right-wing press" through a series of Tory administrations for at least the next three decades (14). These governmental successes showed, perhaps, that Pitt had learned from Bute's and his successors' inept management of the press during the Wilkite disturbances of the 1760s (8–12). See also Kelly, *English Jacobin Novel,* 1–14.

5. Sack, *From Jacobite to Conservative,* 12.

6. See Philp, "Vulgar Conservatism," 43, as well as Goodwin, *Friends of Liberty,* 99–135. Goodwin notes, for example, how in 1792 the Sheffield *Patriot, or Political, Moral, and Philosophical Repository* began to carry extracts of eighteenth-century liberal political theory, including Rousseau's *Social Contract* alongside Locke, Bolingbroke, Montesquieu, and Volney, in addition to news reports and "articles on Anglo-French relations and translations of the fundamental legislative decrees of the French National Assemblies" (224, 225).

7. For an Anti-Jacobin-style attack on the bespectacled "Democrats" and "*Plebeii Philosophi*" Godwin and Holcroft, which is filled with references to their Cynic-style hypocrisy and pride, not least Holcroft's Rousseauean neglect of his son, see [Thomas James Mathias], *The Grove* (first published 1789?): "Still contradict they, by their practice, clear, / What, foes to peace, they pour in ev'ry ear. / Equality they preach, when pow'r they'd gain, / As all decry the thing they would obtain: / The weak misleading, who alone will throng / To listen to the Syren's artful song" (17).

8. From Johnson, *Dictionary of the English Language* (1755), s.v. "Cynick." See also Johnson's definition of "Cynical": "Having the qualities of a dog; currish; brutal; snarling; satirical." The dictionaries of Ash (1775), Spence (1775), Sheridan (1780), and Walker (1791) simply repeat Johnson's definition. Also relevant are the definitions contained in D. Fenning's *Royal English Dictionary; or, A Treasury of the English Language* (1763): "CYNIC, or CYNICAL: "snarling, brutal, or partaking of the qualities of a Cynic philosopher, who was remarkable for his contempt of riches, and rigorous reprehension of vice"; "CYNIC": "a philosopher who valued himself for his contempt of every thing, except morality; a sect founded by Diogenes." Fenning's definitions were still being repeated verbatim twenty years later in Barclay et al., *Complete and Universal English Dictionary On a New Plan* (1782), "CYNIC, or CYNICAL," and "CYNIC," q.v. See also Perry, *Royal Standard English Dictionary* (1775), "Cynic" and "Cynic, Cynical, " q.v.: "a snarling philosopher"; "snarling, satyrical."

9. Preston, *Not in Timon's Manner,* 4–28, 31–33.

10. See Pocock's "Editor's Introduction" to Burke's *Reflections,* vii–lvi.

11. Ibid., x.

12. For other discussions of "prejudice" in Burke, see Weinsheimer, "Burke's *Reflections*"; Garnett, "Hazlitt against Burke"; and Bromwich, "Burke, Wordsworth and the Defense of History."

13. See Colley, *Britons,* 250–81. For the conflict between the cosmopolitan, internationalist optimism of the radical "patriots" (descended from the Wilkite and dissenting portions of the midcentury Opposition) versus the more popular and chauvinist strains of loyalism residing outside radical circles, see Dinwiddy, "England," as well as Radcliffe, "Burke, Radical Cosmopolitanism, and the Debates on Patriotism in the 1790s," and "Revolutionary Writing, Moral Philosophy, and Universal Benevolence in the Eighteenth Century."

14. From "A Letter to William Smith on the Subject of Catholic Emancipation in Burke," *Works,* 6:367.

15. For the 1773 denunciation of Hume and Rousseau in the House of Commons as "members of 'that despicable tribe of skeptics and infidels,'" see Sack, *From Jacobite to Conservative,* 77, in addition to the earlier reference to Wesley.

16. Berlin, "The Counter-Enlightenment."

17. Gumbrecht, "Who Were the *Philosophes*?" 160–70.

18. For Burke's influential deployment of the "perversity" and "futility" theses against the French Revolution's attempts at social change, and their subsequent elaboration, see Hirschman, *Rhetoric of Reaction,* 1–80, 138–39.

19. Keenan, "Twilight of the Political?" #4.

20. Theodor W. Adorno, "Opinion Delusion Society," in *Critical Models: Interventions and Catchwords,* trans. Henry W. Pickford (New York: Columbia University Press, 1995), 108. All subsequent citations will be to this edition and will appear parenthetically in the text.

21. Gumbrecht, "Who Were the *Philosophes*?" 134–35, 146.

22. For the central role of the "artist-intellectual" in England's transition from "aristocratic cosmopolitanism" to "nationalism," see Newman, *Rise of English Nationalism,* 56–60.

23. For the continuity between pre- and post-1790s governmental control of the press, see Black, *English Press in the Eighteenth Century,* 184–88.

24. As Philp notes, however, Burke's and his followers' addresses helped foster a paradoxically eager and participatory conservative movement that attempted to counter radicals' addresses to the people. See Philp, "Vulgar Conservatism," 44.

25. See H. V. F. Somerset's introduction to Burke, *A Note-Book of Edmund Burke,* 3–18. For Burke's extensive training in rhetoric at Trinity College, Dublin, see 14–16. It is fascinating to see how much of the *Reflections*' conceptual framework had been laid out in these notebooks dating from his early residence in London, coinciding roughly with his authorship of the *Vindication of Natural Society* (1756) and the *Enquiry into our Ideas of the Sublime and the Beautiful* (1757), along with his editorship of the *Annual Register,* which he commenced in 1758.

26. From "Several Scattered Hints Concerning Philosophy and Learning Collected Here from My Papers," in Edmund Burke, *A Note-book of Edmund Burke,* ed. H. V. F. Somerset (Cambridge: Cambridge University Press), 91. All subsequent citations will be to page numbers of this edition and will appear parenthetically in the text. For the link between this passage and the *Reflections,* see Damrosch, *Fictions of Reality in the Age of Hume and Johnson,* 187. This same anecdote was discussed by Hume ten years earlier in his essay "Of Moral Prejudices" (1742), published a year before Fielding's "Dialogue of Alexander the Great and Diogenes the Cynic," in the *Miscellanies* (1743). See Hume, "Of Moral Prejudices," in *Essays Moral, Political and Literary,* 539.

27. Hume, "Of Moral Prejudices," in *Essays Moral, Political and Literary,* 540.

28. This metaphor also accords with Kramnick's reading of Burke's "excremental vision" in *The Rage of Edmund Burke,* 184–89.

29. See Radcliffe, "Burke, Radical Cosmopolitanism, and the Debates on Patriotism," 316.

30. James Boyd White also points to the impetus Burke might have had from his French correspondent who had initially urged him to write: "Condescend, sir, to satisfy my doubts, and do not leave under the prejudice of party spirit a young man who was taught in England the danger of all prejudices." From White, *When Words Lose Their Meaning,* 348, n. 12.

31. Gumbrecht, "Who Were the *Philosophes*?" 140. For the Enlightenment's cosmopolitan critique of prejudice, see, for example, Schlereth, *Cosmopolitan Ideal,* 26–28, 64–66.

32. Koselleck, "The Historical-Political Semantics of Assymetric Counterconcepts," 159–61.

33. Berlin, "The Counter-Enlightenment," 1.

34. Apart from Hume, Burke seems to have at least one more precursor in his treatment of prejudice, Berkeley. For Berkeley's notions of "prejudice" and "utility as test of truth" in his arguments against the freethinkers in *Alciphron* (1732), see Dykstal, *Luxury of Skepticism,* 132–45.

35. Lloyd, *Man of Reason,* 1–10. For the implicit gendering of moral philosophy, a tradition written for the most part by male "clerics, misogynists, and puritan bachelors," see Baier, "Trust and Antitrust," 114.

36. Wahrman, "*Percy's* Prologue," 116–23. Though Wahrman dates this "gender panic" from the 1770s, Colley and Johnson have convincingly demonstrated the importance of stabilizing prescriptive gender roles for conservative female writers like More and Hamilton, along with other conservatives. For Hays and Wollstonecraft, see, for example, William Godwin's joint portrait of Mary Wollstonecraft's Rousseauean tutelage under Fuseli in the *Memoirs of the Author of "The Rights of Woman"* (1798): "Smitten with Rousseau's conception of the perfectness of the savage state, and the essential abortiveness of all civilization, Mr Fuseli looks at all our little attempts at improvement, with a spirit that borders perhaps too much upon contempt and indifference. . . . Add to this, that Mr Fuseli is somewhat of a caustic turn of mind, with much wit, and a disposition to search, in every thing new or modern, for occasions of censure. I believe Mary came something more a cynic out of the school of Mr Fuseli, than she went into it" (234). See also Richard Polwhele's description of the "Wollstonecraftian" Mary Hays in *The Unsex'd Females* (1798): "Now stole the modish grin, the sapient sneer, / And flippant HAYS assum'd a cynic leer" (20).

37. For this reading of Burke and the political consequences of gender difference, see, for example, Johnson, *Equivocal Beings,* 1–19, 181–82.

38. For the historical significance of this interpretation of the dependence of commerce upon manners, rather than the other way around, see Pocock, *Virtue, Commerce, and History,* 210.

39. Boulton, *Language of Politics,* 85, 259–60.

40. See Mannheim, "Conservative Thought," 84–119.

41. This seems the greatest single weakness of James Boyd White's otherwise excellent reading of the *Reflections,* from which I have learned a great deal. See White, *When Words Lose Their Meaning,* 212–13.

42. Sloterdijk, *Critique of Cyncial Reason,* xxix.

43. Burke, "Letter to Philip Francis," in *Further Reflections,* 24, 23.

44. Ibid., 24.

45. Ibid.

46. See Boulton, *Language of Politics,* 128–29, as well as Pocock, "Introduction," liii n. 71.

47. Boulton, *Language of Politics,* 251–64.

48. Burke, "Letter to a Member of the National Assembly," in Edmund Burke, *Further Reflections on the Revolution in France,* ed. Daniel E. Ritchie (Indianapolis: Liberty Classics, 1902), 48. All subsequent citations will be to page numbers in this edition and will appear parenthetically in the text.

49. Duffy, *Rousseau in England,* 38.

50. Euben, "Corruption," 222.

51. From "An Appeal from the New to the Old Whigs," in Edmund Burke, *Further Reflections on the Revolution in France,* ed. Daniel E. Ritchie (Indianapolis: Liberty Classics, 1902), 75–76. All subsequent citations will be to page numbers in this edition and will appear parenthetically in the text.

52. See Radcliffe, "Burke, Radical Cosmopolitanism, and the Debates on Patriotism in the 1790s," 329–30.

53. For *Fleetwood,* see Kelly, *English Jacobin Novel,* 237–60; Duffy, *Rousseau in England,* 50–53; Preston, *Not in Timon's Manner,* 46–7; as well as Tysdahl, *William Godwin as Novelist,* 97–125.

54. For the historical rise and fall of the late eighteenth-century type known as the "man of feeling" (taken from Mackenzie's 1771 novel of that name), see, for example, Mullan, *Sentiment and Sociability,* 114–46.

55. For Godwin's ambivalence toward Rousseau's *Confessions,* see Marilyn Butler, *Jane Austen and the War of Ideas,* 52.

56. For example, Godwin set large portions of the novel in Rousseau's beloved Switzerland; includes long discussions about Rousseau by a supposed acquaintance, Macneil; and names Fleetwood's supposed rivals Gifford and Kenrick, after an editor of the *Anti-Jacobin* (John Gifford) and a translator of Rousseau's *Confessions* (William Kenrick).

57. As Tysdahl and Kelly point out, contemporary reviewers vigorously contested Godwin's title-page description of Fleetwood as the "New Man of Feeling." As Sir Walter Scott complains in his review of the novel: "But we have another and a more heavy objection to [Fleetwood], considered as a man of feeling. We have been accustomed to associate with our ideas of this character the amiable virtues of a Harley, feeling deeply the distresses of others, and patient, though not insensible, of his own. But Fleetwood, through the whole three volumes which bare his name, feels absolutely and exclusively for one individual, and that individual is Fleetwood himself." *Edinburgh Review* 6 (April–July 1805): 192–93. See Kelly, *English Jacobin Novel,* 237; Tysdahl, *William Godwin as Novelist,* 104. For a similar response, see the notice in the *Critical Review* 4 (April 1805): 391.

58. Godwin seems to be allegorizing the fortunes of Rousseau's reception in England, where Rousseau/Fleetwood cannot distinguish between friends and enemies, or between supporters like Kenrick and the *Monthly Review* and betrayers like Gifford and the *Anti-Jacobin.*

59. William Godwin, *Fleetwood: or, The New Man of Feeling,* ed. Gary Handwerk and A. A. Markley (Peterborough, Ontario: Broadview, 2001). All citations will be to this edition and will appear parenthetically in the text.

60. See Burke's prediction in the "Letter to a Member of the National Assembly" that the ladies of France will soon be a prey to "dancing masters, fidlers, pattern-drawers, friseurs, and valets-de-chambre" (52).

61. See also Fleetwood's claim that he was a "misanthrope," though "not a misanthrope of the sterner and more rugged class . . . whose voice has the true cynical snarl," but a "conclusion, however erroneous, that I unwillingly entertained" (116). This passage makes especially clear the resemblance between the misanthrope's hasty conclusions and his prejudices.

62. From Essay XII, "Of Deception and Frankness," in *The Enquirer,* 106. The Broadview editors of *Fleetwood* were impressed enough with this parallel that they included these passages in their edition.

63. From book 5, chapter 15, "Of Political Imposture," *Enquiry Concerning Political Justice,* 502, 504.

64. Scott observes: "But it is chiefly in the wedded state that his irritable and selfish habits are most completely depicted." *Edinburgh Review* 6 (April–July 1805): 193.

65. For the parallels between this puppet scene and the Withers incident, see Bruhm, "William Godwin's *Fleetwood,*" 36–37.

66. D'Israeli, *Quarrels of Authors,* 3:16. For other descriptions of Hobbes as selfish Cynic, see also 49, 61, 63, 69. It is interesting that D'Israeli spells "Cynic" and "Cynical" indifferently in both upper- and lowercase, without any distinction between the two.

67. For the French Enlightenment's rather different understanding of public opinion, see, for example, Baker, "Public Opinion as Political Invention," 167–99.

68. See Keenan, "Twilight of the Political?" #14; and Chaloupka, *Everybody Knows,* 201–12.

69. Niehues-Pröbsting, "Modern Reception of Cynicism," 333.

70. Habermas, *Structural Transformation of the Public Sphere,* 27–67, 181–235.

6. Cynicism and Dandyism

1. See *Webster's Revised Unabridged Dictionary* (1913), s.v. "Cynic": "a person who believes that human conduct is directed, either consciously or unconsciously, wholly by self-interest or self-indulgence, and that appearances to the contrary are superficial and untrustworthy." Found at ARTFL Project: Webster Dictionary, 1913.

2. For "insider-cynics," see my discussion in this volume's introduction; and Keenan, "Twilight of the Political?" #4.

3. For a historical-semantic analysis, see Briggs, "The Language of 'Mass' and 'Masses' in Nineteenth-Century England," 34–36.

4. Canto 3, stanza 41, lines 364–69, in Byron, *Byron,* 115–16.

5. *Childe Harold,* Byron's note to line 369, page 140.

6. Drennan, "Lines Addressed to the Author of a Libel on the Players," in *Fugitive Pieces,* 84, lines 61–68.

7. Wilde, *Sebastian Melmoth,* 65.

8. See Goux, "Utility."

9. Hundert, "Mandeville, Rousseau and the Political Economy of Fantasy," 29.

10. Goux, "Utility," 17–18.

11. Walker, *Critical Pronouncing Dictionary* (1791), "Cynick" q.v.: "having the qualities of a dog, churlish, brutal, snarling, satirical" and "a philosopher of the snarling or currish sort, a follower of Diogenes; a snarler, a misanthrope."

12. Or, as Charles Lloyd put it in 1823, ennui was "The child of sensibility, / Begot on cynic apathy, / And . . . by selfish introspection nursed." From "Stanzas on Ennui," in *Poems* (1823), 88, lines 16–18. For the fate of the benevolent misanthrope in the early nineteenth century, see Preston, *Not in Timon's Manner,* 144–76.

13. *OED,* s.v. "cynic." The shift seems to occur sometime between the 1782 Cowper entry ("Blame, cynic, if you can, quadrille or ball") and the 1866 Alger one ("The cynic, who admires and enjoys nothing, despises and censures everything").

14. Seward, "Remonstrance Addressed to William Cowper, Esq. In 1788, On the Sarcasms Levelled at National Gratitude in *The Task,*" in *Poetical Works* (1810), 3:11.

15. See, for example, Hayakawa, *Modern Guide to Synonyms and Related Words* (1968), "distrustful (chary, cynical, disillusioned, jaundiced, mistrustful)": "*Cynical* indicates a disillusioned attitude that has hardened into extreme bitterness, although this may be leavened with resignation: She was *cynical* about her husband's vow to quit drinking. The word can also point to a readiness to be distrustful on the basis of little or no evidence: *cynical* about any account of the altruism and idealism of people younger than he."

16. The earliest dictionary entries featuring "morose" as synonym for "cynical" are Kenrick, *New Dictionary of English Language* (1773), s.v. "cynical"; and Ash, *New and Complete Dictionary of the English Language* (1775), s.v. "cynicalness" (both of which follow Johnson closely otherwise). Webster's *Compendious Dictionary of English Language* (1806) also stresses this dimension of the now-obsolete form "Cynicalness": "moroseness, churlishness."

17. Piozzi, *British Synonymy* (1794), 124–25.

18. See also Whitney and Smith, *Century Dictionary* (1909), s.v. "cynical": "2. Having or showing a disposition to disbelieve in or doubt the sincerity or value of social usages or of personal character, motives, or doings, and to express or intimate the disbelief or doubt by sarcasm, satire, sneers, or other indirection; captious; carping; sarcastic; satirical."

19. Two more pieces of evidence for this semantic shift come from some dictionaries of synonyms dating from the turn of the twentieth century. Soule, *Dictionary of English Synonymes* (1898), s.v. "cynical," lists two sets of synonyms. The first, "carping, censorious, satirical" etc. follows the usual currish meanings of the term; the second

follows the sneering or disbelieving meanings: "contemptuous, derisive, scornful, bitterly unbelieving, pessimistic, misanthropic." Crabb's revised *English Synonymes* (1917), s.v. "misanthropical," adds an entry not in the original Crabb that distinguishes between "misanthropical" and "cynical" in the following way: "Misanthropical implies a morbid psychological condition—often a nervous horror or fear of others, which has some definite external cause. Cynical indicates an intellectual attitude—a disbelief in the goodness of others, and a consequent tendency to sneer. The misanthrope makes himself miserable; the cynic makes others miserable. The misanthropical man separates himself from the rest of human society; the cynical man moves among men sneering. Cynicism is often a characteristic of men of the world who have seen much of the shams and selfishness of society. The misanthropical man is often one who has suffered from some great shock to his belief in human nature."

20. From *World* 189 (August 12, 1756), quoted in Watson, "Lord Chesterfield and 'Decorum,'" 197.

21. As Klein has suggested, citing Trilling's famous study *Sincerity and Authenticity,* this celebration of "sincerity" at the expense of politeness represents Rousseau's greatest contribution to the debate over politeness at the turn of the nineteenth century. See Trilling, *Sincerity and Authenticity;* and Klein, "Politeness and the Interpretation of the British Eighteenth Century," 874.

22. Isaac D'Israeli, "The Pains of Fastidious Egotism," in *Calamities and Quarrels of Authors,* 7 vols., ed. Earl of Beaconsfield (London, 1858–59), 5:42. All subsequent citations will be to this edition and will appear parenthetically in the text.

23. D'Israeli was particularly incensed at Walpole's treatment of Sir Philip Sidney in the amateurish *Catalogue of Royal and Noble Authors.* Walpole first overlooks Sidney's *Defence of Poetry,* then later defends himself by claiming that his forgetting only showed how overrated Sidney's reputation had become. D'Israeli can only exclaim, "How heartless was the polished cynicism which could dare to hazard this false criticism!" (45n). For Walpole's "sickly delicacy," see 46.

24. For dandies and dandyism, see Moers, *The Dandy;* McGann, "The Dandy"; D'Aurevilly, *Of Dandyism and of Beau Brummel;* Rosa, *Silver-Fork School,* 15–54; Adams, *Dandies and Desert Saints.* I would like to thank my UH colleague Natalie Houston for her initial suggestions to investigate the relation of dandyism to Cynicism, and her bibliographical suggestions on the secondary work regarding dandyism.

25. For the dandyish stance of aesthetic detachment as a denial of "vulgar enjoyment," and how this attitude creates a specifically post-Kantian form of cultural distinction not limited to the realm of art, see Bourdieu, *Distinction,* 4–7.

26. For some accounts of how gender, class, and high politics could interact at a moment of domestic crisis in the royal household, see, for example, Wahrman, "Middle-Class Domesticity Goes Public."

27. Hazlitt, "Brummelliana," 430.

28. Moers, *Dandy,* 17–18.

29. Ibid., 18.

30. For *Granby,* see Moers, *Dandy,* 23–24; and Rosa, *Silver-Fork School,* 68–73.

31. Lister, *Granby,* 1:161–162.

32. Edward George Bulwer-Lytton, *Pelham: or The Adventures of a Gentleman,* ed. Jerome J. McGann (Lincoln: University of Nebraska Press), 129–30. All subsequent citations will be to this edition and will appear parenthetically in the text. See also Moers, *Dandy,* 68–83; and Rosa, *Silver-Fork School,* 74–98.

33. Captain William Jesse, *Beaux and Belles of England: Beau Brummell,* 2 vols. (London: Grolier Society, n.d. [1847?], 2: 148. All subsequent citations will be to volume and page number from this edition and will appear parenthetically in the text.

34. Coleridge, "Sonnet IV," in *Poems,* vol. 1: lines 5–7.

35. Definition taken from Noah Webster, *American Dictionary of English Language* (1841), s.v. "cynicism": "the practice of a cynic; a morose contempt of the pleasures and arts of life (Prof. Emerson)." We should note this 1841 edition marks the first appearance of the term "cynicism" in Webster, which had previously included the now-obsolete form "cynicalness."

36. Oliphant, "Mrs. Oliphant on Jane Austen," 216.

37. Ibid., 217.

38. See, for example, Adams, *Dandies and Desert Saints.*

39. Beecher makes his Cynic uppercase throughout this discussion, the better to differentiate him as a "character" or personality type from the ordinary lowercase usage. Nonetheless, Beecher's "Cynic" remains a modern, distrusting, disbelieving post-Diogenical cynic in the manner of D'Israeli's Hobbes.

40. Mackay, *Extraordinary Popular Delusions,* xi.

41. Mackay, "Cynical Ode," in *Interludes and Undertones,* 70–1.

42. See Hanson, "Democracy," 84.

43. For Wilde and dandyism, see, for example, Moers, *Dandy,* 287–314; Gagnier, *Idylls of the Marketplace,* 18–49; Sinfield, *Wilde Century;* Dellamora, *Masculine Desire,* 193–217; Gillespie, "From Beau Brummell to Lady Bracknell."

44. Foucault, *History of Sexuality,* 94, but see 92–102.

45. For the socialist dimension of Wilde's writings, see, for example, Gagnier, *Idylls of the Marketplace,* 3–47, and his essay "The Soul of Man under Socialism."

46. Oscar Wilde, *Picture of Dorian Gray,* ed. Norman Page (Peterborough, Ontario: Broadview, 1998). All subsequent citations will be to page numbers from this edition and will appear parenthetically in the text.

47. Wilde, *Lady Windermere's Fan,* act 3, in Wilde, *Complete Works,* 418.

48. Similarly, Bierce's joking definition from the *Devil's Dictionary* echoes Wilde's second definition and recognizes the manner in which the Cynic is blamed for his visionary gifts: "Cynic: A blackguard whose faulty vision sees things as they are, not as they ought to be."

49. See Freud's interesting discussion of "cynical jokes" in the context of the "salmon mayonnaise" joke and its protest against the sacrifices made to morality in *Jokes and Their Relation to the Unconscious,* 127–37.

50. *Daily Chronicle* review (1890) in Beckson, *Oscar Wilde: The Critical Heritage,* 77.

51. Hawthorne, review in *Lippincott's* (1890) in Beckson, *Oscar Wilde: The Critical Heritage,* 80.

52. See, for example, Pater, "A Novel by Mr. Oscar Wilde," in Beckson, *Oscar Wilde: The Critical Heritage,* 83–86.

53. Hawthorne, in Beckson, *Oscar Wilde, The Critical Heritage,* 80.

54. Cohen, *Talk on the Wilde Side,* 133.

55. For this reading of dandyism as a protest against the conventional Victorian values of utility and means-end rationality, see Gagnier, *Idylls of the Marketplace,* 51–99.

56. Timothy Bewes, *Cynicism and Postmodernity* (London: Verso, 1997). All citations will be to this edition and will appear parenthetically in the text.

57. Bewes's reading is best understood as reflecting a symptomatic Left reaction to "postmodernist" doubts about the progressive unfolding of history. See Brown, *Politics out of History,* 8–9.

58. See Gagnier, *Idylls of the Marketplace,* 90–99; and Dellamora, *Masculine Desire,* 197.

59. Michel Foucault, "What Is Enlightenment?" in *Foucault Reader,* ed. Paul Rabinow (New York: Pantheon, 1984), 41. All subsequent citations will be to this edition and will appear parenthetically in the text. For Baudelaire's transformation of the dandy, see also Gagnier, *Idylls of the Marketplace,* 81–89; and Feldman, *Gender on the Divide,* 97–142.

60. For the differences between Wilde's "hysterization" of the female body and Baudelaire's outright misogyny, see Gagnier, *Idylls of the Marketplace,* 81–83.

61. Foucault, "Politics and Ethics: An Interview," in *Foucault Reader,* 374.

62. Gagnier, introduction to *Critical Essays on Oscar Wilde,* 9.

63. Brown, *Politics out of History,* 102–6.

Epilogue

1. For negations and semantic development, see Gumbrecht, "Who Were the *Philosophes*?" 149.

2. From Fish, "Rhetoric," 204.

3. Empson, *Structure of Complex Words,* 158.

4. Ibid., 156. I have added the bracketed material to the quotations to guide readers through Empson's loose syntax.

5. Ibid., 174. This discussion is specifically about Samuel Johnson's suggestive uses of the word "dog," which are at odds with his Christian beliefs at some level.

6. Ibid., 39.

7. Niehues-Pröbsting, "Modern Reception of Cynicism," 331.

8. Nietzsche, *Beyond Good and Evil,* #26, 38.

9. Stephen, "The Writings of W. M. Thackeray," 373.

10. For the inseparability of political language and political action, see, for example, Farr, "Understanding Conceptual Change Politically," 24–30.

11. For the inherent delays of democratic self-governance due to delays, arguments, and unsatisfying resolutions arising from endless disputes and negotiations over whose will represents "the people," see Keenan, *Twilight of the Political?* #11.

12. Loconte, "Cynicism Won't Win the War in Iraq."

BIBLIOGRAPHY

Dictionaries

Ash, John. *New and Complete Dictionary of the English Language.* London, 1775.

Barclay, James, et al. *A Complete and Universal English Dictionary On a New Plan.* London, 1782.

[Blount, Thomas]. *Glossographia: or A Dictionary Interpreting all such Hard Words.* London, 1656.

Bullokar, John. *An English Expositor: Teaching the Interpretation of the hardest words used in our Language.* London, 1616.

Cawdrey, Robert. *A Table Alphabeticall of Hard Usual English Words.* London, 1604.

Cockeram, Henry. *The English Dictionarie.* London, 1623.

Crabb. *English Synonymes.* Revised and enlarged by John Finley. New York: Harper and Bros., 1917.

Dyche, Thomas. *A New General English Dictionary.* London, 1740.

Elyot, Thomas. *The Dictionary of Syr Thomas Eliot knight.* London, 1538.

Fenning, D. *The Royal English Dictionary; or, A Treasury of the English Language.* 2nd ed., improved. London, 1763.

Hayakawa, S. I. *Modern Guide to Synonyms and Related Words.* New York: Funk and Wagnalls, 1968.

Johnson, Samuel. *A Dictionary of the English Language.* London, 1755.

Kenrick, William. *New Dictionary of English Language.* London, 1773.

Phillips, Edward. *New World of English Words.* London, 1658.

Piozzi, Hester Lynch. *British Synonymy; or, An Attempt at Regulating the choice of Words in Familiar Conversation.* London, 1794. Reprinted in English Linguistics 1500–1800, no. 113. Menston: Scolar Press, 1968.

Rider, John. *Bibliotheca Scholastica: A Double Dictionarie.* London, 1589.

———. *Riders Dictionarie, Corrected and Augmented.* London, 1640.

Soule, Richard. *Dictionary of English Synonymes.* Boston: Little, Brown, 1898.

Thomas, Thomas. *Dictionarium linguae Latinae et Anglicanae.* London, [1587].

Walker, John. *Critical Pronouncing Dictionary and Expositor of the English Language.* London, 1791.

Webster, Noah. *American Dictionary of English Language.* New Haven, 1841.

———. *Compendious Dictionary of English Language.* New Haven, 1806.

Webster's Revised Unabridged Dictionary. Springfield: G&C Merriam Co., 1913. Found at ARTFL Project: Webster Dictionary, 1913, at http://machaut.uchicago.edu/cgi-bin/WEBSTER.page.sh?page=363.

Whitney, William Dwight, and Benjamin Smith. *Century Dictionary.* New York: Century, 1909.

Primary Sources

d'Alembert, Jean Le Rond. "An Essay upon the Alliance betwixt Learned Men, and the Great." In *Miscellaneous Pieces in Literature, History, and Philosophy by Mr. D'Alembert,* 114–76. London, 1764.

Annotations by Sam. Johnson & Geo. Steevens, and the Various Commentators, upon "Timon of Athens." London, 1801.

Bacon, Francis. "The Proficience and Advancement of Learning Divine and Humane." 1605. In *A Selection of His Works,* edited by Sidney Warhaft, 197–271. Indianapolis: Bobbs-Merrill, 1965.

Baldwin, William. *Treatise of Morall Philosophie Wherin Is Contained the Worthy Sayings of Philosophers, Emperours, Kings, and Orators: Their Lives and Answers. Enlarged by Thomas Palfreyman.* 1547–64. Reprint, Gainesville, Fla.: Scholars' Facsimiles and Reprints, 1967.

Bartolus, S. J. *The Learned Man Defended and Reform'd.* London, 1660.

Beecher, Henry Ward. "The Cynic," in "Portrait Gallery," 115–19. In *Lectures to Young Men, on Various Important Subjects,* 105–34. New York, 1853.

Berkenhead, Sir John. *The Assembly-man.* 1663. London, 1681–82.

Bolingbroke, H. St. John. "Of the True Use of Retirement and Study." In *Works,* 2: 339–51. London, 1844.

———. "Reflections upon Exile." In *Works,* 1: 181–200.

Bulwer-Lytton, Edward George. *Pelham: or The Adventures of a Gentleman.* Edited by Jerome J. McGann. Lincoln: University of Nebraska Press, 1972.

Burke, Edmund. *Further Reflections on the Revolution in France.* Edited by Daniel E. Ritchie. Indianapolis: Liberty Classics, 1992.

———. *A Note-Book of Edmund Burke.* Edited by H.V.F. Somerset. Cambridge: Cambridge University Press, 1957.

———. *Reflections on the Revolution in France.* Edited by Conor Cruise O'Brien. New York: Penguin, 1968.

———. "Several Scattered Hints Concerning Philosophy and Learning Collected Here from My Papers." In *A Note-Book of Edmund Burke,* edited by H.V.F. Somerset, 81–98. Cambridge: Cambridge University Press, 1957.

———. *Works.* Rev. ed. 12 vols. Boston: Little, Brown, 1866.

Butler, Samuel. *The Genuine Remains in Verse and Prose of Mr. Samuel Butler, With Notes by R. Thyer.* Vol. 2. Edited by Robert Thyer. London, 1759.

———. *Satires and Miscellaneous Poetry and Prose.* Edited by René Lamar. Cambridge: Cambridge University Press, 1928.

Byron, George Gordon. *Byron: Oxford Authors.* Edited by Jerome McGann. Oxford: Oxford University Press, 1986.

———. *Childe Harold's Pilgrimage.* In *Byron: Oxford Authors,* edited by Jerome McGann, 19–206. Oxford: Oxford University Press, 1986.

Cicero, Marcus Tullius. *Cicero: On Duties.* Edited by M. T. Griffin and E. M. Atkins. Cambridge: Cambridge University Press, 1991.

———. *De officiis.* Translated by Walter Miller. Cambridge: Harvard University Press, 1975.

———. *De oratore.* Vol. 1. Translated by E. W. Sutton. Cambridge: Harvard University Press, 1942.

———. *Tusculan Disputations.* Translated by J. E. King. London: Heinemann, 1927.

Coetlogon, Denis de. *Diogenes's Rambles: Or, Humorous Characters of the Most Noted People at present in the World.* London, 1743.

Coleridge, Hartley. *Poems.* 2 vols. London, 1851.

Combe, William. "Letter to Jean-Jacques Rousseau." In "William Combe, Author of *The Tours of Dr. Syntax.*" In *Notes and Queries,* 4th ser. III (June 19, 1869): 569–73. Reprinted from *Ackermann's Repository of Arts, &c.,* 3rd ser., iii. (1824): 205.

Davenant, Sir William. *Dramatic Works.* Edited by James Maidment and W. H. Logan. 5 vols. Edinburgh, 1873.

The Dicts and Sayings of the Philosophers. 1477. Edited by Curt F. Buhler. Translated by Stephen Scrope, William Worcester, and anonymous. London: Oxford University Press, 1941.

D'Israeli, Isaac. "The Pains of Fastidious Egotism." In *Calamities and Quarrels of Authors,* edited by Earl of Beaconsfield, 7 vols., 42. London, 1858–59.

———. *Quarrels of Authors; or, Some Memoirs for our Literary History.* Vol 3. London, 1814.

Drennan, William. *Fugitive Pieces, in Verse and Prose.* Belfast, 1815.

Erasmus. *Apophthegmes of Erasmus. Translated into English by Nicolas Udall. Literally Reprinted from the Scarce Edition of 1564.* Boston: Roberts, 1877.

Evelyn, John. *Publick Employment and an Active Life with all its Appanages, Such as Fame, Command, Riches, Conversation, &c. Prefer'd to Solitude.* London, 1666.

Fellowes, Robert. "Character of Rousseau." *Monthly Mirror* 8 (August 1799): 71–72.

Fénelon, Francois. *Dialogues of the Dead.* 2 vols. Berwick, 1770.

Fielding, Henry. *Miscellanies by Henry Fielding, Esq.* Vol. 1. Edited by Henry Knight Miller. Middletown, Ct.: Wesleyan University Press, 1972.

Flecknoe, Richard. *Sir Wm. Davenant's Voyage to the Other World: With his Adventures in the Poets Elizium.* London, 1668.

Forrester, James. *The Polite Philosopher: Or, An Essay on that Art Which Makes a Man Happy in Himself and Agreeable to Others.* London, 1736.

Fulwell, Ulpian. *Ars adulandi, or The Art of Flattery.* 1579. Edited by Roberta Buchanan. Salzburg: Institut fur Anglistik und Amerikanistik, [1984?].

Gainsford, Thomas. *The Rich Cabinet.* London, 1616.

Gibbon, Edward. *Memoirs of My Life.* Edited by Georges A. Bonnard. London: Thomas Nelson and Sons, 1966.

Goddard, William. *A mastif whelp with other ruff-Island like Currs fetcht from amongst the Antipedes.* [Dort?] [1598?].

———. *A Satyricall Dialogve or a Sharplye Invective Conference Betweene Allexander the Greate and that Trulye Woman-Hater Diogynes.* [Dort?], [1616?].

Godwin, William. *The Enquirer: Reflections on Education, Manners, and Literature.* A facsimile of the 1797 edition. New York: Garland, 1971.

———. *Enquiry Concerning Political Justice.* Edited by Isaac Kramnick. London: Penguin, 1976.

———. *Fleetwood: or, The New Man of Feeling.* Edited by Gary Handwerk and A. A. Markley. Peterborough, Ontario: Broadview, 2001.

———. *Memoirs of the Author of "The Rights of Woman."* Edited by Richard Holmes, 201–77. New York: Penguin, 1987.

Goslicius, [Laurentius Grimaldus]. *The Counsellor. Exactly Pourtraited in Two Books.* London, 1598.

Guazzo, Stefano. *The Civile Conversation of M. Steeven Guazzo.* Edited by Edward Sullivan. London: Constable, 1925.

Hazlitt, William. "Brummelliana." In *William Hazlitt: Selected Writings,* edited by Ronald Blythe, 430. New York: Penguin, 1985.

Hobbes, Thomas. *Leviathan.* Edited by C. B. Macpherson. New York: Penguin, 1968.

Hoffman, Benneville Ottmar. *Snarl of A Cynic: A Rhyme.* Ephrata, 1868.

Hume, David. *Essays Moral, Political and Literary.* Edited by Eugene Miller. Indianapolis: Liberty Classics, 1987.

"Humility and Pride." *Gentleman's Magazine,* August 18, 1748, 351–52.

Jamieson, Kathleen Hall, and Joseph Cappella. *Spiral of Cynicism.* New York: Oxford University Press, 1997.

Jesse, Captain William. *Beaux and Belles of England: Beau Brummell.* 2 vols. London: Grolier Society, [1844?].

Kant, Immanuel. *Lectures on Ethics.* Translated by Peter Heath. Edited by Peter Heath and J. B. Schneewind. Cambridge: Cambridge University Press, 1997.

Laertius, Diogenes. *Lives of Eminent Philosophers.* Translated by R. D. Hicks. 2 vols. Cambridge: Harvard University Press, 1979.

———. *Lives, Opinions, and Remarkable Sayings Of the Most Famous Ancient Philosophers.* Translated by William Baxter. London, 1688.

Letters from the Westminster Journal. Saturday, March 13, 1741–42. London, 1761.

Lister, Thomas Henry. *Granby.* 2nd ed. 3 vols. London: Henry Colburn, 1826.

Lloyd, Charles. *Poems.* London, 1823.

Lodge, Thomas. *Catharos: Diogenes in his Singularitie.* London, 1591.

Lucian. "The Passing of Peregrinus." In *Works,* translated by A. M. Harmon, 5:1–51. Cambridge: Harvard University Press, 1955.

Lyly, John. *Campaspe.* Edited by G. K. Hunter. The Revels Plays. Manchester: Manchester University Press, 1991.

Lyttelton, Lord (George). *Works.* Edited by George Edward Ayscough. 3 vols. London, 1776.

Mackay, Charles. *Extraordinary Popular Delusions and the Madness of Crowds.* Philadelphia: Templeton Foundation Press, 1985.

———. *Interludes and Undertones.* London: Chatto and Windus, 1884.
Mackenzie, George. *The Moral History of Frugality.* London, 1691.
Mandeville, Bernard. *Fable of the Bees.* 2 vols. Edited by F. B. Kaye. Oxford: Clarendon Press, 1966.
Marmontel, Jean-François. *Memoirs of Marmontel.* First translated 1805. 2 vols. London: H. S. Nichols, 1895.
Marston, John. *The Malcontent.* Edited by George K. Hunter. Manchester: Manchester University Press, 1975.
———. *Poems of John Marston.* Edited by Arnold Davenport. Liverpool: Liverpool University Press, 1961.
[Mathias, Thomas James]. *The Grove. A Satire.* [1789?] 2nd ed. [London?], 1798.
More, St. Thomas. "More's Letter to Ruthall." In *Translations of Lucian,* by St. Thomas More, edited by Craig R. Thompson. In *Complete Works,* 3, pt. 1: 2–9. New Haven: Yale University Press, 1974.
Munda, Constantia. *The Worming of a mad Dogge.* London, 1617.
Nietzsche, Friedrich. *Beyond Good and Evil.* Translated by Walter Kauffman. New York: Vintage, 1966.
Nixon, Richard. "Nixon's Second Watergate Speech." August 15, 1973. http://www.watergate.info/nixon/73-08-15watergate-speech.shtml.
Oliphant, Margaret. "Mrs. Oliphant on Jane Austen." In *Jane Austen: The Critical Heritage,* edited by B. C. Southam, 215–25. London: Routledge, 1968.
Peacham, Henry. *The Garden of Eloquence.* A facsimile of the 1577 edition. Menston: Scolar Press, 1971.
Polwhele, Richard. *The Unsex'd Females: A Poem.* Edited by Gina Luria. A facsimile of the 1798 edition. New York: Garland, 1974.
Review of *Fleetwood,* by William Godwin. *Critical Review* 4 (April 1805): 391.
Review of *The Confessions,* by Jean-Jacques Rousseau. *Monthly Review* 66 (7 June 1782): 530–41.
Review of *The Confessions,* by Jean-Jacques Rousseau. *Monthly Review* 67 (September 1782): 227–33.
Review of "Éloge of Rousseau," by Palissot. *Monthly Review* 60 (February 1779): 136–43.
Review of *Lettre sur les spectacles,* by Jean-Jacques Rousseau. *Critical Review* 7 (January 1759): 48.
Rich, Barnabe. *My Ladies Looking Glasse.* London, 1616.
———. *Opinion Diefied. Discouering the Ingins, Traps, and Traynes, that are set in this Age, whereby to catch Opinion.* London, 1613.
Rousseau, Jean-Jacques. *Basic Political Writings.* Translated by Donald A. Cress. Indianapolis: Hackett, 1987.
———. *The Confessions of J. J. Rousseau, Citizen of Geneva. Part the Second.* Anonymous translation. 3 vols. London, 1790.
———. *Julie, or, The New Heloise: Letters of Two Lovers Who Live in a Small Town at the Foot of the Alps.* Translated by Philip Stewart and Jean Vaché. Hanover, N.H. University Press of New England, 1997.

———. "Narcissus, Or The Self-Admirer. A Comedy." In *The Miscellaneous Works of Mr. J. J. Rousseau,* vol. 2. London, 1767. Reprint, New York: Burt Franklin, 1972.

———. *Rousseau, Judge of Jean-Jacques: Dialogues.* Vol. 1. Edited by Roger D. Masters and Christopher Kelly. Translated by Judith R. Bush, Christopher Kelly, and Roger D. Masters. Hanover: University Press of New England, 1990.

———. Rousseau to Christophe de Beaumont. 1763. Reprinted in *Monthly Review* (March 1763): 224–29.

Scott, Walter. Review of *Fleetwood,* by William Godwin. *Edinburgh Review* 6 (April–July 1805): 192–93.

Seward, Anna. *Poetical Works of Anna Seward.* Edited by Walter Scott. 3 vols. London, 1810.

Shaftesbury, Third Earl of, (Anthony Ashley Cooper). *Characteristics of Men, Manners, Opinions, Times.* Edited by John M. Robertson. 2 vols. Indianapolis: Bobbs-Merrill, 1964.

———. *Notebooks.* In *Philosophical Regimen,* in *The Life, Unpublished Letters, and Philosophical Regimen,* edited by Benjamin Rand, 224–30. New York: Macmillan, 1900.

Shakespeare, William. *Timon of Athens.* Edited by H. J. Oliver. Arden edition of the *Works of William Shakespeare.* Cambridge: Harvard University Press, 1959.

S[harpe], R[oger]. *More Fooles yet.* London, 1610.

Speght, Rachel. *A Mouzell for Melastomus.* London, 1617.

Stafford, Anthony. *Staffords Heavenly Dogge.* London, 1615.

Stanley, Thomas. *History of Philosophy: containing the Lives, Opinions, Actions and Discourses of Philosophers of every Sect.* 3rd. ed. London, 1701.

Swetnam, Joseph. *Arraignment of Lewd, Idle, Froward, and Vnconstant Women.* London, 1615.

Three Parnassus Plays (1598–1601). Edited by J. B. Leishman. London: Ivor Nicholson, 1949.

Tuvill, Daniel. *Essays Politic and Moral* and *Essays Moral and Theological.* Edited by John Leon Lievsay. Charlottesville: Folger Shakespeare Library, [1971].

Vair, Guillaume du. *The Moral Philosophie of the Stoicks.* Translated by Thomas James. 1598. Edited by Rudolf Kirk. New Brunswick, N.J.: Rutgers University Press, 1951.

Voltaire. The *Selected Letters of Voltaire.* Edited and translated by Richard A. Brooks. New York: New York University Press, 1973.

Warren, Arthur. *The Poore Mans Passions And Poverties Patience.* London, 1605.

[Weever, John]. *The Whipping of the Satyre.* In *The Whipper Pamphlets,* pt. 1, edited by Arnold Davenport. Liverpool: University Press of Liverpool, 1951.

Wesley, John. Entry dated Feb. 3, 1776. In *Journal,* vol. 5, edited by Nehemiah Curnock. London: Kelly, 1909–16.

Whitney, Geffrey. *A Choice of Emblemes.* A facsimile of the 1586 edition. Brookfield, Vt.: Scolar Press, 1989.

Wieland, Christoph Martin. *Socrates out of his Senses: Or Dialogues of Diogenes of Sinope.* Translated by Wintersted. London, 1771.

Wilde, Oscar. *Complete Works of Oscar Wilde.* New York: Perennial Library, 1989.

———. *Picture of Dorian Gray.* Edited by Norman Page. Peterborough, Ontario: Broadview, 1998.
———. *Sebastian Melmoth.* London: Arthur Humphreys, 1904.
Wilson, Thomas. *Arte of Rhetorique.* Edited by Thomas J. Derrick. New York: Garland, 1982.

Secondary Sources

Abbott, Don Paul. "Rhetoric and Writing in Renaissance Europe and England." In *Short History of Writing Instruction,* edited by James Murphy, 95–120. Davis: Hermagoras Press, 1990.
Adams, James Eli. *Dandies and Desert Saints.* Ithaca: Cornell University Press, 1995.
Adorno, Theodor W. "Opinion Delusion Society." In *Critical Models: Interventions and Catchwords.* Translated by Henry W. Pickford, 105–22. New York: Columbia University Press, 1998.
———. "Marginalia to Theory and Praxis." In *Critical Models: Interventions and Catchwords,* translated by Henry W. Pickford, 259–278. New York: Columbia University Press, 1998.
Agger, Robert, Marshall Goldstein, and Stanley Pearl. "Political Cynicism: Measurement and Meaning." *Journal of Politics* 23, no. 3 (August 1961): 477–506.
Algra, Keimpe, Jonathan Barnes, Jaap Mansfeld, and Malcolm Schofield, eds. *The Cambridge History of Hellenistic Philosophy.* Cambridge: Cambridge University Press, 1999.
Altman, Joel B. *The Tudor Play of Mind: Rhetorical Inquiry and the Development of Elizabethan Drama.* Berkeley and Los Angeles: University of California Press, 1978.
Ambrus, Gauthier. "La figure du philosophe." In *Rousseau juge de Jean-Jacques: Études sur les dialogues,* edited by Philip Knee and Gérald Allard, 215–25. Ottawa: North American Association for the Study of Jean-Jacques Rousseau, 1998.
Ankersmit, Frank R. "Representational Democracy: An Aesthetic Approach to Conflict and Compromise." *Common Knowledge* 8, no. 1 (2002): 24–46.
Babb, Lawrence. *Elizabethan Malady.* East Lansing: Michigan State College Press, 1951.
Baier, Annette C. "Trust and Antitrust." In *Moral Prejudices: Essays on Ethics,* 95–129. Cambridge: Harvard University Press, 1994.
Baker, Keith Michael. "Public Opinion as Political Invention." In *Inventing the French Revolution.* Cambridge: Cambridge University Press, 1990.
Baldwin, T. W. *Shakespeare's Small Latine and Lesse Greeke.* 2 vols. Urbana: University of Illinois Press, 1944.
Ball, Terence, James Farr, and Russell Hanson, eds. *Political Innovation and Conceptual Change.* Cambridge: Cambridge University Press, 1989.
Barber, Charles. *Early Modern English.* London: André Deutsch, 1976.
Barbier, C. P. "Letters of an Italian Nun and an English Gentleman (1781): A Bibliographical Problem." *Revue de Littérature Comparée* 18, no. 1 (January–March 1954): 75–89.

Barish, Jonas. "Prose Style of John Lyly." *ELH* 23, no. 1 (March 1956): 14–35.

Barker-Benfield, G. J. *The Culture of Sensibility: Sex and Society in Eighteenth-Century Britain.* Chicago: University of Chicago Press, 1992.

Battestin, Martin. *Henry Fielding: A Life.* London: Routledge, 1989.

Beckson, Karl, ed. *Oscar Wilde: The Critical Heritage.* New York: Barnes and Noble, 1970.

Beer, Samuel H. "Two Models of Public Opinion: Bacon's 'New Logic' and Diotima's 'Tale of Love.'" *Political Theory* 2, no. 2 (May 1974): 163–80.

Bender, John, and David Wellbery. "Rhetoricality: On the Modernist Return of Rhetoric." In *Ends of Rhetoric: History, Theory, Practice,* edited by John Bender and David Wellbery, 3–39. Stanford: Stanford University Press, 1990.

Benjamin, Martin. *Splitting the Difference.* Lawrence: University of Kansas Press, 1990.

Berg, Maxine, and Elizabeth Eger, eds. *Luxury in the Eighteenth Century: Debates, Desires, and Delectable Goods.* Houndmills: Palgrave, 2003.

———. "The Rise and Fall of the Luxury Debates." In *Luxury in the Eighteenth Century,* edited by Berg and Eger, 7–27. Houndmills: Palgrave, 2003.

Berlin, Isaiah. "The Counter-Enlightenment." In *Against the Current: Essays in the History of Ideas,* edited by Henry Hardy, 1–24. New York: Penguin, 1982.

Bernstein, Michael André. *Bitter Carnival.* Princeton: Princeton University Press, 1992.

Berry, Christopher. *The Idea of Luxury: A Conceptual and Historical Investigation.* Cambridge: Cambridge University Press, 1994.

Bevington, David. *Tudor Drama and Politics: A Critical Approach to Topical Meaning.* Cambridge: Harvard University Press, 1968.

Bevington, David, and David L. Smith. "James I and *Timon of Athens.*" In *Tragedy's Insights: Identity, Polity, Theodicy,* edited by Luis R. Gamez, 56–87. West Cornwall: Locust Hill Press, 1999.

Bewes, Timothy. *Cynicism and Postmodernity.* London: Verso, 1997.

Black, Jeremy. *English Press in the Eighteenth Century.* Philadelphia: University of Pennsylvania Press, 1987.

Blank, Paula. *Broken English: Dialects and the Politics of Language in Renaissance Writing.* New York: Routledge, 1996.

———. "Languages of Early Modern Literature in Britain." In *Cambridge History of Early Modern English Literature,* edited by David Loewenstein and Janel Mueller, 141–69. Cambridge: Cambridge University Press, 2002.

Blissett, William. "Cynics, Canadians, and *Timon of Athens.*" Paper presented at IAMPE meeting, Vancouver, 1994.

Blum, Carol. *Rousseau and the Republic of Virtue: The Language of Politics in the French Revolution.* Ithaca: Cornell University Press, 1986.

Bolgar, R. R. *The Classical Heritage and Its Beneficiaries: From the Carolingian Age to the End of the Renaissance.* New York: Harper and Row, 1964.

Boose, Lynda. "The 1599 Bishops' Ban, Elizabethan Pornography, and the Sexualization of the Jacobean Stage." In *Enclosure Acts,* edited by Richard Burt and John Michael Archer, 185–200. Ithaca: Cornell University Press, 1994.

Boulton, James. *The Language of Politics in the Age of Wilkes and Burke.* Westport, Ct.: Greenwood Press, 1975.

Bourdieu, Pierre. *Distinction: A Social Critique of the Judgement of Taste.* Translated by Richard Nice. Cambridge: Harvard University Press, 1984.

Boyce, Benjamin. "News from Hell: Satiric Communications with the Nether World in English Writing of the Seventeenth and Eighteenth Centuries." *PMLA* 58 (1943): 402–37.

Branham, Bracht. "Defacing the Currency: Diogenes' Rhetoric and the Invention of Cynicism." In *The Cynics: The Cynic Movement in Antiquity and Its Legacy,* edited by Branham and Marie-Odile Goulet-Cazé, 81–104. Berkeley and Los Angeles: University of California Press, 1996.

———. *Unruly Eloquence.* Cambridge: Harvard University Press, 1989.

———. "Utopian Laughter: Lucian and Thomas More." *Moreana* 86 (1985): 23–43.

Branham, Bracht, and Marie-Odile Goulet-Cazé, eds. *The Cynics: The Cynic Movement in Antiquity and Its Legacy.* Berkeley and Los Angeles: University of California Press, 1996.

Brewer, John. *Party Ideology and Popular Politics at the Accession of George III.* New York: Cambridge University Press, 1976.

Briggs, Asa. "The Language of 'Mass' and 'Masses' in Nineteenth-Century England." In *Collected Essays,* 1:34–54. Urbana: University of Illinois Press, 1985.

Bromwich, David. "Burke, Wordsworth, and the Defense of History." In *A Choice of Inheritance: Self and Community from Edmund Burke to Robert Frost,* 43–78. Cambridge: Harvard University Press, 1989.

Brown, Wendy. *Politics out of History.* Princeton: Princeton University Press, 2001.

Bruhm, Steven. "William Godwin's *Fleetwood:* The Epistemology of the Tortured Body." *Eighteenth-Century Life* 16 (May 1992): 25–43.

Bryson, Anna. *From Courtesy to Civility: Changing Codes of Conduct in Early Modern England.* Oxford: Clarendon Press, 1998.

Butler, Judith. *Gender Trouble.* New York: Routledge, 1990.

Butler, Marilyn. *Jane Austen and the War of Ideas.* Oxford: Clarendon, 1989.

Caputi, Anthony. *John Marston, Satirist.* Ithaca: Cornell University Press, 1961.

Certeau, Michel de. *Practice of Everyday Life.* Translated by Steven Rendall. Berkeley and Los Angeles: University of California Press, 1984.

Chaloupka, William. *Everybody Knows.* Minneapolis: University of Minnesota Press, 1999.

Chorost, Michael. "Biological Finance in Shakespeare's *Timon of Athens.*" *English Literary Renaissance* 21, no. 3 (Autumn 1991): 349–70.

Citrin, Jack. "Comment: The Political Relevance of Trust in Government." *American Political Science Review* 68, no. 3 (September 1974): 973–88.

Clarke, M. L. *Classical Education in Britain: 1500–1900.* Cambridge: Cambridge University Press, 1959.

———. *Greek Studies in England: 1700–1830.* Cambridge: Cambridge University Press, 1945.

Clegg, Cyndia Susan. *Press Censorship in Elizabethan England.* Cambridge: Cambridge University Press, 1997.

Cohen, Ed. *Talk on the Wilde Side.* New York: Routledge, 1993.

Colclough, David. "*Parrhesia:* The Rhetoric of Free Speech in Early Modern England." *Rhetorica* 17, no. 2 (Spring 1999): 177–212.

Coley, W. B., ed. *Contributions to The Champion and Related Writings by Henry Fielding.* Oxford: Clarendon Press, 2003.

Colley, Linda. *Britons.* New Haven: Yale University Press, 1992.

Collinson, Patrick. "Ecclesiastical Vitriol: Religious Satire in the 1590s and the Invention of Puritanism." In *The Reign of Elizabeth I,* edited by John Guy, 150–70. New York: Cambridge University Press, 1995.

Conley, Thomas M. *Rhetoric in the European Tradition.* Chicago: University of Chicago Press, 1990.

Cope, Jackson I. "Rhetorical Genres in Davenant's *First Day's Entertainment at Rutland House.*" *Quarterly Journal of Speech* 45, no. 2 (April 1959): 191–94.

Copeland, Rita. *Rhetoric, Hermeneutics, and Translation in the Middle Ages.* Cambridge: Cambridge University Press, 1991.

Craig, Hardin. "Dryden's Lucian." *Classical Philology* 16 (January–October 1921): 141–63.

Cranston, Maurice. *Jean-Jacques: The Early Life and Work of Jean-Jacques Rousseau 1712–1754.* Norton, 1983.

Damrosch, Leo. *Fictions of Reality in the Age of Hume and Johnson.* Madison: University of Wisconsin Press, 1989.

D'Aurevilly, Barbey. *Of Dandyism and of Beau Brummell.* Translated by Douglas Ainslie. London: J. M. Dent, 1897.

Davenport, Arnold. Introduction to *Poems of John Marston,* edited by Davenport, 1–46. Liverpool: Liverpool University Press, 1961.

Davis, Rose Mary. *Good Lord Lyttelton.* Bethlehem: Times Publishing, 1939.

Dean, James W., Jr., Pamela Brandes, and Ravi Dharwadkar. "Organizational Cynicism." *Academy of Management Review* 23, no. 2 (April 1998): 341–52.

Dellamora, Richard. *Masculine Desire.* Chapel Hill: University of North Carolina Press, 1990.

Dickinson, H. T. *Bolingbroke.* London: Constable, 1970.

Dinwiddy, John. "England." In *Nationalism in the Age of the French Revolution,* edited by Otto Dann and Dinwiddy, 53–70. London: Hambledon Press, 1988.

Dorandi, Tiziano. "Chronology." In *The Cambridge History of Hellenistic Philosophy,* edited by Keimpe Algra, Jonathon Barnes, Jaap Mansfeld, and Malcolm Schofield, 31–54. Cambridge: Cambridge University Press, 1999.

Douglas, Mary. *How Institutions Think.* Syracuse, N.Y.: Syracuse University Press, 1986.

Dudley, Donald R. *History of Cynicism.* Hildesheim: Georg Olms Verlagsbuchhandlung, [1937]. Reprint, 1967.

Duffy, Edward. *Rousseau in England: The Context for Shelley's Critique of the Enlightenment.* Berkeley and Los Angeles: University of California Press, 1979.

Dykstal, Timothy. *Luxury of Skepticism*. Charlottesville: University of Virginia Press, 2001.

Edmond, Mary. *Rare Sir William Davenant*. Manchester: Manchester University Press, 1987.

Empson, William. *The Structure of Complex Words*. London: Chatto and Windus, 1951. Reprint, Cambridge: Harvard University Press, 1989.

Euben, J. Peter. "Corruption." In *Political Innovation and Conceptual Change*, edited by Terence Ball, James Farr, and Russell Hanson, 220–46. Cambridge: Cambridge University Press, 1989.

Farnham, Willard. *Shakespeare's Tragic Frontier: The World of His Final Tragedies*. Berkeley and Los Angeles: University of California Press, 1963.

Farr, James. "Understanding Conceptual Change Politically." In *Political Innovation and Conceptual Change*, edited by Terence Ball, Farr, and Russell Hanson, 24–49. Cambridge: Cambridge University Press, 1989.

Feldman, Jessica R. *Gender on the Divide*. Ithaca: Cornell University Press, 1993.

Finkelpearl, Philip J. *John Marston of the Middle Temple*. Cambridge: Harvard University Press, 1969.

Fish, Stanley. "Rhetoric." In *Critical Terms for Literary Study*, 2nd. ed., edited by Frank Lentricchia and Thomas McLaughlin, 203–22. Chicago: University of Chicago Press, 1995.

Flynn, Thomas. "Foucault as Parrhesiast: His Last Course at the Collège de France." In *Final Foucault*, edited by James Bernauer and David Rasmussen, 102–18. Cambridge: MIT Press, 1991.

Foucault, Michel. "Discourse and Truth: The Problematization of Parrhesia." Six lectures, Berkeley, Calif., October–November 1983, http://foucault.info/documents/parrhesiasts/foucault.diogenes.en.html.

———. *The Foucault Reader*. Edited by Paul Rabinow. New York: Pantheon, 1984.

———. *Hermeneutics of the Subject: Lectures at the College de France, 1981–2*. Edited by Frederic Gros. Translated by Graham Burchell. New York: Palgrave Macmillan, 2005.

———. *History of Sexuality: Vol. 1*. Translated by Robert Hurley. New York: Vintage, 1990.

———. "Nietzsche, Genealogy, History." In *The Foucault Reader*, edited by Paul Rabinow, 76–100. New York: Pantheon, 1984.

———. "Polemics, Politics, and Problemizations." In *The Foucault Reader*, edited by Paul Rabinow, 381–90. New York: Pantheon, 1984.

———. "Theatrum Philosophicum." In *Language, Counter-Memory, Practice*, edited by Donald F. Bouchard, 169. Ithaca: Cornell University Press, 1977.

———. "What Is Enlightenment?" In *The Foucault Reader*, edited by Paul Rabinow, 32–50. New York: Pantheon, 1984.

Fournier, Ron. "Dick Gephardt Says Dean Can't Be Trusted." Associated Press, January 14, 2004.

Fox, Adam. *Oral and Literate Culture in England: 1500–1700*. Oxford: Clarendon Press, 2000.

France, Peter. *Politeness and Its Discontents.* Cambridge: Cambridge University Press, 1992.

Freud, Sigmund. *Jokes and Their Relation to the Unconscious.* Translated by James Strachey. New York: Norton, 1989.

Gagnier, Regenia, ed. *Critical Essays on Oscar Wilde.* New York: G. K. Hall, 1991.

———. *Idylls of the Marketplace.* Stanford: Stanford University Press, 1986.

Garnett, Mark A. "Hazlitt against Burke: Radical Versus Conservative." *Durham University Journal* 81, no. 2 (1989): 229–40.

Gillespie, Michael Patrick. "From Beau Brummell to Lady Bracknell: Reviewing the Dandy in *The Importance of Being Earnest.*" *Victorians Institute Journal* (1993): 119–42.

Goldfarb, Jeffery. *The Cynical Society.* Chicago: University of Chicago Press, 1991.

Goldsmith, M. M. "Faction Detected: Ideological Consequences of Robert Walpole's Decline and Fall." *History Today* 64 (1979): 1–19.

Goodman, Dena. *The Republic of Letters: A Cultural History of the French Enlightenment.* Ithaca: Cornell University Press, 1994.

———. "Pigalle's *Voltaire nu:* The Republic of Letters Represents Itself to the World." *Representations,* no. 16 (Autumn 1986): 86–109 n. 28.

Goodwin, Albert. *Friends of Liberty.* Cambridge: Harvard University Press, 1979.

Goux, Jean-Joseph. "Utility: Equivocation and Demoralisation." *Discourse* 23, no. 3 (2001): 3–23.

Grafton, Anthony. *Defenders of the Text.* Cambridge: Harvard University Press, 1991.

Grafton, Anthony, and Lisa Jardine. *From Humanism to the Humanities.* London: Duckworth, 1986.

———. "'Studied for Action': How Gabriel Harvey Read His Livy." *Past and Present* 129 (November 1990): 30–78.

Gray, Hanna H. "Renaissance Humanism: The Pursuit of Eloquence." *Journal of the History of Ideas* 24, no. 4 (1963): 497–514.

Griffin, Miriam. "Cynicism among the Romans." In *The Cynics: The Cynic Movement in Antiquity and Its Legacy,* edited by Bracht Branham and Marie-Odile Goulet-Cazé, 190–204. Berkeley and Los Angeles: University of California Press, 1976.

Grimsley, Ronald. *Jean d'Alembert.* Oxford: Clarendon Press, 1963.

Gumbrecht, Hans Ulrich. "A History of the Concept 'Modern.'" In *Making Sense in Life and Literature,* 79–110. Minneapolis: University of Minnesota Press, 1992.

———. "Who Were the *Philosophes*?" In *Making Sense in Life and Literature,* 133–77. Minneapolis: University of Minnesota Press, 1992.

Gunn, J. A. W. *Beyond Liberty and Property: The Process of Self-Recognition in Eighteenth-Century Political Thought.* Kingston: McGill-Queen's University Press, 1983.

Guy, John. "The Henrician Age." In *Varieties of British Political Thought, 1500–1800,* edited by J. G. A. Pocock, 13–46. Cambridge: Cambridge University Press, 1993.

———. "The Rhetoric of Counsel in Early Modern England." In *Tudor Political Culture,* edited by Dale Hoak, 292–310. Cambridge: Cambridge University Press, 1995.

Habermas, Jurgen. *The Structural Transformation of the Public Sphere: An Inquiry into a Category of Bourgeois Society.* Translated by Thomas Burger with Frederick Lawrence. Cambridge: MIT Press, 1989.

Hadot, Pierre. *Philosophy as a Way of Life.* Edited by Arnold I. Davidson. Translated by Michael Chase. Cambridge: Blackwell, 1995.

———. *What is Ancient Philosophy?* Translated by Michael Chase. Cambridge: Harvard University Press, 2002.

Hankins, James. *Plato in the Italian Renaissance.* 2 vols. Leiden: E. J. Brill, 1990.

Hanson, Russell. "Democracy." In *Political Innovation and Conceptual Change,* edited by Terence Ball, James Farr, and Hanson, 68–89. Cambridge: Cambridge University Press, 1989.

Hardin, Richard. "Marston's Kinsayder: The Dog's Voice." *Notes and Queries* 29 (1982): 134–35.

Havens, George R. *Voltaire's Marginalia on the Pages of Rousseau: A Comparative Study of Ideas.* New York: Haskell, 1966.

Hawthorne, Julian. Review of *Dorian Gray,* by Oscar Wilde. *Lippincott's* (1890). In *Oscar Wilde: The Critical Heritage,* edited by Karl Beckson, 80. New York: Barnes and Noble, 1970.

Hexter, J. H. "Education of the Aristocracy in the Renaissance." In *Reappraisals in History,* by Hexter, 45–70. New York: Harper and Row, 1961.

Hill, Christopher. "The Many-Headed Monster." In *Change and Continuity in Seventeenth-Century England,* 181–204. Cambridge: Harvard University Press, 1975.

Hirschman, Albert O. *The Rhetoric of Reaction.* Cambridge: Harvard University Press, 1991.

Hock, Ronald F., and Edward N. O'Neil. *The Chreia in Ancient Rhetoric.* Vol. 1, *The Progymnasmata.* Atlanta: Scholars Press, 1986.

Horne, R. C. "Voices of Alienation: The Moral Significance of Marston's Satiric Strategy." *Modern Language Review* 81, no. 1 (1986): 23–25.

Howell, Wilbur Samuel. *Eighteenth-Century British Logic and Rhetoric.* Princeton: Princeton University Press, 1971.

Hundert, Edward. *Enlightenment's Fable.* Cambridge: Cambridge University Press, 1994.

———. "Mandeville, Rousseau and the Political Economy of Fantasy." In *Luxury in the Eighteenth Century: Debates, Desires, and Delectable Goods,* edited by Maxine Berg and Elizabeth Eger, 28–40. Houndmills: Palgrave, 2003.

Hunter, G. K. Introduction to *Campaspe,* by John Lyly, edited by G. K. Hunter, 1–43. Manchester: Manchester University Press, 1991.

———. *John Lyly: The Humanist as Courtier.* Cambridge: Harvard University Press, 1962.

Ingram, Martin. "Ridings, Rough Music and Mocking Rhymes in Early Modern England." In *Popular Culture in Seventeenth-Century England,* edited by Barry Reay, 166–97. London: Croom Helm, 1985.

Jacob, James R., and Timothy Raylor. "Opera and Obedience: Thomas Hobbes and 'A Proposition for Advancement of Moralitie' by Sir William Davenant." *Seventeenth Century* 6 (1991): 205–50.

Jamieson, Kathleen Hall, and Joseph Cappella. *Spiral of Cynicism.* New York: Addison-Wesley, 1996.

Jardine, Lisa, and Anthony Grafton. "'Studied for Action': How Gabriel Harvey Read His Livy." *Past and Present* 129 (November 1990): 30–78.

Javitch, Daniel. *Poetry and Courtliness in Renaissance England.* Princeton: Princeton University Press, 1978.

Johnson, Claudia. *Equivocal Beings: Politics, Gender, and Sentimentality in the 1790s.* Chicago: University of Chicago Press, 1995.

Jones, Richard Foster. *The Triumph of the English Language: A Survey of Opinions Concerning the Vernacular from the Introduction of Printing to the Restoration.* Stanford: Stanford University Press, 1953.

Jowett, John. "Middleton and Debt in *Timon of Athens.*" In *Money and the Age of Shakespeare,* edited by Linda Woodbridge, 219–35. New York: Palgrave Macmillan, 2003.

Kahn, Coppélia. "'Magic of Bounty': *Timon of Athens,* Jacobean Patronage, and Maternal Power." *Shakespeare Quarterly* 38 (1987): 34–57.

Keenan, Alan. *Democracy in Question.* Stanford: Stanford University Press, 2003.

———. "The Twilight of the Political? A Contribution to the Democratic Critique of Cynicism." *Theory & Event* 2, no. 1 (1998), http://muse.uq.edu.au.ezproxy.lib.uh.edu/journals/theory_and_event/v002/2.1keenan.html.

Keener, Frederick M. *English Dialogues of the Dead.* New York: Columbia University Press, 1973.

Kelly, Gary. *English Jacobin Novel.* Oxford: Clarendon Press, 1976.

Kennedy, George A. *The Art of Rhetoric in the Roman World.* Princeton: Princeton University Press, 1972.

———. *A New History of Classical Rhetoric.* Princeton: Princeton University Press, 1994

Kernan, Alvin. *The Cankered Muse: Satire of the English Renaissance.* Hamden, Ct.: Archon, 1976.

Kinney, Daniel. "Heirs of the Dog: Cynic Selfhood in Medieval and Renaissance Culture." In *The Cynics: The Cynic Movement in Antiquity and Its Legacy,* edited by Bracht Branham and Marie-Odile Goulet-Cazé, 294–328. Berkeley and Los Angeles: University of California Press, 1976.

Klein, Lawrence. "Politeness and the Interpretation of the British Eighteenth Century." *Historical Journal* 45, no. 4 (2002): 869–98.

———. *Shaftesbury and the Culture of Politeness.* Cambridge: Cambridge University Press, 1994.

Knight, G. Wilson. *Wheel of Fire.* New York: Meridian, 1957.

Konstan, David. "A Dramatic History of Misanthropes." *Comparative Drama* 17, no. 2 (Summer 1983): 97–123.

Koselleck, Reinhart. "Begriffsgeschichte and Social History." In *Futures Past: On the Semantics of Historical Time,* by Kosellack, translated by Keith Tribe, 73–91. Cambridge: MIT Press, 1985.

———. *Critique and Crisis: Enlightenment and the Pathogenesis of Modern Society.* Cambridge: MIT Press, 1988.

———. *Futures Past: On the Semantics of Historical Time*. Translated by Keith Tribe. Cambridge: MIT Press, 1985.

———. "The Historical-Political Semantics of Asymmetric Counterconcepts." In *Futures Past: On the Semantics of Historical Time*, by Kosellack, translated by Keith Tribe, 159–97. Cambridge: MIT Press, 1985.

Kramnick, Isaac. *Bolingbroke and His Circle*. Ithaca: Cornell University Press, 1968.

———. *The Rage of Edmund Burke: Portrait of an Ambivalent Conservative*. New York: Basic, 1977.

Kristeller, Paul Oskar. "The Active and the Contemplative Life in Renaissance Humanism." In *Arbeit Musse Meditation: Betrachtungen zur Vita Activa und Vita Contemplativa*, edited by Brian Vickers, 132–52. Zurich: Verlag der Fachvereine Zurich, 1985.

Krueger, Derek. "The Bawdy and Society: The Shamelessness of Diogenes in Roman Imperial Culture." In *The Cynics: The Cynic Movement in Antiquity and Its Legacy*, edited by Bracht Branham and Marie-Odile Goulet-Cazé, 222–39. Berkeley and Los Angeles: University of California Press, 1976.

Langford, Paul. *A Polite and Commercial People*. New York: Oxford University Press, 1989.

Lechner, Joan Marie. *Renaissance Concepts of the Commonplaces*. New York: Pageant Press, 1962.

Lerner, Michael. *The Politics of Meaning: Restoring Hope and Possibility in an Age of Cynicism*. New York: Addison-Wesley, 1996.

Lewis, C. S. *English Literature in the Sixteenth Century Excluding Drama*. Oxford: Clarendon Press, 1954.

Lewis, Wyndham. *The Lion and the Fox: The Role of the Hero in the Plays of Shakespeare*. New York: Barnes and Noble, [1966].

Lievsay, John Leon. "Some Renaissance Views of Diogenes the Cynic." In *Joseph Quincy Adams: Memorial Studies*, edited by James G. McManaway, Giles E. Dawson, and Edwin E. Willoughby, 447–55. Washington: Folger Library, 1948.

———. *Stefano Guazzo and the English Renaissance, 1575–1675*. Chapel Hill: University of North Carolina Press, 1961.

Litt, Edgar. "Political Cynicism and Political Futility." *Journal of Politics* 25, no. 2 (May 1963): 312–23.

Lloyd, Genevieve. *The Man of Reason*. 2nd ed. Minneapolis: University of Minnesota Press, 1993.

Loconte, Joseph. "Cynicism Won't Win the War in Iraq." "Heritage Foundation Policy Research and Analysis." http://www.heritage.org/Press/Commentary/ed100104a.cfm.

Long, A. A., ed. *Cambridge Companion to Early Greek Philosophy*. Cambridge: Cambridge University Press, 1999.

———. "Scope of Early Greek Philosophy." In *Cambridge Companion to Early Greek Philosophy*, edited by A. A. Long, 1–21. Cambridge: Cambridge University Press, 1999.

———. "The Socratic Tradition: Diogenes, Crates, and Hellenistic Ethics." In *The Cynics: The Cynic Movement in Antiquity and Its Legacy,* edited by Bracht Branham and Marie-Odile Goulet-Cazé, 28–46. Berkeley and Los Angeles: University of California Press, 1976.

Luhmann, Niklas. "Work of Art and the Self-Reproduction of Art." In *Essays on Self-Reference,* 191–214. New York: Columbia University Press, 1990.

Mace, Nancy. *Henry Fielding's Novels and the Classical Tradition.* Newark: University of Delaware Press, 1996.

MacIntyre, Alasdair. *Short History of Ethics.* New York: Collier, 1966.

Malkin, Edward E. "Rousseau and Epictetus." *Studies on Voltaire and the Eighteenth Century* 106 (1973): 113–55.

Mannheim, Karl. "Conservative Thought." In *Essays on Sociology and Social Psychology,* edited by Paul Kecskemeti, 74–184. London: Routledge, 1953.

Mansfeld, Jaap. "Sources." In *Cambridge Companion to Early Greek Philosophy,* edited by A. A. Long, 22–44. Cambridge: Cambridge University Press, 1999.

———. "Sources." In *Cambridge History of Hellenistic Philosophy,* edited by Keimpe Algra, Jonathon Barnes, Mansfeld, and Malcolm Schofield, 3–30. Cambridge: Cambridge University Press, 1999.

Marrou, Henri. *The History of Education in Antiquity.* Translated by George Lamb. Madison: University of Wisconsin Press, 1982.

McCarthy, Jeanne H. "Elizabeth I's 'picture in little': Boy Company Representations of a Queen's Authority." *Studies in Philology* 100, no. 4 (Fall 2003): 425–62.

McConica, James Kelsey. *English Humanists and Reformation Politics under Henry VIII and Edward VI.* Oxford: Oxford University Press, 1965.

McGann, Jerome J. "The Dandy." *Midway* (1960): 3–18.

McKeon, Michael. "Politics of Discourses and the Rise of the Aesthetic in Seventeenth-Century England." In *Politics of Discourse,* edited by Kevin Sharpe and Steven N. Zwicker, 35–51. Berkeley and Los Angeles: University of California Press, 1987.

McKillop, Alan D. "Local Attachment and Cosmopolitanism—The Eighteenth-Century Pattern." In *From Sensibility to Romanticism,* edited by Frederick W. Hilles and Harold Bloom, 191–218. New York: Oxford University Press, 1965.

McLean, Gerald. Introduction to *Culture and Society in the Stuart Restoration.* Cambridge: Cambridge University Press, 1995.

McManaway, James G., Giles E. Dawson, and Edwin E. Willoughby, eds. *Joseph Quincy Adams: Memorial Studies.* Washington: Folger Library, 1948.

McRae, Andrew. *Literature, Satire, and the Early Stuart State.* Cambridge: Cambridge University Press, 2004.

Miller, Arthur H. "Political Issues and Trust in Government: 1964–1970." *American Political Science Review* 68, no. 3 (September 1974): 951–72.

Miller, Henry Knight. *Essays on Fielding's "Miscellanies."* Princeton: Princeton University Press, 1961.

———. "General Introduction." In *Miscellanies by Henry Fielding, Esq,* 1:xi–xlix. Middletown, Ct.: Wesleyan University Press, 1972.

———. "The Paradoxical Encomium with Special Reference to Its Vogue in England, 1600–1800." *Modern Philology* 53, no. 3 (1956): 145–78.

Minar, David W. "Public Opinion in the Perspective of Political Theory." *Western Political Quarterly* 13, no. 1 (March 1960): 31–44.

Moers, Ellen. *The Dandy.* Lincoln: University of Nebraska Press, 1960.

Moles, John L. "Cynic Cosmopolitanism." In *The Cynics: The Cynic Movement in Antiquity and Its Legacy,* edited by Bracht Branham and Cynthia-Odile Goulet-Cazé, 105–20. Berkeley and Los Angeles: University of California Press, 1996.

———. "Cynics and Politics." In *Justice and Generosity,* edited by Andre Laks and Malcolm Schofield, 129–58. Cambridge: Cambridge University Press, 1995.

———. "*Honestius Quam Ambitiosius?* An Exploration of the Cynic's Attitude to Moral Corruption in His Fellow Men." *Journal of Hellenic Studies* 103 (1983): 103–23.

Momigliano, Arnaldo. "Freedom of Speech in Antiquity." In *Dictionary of the History of Ideas,* vol. 2, edited by Philip P. Wiener, 252–63. New York: Charles Scribner's Sons, 1973.

Monsarrat, Gilles D. *Light from the Porch: Stoicism and English Renaissance Literature.* Paris: Didier-Erudition, 1984.

Morgan, Teresa. *Literate Education in the Hellenistic and Roman Worlds.* Cambridge: Cambridge University Press, 1998.

Mullan, John. *Sentiment and Sociability: The Language of Feeling in the Eighteenth Century.* Oxford: Clarendon Press, 1988.

Nadel, George. "Philosophy of History before Historicism." *History and Theory* 3, no. 3 (1964): 291–315.

Navia, Luis E. *Philosophy of Cynicism.* Westport, Ct.: Greenwood Press, 1995.

Nethercot, Arthur. *Sir William D'Avenant.* Chicago: University of Chicago Press, 1938.

Newman, Gerald. *The Rise of English Nationalism.* New York: St. Martins, 1987.

Niehues-Pröbsting, Heinrich. "The Modern Reception of Cynicism: Diogenes in the Enlightenment." In *The Cynics: The Cynic Movement in Antiquity and Its Legacy,* edited by Branham and Marie-Odile Goulet-Cazé, 329–65. Berkeley and Los Angeles: University of California Press, 1996.

O'Dair, Sharon. *Class, Critics, and Shakespeare: Bottom Lines on the Culture Wars.* Ann Arbor: University of Michigan Press, 2000.

Olson, Mancur. *The Logic of Collective Action.* Cambridge: Harvard University Press, 1971.

Ong, Walter J. "Latin Language Study as a Renaissance Puberty Rite." *Studies in Philology* 56, no. 2 (April 1959): 103–24.

———. "Tudor Writings on Rhetoric." *Studies in the Renaissance* 15 (1968): 39–69.

Parkin-Speer, Diane. "Freedom of Speech in Sixteenth Century English Rhetorics." *Sixteenth Century Journal* 12, no. 3 (Autumn 1981): 65–72.

Pater, Walter. "A Novel by Mr. Oscar Wilde." In *Oscar Wilde: The Critical Heritage,* edited by Karl Beckson, 84–85. New York: Barnes and Noble, 1970.

Patterson, Annabel. *Censorship and Interpretation: The Conditions of Writing and Reading in Early Modern England. With a New Introduction.* Madison: University of Wisconsin Press, 1984.

Pauls, Peter. "Shakespeare's *Timon of Athens* and Renaissance Diogeniana." *Upstart Crow* 3 (1980): 54–64.

Payne, Harry C. *The Philosophers and the People.* New Haven: Yale University Press, 1976.

Peltonen, Markku. *Classical Humanism and Republicanism in English Political Thought: 1570–1640.* Cambridge: Cambridge University Press, 1995.

Pennock, J. Roland, and John W. Chapman, eds. *Compromise in Ethics, Law, and Politics: Nomos XXI.* New York: New York University Press, 1979.

Pfeiffer, Rudolf. *History of Classical Scholarship.* Oxford: Clarendon Press, 1976.

Phillips Mark Salber. *Society and Sentiment.* Princeton: Princeton University Press, 2000.

Philp, Mark. "Vulgar Conservatism." *English Historical Review* 110, no. 435 (February 1995): 42–69.

Pincombe, Michael. "Lyly's *Campaspe* and the Tudor 'Owlglass.'" *Notes & Queries,* n.s., 44, no. 1 (1997): 30–32.

———. The *Plays of John Lyly: Eros and Eliza.* Manchester: Manchester University Press, 1996.

Pocock, J.G.A. "Burke and the Ancient Constitution: A Problem in the History of Ideas." In *Politics, Language, and Time: Essays on Political Thought and History,* 202–32. Chicago: University of Chicago Press, 1971.

———. "Cambridge Paradigms and Scotch Philosophers." In *Wealth and Virtue,* edited by Istvan Hont and Michael Ignatieff, 243. Cambridge: Cambridge University Press, 1983.

———. "Clergy and Commerce: The Conservative Enlightenment in England." In *L'Età dei Lumi,* edited by R. Ajello, 525–62. Naples: Jovene, 1985.

———. "Enthusiasm: The Antiself of Enlightenment." In *Enthusiasm and Enlightenment in Europe, 1650–1850,* edited by Lawrence E. Klein and Anthony J. La Vopa, 7–28. San Marino: Huntington Library Publications, 1998.

———. "The Imperial Crisis." In *Varieties of British Political Thought, 1500–1800,* ed. Pocock, 246–82. Cambridge: Cambridge University Press, 1993.

———, ed. *Reflections on the Revolution in France.* By Edmund Burke. Indianapolis: Hackett, 1987.

———, ed., with Gordon J. Schochet and Lois G. Schwoerer. *Varieties of British Political Thought, 1500–1800.* Cambridge: Cambridge University Press, 1993.

———. *Virtue, Commerce, and History: Essays on Political Thought and History, Chiefly in the Eighteenth Century.* Cambridge: Cambridge University Press, 1985.

Pocock, J.G.A., and Gordon J. Schochet. "Interregnum and Restoration." In *Varieties of British Political Though 1500–1800,* edited by Pocock, with Schochet and Lois G. Schwoerer, 146–79. Cambridge: Cambridge University Press, 1993.

Potkay, Adam. *Fate of Eloquence in the Age of Hume.* Ithaca: Cornell University Press, 1994.

Preston, Thomas R. *Not in Timon's Manner: Feeling, Misanthropy, and Satire in Eighteenth-Century England.* University: University of Alabama Press, 1975.

Radcliffe, Evan. "Burke, Radical Cosmopolitanism, and the Debates on Patriotism in the 1790s." *SECC* 28 (1998): 311–39.

———. "Revolutionary Writing, Moral Philosophy, and Universal Benevolence in the Eighteenth Century." *Journal of the History of Ideas* 54, no. 2 (April 1993): 221–40.

Rawls, John. *Political Liberalism.* New York: Columbia University Press, 1996.

Relihan, Joel C. *Ancient Menippean Satire.* Baltimore: Johns Hopkins University Press, 1993.

———. "Menippus in Antiquity and the Renaissance." In *The Cynics: The Cynic Movement in Antiquity and Its Legacy,* edited by Bracht Branham and Marie-Odile Goulet-Cazé, 265–93. Berkeley and Los Angeles: University of California Press, 1996.

Review of Dorian Gray, by Oscar Wilde. *Daily Chronicle.* In *Oscar Wilde: The Critical Heritage,* edited by Karl Beckson. 72. New York: Barnes and Noble, 1970.

Richards, Jennifer. *Rhetoric and Courtliness in Early Modern Literature.* Cambridge: Cambridge University Press, 2003.

Riggs, David. *Shakespeare's Heroical Histories: Henry VI and Its Literary Tradition.* Cambridge: Harvard University Press, 1971.

Robinson, Christopher. *Lucian and His Influence in Europe.* Chapel Hill: University of North Carolina Press, 1979.

Roddier, Henri. *J.-J. Rousseau en Angleterre au XVIII siècle.* Paris: Boivin, 1950.

Rogers, Nicholas. *Whigs and Cities: Popular Politics in the Age of Walpole and Pitt.* Oxford: Clarendon Press, 1989.

Rosa, Matthew. *Silver-Fork School.* New York: Columbia University Press, 1936.

Rowlands, Samuel. *Diogenes Lanthorne.* London, 1608.

Rudé, George. *Wilkes and Liberty.* Oxford: Clarendon Press, 1962.

Rummel, Erika. *Erasmus as a Translator of the Classics.* Toronto: University of Toronto Press, 1985.

Saccio, Peter. *Court Comedies of John Lyly: A Study in Allegorical Dramaturgy.* Princeton: Princeton University Press, 1969.

Sack, James. *From Jacobite to Conservative.* New York: Cambridge University Press, 1993.

Sanderson, John. *"But the People's Creatures": The Philosophical Basis of the Civil War.* Manchester: Manchester University Press, 1989.

Sayre, Farrand. *The Greek Cynics.* Baltimore: J. H. Furst, 1948.

Scanlan, Timothy M. "Jean-Jacques Rousseau and Diogenes the Cynic." *USF Language Quarterly* 15, nos. 1–2 (1976): 23–24.

Schlereth, Thomas. *Cosmopolitan Ideal in Enlightenment Thought: Its Form and Function in the Ideas of Franklin, Hume, and Voltaire, 1694–1790.* Notre Dame: University of Notre Dame Press, 1977.

Schochet, Gordon. "Why Should History Matter?" In *Varieties of British Political Thought, 1500–1800,* edited by J.G.A. Pocock, with Schochet and Lois G. Schwoerer, 324–32. Cambridge: Cambridge University Press, 1993.

Scragg, Leah. "*Campaspe* and the Construction of Monarchical Power." *Medieval and Renaissance Drama in England* 12 (1999): 59–83.

Seigel, Jerrold E. *Rhetoric and Philosophy in Renaissance Humanism: The Union of Eloquence and Wisdom, Petrarch to Valla.* Princeton: Princeton University Press, 1968.

Sekora, John. *Luxury: The Concept in Western Thought, Eden to Smollett.* Baltimore: Johns Hopkins University Press, 1977.

Shankar, S. "Translating Modernity." Lecture, University of Houston, December 5, 2003.

Sharpe, Kevin. *Reading Revolutions: The Politics of Reading in Early Modern England.* New Haven: Yale University Press, 2000.

Sharpe, Kevin, and Steven N. Zwicker, eds. *Politics of Discourse.* Berkeley and Los Angeles: University of California Press, 1987.

Simon, Joan. *Education and Society in Tudor England.* Cambridge: Cambridge University Press, 1966.

Sinfield, Alan. *Wilde Century.* New York: Columbia University Press, 1994.

Skinner, Quentin. "The Principles and Practice of Opposition: The Case of Bolingbroke versus Walpole." In *Historical Perspectives: Studies in English Thought and Society,* edited by Neil McKendrick, 93–128. London: Europa Publications, 1974.

———. *Reason and Rhetoric in the Philosophy of Hobbes.* Cambridge: Cambridge University Press, 1996.

Skura, Meredith Anne. *Shakespeare the Actor and the Purposes of Playing.* Chicago: University of Chicago Press, 1993.

Sloterdijk, Peter. *Critique of Cynical Reason.* Translated by Michael Eldred. Minneapolis: University of Minnesota Press, 1987.

Smith, Nigel. *Literature and Revolution in England, 1640–1660.* New Haven: Yale University Press, 1994.

Somerset, H. V. F. Introduction to *A Note-Book of Edmund Burke,* edited by Somerset, 3–18. Cambridge: Cambridge University Press, 1957.

Spencer, Theodore. "The Elizabethan Malcontent." In *Joseph Quincy Adams: Memorial Studies,* edited by James G. McManaway, Giles E. Dawson, and Edwin E. Willoughby, 523–35. Washington: Folger Library, 1948.

Starobinski, Jean. "Diogène dans *Le Neveu De Rameau.*" *Stanford French Review* 8, nos. 2–3 (Fall 1984): 147–65.

———. *Jean-Jacques Rousseau: Transparency and Obstruction.* Translated by Arthur Goldhammer. Chicago: University of Chicago Press, 1988.

———. "The Word *Civilization.*" In *Blessings in Disguise; or, The Morality of Evil,* translated by Arthur Goldhammer, 1–35. Cambridge: Harvard University Press, 1993.

Stephen, Leslie. "The Writings of W. M. Thackeray." In *Works of William Makepeace Thackeray,* 1878–79. Reprinted in *Thackeray: Critical Heritage,* edited by Geoffrey Tillotson and Donald Hawes, 358–83. London: Routledge and Kegan Paul, 1968.

Struever, Nancy. *Language of History in the Renaissance.* Princeton: Princeton University Press, 1970.

Tambling, Jeremy. "Hating Man in *Timon of Athens.*" *Essays in Criticism* 50, no. 2 (April 2000): 145–68.

Thompson, Craig. Introduction to *Translations of Lucian,* by St. Thomas More, edited by Thompson. In *Complete Works,* 3, pt. 1: xvii–lxxii. New Haven: Yale University Press, 1974.

Tosh, John. "What Should Historians Do with Masculinity? Reflections on Nineteenth-Century Britain." *History Workshop Journal,* no. 38 (1994): 174–202.

Trilling, Lionel. *Sincerity and Authenticity.* Cambridge: Harvard University Press, 1972.

Tysdahl, B. J. *William Godwin as Novelist.* London: Athlone, 1981.

Vickers, Brian, ed. *Arbeit Musse Meditation: Betrachtungen zur Vita Activa und Vita Contemplativa.* Zurich: Verlag der Fachvereine Zurich, 1985.

———. *In Defence of Rhetoric.* Oxford: Clarendon Press, 1988.

———. "'The Power of Persuasion': Images of the Orator, Elyot to Shakespeare." In *Renaissance Eloquence,* edited by James J. Murphy, 411–35. Berkeley and Los Angeles: University of California Press, 1983.

———. *Shakespeare, Co-Author.* Oxford: Oxford University Press, 2002.

Voisine, Jacques. *J. -J. Rousseau en Angleterre a L'Époch Romantique.* Paris: Didier, 1956.

Wahrman, Dror. "Middle-Class Domesticity Goes Public: Gender, Class, and Politics from Queen Caroline to Queen Victoria." *Journal of British Studies* 32, no. 4 (October 1993): 396–432.

Wahrman, Dror. "*Percy's* Prologue: From Gender Play to Gender Panic in Eighteenth-Century England." *Past and Present* 159 (May 1998): 113–60.

Warner, Michael. *Publics and Counterpublics.* New York: Zone, 2002.

Watson, Melvin R. "Lord Chesterfield and 'Decorum.'" *Modern Language Notes* 62, no. 3 (March 1947): 197–98.

Weber, Samuel. *Institution and Interpretation.* Minneapolis: University of Minnesota Press, 1987.

Weinbrot, Howard D. *Menippean Satire Reconsidered: From Antiquity to the Eighteenth Century.* Baltimore: Johns Hopkins University Press, 2005.

Weinsheimer, Joel. "Burke's *Reflections:* On Imitation as Prejudice." *Southern Humanities Review* 16, no. 3 (1982): 223–34.

White, James Boyd. *When Words Lose Their Meaning.* Chicago: University of Chicago Press, 1984.

Wilcher, John. *Writing of Royalism, 1628–1660.* Cambridge: Cambridge University Press, 2001.

Williams, Raymond. *Marxism and Literature.* New York: Oxford University Press, 1977.

Wilson, Kathleen. *The Sense of the People: Politics, Culture, and Imperialism in England, 1715–1785.* New York: Cambridge University Press, 1995.

Wiseman, Susan J. "'History Digested': Opera and Colonialism in the 1650s." In *Literature and the English Civil War,* edited by Thomas Healy and Jonathan Sawday, 189–208. Cambridge: Cambridge University Press, 1990.

Woodfine, Philip. *Britannia's Glories: The Walpole Ministry and the 1739 War with Spain.* Royal Historical Society Studies in History. New series. Woodbridge: Boydell Press, 1998.

———. "Government Harassment of the Press in the Late 1730s." *Journal of Newspaper and Periodical History* 5, no. 2 (1989): 20–34.

Wright, Ernest Hunter. *Authorship of "Timon of Athens."* New York: Columbia University Press, 1910.

Zaller, Robert. "Breaking the Vessels: The Desacralization of Monarchy in Early Modern England." *Sixteenth Century Journal* 29, no. 3 (Autumn 1998): 757–78.

Zwicker, Steven. *Lines of Authority.* Ithaca: Cornell University Press, 1993.

INDEX